THE EMERGENCE OF MAN

THE EMERGENCE
OF MAN

Third Edition

JOHN E. PFEIFFER

HARPER & ROW, PUBLISHERS
New York   Hagerstown   San Francisco   London

Special Projects Editor: Marlene Ellin
Project Editor: Pamela Landau
Designer: Gayle Jaeger
Production Supervisor: Stefania J. Taflinska
Compositor: P & M Typesetting, Incorporated
Printer and Binder: The Murray Printing Company
Art Studio: Danmark & Michaels, Inc.

The Emergence of Man, Third Edition

Library of Congress Cataloging in Publication Data

Pfeiffer, John E.   Date—
   The emergence of man.

   Bibliography: p.
   Includes index.
   1. Human evolution.   2. Man, Prehistoric.
3. Society, Primitive.   I. Title.
GN281.P45   1978   573.2   77–12804
ISBN 0–06–045196–3

CONTENTS

ILLUSTRATIONS

PHOTOGRAPHS

DIAGRAMS

MAPS

PREFACE

One of the most rapidly expanding areas in anthropology, and for that matter, in the entire range of the social sciences, is the study of prehistory — the enormous time span from the appearance of the first members of the family of man some 15 million years ago to the invention of writing around 3500 B.C. The evidence continues to mount, month by month. It includes new finds of human and prehuman fossils, new sites where our remote ancestors camped and butchered their prey, new deductions about the origins and development of tool use, language, and communal living among early hunting-gathering societies.

Human evolution has had a sweep and rhythm of its own. It started inauspiciously and very slowly. Prospects hardly seemed bright for the breeds of small chimpanzeelike creatures which began to move out of their dense ancestral forests toward wide-open savanna lands. And for millions of years thereafter, nothing much seems to have happened, at least as far as we can tell from the fossil record. Then, as life on savannas somehow became more and more complicated, the rate of evolution started accelerating, still slowly at first, but faster and faster, with an extra burst beginning about 40,000 to 50,000 years ago when a modern type of people spread throughout the earth.

Their story, which continues to unfold in our times, has guided the organization of this book. My first objective was to bring together in a single narrative section recent discoveries in archeology, geology, and other disciplines which bear more or less directly on the emergence of human beings from near apes — on the rise not only of a new species, but also of a new kind of evolution that involved more than purely physical adaptations. The first eleven chapters present some of the information we have about this process. They cover mainly inanimate evidence, fossil bones and flint artifacts excavated from representative major sites.

The second section of the book focuses on the present and future, on the living research which is contributing to our understanding of human origins and which can be expected to contribute increasingly to it during the next decade of discovery. It would have slowed or interrupted the pace of the first section to present these studies in the wealth of detail they deserve; they demand special attention and emphasis in their own right. The chapters in this section are devoted to descriptions of experimental techniques and intensive observations of existing rather than extinct primates—human and nonhuman hunter-gatherers and city dwellers—whose behavior makes prehistory come alive because it approximates basic features of behavior in times long past. Essentially, the purpose behind these chapters is to reconstruct certain life styles that have vanished in order to obtain a deeper insight into contemporary life styles and the knowledge to shape the future in a more sophisticated way.

Editor's Note

We have kept the title *THE EMERGENCE OF MAN* unchanged from the second edition because we want our readers to know that this is the third edition of a book with which they are familiar. However, we admit to feeling uncomfortable with the title because it is inexact—this book is obviously not just about "men" but about the physical and cultural development of both men and women. We hope our readers will understand that we use "man" in the generic sense.

ACKNOWLEDGMENTS

As the remote past takes on a wider scope and significance, more schools are providing fuller accounts of what happened in prehistory to more pupils and at an earlier age, often in the eighth and ninth grades. High school and college students are exposed to knowledge once offered only to graduate students. Above all, many barriers are being broken down, notably the barriers which separate academic departments and which have done so much to frustrate the study of human evolution and human behavior. Findings about life in prehistoric times bear on problems in neurophysiology, psychology, psychiatry, animal behavior, and architecture—and research in these areas, in turn, bears on problems in archeology and anthropology.

In presenting and coordinating material from such diverse sources, I have received help from many persons. I was fortunate in meeting Sherwood Washburn of the University of California, Berkeley, early in the preparation of this book. He indicated the nature of the work ahead in its full complexity, advised me in the planning of research and interviews, and has kept me posted on progress in his own research and in the research of his students and associates. Throughout the writing of the book Clark Howell, also of the University of California, has given most generously of his time, sharing his extensive knowledge and experience and evaluating controversial points in a field where controversies are common and evaluation is exceedingly tricky.

My debt to François Bordes of the Laboratory of Quaternary Geology and Prehistory of the University of Bordeaux is particularly difficult to acknowledge. It is not only what I learned from him about excavating methods and the analysis of artifact assemblages of Neanderthal people, although that was considerable, but also what he conveyed simply by being himself—a feeling for the honesty, passion, and imagination that go into creative research. For the sheer flow of stimulating ideas and a glimpse of future trends, I owe a great deal to Lewis Binford of the University of New Mexico, perhaps the most articulate and forceful representative of the new archeology, a discipline in which relatively sophisticated mathematical techniques will play a far larger role than they have in the past. At Harvard, Hallam Movius contributed a great deal to the archeological sections of this book, conveying basic ideas as well as factual information.

I also received other kinds of help. A number of investigators contributed to my archeological education by permitting me to work with them on actual excavations, on the theory that first-hand experience is essential in writing about any area of research. My most extensive digging was done with Francois Bordes at Combe Grenal, Andre Leroi-Gourhan of the University of Paris at Arcy-sur-Cure in the Yonne Valley, and Cynthia Irwin-Williams of Eastern New Mexico University in the foothills of the Rockies near Denver. Mary Leakey and the late Louis Leakey of the Center for Prehistory and Archaeology in Nairobi, Kenya, served as my guides during a visit to the Olduvai Gorge.

Revil Mason and Phillip Tobias of the University of the Witwatersrand in Johannesburg, Ray Inskeep of Oxford University, and Ronald Singer of the University of Chicago showed me South African sites, including those of *Australopithecus* and several Bushman art caves. Desmond Clark, one of Washburn's colleagues at the University of California, led me through some formidable back country during a search for new sites in the Karonga district of northern Malawi; and J. Gonzales Echegaray and M. A. Garcia-Guinea of the Santander Museum of Prehistory and Archaeology conducted me through Altamira and other art caves in northern Spain. My observations of nonhuman primates in the wild included several weeks spent in East Africa with Irven DeVore of Harvard University following baboon troops in Nairobi Park and the Amboseli Game Reserve.

Checking for accuracy and proper emphasis is a major task in a book like this one which draws on so many areas of research. I am reasonably sure that most errors have been found and corrected, since every chapter has been read critically by four to eight persons. I take full responsibility, however, for any errors that remain. Bernard Campbell of Cambridge University and Clark Howell read the entire book, and their suggestions have done much to improve the text.

The following are among the other investigators who provided me with information during interviews, or read individual chapters or sections of chapters: Emiliano de Aguirre, Museo Nacional de Ciencias Naturales, Madrid; Mary Ainsworth, University of Virginia; Owen Aldis, Behavioral Science Research Fund, Menlo Park, California; Anthony Ambrose, Behavior Development Research Unit, St. Mary's Hospital, London; Richard Andrew, Sussex University, England; Ofer Bar-Yosef, Hebrew University, Jerusalem; Alex Bavelas, University of British Columbia; Joseph Birdsell, University of California at Los Angeles; Ben Blount, University of Texas; John Bowlby, Tavistock Clinic, London; Robert Braidwood, University of Chicago; Charles Brain, Transvaal Museum, Pretoria, South Africa; Harvey Bricker, Tulane University; Don Brothwell, University College London; Karl Butzer, University of Chicago; David Bygott, Cambridge University; Michael Chance, University of Birmingham, England; Glen Cole, Field Museum of Natural History, Chicago; Desmond Collins, University of London; Shirley Coryndon, British

Museum of Natural History; Don Crabtree, Idaho State University **xvii**
Museum; Lya Dams, Brussels, Belgium; Raymond Dart, Institute for the
Achievement of Human Potential, Philadelphia; Woodrow Denham,
University of California; Patricia Draper, University of New Mexico;
John Eisenberg, National Zoological Park, Smithsonian Institution;
Richard Estes, Philadelphia Academy of Natural Sciences; Brian Fagan,
University of California, Santa Barbara; Robert Fagen, University of
Illinois; William Farrand, University of Michigan; Kent Flannery, University of Michigan; Roger Fouts, University of Oklahoma; Robin Fox,
Rutgers University; Leslie Freeman, University of Chicago; Allen and
Beatrice Gardner, University of Nevada; the late Dorothy Farrod, Villebois,
Lavalette, France; Norman Geschwind, Harvard Medical School; Eugene
Giles, University of Illinois; Ian Glover, Institute of Archaeology, London;
Richard Gould, University of Hawaii.

Also David Hamburg, Stanford University Medical Center; Annette
Hamilton, Macquarie University, Australia; Jack Harlan, University of
Illinois; Henry Harpending, University of New Mexico; Richard Hay,
University of California, Berkeley; June Helm, University of Iowa; Gordon
Hewes, University of Colorado; the late Eric Higgs, Cambridge University,
England; Robert Hinde, Cambridge University; Charles Hockett, Cornell
University; Nancy Howell, University of Toronto; Corinne Hutt, University of Keele, England; Dell Hymes, University of Pennsylvania;
Glynn Isaac, University of California, Berkeley; Arthur Jelinek, University of Arizona; Peter Jewell, University College, London; Carl Johanson, Cleveland Museum of Natural History; Clifford Jolly, New York
University; Nicholas Blurton Jones, Institute of Child Health, London;
Sheldon Judson, Princeton University; Charles Keller, University of
Illinois; Jack Kelso, University of Colorado; William Kessen, Yale University; Richard Klein, University of Chicago; Melvin Konner, Harvard
University; Ronald Lampert, Australian National University; Jan Lancaster, University of New Orleans; Jane van Lawick-Goodall, Nairobi,
Kenya; Foss and Helen Leach, University of Otago, New Zealand; Richard
Leakey, National Museums of Kenya; Richard Lee, University of Toronto;
the late Eric Lenneberg, Cornell University Medical College, New York;
Jerome Lettvin, Massachusetts Institute of Technology; William Longacre,
University of Arizona; Henry de Lumley, University of Aix-Marseilles,
France.

Also Paul MacLean, National Institute of Mental Health; Vincent
Maglio, Rutgers University Medical School; Brian Maguire, University of
the Witwatersrand, Johannesburg, South Africa; Alan Mann, University
of Pennsylvania; Peter Marler, Rockefeller University; Robert Martin,
University College, London; John Mawby, Deep Springs College, California; Ernst Mayr, Harvard University; David McNeill, University of
Michigan; Patrick McGinnis, Cambridge University; George Miller,
Rockefeller University; John Mulvaney, Australian National University;
John Napier, Royal Free Hospital, London; Walle Nauta, Massachusetts

Institute of Technology; Kenneth Oakley, British Museum of Natural
History; Armand Oppenheimer, Columbia University; Bryan Patterson, Harvard University; Jean Perrot, French Archaeological Mission, Jerusalem; Nicolas Peterson, Australian National University; Anthony Pfeiffer, Rutgers University; David Pilbeam, Yale University; David Premack, University of Pennsylvania; Karl Pribram, Stanford University Medical Center; John Price, Maudsley Hospital, London; William Redican, University of California, Davis; Vernon Reynolds, Oxford University; John Robinson, University of Wisconsin; Thelma Rowell, Makerere University College, Kampala, Uganda; James Sackett, University of California at Los Angeles; Earl Saxon, University of Durham; George B. Schaller, New York Zoological Society; Carmel Schrire, Rutgers University; Ann and Gale Sieveking, British Museum; George Silberbauer, Monash University, Australia; Elwyn Simons, Yale University; Philip Smith, University of Montreal; Ralph and Rose Solecki, Columbia University; Denise de Sonneville-Bordes, University of Bordeaux; Augustus Sordinas, Memphis State University; John Speth, University of Michigan; Axel Steensberg, University of Copenhagen; Theodor Strehlow, University of Adelaide, Australia; Alan Swedlund, University of Massachusetts, Amherst; James Tanner, Institute of Child Health, London; Geza Teleki, Pennsylvania State University; Harold Thomas, Harvard University; Alan Thorne, Australian National University; Lionel Tiger, Rutgers University; Niko Timbergen, Oxford University; Robert Trivers, Harvard University; Jorgen Troels-Smith, National Museum of Copenhagen; Peter Ucko, Institute for Aboriginal Studies, Canberra; John Waechter, Institute of Archaeology, London; Lawrence Wells, University of Cape Town, South Africa; Peter White, University of Sydney; Polly Wiesner, University of Michigan; Edwin Wilmsen, University of Michigan; John Witthoft, University of Pennsylvania; Martin Wobst, University of Massachusetts, Amherst; Richard Wrangham, University of Bristol; Henry Wright, University of Michigan; Richard Wright, University of Sydney; Vero Wynne-Edwards, University of Aberdeen, Scotland; John Yellen, George Washington University; J. Z. Young, University College, London; and Adrienne Zihlman, University of California, Santa Cruz.

I am most grateful to Jeannette Hopkins. She has improved the style and clarity of my writing, and I am fortunate to have had the benefit of her experience and creative editing. Marlene Ellin, special projects editor, helped considerably in planning and guiding this third edition to completion.

Finally, in connection with the third edition, special acknowledgment is due to Alan Mann of the University of Pennsylvania. He not only corrected statements which were just plain wrong, but he also suggested the inclusion of new material which he considered particularly interesting to students and particularly relevant to the questions they ask.

PICTURE CREDITS

THE EMERGENCE OF MAN

Role of the savanna in prehistory; man's 15 million years as a wild animal; formation and persistence of archeological sites; worldwide search for new sites; element of chance and a lucky find; outline of the human story; nature of human evolution; archeology and living prehistory

PROLOGUE TECHNIQUES AND PROSPECTS IN THE SEARCH FOR MAN

Parts of the past still endure in Africa in stretches of relic wilderness wide as inland seas. There is a hilltop in Kenya's Amboseli Game Reserve, for instance, where you look west across a savanna that extends bright and yellowish brown and bone-dry as far as the eye can see. This is usually an empty semidesert land with a few flat-topped fever trees and nothing abroad but dust devils, little whirlwinds which appear out of nowhere as brown spiral puffs and spin along for a distance and then vanish.

But a change takes place during certain dry-season days. The land becomes a great gathering place, and the Amboseli hilltop becomes an observation post. There is a massive coming together of species, as if to a sanctuary or an Ark. Streams of animals move toward a place not far from the foot of the hill, a large pool of stagnant green-gray water.

I remember watching the scene one glaring mid-July morning. A herd of zebras was already drinking at the edge of the pool while not yet at the edge, wildebeests with curved horns and high shoulders moved slowly in a single file as if queuing up for their turn and behind them more animals and still more stretched back until all I could make out were black specks in the far distance. Suddenly the zebras panicked, perhaps at a rustle in the low bushes nearby, and dashed from the pool. Then some of the wildebeests waded in, drank, and left; a herd of gazelles took their place and left after another brief panic; half a dozen ostriches, two troops of baboons, and a lone giraffe followed, and on and on all day till sunset.

This is the part of Africa that is dying, the wild and primeval part, the Africa that once belonged to animals other than man. This Africa produces a strange sort of double vision or double perspective, a sense of being in two worlds. One world, of course, is completely alien. The savanna and all that is going on there are so different from anything the observer has known that it might just as well be happening on another planet. One is a spectator, uninvolved, uncommitted, trying to take it in. **1**

The other world, where an undercurrent of nostalgia stirs, is like a place known long ago and revisited. One responds to it for the same reason that one responds to all lonely places—whether during walks along beaches with no one in sight, camping out in a ravine in the desert, going off paved highways to dirt roads, on tracks into the interior, or going into trackless areas, heading for lakes and canyons with waterfalls and no roads leading to them. Something is lost by living too long away from such places. A feeling of belonging to the wilderness persists, and the feeling is strongest and most moving in Africa because that is the land of man's ancestors.

They lived on African savannas as animals among animals. They were once part of the great processions that approached water holes along ancient trails and waited their turn during times of thirst. They stepped aside unhurried and without looking up as wildebeests and zebras moved by, strode through herds of gazelles, and chased the baboons, their closest relatives in the crowd. They came to drink and bolted in panic when there were sounds in the bushes. And sometimes near the edges of stagnant waters they became victims of lions and other predators.

This way of life is not remote. Hominids, or members of the human family, have spent 10 to 15 million years foraging on savannas and only a few thousand years living in cities. They have been wild animals for 10 to 15 million years and domesticated animals, or rather partly domesticated animals, for a fraction of one percent of that span. In a basic sense, far from having arrived, they are just beginning to find their way, their place in the scheme of things.

This is the point of the statement that we are the missing link between anthropoid apes and human beings. The assumption that we are already fully human is open to argument. It leads to questions which are difficult to answer, for example, the question of why we so frequently behave in a fashion which we ourselves consider inhuman. Such contradictions emphasize the need for a shift in viewpoint. The sense of urgency about things to come demands a harder and longer look at the way things were. We must look backward as well as forward.

In a time when the accent is more and more on what the future may bring, on visits to other planets and the problem of surviving and evolving on our own planet, research on the remote past is beginning to come into its own. Investigators are engaged in an expanding effort to look at the past more realistically, and a major part of that effort is the search for fresh evidence about human origins. Everything suggests that the events of prehistoric times are as important in understanding the species as the events of infancy and early childhood are in understanding the individual.

Man among
mammals

The marks of the past may endure for long periods. Imagine a prehistoric twilight with hunters living and settling by a stream. They scoop a hollow place in the earth for a hearth, sharpen old flints and shape new ones, eat by the fire and come close for warmth, curling up at the edge of the fire to sleep. After a stay of a few days or a few weeks, they abandon camp as the seasons change. Leaves and branches fall and form new earth; winds blow in dust and sand and volcanic ash. The area is flooded, and a lake appears. Sediment drifts down through the waters and settles and accumulates on the bottom.

Then the lake dries up, and another cycle starts. Decades pass and centuries and millennia, and something endures. The original occupation floor may be preserved like a flower pressed between pages of a diary or a fossil imprint of a fern on rock. Discarded tools, charred bones, and the remains of fires that sputtered out long ago are traces of camps where people stayed awhile and disturbed the earth and then moved on. There are sites where living patterns have persisted for as long as 2 to 3 million years.

A worldwide search is under way for new sites which will reveal more about the ways of creatures in the first throes of becoming human. Every lead is followed up, every tale of fields and caves rich in ancient fossils (which usually turn out to be the bones of modern ani-

3

mals). Expeditions are searching in backcountry bordering lakes in the
4000-mile African Rift Valley, on slopes rising from the flat plains of
northern Thailand, among the foothills of the Rockies and Himalayas
and Urals, along the Mediterranean coast, in the deserts of Australia,
and in valleys gouged out of the plateaus of central Spain.

Expeditions are part adventure and part sheer drudgery. Work in
the field often begins with the inspection of geological maps indicating
where promising deposits lie, exposed or near the surface; ancient lake
sediments or dunes or river banks may include the remains of prehistoric camps and campers. The next step may involve aerial photographs of the mapped terrain, pairs of photographs placed edge to edge
and looked at through a stereo viewer so that trees, cliffs, gullies, hills,
and other features appear sharp and in three dimensions, as if one were
flying over the region on a clear day.

The latest advance in the technology of site searching involves
remote-sensing eye-in-the-sky satellites. Equipped with television-type
scanning devices, they view the world from heights of about 500 miles
and take synchronized photographs in green, red, and infrared light every 25 seconds, each photograph covering an area of about 10,000
square miles (100 miles on a side). Some of the photographs, specifically
the ones covering the Chaco Canyon National Monument region of
New Mexico, are being studied in intensive detail for use in identifying
places where people lived many thousands of years ago, extinct river
beds and lakes, soils rich in organic matter and clays, hidden springs
and other water sources, fine debris at the bottom of cliffs, stream and
beach gravel, and wind-deposited sands which may contain ancient artifacts. In this way, the insights gained in the course of checking a region already well known archeologically can be used to examine features of satellite photographs of lesser known regions.

The real work starts after photography and other techniques have
pinpointed a number of likely areas for detailed on-the-ground surveying. Since most unexplored regions are located far off the beaten track
in country too rugged even for Land Rovers, surveying means getting
out and walking. On a typical day you wake at sunrise, tramp through
brush and brambles, bending low to avoid the thorns, half slide and
half fall down the steep steps of ravines, follow the courses of dried-out
stream beds, and then try to find your way back before nightfall. You
may walk 15 miles or more in 8 hours, with about 40 minutes off to eat
and rest, and that goes on day after day for as long as it takes to cover
an area systematically.

Every search is a gamble, and many searches end with little or
nothing to show for them. Under such conditions, when success comes,
it is especially sweet. For example, an important site was discovered a
number of years ago by Desmond Clark of the University of California
in Berkeley just as he was on the verge of quitting. The setting is one of

the wildest and most magnificent in Africa, near the southern end of Lake Tanganyika where the Kalambo River winds sluggishly through a high valley, moves faster as it nears the edge of a cliff, and plunges 700 feet into a dark tropical canyon. One morning Clark was walking back from the falls along the spillway gorge when, after nearly falling into a pit dug by natives to trap wild pigs, he happened to look down at a point where the river makes a sharp meander.

"I almost missed the place completely," he recalls. "The grass, which is normally about 8 feet high and thick as your finger, had been burned off, revealing a sheer erosion cut in the river bank, and you look at practically every sheer cut. This one was touch and go, but I did look. I hung on to a couple of roots, lowered myself over the edge, and found some nice tools dating back to the Middle Stone Age of Africa about 25,000 to 30,000 years ago. Then I dropped to the bottom, where still older tools, hand axes and cleavers, were sticking out from the bank as well as pieces of carbonized wood. I could hardly believe that it was the real thing."

Clark came back three years later for a full-scale effort. Modern excavating techniques demand time and patience because thousands of tools, flakes, and other objects are uncovered bit by bit with trowels and brushes. Furthermore, one never knows how long a dig will take, how much time one will need to pass through layer after layer until reaching bedrock. It required nearly 12 months of digging over several seasons to do the job at Kalambo, and many excavations take a great deal longer.

The general practice is not to excavate a site completely, because of the peculiar nature of archeological evidence. In other sciences experiments can always be repeated and results checked. Astronomers can always make new observations of the sun and planets; biologists have an ample supply of organisms for continuing laboratory studies. Once an archeologist excavates a site, however, there can be no checking or retracing of steps. That particular arrangement of buried objects is unique. There is no other arrangement like it, and it can never be fully recreated again. Clues missed because of carelessness or ignorance are gone forever.

An appalling amount of information has been lost because of bad practices in the not very remote past. Profit-minded diggers have destroyed many fine sites simply to obtain a few beautifully worked flint or bone tools to sell to museums, tourists, or private collectors by using rush tactics to complete in a few hours excavations which should have been carried out for weeks. One notorious plunderer was caught in the act of trying to remove a section of the ceiling of a French rock shelter, a section containing a sculpted fish. The organized looting of archeological sites is an international scandal and will no doubt continue for a long time despite laws prescribing punishments for offenders. The

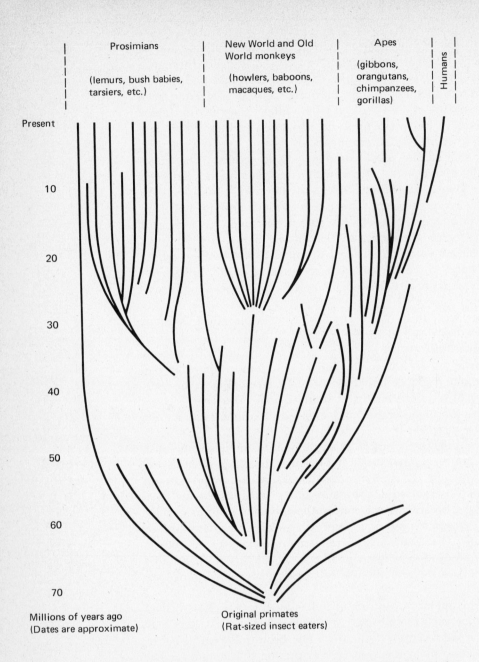

Prosimians

(lemurs, bush babies, tarsiers, etc.)

New World and Old World monkeys

(howlers, baboons, macaques, etc.)

Apes

(gibbons, orangutans, chimpanzees, gorillas)

Humans

Present

10

20

30

40

50

60

70

Millions of years ago
(Dates are approximate)

Original primates
(Rat-sized insect eaters)

laws are not always strictly enforced; government officials often look the other way and sometimes do nothing to prevent the purchase of looted material by museum directors and other collectors whose desires for objects of art keep the looters in business.

Such problems aside, the normal difficulties of excavating are

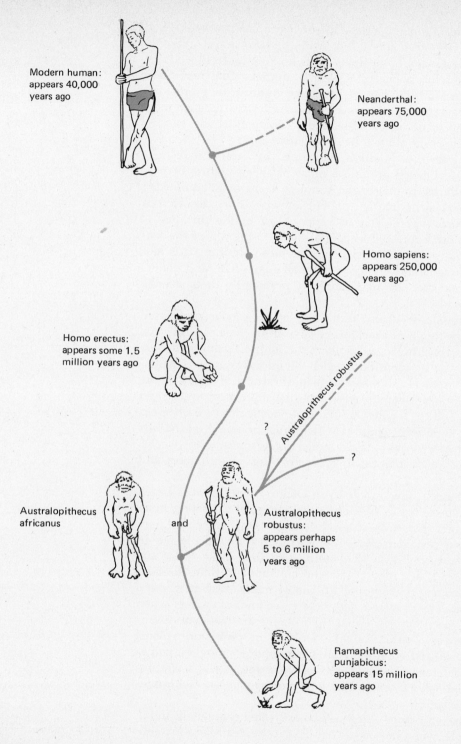

Evolution of man in Europe, Asia, and Africa from about 70 million years ago to the present

Modern human: appears 40,000 years ago

Neanderthal: appears 75,000 years ago

Homo sapiens: appears 250,000 years ago

Homo erectus: appears some 1.5 million years ago

Australopithecus robustus

?

?

Australopithecus africanus

and

Australopithecus robustus: appears perhaps 5 to 6 million years ago

Ramapithecus punjabicus: appears 15 million years ago

7

enough to tax the ingenuity and patience of legitimate workers. Even seasoned archeologists have discarded evidence and have gathered what they could see easily—large items such as flint projectile points, butchering tools, and the bones of big-game animals. One result has been an overemphasis on the role of big-game hunting in prehistoric survival. Because big-game hunting is a male activity and because most archeologists happen to be males who tend to reconstruct the past in their own image, this point of view has been fostered.

A technique known as flotation, developed by Danish investigators half a century ago, helps provide a more balanced picture of prehistoric survival patterns. In one of the simplest forms of flotation, dirt from excavated layers is poured into a bucket with a window-screen bottom which is partly submerged in water. Most of the dirt passes through the screen, but lightweight material floats to the top of the water in the bucket and is scooped off with a fine mesh strainer. This material may include fragmentary remains of small game, fish, and plants, and analyses indicate that the major part of prehistoric diets usually consisted of such foods.

Another increasingly useful technique is the analysis of fossil pollen, grains whose tough outer coatings have been preserved in such fine detail that grasses, shrubs, oak, holly, pine, juniper, palm, and dozens of other plants can be identified under the microscope. It is painstaking work. Each grain is examined at magnifications of 400 to more than 1500 times for size, shape, types, and distribution of spiny and rodlike extensions, and for a wide variety of surface features. Each grain has about 40 to 50 significant features which must be noted. Hundreds of grains may be analyzed daily, and a project may continue for weeks. The results provide invaluable aid in reconstructing past climates and environments.

In New Zealand, at the University of Otago, Dunedin, Foss Leach and his associates specialize in developing new ways of extracting more and more information from archeological deposits. One procedure uses the observation that certain mollusks which prehistoric people ate in large quantities show shell growth patterns like tree rings. Since the rings tend to be formed at a regular rate and are about 20 times broader in summer than winter, microscopic studies of many excavated shells indicate when the mollusks were caught and eaten and, of course, when the particular site was occupied. Other experiments are based on examinations of fish scales, teeth, stonelike remains of prehistoric plants known as plant opals, and other material. Contemporary diggers, knowing of such research, generally leave one fourth to one half of a site undug for future workers who will come with more advanced techniques and greater knowledge.

In exceptional situations, sites may be excavated completely and in a hurry, for example, when they are scheduled to be destroyed for non-archeological reasons, which is happening more and more frequently as construction crews build new homes and highways for expanding populations. Work was halted for five months during the building of new apartments on the French Riviera when bulldozers exposed tools and other signs of a prehistoric encampment. In this case, as in the case of Nile Valley sites flooded by the Aswan Dam in Egypt, the objective was to recover as much evidence as possible in a limited time.

Emotional involvement and feuding of various types, by no means unknown in other sciences, reach a strikingly high level among prehistorians, an occupational ailment which may have something to do with the sustained loneliness of digging and the difficulty of obtaining solid evidence. "I can't account for it," says an anthropologist who has been in the thick of a number of heated debates, "but there is something about exploring the past that affects you. It seems that every time people find a human bone they go crazy on the spot." Traces of the remote past affect us strongly, for reasons which have yet to be determined.

The human story is known in broad outline. The hominids of 10 to 15 million years ago were small, probably hairy creatures—considerably less than human, but something more than apes. Most investigators assume that they were moving out of dense ancestral forests into open woodlands and savanna grasslands. They probably used tools such as digging sticks and clubs and walked upright a good deal of the time as they carried their tools. Furthermore, although monkeys and apes lived almost exclusively on plant foods in those days as they do now, the odds are that the tool users' diet was rather more inclusive and consisted of appreciable proportions of meat—everything from insects, snakes, lizards, and rodents to antelopes and other herd animals—as well as of plants.

The very variety of their diet demanded a wide knowledge about other wild species. Fruits, nuts, cereal grasses, and other plants ripened at different times in different places. Some plants were poisonous, and it must have taken long periods of trial and error and many mysterious deaths to learn the hard way which species to avoid. It also took time to learn the habits of birds and other small and large prey, particularly those built-in habits which made them vulnerable to snares, traps, pitfalls, and ambushes. There was a premium on cooperation, the sharing of food and knowledge, and group defenses against lions and other established killers encountered in the savanna during the food quest.

Change came slowly in the beginning. The most advanced hominids of about 5 million years ago had brains perhaps half again as large as those of their remote ancestors, and although brain size is by no means an infallible criterion, it does provide a rough index of evolutionary progress in the primate line. Three million years later, however, it was a different story. By that time, brain sizes had more than dou-

bled, putting them in the modern size range; the first members of the
genus *Homo* had appeared.

The rise of *Homo sapiens* is intimately connected to the rise of increasingly complex social organizations and methods of obtaining food. Our kind began to dominate the scene more than 100,000 years ago, and ever since then cultural evolution has been moving at an accelerating rate. The final phase of prehistory, the last twentieth or so of the long journey from the newcomers on the savanna to modern people, includes the oldest traces of religion and art. It also includes the high point in the development of the hunt, the mass killing of herd animals by many bands or on a tribal basis; after which there was a decline of the hunt as an activity essential to the community, a decline that began some 10,000 years ago with the invention of agriculture. The invention of writing about four or five millennia later may be taken as the official end of prehistory.

Something unprecedented happened during the course of these and subsequent events, something that acquires special meaning in the light of all that happened before the appearance of human beings. Their evolutionary position involves two apparently contradictory truths, namely, that they have much in common with other animals (far more than is generally realized) and, at the same time, that they represent another order of being. Humans are not merely a new species but the pioneers of an entirely new kind of evolution.

All previous species, some 500 million extinct as well as surviving forms, evolved by mutation and natural selection. And all species, from whales and giant redwood trees to tadpole-shaped viruses so small that several billion of them would fit comfortably into a sphere no bigger across than the period at the end of this sentence, share certain basic similarities at the molecular level. They transmit their characteristics from generation to generation in the form of genes, discrete and highly organized molecules of hereditary materials known as nucleic acids, almost always the one known as DNA (short for deoxyribonucleic acid).

There are other similarities. The DNA generally comes in the form of a double helix, two long atomic chains interconnected and tightly coiled into a spiral-staircase structure, and includes large numbers of the same four nitrogen-containing units or bases: adenine (A), thymine (T), cytosine (C), and guanine, (G). The order in which these units occur in the DNA of a particular species determines the nature of that species. The bases may be thought of as a kind of genetic alphabet, letters which spell out the specifications for organisms and control the manufacture of proteins that form living tissue. Imagine a series of DNA molecules, genes, uncoiled to produce long strings of bases attached to one another. A string starting C-A-G-T-T-A might represent the instructions for the shaping of an amoeba, and strings starting C-G-

A-C-T-G and A-C-C-T-A-G might represent a monkey and an elephant. **11**

A complete collection would consist of some 10 million such strings, one for each existing species. Furthermore, although there are some exceptions, the general rule is that the more complicated an organism, the longer the genetic message it transmits to its offspring, that is, the more instructions required for the building of future generations. The total length of all the DNA chains in some viruses is less than 1/25,000 of an inch, while it takes about 5 feet of DNA to make a person.

Living things are designed to maintain the integrity of the hereditary material. DNA molecules with their bases in proper order are duplicated over and over again in generations of sperm and egg cells, and the duplicating mechanisms may work with wonderful accuracy. They may turn out a million or more highly organized molecules in succession, each one made up of millions and millions of atoms and each one a faithful copy of the one before it, within close biological tolerances.

This process reflects a massive conservatism, a way developed over the ages to preserve things as they are, to maintain distinct and unchanging species. Powerful biological forces resist change. No other process is so nearly flawless; certainly no man-made machine can approach it. But sooner or later a slip-up or mutation occurs on the genetic assembly line. It may be a very small change, perhaps a missing base or two, or a "misspelling" in the form of a change of base order, say, from A-T-C-G to A-G-C-T.

A DNA molecule departs in a small way from inherited genetic blueprints, and that makes all the difference. If there were no slip-ups, no mutations, the highest form of life today, assuming life could exist at all, might be a single-celled organism. Evolution, the "force like a hundred thousand wedges" which so impressed Darwin, exists simply because nothing is perfect, not even the chemical operations of heredity, which represent the closest thing to perfection, to infallible reproduction, that we know of.

New species are formed in isolation, under conditions which permit a measure of independent evolution. In the vast majority of cases the first steps take place when geographic barriers, anything from a stream that cannot be crossed to an ocean or a range of mountains, divide parts of the ancestral species from one another. The separated subpopulations begin to undergo distinctive changes. Mutations which would formerly have spread throughout the ancestral population now accumulate on either side of the barrier. Furthermore, since no two environments are exactly alike, the adaptations called for on either side of the barrier will differ in certain respects.

After a sufficient number of generations, the net effect is two genetically incompatible subpopulations. The differences between them have become so great that even if the barrier is removed or crossed they can no longer interbreed to reproduce generations of viable offspring.

At this point a new species is said to have arisen. Darwin studied such a case on the Galapagos Islands which lie in the Pacific Ocean about 600 miles from the nearest mainland, the coast of Ecuador. The islands were inhabited by more than a dozen species of finches, all of them the descendants of a colony of finches presumably blown to the islands by high winds and all of them sufficiently isolated from one another to develop different adaptations and species status.

The Galapagos finches provide a good model for the origin of species throughout the course of evolution; new species are still being formed. The Grand Canyon in northern Arizona separates two kinds of squirrel which had a common ancestor centuries ago and have been diverging genetically ever since. The question is whether the squirrels have yet become sufficiently different to be classified as different species, but they seem to be heading in that direction.

Human beings are subject to the same evolutionary forces that shaped and are shaping their fellow species. The geography of their speciation, the specific barriers that isolated hominid populations at various times in the past, is unknown. But there were barriers, and we are the result of them. Like all other creatures, we arose by the processes of mutation and natural selection, and we continue to depend on our genes. The big difference is that in other creatures genetic evolution plays the major role, while in us cultural evolution has developed to an unprecedented degree.

The things other species need to survive, to escape and kill and adapt, are generally built in as part of their bodies. Their genes determine the growth of fur, horns, scales, claws, wings, and so on. We learn and pass accumulating knowledge as well as genes from generation to generation; we make a wide variety of shelters and weapons and, to an increasing extent, our own environments. Culture permitted our ancestors, a single species, to spread throughout the world, to live and reproduce in high mountain valleys, semideserts, tropical rain forests, and subzero Arctic regions. Of course, genes continue to operate in us, just as learning may play an important role among other species. After all, we inherit our brain, and it, more than anything else, makes us human. But in our world, learning and tradition have acquired a new order of importance.

This is a relatively recent trend. In the earliest hominid days on the savanna our ancestors were still very much genetic creatures in the sense that heredity played a far greater part in their activities than it does in ours. The way was prepared for new possibilities sometime during the development of social organization and the accompanying expansion of the brain during the past few million years. About 100 millennia ago, culture began overtaking genetics as the major determinant in human behavior.

The most important development of all, a kind of overgrowth or hypertrophy of culture, is even more recent. All other species are basically standpatters. They tend to live today very much the way they lived yesterday, assuming, of course, that the environment does not change. Given reasonably stable conditions, a favorable climate, plenty of food, and no human beings in the area, even chimpanzees—the animals most like us—would continue living in the same way indefinitely. The point is that they adapt, and in the process of adapting, they do not change their forests. This is what we mean by saying they are in balance with nature.

The same cannot be said for us as we have evolved in our times. Stability is not for us. When we settle down, forests are felled and earth is moved and the world begins changing radically. As the only species to produce major changes in the environment, we try to adapt in a difficult and unique situation. In effect, we create increasingly complex environments, which demand continual adaptations and readaptations. Moreover, the tendency is not to minimize change but to seek it out and discover and invent it. We have created in ourselves a new chronic restlessness, a process which continually works against equilibrium, an antihomeostasis. At present it seems that our genes can barely keep up with the pace of cultural change.

Science offers no problem more complex than that of reconstructing the events and forces which have produced this condition, perhaps the outstanding characteristic of human evolution. This book is concerned with prehistory, with nomadic hunters and gatherers. It follows their evolution to the point when they are just beginning to settle down on farms. Subsequent events mark the coming of writing and records, the end of prehistory. The first part of the book deals chiefly with archeological evidence about extinct species, with artifacts and fossils and other material dug out of the earth. The second part, starting with Chapter 12, focuses on another important and closely related area of study, living prehistory, which provides clues to the past as revealed by the behavior of existing species.

Much can be learned from other members of the order of primates, which includes monkeys and apes. Recent investigations show that their behavior in their native forests and savannas may be surprisingly human. They have traditions, often rather sophisticated traditions, and leaders and hierarchies, and they spend considerable time trying to maintain or improve their social status. When an opportunity arises, some of them will break their vegetarian diets and eat meat, even hunting upon occasion. Savanna-dwelling monkeys have evolved ways of defending themselves against predators which may well have been used by early hominids.

As wildernesses vanish, investigators are taking a look at the last surviving bands of hunter-gatherers, people still living much as our ancestors lived 40,000 or more years ago. They still endure without agri-

culture in desert places, where they have been forced to live and where
they fare much better than one might expect, thus demonstrating once
again the capacity of humans to make their way under demanding conditions. Investigators are also studying people in cities and suburbs.
New knowledge about such things as the bond between a mother and
her infant, the nature of language and how children acquire it, and
mass aggressiveness as a predominantly male characteristic inevitably
deepens the understanding of the past because it is rooted in the past.

Contemporary research in living prehistory and archeology looks
in both directions. It is relevant to the present and future as well as to
the past. The study of prehistory presents modern times in a wider perspective so that we see ourselves more dispassionately in the light of
remote origins, and above all so that we may rid ourselves of at least a
few of the cliches and preconceptions that hold us down. We live with
the past and always, to some extent, in it; we explore it to learn more
about ourselves and what we may become.

CHAPTER 1   PRIMATE ORIGINS

A decade ago two excavators made an important find on Purgatory Hill, not far from the Fort Peck Reservoir in northeastern Montana. Leigh Van Valen of the American Museum of Natural History and Robert Sloan of the University of Minnesota were working at a bone-dry and eroded site. Long ago a stream flowed there through abundant forests. Animals died near the banks. When the banks collapsed or heavy rains came, they were swept downstream to a place where a large slow eddy had formed. Their bodies swirled on the lee side of the eddy, sank, and settled on a bed of clams. Over the ages sediments filtered down to cover everything.

Today the site is a compacted rocky conglomerate of clam shells, minerals, and bits of fossil embedded in a silty matrix. Van Valen and Sloan tossed chunks into hundred-pound sacks and rolled the sacks down the steep hillside to a truck at a nearby reservoir. They poured the rock into fine mesh screens, washing it in the lake until the matrix dissolved. The remainder went to a University of Minnesota laboratory to be dumped into a bathtub-sized vat of dilute acetic acid. The acid dissolved the clam shells, leaving a mixture which included, among other things, the fragmentary remains of extinct species.

The Montana project yielded important prehistoric remains after scientists had removed more than 30,000 pounds of rock from Purgatory Hill and sifted through the debris. The most striking find consisted of half a dozen molar and premolar teeth, bits of bony fossil 65 million years old, each about the size of the head of a paper book match. These were traces of the earliest known primates, the order that includes monkeys and apes and humans. Since then other investigators have been working sites in the same geological formation as that represented at Purgatory Hill. William Clemens of the University of California in Berkeley and his associates have found more than a hundred teeth and two dozen lower jaw bones of the early primate genus known as *Purgatorius*.

15

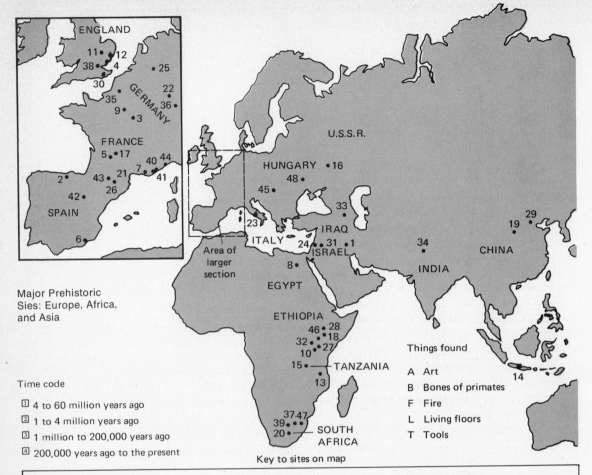

Major Prehistoric
Sies: Europe, Africa,
and Asia

Things found

A   Art
B   Bones of primates
F   Fire
L   Living floors
T   Tools

Time code

[1] 4 to 60 million years ago

[2] 1 to 4 million years ago

[3] 1 million to 200,000 years ago

[4] 200,000 years ago to the present

Key to sites on map

1. Ali Kosh [4] L, T	18. Lake Turkana site [2] B, T	35. St. Acheul [3] T
2. Altamira [4] A, T	19. Lantian site [3] B	36. Steinheim [4] B
3. Arcy [4] B, F, L, T	20. Makapan [2] B	37. Sterkfontein [2] B, T
4. Clacton-on-Sea [3] T	21. Mas D'Azil [4] A, T	38. Swanscombe [4] B, T
5. Combe Grenal [4] F, L, T	22. Mauer site [3] B	39. Taung [2] B
6. Cueva de Ambrosio [4] B, F, T	23. Monte Circeo [4] B, T	40. Terra Amata [4] F, L, T
7. Escale cave [3] B, F, L, T	24. Mt. Carmel [4] B, F, T	41. Lazaret [4] F, L, T
8. Fayum Depression [1] B	25. Neanderthal [4] B	42. Torralba-Ambrona [3] B, F, L, T
9. Pincevent [4] A, F, L, T	26. Niaux [4] A, T	43. Tuc d'Audoubert [4] A, T
10. Fort Ternan [1] B	27. Olduvai Gorge [2] B, L, T	44. Vallonet cave [3] B, T
11. High Lodge [4] T	28. Omo [2] B, T	45. Vertesszöllos [3] B, F, L, T
12. Hoxne [4] T	29. Peking Man [3] B, F, T	46. Lothagam [1] B
13. Isimila [4] F, L, T	30. Piltdown (discredited)	47. Swartkrans [2] B
14. Java site [3] B	31. Qafzeh [4] B, F, T	48. Molodova [4] B, T, L, F
15. Kalambo Falls [4] B, F, L, T	32. Rusinga Island [1] B	
16. Kostenki [4] A, B, F, L, T	33. Shanidar cave [4] B, F, L, T	
17. La Chapelle-aux-Saints [4] B, T	34. Siwalik Hills [1] B	

The coming of primates has its own prehistory. It was part of a much earlier sequence of events which includes the rise and fall of reptiles, the rise of mammals, and a global splitting up of continents. Reptiles dominated the earth some 225 million years ago, when the first dinosaurs appeared along with the first ancestors of mammals. At the time, the world was literally one world. No separate continents existed, only a great single land mass or island in the midst of a great single ocean, a supercontinent known as Pangea.

But divisive stresses were already at work. Cracks or rifts were appearing deep in the earth, under the land mass and under the ocean. The earth started splitting into some twenty huge blocks of land or plates, along flaw lines possibly built into the planet during its formation 4 to 5 billion years ago. The first plate to break away from the supercontinent of Pangea was India-Antarctica, which formed a single block. By 200 million years ago there were three plates, India and Antarctica having drifted apart, while South America-Africa was attached to North America-Europe-Asia at only one place, Gibraltar. In one of the most recent developments, North America separated from Europe-Asia and attached itself to South America, which had previously separated from Africa. (The process is continuing; within 10 million years or so, parts of Somaliland-Kenya-Tanzania are scheduled to become an island off mainland Africa, and a piece of southern California including Los Angeles will have broken off and started drifting toward San Francisco.)

These changes had a major impact on all subsequent evolution. The breaking up of Pangea produced an island effect, creating huge blocks of land and isolating large groups of species from one another. Isolation is one of the main factors promoting rapid and diverse evolution. Such conditions favor the appearance of new adaptations and new orders of creatures, since they have a chance to develop on their own in many different environments. Certainly the class of mammals spread widely and produced a rich variety of orders, more than 30 including the primates.

The first mammals, the remote ancestors of whales and tigers and human beings, were beady-eyed, bewhiskered, long-snouted creatures no bigger than your little finger. They may have existed for 130 million years before beginning to increase about 70 million years ago. They scurried and snuffled through fallen leaves and undergrowth for their food, which was chiefly insects. They probably also devoured mostly anything else that was edible. Most seem to have been night feeders who spent the day huddled in nests and burrows. Unimpressive and inconspicuous, they had good reason to walk small. Giants were abroad.

Triceratops, a three-horned plant eater of about 5 tons with a head 7 feet long, and other dinosaurs dominated the earth. Recent studies by Robert Bakker of Harvard University suggest that dinosaurs were

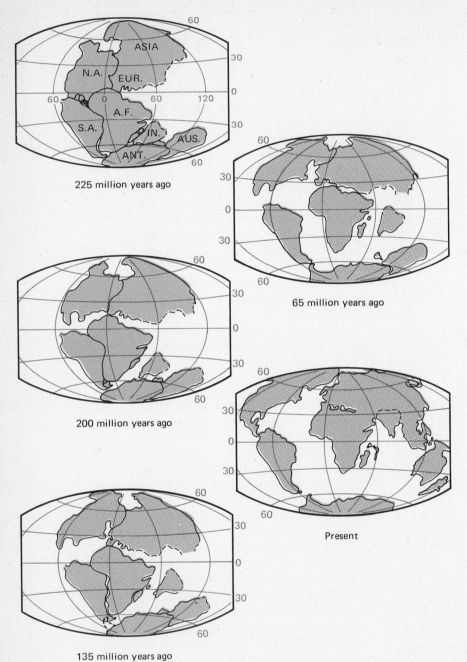

225 million years ago

200 million years ago

135 million years ago

65 million years ago

Present

Breakup of the
universal continent,
Pangea

not the sluggish, lumbering, cold-blooded animals described in textbooks. Rather more like mammals than reptiles, they were warm-blooded and swift-running. Furthermore, they did not vanish in a sudden twilight-of-the-gods melodrama, inundated en masse in waves of white-hot lava or dying of thirst, as pictured in the fantasy clichés of Hollywood and Disney and the comic strips. According to Bakker, they passed gradually in relatively quiet times "with the draining of shallow seas on the continents and a lull in mountain-building activity in most parts of the world." Incapable of changing with changing times, they produced fewer and fewer offspring in successive generations. Mammals finally came into their own after more than 100 million years in the shadows.

The earliest primates, small rodent-like creatures known as prosimians or premonkeys, lived in a time of rising temperatures and extensive forests. Today's dwindling forests, stretches or patches of woodland among cities and deserts and eroded regions and farms, are mere remnants of what used to be. A belt of almost continuous tropical and subtropical forests thousands of miles wide extended from Seattle and Vancouver to southern Argentina and Chile, from London to Cape Town, from Japan to southern Australia. In the Sahara, woodlands and savannas and lakes existed where desert is now. There were crocodiles, palm trees, and swamps in England, France, and the northwestern United States.

Prosimians had to adapt in the dense foliage and branches and canopies of the forests, and how they did it is of direct concern to humans. Humans are forest creatures to the extent that their basic structures, brain, sense organs, limbs, and reproductive system, evolved in the forests. Later developments generally called for modifications and elaborations of those structures rather than for totally new ones. Preadaptation, the evolution of features in one environment which also happen to be as appropriate or even more so in a future environment, has been important in the shaping of all species, including humans.

Life in the trees offered interesting evolutionary possibilities, largely because it was not a complete exploitation of the third dimension as is the flight of birds. Flying, which puts a premium on lightness, produced small and highly specialized species. As in man-made flying machines, every fraction of an ounce of weight that could be dispensed with was. One result has been a brain incorporating within a small space circuitry far more compact than anything yet designed by engineers concerned with minicomputers and solid-state physics. It coordinates elaborate nesting and mating behavior, communications, keen eyesight, and swift maneuvers in space. It gained compactness at the price of some flexibility—bird behavior tends to have a set, stereotyped quality.

Life on the ground provided another range of opportunities. Proceeding at a different pace, it did not need to be as automatic. It permitted the development of big bodies and big brains and offered the possibility of flexible, adjustable behavior based to a greater degree on learning. There was time on the ground for watching, pausing, and a measure of preparation. Species could prowl about and lie in wait. Lying in wait demands control and the delay of reflexes and, at the same time, a readiness for swift responses. Inhibition achieved through regulatory centers in the nervous system serves the survival of animals that can bide their time. On the other hand, the challenge and complexity of general navigation hunting, and escaping were not as great on the ground as in free flight.

Life in the trees combined certain features of earthbound and aerial modes of existence. Species could evolve with brains large enough to handle considerable learning and to accommodate the built-in circuitry for advanced visual powers and sensory and muscular coordination. Even more significant, life in the trees introduced a unique feature, a new and chronic psychological insecurity or uncertainty. The ground is reasonably broad and solid, a dependable platform; the air is consistently insubstantial and must be coped with accordingly. The uncertainty in the trees stemmed from unpredictable changes between solid and aerial states. The environment was full of discontinuities, surprises. From a ground dweller's point of view, such a life would be roughly equivalent to speeding through tall dense grasses without being able to see more than a few feet ahead and suddenly coming upon a gaping hole too wide to cross. Such hazards, numerous and scattered at random over the terrain, require frequent swift decisions about how far to jump and in what direction. To live in trees, with such gaps between branches, is to be confronted continually with emergencies.

In addition, branches are never absolutely reliable as launching or landing sites, or even as resting places. A branch may be firm and solid as the ground itself, or it may sway, give, or break because it is too small or brittle to bear weight. One of the most amazing recoveries from a serious and seemingly unavoidable accident has been described by Ray Carpenter of Pennsylvania State University, a pioneer observer of primate behavior. One day in Thailand he saw a female gibbon swinging out on a limb and preparing for a take-off leap to another tree. At just that instant, the limb snapped off, leaving a stub about 6 inches long. The ape was suspended in space for a split second. "As the limb broke and fell, the gibbon recovered by turning almost in midair and catching the remaining stub of the branch. With extreme rapidity she swung around under and then on top of the [stub] and then, with only a slight loss of time and momentum, jumped outward and downward 30 feet to an adjacent tree top."

First mammal:
200,000,000-year-old
insect eater, about
the size of a little
finger, as
reconstructed by
Robert Bakker of
Harvard University

Dime-sized jawbone:
evidence from
southern Africa for
first mammal

Water hole at
Amboseli: early man
lived on such
savannas

A supreme trapeze artist, the product of hundreds of thousands of generations of evolution, the gibbon had managed to avoid trouble by a swift and superbly executed maneuver. While such agility in three dimensions is typical of many tree dwellers, the prosimians that took up life in the forests about 65 million years ago had some unique traits. Probably, almost from the beginning, they had fingers rather than the claws which are characteristic of such primitive species as the present-day long-tailed tree shrews of Southeast Asia. Tree shrews, incidentally, resemble both rodents and primates, so that paleontologists have shifted them from one order to the other several times. The latest and probably final decision is that they are not primates. Some tree shrews go abroad only at night, and all of them are vicious fighters and voracious eaters, consuming their own weight or more in food each day.

A recent theory by Matt Cartmill of Duke University accounts for a number of early primate developments. He believes that prosimian fingers evolved as an aid to the food quest, since they favor "cautious well-controlled movements in pursuit of prey on slender supports." The prey consisted primarily of insects, and the slender supports included creeping vines and small branches, which would be encountered while foraging among shrubs, bushes, and trees. As grasping elements, fingers equipped with flattened nails and a thumb capable of moving opposite to the other four digits to form a locking grip were useful for predation in those environments.

Other changes came with the increasing exploitation of insects

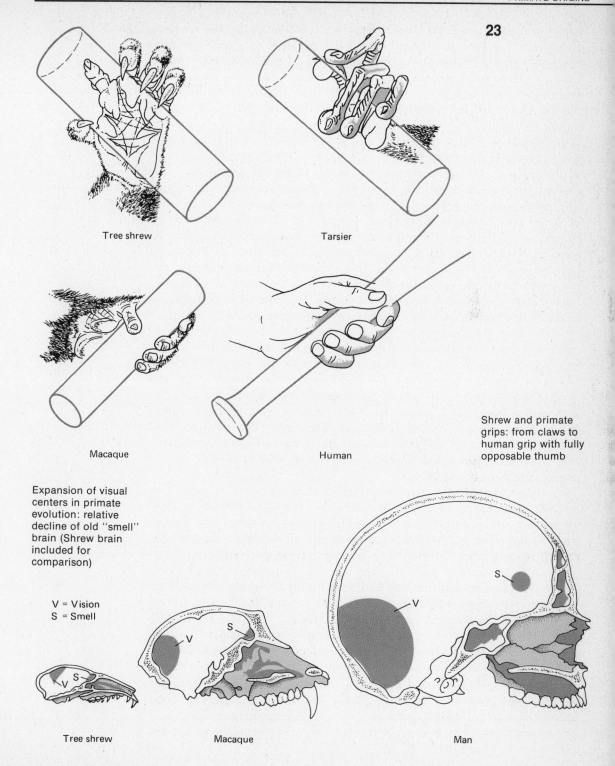

Tree shrew

Tarsier

Macaque

Human

Shrew and primate grips: from claws to human grip with fully opposable thumb

Expansion of visual centers in primate evolution: relative decline of old "smell" brain (Shrew brain included for comparison)

V = Vision
S = Smell

Tree shrew

Macaque

Man

and forest environments. While preprimate mammals tended to have
small eyes on the sides of an extended and tapering snout, in prosimians the eyes became larger, perhaps as an adaptation to let in more
light and improve nighttime vision. Furthermore, the eyes moved forward like twin headlights as the snout retreated, which results in better
depth perception, an enormous advantage complementing the use of
hands and fingers for close manipulative work. Although three-dimensional vision is limited to distances of about 10 feet, it contributes also
to accuracy and sure-footedness in leaping from bough to bough.

These and other developments were intimately connected with
the development of more elaborate brains. In particular, moving about
in a rich three-dimensional arboreal environment favored the expansion
of the cerebral cortex, or outer bark of the brain. This structure arose in
response to an earlier adventure in evolution, a rudimentary pinhead-
sized patch of cells on the brain surfaces of the first creatures that came
out of the sea and took up life on land. But with the rise of mammals,
the cortex really began coming into its own as an organ for coordinating
highly complex behavior, analyzing messages flowing in from the sense
organs, and sending messages of its own to the muscles.

Although the prosimian brain was only the size of a pea in a 2-
inch skull by this stage of evolution, the cortex had spread like a gray
tide over the brain's surface, and it consisted of a thin sheet of millions
of nerve cells. One cortical area was located toward the front of the
head. The most important part of the so-called smell brain, it had a long
and respectable history dating back to creatures which guided themselves primarily with the sense of smell. The newer part of the cortex,
located at the back of the brain, had expanded to deal with the increasing amount of visual information involved in the successful perfor-
mance of arboreal acrobatics.

Improved grasping preceded improved thinking, in line with an
ancient evolutionary tradition. Muscle and the special senses such as
sight and smell, movement and sensation, are primary, and nerves
evolved to serve them. The predominance of the brain and of intelligence, language, and discovery, is a very recent development.

A major turning point in the history of primates occurred about
35 million years ago. Prosimians had been highly successful for millions
of years, multiplying, spreading widely, and dominating the vast forests
of the times. Then they began declining rapidly, probably because of
intense competition from other primates, from monkeys and apes. Geological changes that had begun long ago and had helped accelerate the
passing of the dinosaurs were approaching a climax.

The weight of sediments accumulating on the floor of the great
sea that stretched from Spain to Malaya caused a sagging in some
places, an upward buckling in others, and the appearance of island
ridges which were to become the Alps. Mountain-building processes

elsewhere gave rise to precursors of the Himalayas, Rockies, and Andes. The net effect was a further splitting up of the lands, continuing a process that dates back to the beginning of continental drift. New land masses came into being, creating new environments and zones for new species. A similar fragmenting affected parts of the forest belt; the trees dwindled in various localities, giving way to open grasslands which also offered zones for new species. All the changes offered new evolutionary opportunities. Elephants, deer, rhinoceroses, and other modern mammals appeared together with monkeys and apes.

In this period, the Egyptian coast of the Mediterranean extended some hundred miles farther inland, so that part of the Spain-to-Malaya sea covered areas where Cairo and the Pyramids stand today. Coastal plains and savannas merged with thick and humid tropical forests through which sluggish swamp-lined rivers moved to the shallow sea. The rivers carried the bodies of many animals, and their sands buried the bodies. In relatively recent times lava from the depths of the earth forced its way to the surface, and cracks in the earth's crust formed steep cliffs and ridges.

The region called the Fayum Depression, a wasteland on the eastern edge of the Sahara, is one of the world's richest fossil-primate sites. Between the turn of the century and 1960, collectors had found only 7 pieces of primate remains in the Fayum, but since 1960 more than 200 have been found in expeditions headed by Elwyn Simons of Yale University. Among the finds is part of a lower jaw, which may represent the earliest known ancestor of living monkeys, a diagnosis based largely on tooth studies. It had 32 teeth, like most present-day monkeys, as compared with 34 teeth for most prosimians, and a special 4-cusp pattern also typical of monkeys (although this pattern is absent from the molar teeth). It was probably about the size of a small cat, which is large enough for a prosimian, although not for a monkey, in accord with the general trend toward increasing size among primates.

Within 10 million years, monkeys had spread throughout the forests and developed the basis for an entirely different kind of viewing and dealing with the world. Every change was part of a complex of interrelated changes, part of an emerging evolutionary pattern. The sense of smell declined in importance. A generation or two ago, investigators said that this decline was due to the impossibility of making or following clear-cut scent trails in the trees and that arboreal primates could not use the sense of smell to detect sharply defined, coherent, and directional patterns in the broken-up context of leaves and branches and the gaps between them. This turns out not to be the case since primates and other arboreal species mark out clearly defined territories and trails by urinating at strategic spots, and they distinguish friend from foe by these odors.

In comparison with sight, however, the sense of smell assumed a

Fayum Depression, Egypt: searching for fossils

secondary position. The olfactory nerve, which carries signals from nose to brain, decreases in diameter, a development indicated by comparative measurements of the holes in the nasal part of the skull through which the nerve passes. (This is recapitulated in human growth: some olfactory-nerve cells begin dying off even before birth, and about half of them have died by middle age.)

Hands and sense organs evolved together, each development accelerating the other in an involved feedback relationship. Hands acquired a considerably richer supply of nerve cells and fibers concerned with the sense of touch. Fingers became more and more mobile and ca-

Fayum Depression, Egypt: fossil being prepared for removal

pable, not only of moving faster but also of assuming a far greater variety of positions. They were used increasingly for getting food and, even more important, for picking up objects, bringing them closer, and turning them around to examine them from all angles. The ability to manipulate in this way was new in the history of terrestrial life, and it reached a high point in the monkey family.

In fact, from one point of view the monkey's universe was the first to contain full-fledged objects. The very notion of objects in an environment made up of separate and distinct things some of which could be moved for one's own purposes came with the simian way of life, with a superbly developed visual sense and advanced manipulative powers. The world was objectified, or fragmented into things which stood out from the background, as it had never been before. Eyes placed at the sides of the head see landscapes as two-dimensional flat sheets and respond to motion across the sheets; they are poorly designed to detect what does not move or what moves slowly and directly toward the observer rather than across the field of vision.

A more and more complete picture of reality, a revelation, came with the movement of the eyes from a side to an up-front position and with color vision, which developed to an advanced stage among monkeys. Imagine that you can see things in two dimensions only. You are standing on a plain looking toward a place where animals move among tall grasses and shrubs, and everything has a flat stage-set quality, some of the animals merging in part with the landscape and others well camouflaged and entirely invisible.

Then as you watch you acquire stereoscopic and color vision and the scene changes. The scene begins to take on depth, slowly at first and more rapidly later, as shapes and shadows seem to move forward and backward and assume their natural places. Animals and objects which were visible but not in full perspective begin to stand out more completely as distinct entities. Animals and objects invisible in two-dimensional black-and-white viewing become increasingly visible with the appearance of a richer and richer variety of colors, so that even at a distance you get the feeling of almost being among them.

Something like this happened gradually during primate evolution. Color vision helped to detect predators and later, when primates themselves became increasingly predatory, to detect potential prey. Marcel Hladik and Georges Pariente at the National Museum of Natural History in Brunoy, France, are investigating the possibility that color vision played and plays a role in selecting food. Preliminary studies of monkeys sharing the same forest areas in Ceylon and Panama indicate that they tend to exploit foods of different colors, and that different species may be sensitive to these preferred colors.

Our visual apparatus is a direct heritage from life in the trees. It has changed little since the days when monkeys were the earth's high-

est primates. The structure of the monkey brain reflected the increasing
emphasis on vision. The cortex expanded considerably, perhaps about
two to three times, burying most of the old smell-brain centers. Although a large part of the expansion involved the visual cortex at the
back of the brain, other areas were affected; for example, certain areas
concerned with the control of finger movements—a tiny strip of cortex
on the right side of the brain controlling the fingers of the left hand and
a corresponding left-side strip controlling the right hand. The degree of
detail on the map of the cortex depends on the evolutionary status of
the species.

Judging by contemporary prosimians, ancestral forms must have
operated their fingers en masse, in one gross movement. That is, they
could not move fingers individually but moved them all together as a
single mechanism. When they curved their hands to make a grip, nerve
signals passed from the finger-control maps on the brain's surface to
appropriate muscles in the hands, and the muscles contracted. Such
generalized action did not require an elaborately organized map and
consisted mainly of a general five-finger area. But judging by observations of living species, monkeys evolving 30 million years or more ago
moved their fingers far more freely and independently; among other
things, they could bring thumb and forefinger together to pick up small
objects such as insects and seeds. Their cortical maps evolved accordingly, including, instead of one five-finger area, five separate one-finger
areas for more precise digital control.

Generally speaking, the finer the detail, the larger mapping area
required, a principle which applies to the wrist, arm, foot, toes, and
other parts that became more mobile among monkeys. Furthermore, as
the skin incorporated a richer supply of nerve cells registering the sense
of touch, touch maps also became larger and more detailed. The expansion of the cortex was the net effect of the expansions of many kinds of
maps. It also included larger association areas, areas devoted to the
swift analysis of information flowing from many sense organs, those
recording the state of affairs within as well as outside the body, and
from noncortical brain structures such as the cerebellum, attached to the
brain stem at the back of the head, which coordinates balance and the
tensions of more than 150 pairs of opposing muscles.

The brain, in short, was modified to serve the needs of a new
kind of animal. It included structures designed to coordinate at extremely rapid rates the movements of muscles and sets of muscles involved in complex manipulations, climbing, leaping, chasing, and being
chased. These structures could take orders from the cortex. But they also
had to be capable of automatic operations on their own because monkeys are restless, agile, and lightweight, and they often move so fast
that there is no time for deliberation. Their entire behavior pattern rep-

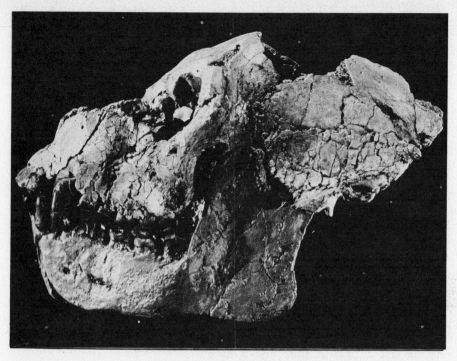

Aegyptopithecus:
representative of
earliest known apes

resented and represents a special and highly dynamic adaptation to the forests.

There were other kinds of primates in the trees. The pressure is always on in evolution. Life does not stay put but tends always to become more diverse, to develop new forms adapted to new and varied conditions. Sometimes it is a matter of occupying new places, filling hitherto empty living zones—as, for example, when fish invaded the land more than 350 million years ago or when prosimians and some rodents took to the trees. In other cases it may involve a new time zone, as when certain species of early mammals exploited the possibilities of nocturnal feeding. Another type of adaptation, another major variation of the primate theme, arose at about the same time monkeys appeared on the scene or perhaps somewhat later. The Fayum Depression has also yielded remains of the earliest known members of the ape family, species which developed a different approach to the forest world and a different type of biological organization.

A large part of the difference involved ways of using branches to obtain food. Most of the food in trees hangs at the ends of branches where it is beyond the reach of many animals and has the best chances of not being eaten. (This is its evolution for survival.) But apes have an ingenious way of getting at such places. A characteristic posture of an

ape in a tree is very roughly that of a monkey which has slipped and
saved itself by hanging on with its hands.

But what represents an emergency for the monkey has become an important form of behavior for the ape. In the structure of their wrists, arms, elbows, and shoulders, they are adapted for hanging suspended full length under branches and for walking on top of them as well, as monkeys generally do. In fact, feeding far out on slender branches is easier for apes than it is for monkeys; monkeys are lighter, but they must go on four feet. Sherwood Washburn of the University of California in Berkeley, a leading investigator of primate evolution and behavior, points out that an ape can distribute its weight strategically among three branches by holding fast with two feet and a hand and reaching out for a succulent piece of fruit with its free hand; "This is a distinctive behavior pattern of apes which can hang comfortably with one arm and do things with the other arm. Only an ape could have any possible reason for designing a bus or a subway train with straps."

But no ape is as good as the gibbon at swinging along through the trees. Using its powerful arm and shoulder muscles, it can propel itself 30 feet or more in one fluid movement, one of the most spectacular aerial maneuvers among nonflying animals. But in the course of evolving such talents, it had to stay small for the same reason that birds are small, to assure lightness and maximum mobility. (Gibbons are lighter than many monkeys, weighing only about 10 to 15 pounds.)

If all apes had gone the way of the gibbon, today's most advanced primates would be master aerialists rather than intellectuals. Some species followed another line of development, involving an evolutionary compromise between body weight and acrobatic skill. The most obvious advantage of being big was to discourage predators. The smallest prosimians and monkeys are fair game for the most abundant carnivores, small carnivores like snakes and eagles and jackals. (If they have any choice, large carnivores do not bother to eat such small game.) But only leopards, lions, and other big cats take on orangutans, chimpanzees, and the largest monkeys such as baboons. And nothing goes after gorillas but humans, who go after everything.

There may have been another reason for becoming bigger. The fossil record indicates that apes began spreading widely in Africa about 25 million years ago, reached a peak about 10 million years later with a record number of species, mostly relatively small forms, and then went into a sharp decline. The reasons for the decline are not at all clear. The number of species of arboreal monkeys seems to have increased enormously as the number of ape species decreased, which is somewhat surprising since apes had better brains. Apparently superior intelligence is not always enough.

Monkeys may have evolved more advanced social organizations than apes, perhaps because their troops tended to be larger and demanded more discipline and coordination. Another possibility, suggested by Robert Martin of University College, London, is based on observations of present-day species. Monkeys generally use food more efficiently than apes, grinding plant materials more thoroughly and thus permitting more complete digestion. Some species have compartments in their stomachs which are specialized to break down leafy foods; others, like the baboon, aid processes of digestion by softening food in cheek pouches before swallowing it. When competition for food is intense, as it might well have been 15 million years ago in African forests, any advantage in obtaining energy from food pays off handsomely in terms of survival.

So apes may have become bigger in self-defense, a point reinforced by the fact that in Asia, where arboreal monkeys are few, apes have remained relatively small. In Africa, gorillas and their ancestors may have specialized in highland-mountain living, while chimpanzees foraged mainly in lower woodland-orchard regions. Big primates roamed more widely and spent more time on the ground as well as in the trees, partly because they had less to fear and partly because they needed more food and had to travel farther for it. (Most monkeys possess home ranges of a fraction of a square mile to 3 square miles or so; apes move over a territory of 15 to 20 square miles, except for the little gibbon, whose range is at the low end of the monkey scale.) In other words, they encountered a wider and more varied environment.

Their evolving anatomy permitted a greater variety of movements. New nerve pathways developed in consequence—the cerebral expression of new possibilities. New cortical pathways appeared. The possible routes along which nerve signals may pass from sense organs to muscles increased enormously. The cortex is in part an organ of analysis, a dense feltwork of billions of nerve cells which lies between stimulus mechanisms and response mechanisms, between experience and action. Its complexity reflected the new complexity of the apes' world.

The ape brain responded to a new way of life and expanded with increased body size. As usual, the cortex expanded most. In early prosimians, as in most present-day prosimians, it tended to be a smooth gray sheet, since it lay almost entirely on the surface of the brain. But among apes it became wrinkled and folded primarily because of increasing variety of movement, the increasing role of hand-eye coordination, demanded more nerve pathways for the transmission and analysis of information. To meet this demand, natural selection favored the maximum cerebral tissue within the confines of a given skull capacity, so that the cortex spread down into crevices in the underlying white matter, a process already evident among monkeys. Perhaps 25 to 30 percent of the ape cortex is buried in the crevices as compared with 7 percent for monkeys.

The evolving cortex expressed another important trend, a greater and greater stress on inhibition, on the art of not doing things. This is implicit in the multiplicity of alternatives confronting advanced species. Choosing a course of action demands the ruling out of many possibilities. It also demands time, deliberation, and delay. Life becomes less automatic and depends to a greater extent than ever before on learning, and learning is an inevitable consequence of complexity in evolution. It became increasingly important among higher species whose environments offered a wider and wider range of choices.

Many forces shaped primates during the period from 25 to 70 million years ago. Important parts of the record are still missing; for example, we do not know what happened during the transition time when prosimians evolved into monkeys and apes. The earliest known species, represented by fossils in deposits of the Fayum, had obviously done considerable evolving before that.

But the record is clear on one point. Primates were evolution's most promising way of adapting mammals, inheritors of the earth after the decline of the dinosaurs, to the uncertainties and challenges of life in the trees. Something more happened in the process of adaptation. Some species were equipped not only for forest dwelling but also for a new and bold adventure, the invasion of open country which foreshadowed the coming of man.

Spread of savannas; nature of prehuman apes, an ancestor near Lake Victoria; significance of the small teeth of *Ramapithecus;* advantages of bipedalism; tool use among prehumans and modern chimpanzees; new fossil finds

CHAPTER 2 FIRST MEMBERS OF THE HUMAN FAMILY

Our ancestors arose 15 million years ago in the slowly changing subtropics of the Old World. The restlessness in the earth, a heritage from earlier periods, continued as the crust buckled and pushed up sediments thousands of feet thick that had accumulated on the floors of ancient seas. The buckling produced great mountain chains and intermontane valleys, including the great ranges of the Alps and Himalayas. Gases, ash, and lava poured out of volcanic craters, and increased rains produced intense erosion along the slopes of mountains and foothills. Worldwide annual temperatures fell, perhaps by as much as an average of 5 degrees Fahrenheit or so.

A broad forest extended from the west coast of Africa to the East Indies, but not the solid unbroken forest of former times. The savanna was on the move. Grasses spread in a slow tide among the trees, and there were dry plains wide as oceans, particularly on the lee side of newly formed highlands. Penetrating into the plains were dark peninsular stretches of gallery forest. In a sense nature was more natural then, the wilderness was wilder than it has ever been since. It might have been an Eden of a sort except for, or perhaps because of, the fact that humans had not yet put in an appearance.

But their coming, the increasing exploitation of savanna lands, was imminent. Most primates spent most of their lives in the shade, leading enclosed lives inside green caves of leaves and vines. They found pathways high in the forests, trails for leaping and swinging in the canopies of trees, familiar branches and footholds among dense foliage. They avoided more exposed places such as open woodlands where trees were somewhat fewer and farther between. Most of all, they avoided the wide-open, bright, uneasy places where savanna grasses rustled at the very edges of the woodlands.

Of course, then as now a few individuals were always ready to push their luck and investigate alien terrain. Such explorers have long **33**

had a special influence on the course of mammalian evolution, a point
emphasized by John Christian of the Albert Einstein Medical Center in
Philadelphia. He indicates that as a rule they tend not to be high-ranking members of groups: "It seems that the dominant core of a population or species is rarely primarily involved in the evolutionary process." In other words, evolving is a business for adventurers. More
often than not the adventurers are thwarted young males who have not
found places for themselves in the ranks of established hierarchies and
are driven out of the group's central area and practically forced to investigate action at the edges of things.

Restless young prehominids, like their counterparts among many
other species, probably spent considerable time playing I-dare-you
games and trying out environments which primates had not exploited.
But it took more than that to bring about full-scale permanent changes.
Moving out of relatively safe forests into the favorite hunting grounds
of the big cats and other predators probably was prompted by the problem of getting enough food.

It could have been a matter of warmer and drier climates, less
rainfall, and dwindling forests; or perhaps the forests were not shrinking, but primate populations were on the increase. Both possibilities
have been suggested and the evidence is insufficient to make out a
solid case for either one of them. At any event, the effect was the
same—too many individuals for the available food supply. The hominid
story from this stage on seems to be an increasing exploitation of increasingly open terrain.

The evidence indicates what sort of primate gave rise to humans.
In tests based on comparisons of the chemical nature of proteins taken
from the blood of living primates, if certain proteins from two species
react to about the same degree with an appropriate antiserum, the implications are that they are closely related chemically and that a close
evolutionary relationship may exist between the two species. Proteins
from two remotely related species, on the other hand, may react differently with the same antiserum, and the extent of the difference can be
measured with some precision.

Such tests show not only that humans are more closely related to
apes than to monkeys but also that they are more closely related to the
chimpanzee and gorilla than to the orangutan and gibbon, an observation which confirms the results of detailed anatomical studies. According to Morris Goodman of Wayne State University in Detroit, an authority on the comparative blood chemistry of primates, the kinship can
be expressed even more strongly. He believes that as far as protein research is concerned, the chimpanzee and gorilla are closer to humans
than they are to other apes.

Tests involving heredity-transmitting chromosomes and other
substances tend to support Goodman's findings. So do studies of pri-

mate parasites. Varieties of fleas, lice, and mites which live on humans and chimpanzees and gorillas leave gibbons and orangutans alone. Similarly, species of organisms causing malaria in humans do not affect the gibbon and orang, although some of them may produce a disease among chimpanzees and gorillas. It seems that certain parasites which infest humans, chimpanzees, and gorillas today had a common ancestor which is distinct from the same common ancestors of gibbon and orang parasites, and the same sort of family tree applies to the primates themselves.

The first hominids, the first members of the human family, certainly differed from any existing ape. Perhaps they looked something like the pygmy chimpanzee which lives south of the Congo River—a "slender animal with long, thin arms and legs, strongly suggestive of a tailless spider monkey." David Pilbeam, who works closely with Elwyn Simons at Yale, speculates that they may have weighed as little as 30 to 45 pounds, stood 3 feet or less tall, and had a brain of some 250 cubic centimeters, about 1/6 the size of the brain of modern persons.

Our earliest ancestors were probably creatures like this who spent a good deal of time in trees and slept in trees at night. Increasingly they came down to the ground during the day, foraging for plant foods. That means they naturally moved away from denser parts of the forests, where plants were scarce because little sunlight penetrated the trees, to opener forest territory where sunlight and plants were more abundant, to woodlands and grassy areas near seasonally flooded lakes and rivers within the forests. At times they may have ventured away from the last stands of trees at forest fringes out into wide grassy savannas, foraged there for a while, and scampered back into the forests.

Since food tends to be more widely dispersed in open country, the results were a wider-ranging type of primate and significant changes in posture and walking. Apes used their feet not only as supports but also as grasping devices, for example, while eating fruit at the ends of slender branches. Furthermore, they naturally assumed a bent-forward posture, were capable of two-footed walking (but rarely and not for long periods), and usually moved along on their hands as well as on the soles of their feet. Their feet were not fully specialized for support, nor their hands for grasping.

A more complete division of labor was taking place among the first hominids. It was the beginning of the process which eventually resulted among other things in the human stride, a unique primate development involving a series of precisely controlled and timed operations. The stride starts with arch and toe acting as a lever, lifting the body gradually until it rises several inches above its standing height. Measurements show that at this point the average person remains in a delicate balance for about two tenths of a second as the entire weight rests on the foot. Then a final push, which lasts less than half that time, pro-

Pygmy chimps, mother and child: earliest hominids may have looked something like this

pels the person forward so that the other foot glides in for a smooth rather than a jarring landing.

The search continues for direct fossil evidence to document the evolution of the human stride and other hominid features. The ideal situation would be to have a record as ample as that which exists for the evolution of the horse, a series of fossils which shows the gradual change from a collie-sized creature with short chunky teeth and 14 toes each with its own hoof to the modern long-toothed, 4-hooved species.

Unfortunately, the hominid record is still far less detailed, although recent years have seen some important new finds and new interpretations of old finds.

One development involves an incredibly churned-up part of East Africa, the region around Fort Ternan in Kenya about 40 miles east of Lake Victoria, where violent movements in the earth have formed a complex and heavily eroded system of hills and valleys. In 1961, the late Louis Leakey, director of the National Museums' Center for Prehistory and Paleontology in Nairobi and the most widely known searcher for hominid remains, started digging on the slope of one of the hills at a site discovered by a local orange grower, who was looking for mineral deposits and found fossils instead. The site is rich, having already yielded more than 10,000 bones in an area about the size of a large living room. Leakey believed that it may once have been a place where waters, and occasionally poisonous gases, rose up from fissures deep in the earth, and that the gases killed animals coming to drink. (He knew of several such places in the Congo.) During his first season of digging he found the remains of a pygmy giraffe, a pygmy elephant, numerous antelopes, and an unusual variety of primates.

Geologists at the University of California in Berkeley have dated the group of extinct species by dating samples of volcanic rock found with them. Atoms of radioactive potassium in the rock break down spontaneously into the inert gas argon. The gas is trapped in rock crystals after the lava cools (there is no gas to start with) and accumulates at a steady rate which can be measured with the aid of devices capable of detecting fractions of a billionth of an ounce of material. According to this radioactive-clock technique—which, incidentally, has also been used to date crystalline rocks brought back from the moon—the Fort Ternan fossils are about 14 million years old, give or take a few hundred thousand years.

Examination of the primate specimen, which includes part of an upper jawbone and several associated teeth, reveals certain distinctively human features. The proportions of the reconstructed jaw indicate a shortened face with a very much reduced snout; the curvature of the jaw suggests a widely arched dental arc rather than the narrow U-shaped arc typical of recent apes. These and other characteristics, such as the smallness of the teeth, can be interpreted in two ways. They are human characteristics in themselves, but that does not necessarily mean that this particular primate was a member of the human family.

Many types of apes existed 14 million years ago, and this diversity implies a wide range of physical characteristics—long faces and intermediate-sized faces as well as shortened faces, differently shaped dental arcs, different-sized teeth and so on. Thus certain primate species may have had a few hominid traits without being hominids in many other respects and without belonging to the human line. On the other hand, Leakey announced that the Fort Ternan specimen exhibits enough hominid features to qualify as an entirely new variety of primate, which helps fill "an enormous gap in the panorama of . . . development," the gap between apes and creatures like ourselves.

The announcement proved of special interest to Elwyn Simons, whose digging in the Fayum region of Egypt is only part of a long and continuing investigation of primate evolution. He had spent considerable time studying hundreds of fossils from sites throughout the world in an effort to avoid the bad habit which affects paleontologists as well as others—overestimating the importance of one's own work. Since it is generally more satisfying to discover something new than to confirm someone else's discovery, paleontologists often make too much of their finds. The tendency is to interpret small differences in tooth size and other factors, differences that fall within the normal range of individual variation, as signs of a new genus or at least a new species. In an extreme case, North American grizzly bears, now recognized as members of a single species which also includes Old World varieties, were once divided into more than 20 species.

Aware of a similar tendency in primate studies, Simons recognized the Fort Ternan specimen as a hominid but not as a new genus or even a new species. He pointed out that the collection at Yale's Peabody Museum included an upper-jaw fragment and four teeth of the same sort of creature which a native worker had found about three decades earlier in foothills of the Himalayas, in the Siwalik Hills of the Punjab Province of northern India. Furthermore, he had already reconstructed the jaw and estimated the size of a missing canine tooth by the size of the empty socket. This hypothetical tooth turned out to be an almost perfect match with a real canine tooth found at the Kenya site.

Not long after the Fort Ternan announcement, Simons launched a more intensive survey of previously found material stored in museums, and gained as much fresh information as had been obtained during the previous search for new evidence in the field. For one thing, he "discovered" still another specimen of the same hominid species. That is, he reclassified an upper-jaw fragment which had been found in the Punjab hills about half a century ago, kept in the Calcutta collection of the Geological Survey of India ever since, and identified mistakenly as belonging to an extinct ape.

At this point the reexamination of old finds took a new turn. The Yale investigator noted that the three specimens, one from East Africa and two from India, were all parts of upper jawbones, a curious observation because collectors generally find more lower jawbones, which are denser and more compact and hence more resistant to decomposition. He began to wonder whether some lower jawbones had actually been found and duly tucked away on museum shelves, but not recognized for what they were. As frequently happens in research, asking the right question is more than half the battle. No sooner had Simons decided on what to look for than he found it, and in his own museum.

The Yale collection included three specimens, all lower-jaw fragments with molar teeth, all found in India years ago, and all classified as remains of a special genus of fossil ape. But the fragments fitted neatly with corresponding upper-jaw fragments already identified tentatively as those of a creature on the direct line of human descent. If future studies confirm such conclusions, this phase of the work will eliminate an entire genus and several species from fossil records, a fitting climax to a survey which has helped clear away some of the debris of primate nomenclature and furnished for the first time a plausible reconstruction of the remote stages of human evolution.

One of our earliest known ancestors consisted of a single species with the official title *Ramapithecus punjabicus*. (*Rama* is the name of a hero in Hindu mythology, the incarnation of the deity Vishnu; *pithecus* is Greek for "ape"; and *punjabicus* signifies the part of India where typical material was first discovered.) Not many *Ramapithecus* specimens have been recovered so far, a total of some 15 jaw fragments and more than 40 teeth, representing perhaps 12 to 20 individuals. But that is enough to serve as the basis for a number of interesting speculations. For example, fossil traces occur not only in Africa and India but also in the coal beds of Hunan Province in China, the Jura Mountains of southern Germany, and perhaps in Hungary, Greece, Turkey, and Spain. It is possible that members of this and related species moved about freely in the world's savannas and forests. If this assumption is correct, if widespread distribution is any criterion, they must have been highly adaptable and quite capable of dealing with a variety of circumstances.

Current thinking about the way *Ramapithecus* lived is based in part on studies of the teeth, including the small canines, which have been used to support different theories. According to the oldest theory, small hominid canines are a sign of habitual tool use. Many primates have large canines and put them to good use for purposes indicated, for example, by the behavior of the type of baboon in the savannas of Kenya in Africa, another primate whose ancestors turned from tree dwelling to life on the ground. Under conditions of tension a male baboon in his prime will stop, face an opponent, open his mouth wide in a prodigious yawn, and flash a set of four huge and sharp canines. There is nothing particularly subtle about this gesture. It is a direct threat and warning. It says more clearly than words that the opponent is likely to be ripped if he does not get out of the way.

The flashing of canine teeth serves as an effective symbol. More often than not trouble is avoided and the opponent does indeed get out of the way. When threats and warnings fail, however, these teeth may go into action. They are a baboon's most formidable weapons, and in the last analysis his position in the social order of the troop depends on how well he can fight. Apes as well as baboons, and for that matter carnivores such as lions and tigers, also use them in dismembering prey and shredding plant food. Gorillas have been seen ripping the tough outer layers off bamboo shoots to get at the pith inside, in a kind of banana-peeling operation.

But *Ramapithecus* was not equipped with such large, deep-rooted slashing and puncturing devices. The canines were small like ours and had smaller and more shallow roots, all of which has certain fundamental implications in the light of evolutionary theory. Since the survival of a species depends on vigorous offensive and defensive action, on eating and not being eaten, the body can include no superfluous structures, and generations of development ensure that every part of every individual is shaped for maximum efficiency. There must be a reason for every significant change. Bony armor does not become thinner or movement slower unless compensating factors come into play.

In this context the reduction of the canine teeth was interpreted to mean that *Ramapithecus* males had other ways of taking care of themselves. Darwin drew a similar conclusion a century ago: "The early male forefathers of man were . . . probably furnished with great canine teeth; but as they gradually acquired the habit of using stones, clubs, or other weapons for fighting with their enemies or rivals, they would use their jaws and teeth less and less." In other words, canines became smaller, because they were no longer needed for attack and defense.

Recent studies suggest a more plausible theory, which depends neither on the assumption of early and extensive hominid tool use nor on the notion of a tooth-and-claw struggle for existence. The theory involves original research by Clifford Jolly of New York University on fossil baboons, extinct relatives of so-called gelada baboons which today live on the high treeless plateaus of central Ethiopia. He notes, among other things, that the canines of males tended to become somewhat smaller and shorter in the course of their evolution than the canines of males belonging to a species of savanna-dwelling baboon.

Since these primates do not use weapons, some factor other than fighting must be at work, and Jolly believes the difference is primarily a matter of diet. Gelada baboons eat an unusually high proportion of grass seeds, stems, and other tough plant tissues, and their extinct relatives probably consumed similar foods. Such material must be ground up and calls for a powerful chewing action. And that, in turn, poses a mechanical problem, since large canine teeth tend to interlock, making side-to-side jaw movements less efficient. This problem has put an evolutionary premium on those males with smaller and smaller canines; this reduces chances of interlocking and permits more complete grinding, and the same changes occurred in times past among early hominids, who also had to cope with increasing quantities of tough plant foods as they foraged increasingly on the ground.

This argument does not rule out the possibility that early hominids used weapons. Indeed, if we can judge by the behavior of chimpanzees today, the odds are that they did—and that may have had an indirect bearing on canine reduction. The fact that our ancestors were quite capable of wielding weapons probably permitted the evolution of considerably smaller canine teeth without a great disadvantage in fighting and defense. The main point about Jolly's theory is that it focuses on diet rather than fighting. Other theories, such as that of Frederick Szalay of the City University of New York, stress the reshaping as well as the reduction of the canines and the role of meat eating rather than seed eating.

Another feature and major problem of hominid behavior concerns the development of an upright posture and walking in the human line. Many theories have been offered to explain why a two-footed gait should have developed in the first place. The value of this new form of primate locomotion is not at all self-evident. It is certainly not an inevitable consequence of coming down to earth from the trees, and the example of the baboon, among other species, shows that primates can live on the ground without walking upright. As a matter of fact, an upright posture has several important disadvantages. Animals balancing themselves on two feet are easier to knock over, more conspicuous, and less agile when it comes to dodging and feinting and other escape tactics.

So there must have been advantages, and they must have been enormous advantages to overcome all the drawbacks, the illogic, and the awkwardness of bipedalism. Certain theories turn out to be quite inadequate to account for so drastic a change in locomotion. For example, primates often stand erect for a time when circumstances demand it, say, when they want a better view of the surrounding terrain. This is a familiar sight in the Amboseli Game Reserve, where baboons, including infants no more than two or three months old, often stand up on their hind legs at the sound of a passing car or to keep track of the rest of the troop.

Such conduct is common among baboons and other grounddwelling primates. In fact it has been cited in support of the reconnaissance theory of human bipedalism, which holds that savanna-exploring hominids were frequently killed by lions and other predators lurking in tall grasses, that evolution put a premium on standing erect as a way of spotting predators at a distance and avoiding them, and that a by-product of standing erect was the release of the hands for use in coping with the environment. But these advantages are not big enough. The theory does not clarify the main problem. It presents a convincing argument for the benefits of occasional but not habitual bipedalism, without indicating what type of living conditions could have made reconnaissance so important that it brought about a radical departure from conventional patterns of primate locomotion.

Better arguments exist for the notion that walking on two feet evolved as a way of carrying food more efficiently. There is plenty of evidence for such behavior among primates of all ages. Jane Goodall of the Gombe Stream Research Center on the shores of Lake Tanganyika, Africa, spent more than ten years observing chimpanzees in the forests of northwest Tanzania (an operation that had to be curtailed in 1975 after Zaire guerillas kidnapped, and eventually released, four members of the Center's research group). She has seen the apes "loading their arms with choice wild fruits, then walking erect for several yards to a spot of shade before sitting down to eat."

These and many similar examples are sufficient to show that apes and monkeys can walk upright upon occasion just as we can go on all fours when the demand arises, as in clambering up a steep bank or moving along under low branches or crawling through low passages in caves. Other special forces and circumstances favored the shift from part-time to full-time bipedalism. In this connection meat eating and sharing may be significant. Killing even a small animal may provide hunters with ten or fifteen pounds of meat, which is more than they can eat and may be worth carrying back to camp or home base. The record certainly indicates that meat eating inevitably led to greater sharing, and that meant carrying food over long distances—a development which could have contributed to the selection of populations made up of individuals who could walk several miles while carrying one or more small animals.

Another possibility is that more basic forces were at work even earlier. For one thing, the very fact that hominids foraged increasingly on the ground, where food tends to be dispersed, may have encouraged new forms of locomotion. Bipedalism happens to be a comfortable and convenient way of covering large areas, once it has been developed. It would also be promoted by the use of tools, a theory that differs from most other theories, which assume that erect posture came first and that the release of the hands was a secondary bonus effect. The notion that things also worked the other way around was originally suggested by Darwin.

Tool use may have favored the shift to full-time bipedalism. Tools opened up many possibilities, not only in defense against predators but also in digging up and preparing food. So bands composed of individuals which could stand and walk upright more easily and for longer and longer periods, and hence had their hands free increasingly for tool use, flourished rapidly at the expense of bands less fitted to survive in the savanna.

Assuming that this is what happened, the problem is how tool use itself evolved. There are clues to a possible answer. Imagine an adventurous hominid or prehominid, a primitive *Ramapithecus* perhaps, looking for food in the savanna and wandering too far and suddenly being confronted by a predator directly in the escape route to the nearest trees. Such encounters could have been frequent in the beginning. They are by no means rare nowadays. One hardly ever observes actual attacks, which are generally carried out at night, but a leftover leg or some other fresh piece of primate carcass lying in the savanna dust the next morning indicates the failure of escape tactics. Also, examinations of the droppings of leopards and other big cats indicate that monkeys are well preyed on.

At one time, our ancestors had no effective way of fighting back when brought to bay by large predators. But they may well have developed special forms of display, or bluffing behavior, which helped them delay attacks and even get away in some cases. The trick among all animals in all such emergencies is to make themselves look more frightening, often by increasing apparent stature. Puffer fish double or triple their body size by inflating themselves into globes; birds may ruffle their feathers and puff out their chests and spread their wings wide; cats arch their backs and their fur stands on end.

All such reactions are natural in the sense that they tend to be automatic, or hereditary, and that they consist essentially of mechanical and physiological changes in body structure. But it is possible that a new principle may have been at work in the displays of prehominids and that they began to reach out for something external, something not built in and not part of the body which would help them to appear bigger and more formidable. In other words, they may originally have put up a bluff by artifical means, using branches or clumps of tall grass or perhaps long bones to enlarge their body images.

The general tendency to pick up and wave things is common among contemporary apes. When chimpanzees and gorillas are aroused, they often grab a nearby stick or branch and swing it about in a vigorous, random flailing motion. Goodall reports that on rare occasions playing with branches may take on a strange, ritualistic quality. A big male chimpanzee may become tremendously excited, break a branch off a tree, brandish it about, and rush down a mountain slope (often on two feet) dragging it behind him. Then he rushes up the slope and repeats the action several times. The significance of this behavior is not known, but sometimes other males will join the fun in a mass "branch-waving display . . . calling, tearing off and waving large branches, hurling themselves to the ground from the trees."

Branch-waving plays a less mysterious role when chimpanzees are frustrated or angry with one another, in which case shaking branches is part of displays that may include slapping or stamping on the ground and high-pitched screaming. They have been seen charging at one another with sticks in their hands, and although in general they simply threaten and do not strike, they sometimes use sticks to attack one another. The apes also show a special concern with branches when

they climb into a tree where they expect to spend some time, either to
build a nest for the night or to play with another chimpanzee. They move from limb to limb, breaking off dead branches and dropping them to the ground below, as if they were clearing away deadwood so that the tree would be a safe place for maneuvering.

Apes have an ample repertoire of basic branch-handling activities and manipulations, which they use in different combinations and sequences under different circumstances. Although no one has ever reported seeing a real-life encounter between an armed ape and a predator, a Dutch zoologist produced an analogous situation experimentally in the Congo. Adriaan Kortlandt of the University of Amsterdam arranged things so that a stuffed dummy leopard could be pulled out of some shrubbery and into a meadow when a troop of wild chimpanzees was being observed.

Here is how he describes one such confrontation when the stuffed leopard appeared with a chimpanzee-doll victim in its claws: "There was a moment of silence first. Then hell broke loose. There was an uproar of yelling and barking, and most of the apes came forward and began to charge at the leopard. . . . Some charges were made barehanded; in others the assailants broke off a small tree while they ran toward or past the leopard, or brandished a big stick or broken tree in their charge, or threw such a primitive weapon in the general direction of the enemy. . . . Both when attacking and when looking at the leopard, the apes again and again uttered a special blood-curdling type of barking yell."

For all the sound and fury, however, it was more a mobbing type of display calculated to harass the leopard and make it go away than a practiced and skillfully directed use of weapons. Clubs were brandished and hurled, but there were no actual hits. The interesting thing about all this is that the chimpanzees were forest dwellers, and attacks from leopards and other predators tend to be infrequent in forests.

In later studies Kortlandt reports far more direct action among wild chimpanzees living in the sort of open savanna country in Guinea, where predators are more common. There was no doubt about the chimpanzees' objectives under these conditions. They beat up the dummy leopard with repeated and well-aimed heavy blows using clubs up to six feet long. Goodall has seen chimpanzees throwing stones at baboons; they seldom hit their targets although some individuals are more accurate than others. The implication is that early hominids may also have used clubs and missiles from time to time.

Some investigators have another explanation for the origins of tool use, an explanation which accents the search for food rather than defense. According to Leakey, evidence for the food hypothesis may already have been uncovered in the form of the broken shinbone of an oxlike animal found at Fort Ternan. The break is the depressed or indented kind which might have been produced by a rock, and suggests **45** that perhaps a hungry *Ramapithecus* wielded the rock to make a meal of the bone marrow, although similar breaks have been found among bones in leopard lairs. The effort to check such possibilities indicates why analyzing fractured fossil bones is an important phase of present-day research.

Tools could have been used in gathering plant foods. During dry periods, baboons may use their fingers to dig holes as big as 15 inches deep and 2 feet across to get at succulent roots and tubers; but, as far as we know, they have not discovered that the job would be considerably easier with the aid of a sturdy stick or a sharp rock. On the other hand, hominids or prehominid apes might well have learned the trick, since they were probably rather skillful in working with tools.

They might also have learned to use probes, perhaps somewhat as wild chimpanzees do today. The observations of Goodall in Tanzania do much to weaken a notion supported over the years by many investigators from Benjamin Franklin and Friedrich Engels to modern anthropologists, namely, that although other animals may upon occasion use tools, man is the only regular maker of tools. Chimpanzees also make tools to obtain one of their favorite foods, termites. During most of the year, termite hills are covered with a thick concretelike shell to protect them from birds, monkeys, and other termite eaters. But in late October or early November, just before the onset of the rainy season, worker termites drill holes through the shell, destroying all but the outermost fraction of an inch—so that they can emerge quickly when the rains come, being their nuptial flights, and found new colonies.

While the termite operates by instinct, the chimpanzee operates by insight. He has learned when a termite hill is ripe for exploitation and where the thinly covered holes are. Then he takes a bit of vine or a slender stick, trims it neatly and carefully by pulling off leaves and side shoots, breaks it off to a length of 6 to 12 inches, and approaches the hill. After licking the probe, he pokes it through the shell and into one of the holes, and waits a moment or two. When he draws the probe out, termites are clinging to it and he licks them off as gleefully as a child with a lollipop. (Incidentally, Goodall has eaten termites and finds them "rather flavorless.")

In such foraging, chimpanzees may plan ahead. For example, they do not always find a promising termite hill and then proceed to make a probe. They may make the probe first, anticipating a meal of termites, although neither termites nor termite hills are in sight. One chimpanzee carried a suitably prepared stick in its mouth for half a mile, inspected eight hills without finding a good one, and then dropped the tool. So these apes seem to have the basic concept of a tool as something to be shaped for a situation that has not yet materialized, and there is reason to believe that *Ramapithecus* was at least as ingenious.

Prehuman tool user:
Gombe chimpanzee
probing for termites

In any case, the use of implements as accessories or extensions of the body bears a direct relationship to developments that had taken place beforehand in the trees. Part of the story, of course, concerns the sort of dexterity required to grasp and pull branches and to swing along from branch to branch. But the coming of stereoscopic color vision was an even more important factor. As already indicated, objects acquired a new meaning, a new reality, with the appearance of highly advanced visual mechanisms. They were viewed in full perspective and tended to leap out of the background more completely and vividly for primates than for other visually inferior animals. To put it another way, primates acquired richer and more detailed perceptions, and it is precisely this faculty, more than anything else, which created a heightened awareness of objects as distinct and clear-cut entities capable of serving as display elements and ultimately as tools.

47

Once the new way of life caught on, once its advantages were proved in the field as it were, it achieved a new kind of momentum of its own. The relationship between tool use and bipedalism acquired a two-way self-reinforcing quality. It was not only that increased tool use brought about the selection of changes in body structure which made for more efficient bipedalism. More efficient bipedalism, in turn, freed the hands more and more for increased tool use and provided more time for acquiring new manipulative skills. In such a developing process it becomes increasingly difficult to distinguish cause and effect.

The process yielded further advantages as by-products. Walking erect resulted in a continuous and more panoramic view of the savanna, an increased ability to see things coming and to detect and anticipate danger. Looking ahead from an elevated position may also have extended the sense of the future. So there is something to the reconnaissance theory. There is also something to the food-carrying theory, although, since food is generally eaten on the spot, it may have been more important to be able to carry infants than food. If bipedalism produced a foot designed above all for support and with greatly reduced grasping capacities, infants could no longer have clung as effectively to their mothers and would have had to be carried. In fact, the one case that I have seen of upright walking among baboons involved a mother who from time to time was forced to move a few steps on two feet so that she could support her infant.

Another indirect benefit of bipedalism may have been that it helped discourage the most dangerous predators, the big cats. A predator knows its prey from repeated encounters and repeated successes and failures in the hunt, and part of that knowledge in early hominid times must have been a firmly ingrained image of prey as four-footed animals. George Schaller of the New York Zoological Society, who has observed tigers in India, lions in Tanzania, and gorillas in the Congo, comments on this possibility: "Some big cats turn into man eaters, a fact interesting chiefly because it is so rare. They hunt by lying in wait or approaching stealthily and bounding on the victim's back, and they bite at the neck. Man is bipedal and thus does not furnish a good target, a good horizontal plane for the cats to jump on. Perhaps that is one thing that deters them today, and deterred them in the past."

These and other such ideas are mostly speculation, neither proved nor universally accepted. *Ramapithecus* is known from teeth and jaws. We have no foot, leg, or pelvic bones to indicate whether this primate was more proficient than present-day apes at walking about on two feet. The argument for tool-use rests on circumstantial evidence. Efforts have been made to trace the hominid line back further than 14 million years, the date established at Fort Ternan. A date of 20 million years has been estimated for certain fossil primate specimens, including some found on Rusinga Island in Lake Victoria, long a favorite hunting ground of Leakey and his wife Mary, an accomplished investigator in her own right. But most specialists feel that the specimens are the remains of an ape rather than a hominid.

Other investigators favor a more recent date. Washburn, for example, cites biochemical studies of primate blood proteins conducted by Vincent Sarich at the University of California as part of his argument that hominids and apes did not emerge as separate lines until 5 million years ago. But the tendency is to stick with an estimate of about 15 million years and, for the time being, with *Ramapithecus* as the best available candidate for hominid ancestry.

CHAPTER 3 THE UNFOLDING STORY OF HUMAN EVOLUTION

Ramapithecus stands isolated in time, a face or the shadow of a face seen in the far distance, a creature partly imaginary in the sense that many of its features are still speculative. But a clearer picture of early pre-human species is beginning to emerge based largely on new fossil remains which Pilbeam and other investigators are finding during annual expeditions to the Siwalik Hills. The region has yielded between 150 and 200 primate specimens as well as thousands of specimens of other animals.

Human evolution proceeded in a period of unprecedented unrest, as it still does. The climate became cooler and drier, a change marked by the dwindling of seas and the spread of savannas, deserts, and semi-deserts. The vast sea that stretched from Spain to Malaya 70 million years ago when the first primates appeared, the sea that was itself the remnant of an even more extensive earlier sea, continued to shrink toward its present-day dimensions, leaving the Mediterranean and three smaller "puddles," the Black, Caspian, and Aral seas. By 15 million years ago, the time of the first varieties of *Ramapithecus* and presumably other small upright primates, there were large stretches of open country in Eurasia.

The trend toward cooler, drier conditions accelerated starting about 3 million years later, and with it the pace of change. The further expansion of open country, into eastern and central Europe among other regions, resulted in a new evolutionary radiation, a sharp increase in the number of species adapted to life outside the forests—rodents, horses, pigs, oxen, and primates as well. Specialized tree dwellers, including the ancestors of modern chimpanzees and gorillas, continued to live their entire lives in island or residual forests, some species confining themselves chiefly to a single grove of trees.

Our ancestors evolved in the wide-open spaces. They devoted less and less time to woodlands, more and more time to savannas rich **49**

Baboons, like early man, keeping lookout over savanna

in grasses, seeds, and tender shoots. In the process they probably had increasing encounters with predators. The arboreal life was not yet completely abandoned, however. At first they may have continued sleeping in trees among the woodlands where they returned every night. Later, when they no longer returned to the woodlands, they slept in groves out in the savanna. When trees were not available they most likely chose places where predators could not follow, perhaps spending their nights on the ledges of cliffs, facing the cliff wall as some baboons do in the twentieth century.

Exploiting grassy savannas and semiarid regions demands wider ranging. Early hominids presumably had to cover a relatively wide area on the principle that vegetation was sparse, and the sparser the vegetation the farther an individual must travel to obtain its quota of food. In fact, the energy spent ranging in search of food increased the required quota. Our ancestors were probably on the move a good part of the day. They may have made increasing use of digging sticks and pointed rocks to get at tubers containing water and other buried food. The rocks and digging sticks could also have served as weapons to ward off carnivores, which were busy in their own ways exploiting food sources to the utmost.

The most recent *Ramapithecus* remains have been found in deposits about 9 million years old, but conclusive evidence for the next stage of hominid evolution is dated 4 or 5 million years later. For reasons yet to be determined, all the evidence turns up in Africa. We know that the continent of Africa experienced one of the most spectacular series of up-heavals in the history of the earth. The southernmost part of the continent remained quiet, geologically speaking, having had its period of fire and brimstone some 150 million years ago, when volcanoes erupted everywhere and buried it beneath more than 6000 feet of lava. But trouble came in more northerly regions, where the earth's interior was rumbling and unstable and where there were and still are marks of the continuing splitting up of continents.

Traces of what happened can be seen today in Kenya, less than an hour's drive out of Nairobi, from the edge of a cliff overlooking a valley 50 miles across. At the other side is another cliff, and in between, on the valley floor 1500 feet below, are signs of a time when the earth tossed like an angry sea. Here the waves and the churnings are frozen in solid rock: Mount Eburru, black and craggy and flat along the top, a volcano that may become active again; Mount Longonot, with its peak hidden in clouds and long sloping terraces formed by ancient lava flows; domes like the tops of bubbles about to burst and craters where bubbles burst ages ago; and Lake Naivasha, with no visible outlet, drained by deep fissures.

This shattered landscape, one result of the drifting of land masses throughout the world, is part of a far-flung fracture zone, the Great Rift Valley, extending about 4000 miles from the Zambezi River area of Mozambique in the south, up through East Africa and Ethiopia, and north as far as the Valley of the Jordan in Israel. The Jordan River, the Dead and Red seas, Lakes Edward and Albert and Tanganyika and Malawi are some of the places where water has filled steep, parallel-sided valleys along the fracture lines of the Rift.

The rifting reached its height between 2 and 5 million years ago. The earth has not yet recovered; it still trembles and heaves in response to forces deep inside. Steam hisses from vents and fissures on the slopes of Mount Eburru, and local farmers use it to cook potatoes and, in condensed form, to water livestock. Some 2000 miles away, in the floor of the Red Sea offshore from Mecca more than a mile deep, are cracks out of which flows water at temperatures as high as 133 degrees Fahrenheit and ten times saltier than the sea water above it, cracks associated with continuing Rift activity and the shaping of a new ocean where the Red Sea and the Gulf of Aden are now. In fact, in this area, the Rift Valley is widening at a rate of about half an inch a year. The process is under way in the current formation of the island-to-be (mentioned in Chapter 1) consisting of parts of Somaliland, Kenya, and Tanzania.

As regards human evolution, the effects of rifting in Africa are more difficult to specify than the effects of the increase of deserts and semideserts—but the movements of hominids were certainly altered. Traditional migration routes had to be abandoned and new ones established. Before the rifting, Africa was essentially a broad plain created by the erosion of ancient mountain ranges, a plain rising gradually to heights of more than a mile. The top of the rise formed a continental divide running north and south, waters of the Congo Basin draining west off the slopes into the Atlantic Ocean, and other waters draining east into the Indian Ocean. Rivers tended to separate hominid populations from one another, to restrict their movements to zones running east and west. (Apes are afraid of water when they cannot see bottom, and they will not cross a stream that is more than 1 foot deep and more than 20 feet or so wide.)

Rifting changed that pattern. Instead of flowing in a west-to-east direction from the divide to the Indian Ocean, rivers tended to flow north and south along Rift lines and drained internally in Rift valleys. So hominid bands could also move more freely along new north-south migration routes, although the all-important question of timing remains to be answered. Did populations of advanced hominids evolve on the plains of southern Africa and spread to the north when the rivers shifted, did they evolve in East Africa and spread south, or did they evolve in both regions and mingle? Some investigators suspect that post-Rift migrations were from south to north, but the evidence is so sparse that no one really knows.

The picture becomes even more complicated when one considers that rifting closed certain routes while it opened others. In pre-Rift times a land bridge connected Asia and Africa, so that it was possible to move directly from Egypt or the Sudan or Ethiopia across Saudi Arabia into Iran and India. But that bridge was broken by the formation of the Red Sea. Furthermore, studies of closely related species of trees, mollusks, and birds now separated by 500 miles of hot, dry terrain suggest that the rising of Rift mountains cut West Africa from East Africa and isolated populations that once mingled freely.

Millions of years passed between the heyday of *Ramapithecus* and the next phase of the fossil record. Then the story picks up again, and it is a new story based on new evidence, much of it discovered during the past two or three years. A different kind of human ancestor emerges. Imagine that you are in a helicopter flying high over an African savanna late one hot prehistoric afternoon. From that perspective things appear very much as they do today. You look down on a dry grassy plain, straw colored except for scattered bushes and trees, dark green clumps near swamps and water holes, and the lone winding ribbon of green that marks the course of a large river where it empties into a lake.

Coming down for a closer view and hovering at the edge of the trees along a stretch of the river, you might at first sight see nothing unusual, nothing to indicate that you are not in the twentieth century. There might be many familiar-looking birds and monkeys performing in the trees, as well as hyenas, antelopes, giraffes, and perhaps a hippopotamus wallowing in the mud—all of them very much like today's varieties. Then you notice some strange animals—little three-toed horses grazing near the trees and a herd of elephants with two tusks in their lower jaws and two in their upper jaws.

But the most surprising sight of all would lie in another direction. You turn, the trees at your back, look out over the wide savanna, and see a troop of creatures heading for the forest. They have not yet come close, but even at a distance there is something familiar about them. They move like people. They walk fully upright, their arms swinging freely at their sides. A mother runs over to a group of scuffling children and scolds as she snatches her child away. The leader strides forward confidently with the alert no-nonsense attitude of a sheriff in a Western making sure the coast is clear.

As he approaches and you see him clearly for the first time you are shocked. Judging by his gait and posture and by the general feeling of humanness about the troop, you expect to confront a being similar to yourself. But he is surprisingly small, 4 feet tall, about the size of a modern child of 7 or 8 years. Even more surprising is his alien and disturbing face. His jaw and mouth are thrust forward with the trace of a muzzle. He has a low forehead and flattish nose and a remote half-wild look which is not human and yet somehow reminds you of humanity. The troop reaches the water hole and begins climbing into the trees to prepare for the night as the sun is setting.

The earliest known trace of these creatures exists in the form of an age-blackened bit of lower jawbone from Africa, announced in 1971 by Bryan Patterson of Harvard's Museum of Comparative Zoology. The specimen was studied on and off for nearly four years, ever since it was found one scorching August afternoon lying on a sun-baked clay slope of Lothagam Hill in the Kenya badlands near the southwestern end of Lake Turkana (formerly Lake Rudolf), part of the African Rift Valley.

The significance of the discovery was immediately evident to Patterson and his associates, who had been searching in the general region because of its promising fossil-bearing sediments. But their work had just begun. First of all, whenever an important fossil is found, efforts are redoubled to find further evidence on the spot, hopefully including other pieces of the same specimen. In this case, the Harvard investigators and a dozen workers recruited from a tribe of local nomads spent the better part of a month digging and sifting through tons of deposits, with only a lone unexciting monkey premolar tooth to show for their trouble.

So all the information had to come from the original specimen in detailed laboratory studies, and part of the job was to identify it as definitely as possible. Patterson went mainly by the shape of the jawbone, and the shape and wear patterns of the single tooth remaining in place, a molar. For example, the tooth's grinding surface was worn unevenly,

included a number of deep pits, and showed extensive wear on the
sides where the tooth had fitted against neighboring teeth. These characteristics and others are rare among apes but typical of creatures far
more like man than any other previous primate—members of the genus
Australopithecus or southern ape.

The Lothagam fossil yielded further information. The genus included two species: *Australopithecus africanus,* which was about 4 feet
tall, and the somewhat taller and heavier *Australopithecus robustus.* The
main clue to distinguishing one species from the other was the striking
difference in the size of the back teeth. As far as the front teeth were
concerned, there was little basis for a choice. *Robustus* has considerably
larger premolars and molars. The single Lothagam tooth is of *africanus*
dimensions. The smallish size of the jawbone hints that it may have
been that of a female.

The most striking thing about the specimen turns out to be its
age. Unfortunately, the deposits in which it was found contain no volcanic rock suitable for dating by the potassium-argon technique. But
they do contain remains of elephants, which were evolving swiftly during early *Australopithecus* days and hence provide a relatively sensitive
index to the passage of time. Vincent Maglio of Princeton University
found a massive four-tusked variety of elephant in the Lothagam deposits; nearby deposits bearing somewhat less primitive, somewhat
more recent elephants had been dated by the potassium-argon radioactive clock. By conservative estimates, the jawbone is more than 5 million years old, which makes it at least a million years older than the
previously oldest known *Australopithecus* specimen.

This find is only one of a series of recent finds which are providing a fuller picture of the near humans or prehumans of Africa. The
new work confirms and vindicates the insights of an investigator who
recognized the importance of such fossils nearly half a century ago,
about a generation before the time was ripe for acceptance of his ideas.
Australopithecus remains were first discovered in the southern part of
Africa by Raymond Dart, professor of anatomy at the Medical School of
the University of the Witwatersrand in Johannesburg. One afternoon in
1924, he received two crates filled with fossil-bearing rocks collected by
a miner at a limestone quarry in the village of Taung ("place of the
lion" in Bantu) near the edge of the Kalahari Desert about 200 miles
away. He was expected at a wedding and was wrestling with a stiff
winged collar at the time, but he promptly tore if off and began examining the material.

The quarry had already yielded the skull of a baboon, among
other things, and there was always the possibility of finding something
more interesting, say, the remains of a more advanced primate. This is
precisely what happened. A large block which had been blasted out of a
tunnel-like cave in a limestone cliff contained the cast of a large brain

case and major parts of a skull and jaw. Dart speculated that "the face might be somewhere there in the block." He went to work with hammer and chisel, and for the most delicate work he used one of his wife's knitting needles.

In a subsequent report he recalls the long process of separating the fossil bones from their matrix of sand and lime: "No diamond cutter ever worked more lovingly or with such care on a priceless jewel—nor, I am sure, with such inadequate tools. But on the seventy-third day, December 23, the rock parted. I could view the face from the front, although the right side was still imbedded. [The complete extraction process took more than four years.] The creature which had contained this massive brain was no giant anthropoid such as a gorilla. What emerged was a baby's face, an infant with a full set of milk teeth and its permanent molars just in the process of erupting. I doubt if there was any

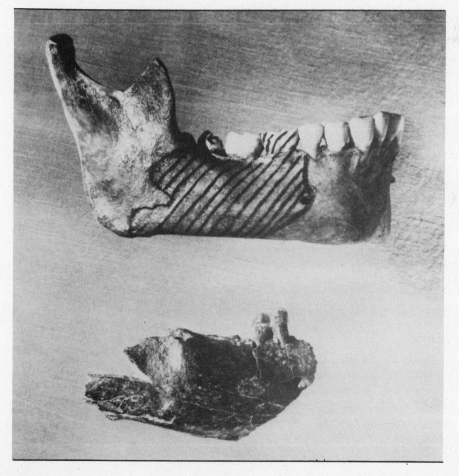

New fossil: bottom-*Australopithecus* jawbone fragment more than 5 million years old. Top-modern jawbone showing location of fragment

parent prouder of his offspring than I was of my Taung baby on that
Christmas."

About five weeks later, the South African anatomist announced his find in a paper published in the British journal *Nature*. The report noted that the canine teeth of the Taung specimen were small, and that this implied an upright posture and increasing use of the hands and the probable use of tools and weapons. It also noted the significance of the fact that the specimen had been found in a desertlike site where life must have been difficult and must have required "enhanced cerebral powers" for survival. Dart described the specimen as that of an "ultra-simian and prehuman stock," "a manlike ape," and officially christened it *Australopithecus africanus,* the first representative of a new species.

His report also made a strong case for Africa as the continent where humans first appeared, a point first emphasized by Darwin. More specifically, it suggested that humans have arisen in dry and grassy savannas rather than in dense tropical forests, as many anthropologists believed. Food was so abundant in the forests and life so easy that apes faced no major challenges and remained apes. "For the production of man a different apprenticeship was needed to sharpen the wits and quicken the higher manifestations of intellect—a more open veldt country where competition was keener between swiftness and stealth, and where adroitness of thinking and movement played a preponderating role in the preservation of the species."

It was a typical example of a report written too soon for contemporary thinking. Dart's general conclusions were right, but they came at the wrong time. *Ramapithecus* had not yet been identified, and it was widely assumed that walking on two feet and tool use could not be expected among apes, even among humanlike apes. Most investigators, including Dart's former teacher, Elliot Smith, at University College in London regarded the Taung baby as an ape not on the line that led to humans but more like the chimpanzee or gorilla. So they were less interested in discussing its nature than in the fact that it had been discovered so far south and in a desertlike region.

Furthermore, all eyes then were on Asia, where the earliest known traces of humans at that time had been found. So far as most anthropologists were concerned, Dart was working in the wrong part of the world. They also felt that he had found the wrong kind of human ancestor. *Australopithecus* had a small brain, weighing perhaps a pound, or about a third as much as the brain of modern people, and that did not fit in with prevailing theory. According to Elliot Smith and most of his colleagues, the brain was a kind of pacemaker in evolution, and people had arisen from apelike species, which had big brains to start with, and then had proceeded to take advantage of this favorable beginning by evolving to human status.

There was some evidence for this theory. In 1913, the British lawyer and part-time antiquarian Charles Dawson reported that he had discovered the remains of an individual with a human skull and an apelike jaw in a gravel pit in the village of Piltdown near the eastern coast of England. This material, together with skull fragments and apelike teeth which Dawson found later in a field 2 miles away, puzzled many investigators because the contrast between the humanness of the skull and the apishness of the jaw was so great. But since the remains tended to confirm the theory of the brain as pacemaker, they were more readily accepted at face value.

Dart had to wait until the time was ripe for his point of view, until the weight of accumulating evidence and the exposure of Piltdown man as a fraud forced other workers to recognize that his southern apes were actually full-fledged hominids. The first confirmation came a dozen years later from a site nearer home, 30 miles west of Johannesburg. It lies in the Transvaal with its wide, dry rolling plains, waist-high golden grasses, clumps of trees, and a dryness so prevalent that there is a joke about what to do when you fall into a South African river—you get up and brush yourself off.

The land here, as in many parts of Africa, is itself a prehistoric relic. It must have looked much the same in the time of *Australopithecus* and earlier, though the grasses are less hostile now, lions and other predators having been driven out and confined together with their prey to game reserves far from the city. One of the few wet waterways of the region, the Klip River, winds through a broad valley and rises from a swamp. Not far from the swamp, on a farm known as Sterkfontein, is a kopje, or little hill, with a long history.

The hill is a block of limestone formed some 2 billion years ago when Africa was submerged beneath a shallow sea, covered by more than 6 miles of sediments and lava, and then exposed by erosion. Waters seeped down through cracks in the rock and dissolved away deposits containing calcium, producing small cavities at first and later a system of deep caves. One of the caves still exists; the others have crumbled away. Limestone quarrymen moved into its several hundred yards of underground passages more than 60 years ago. There they found fossils, many of which were sold to tourists on Sundays when the mine was open to the public. Also on sale was a guidebook, which included an invitation: "Come to Sterkfontein and find the missing link."

One Sunday visitor took the invitation literally—Robert Broom, a Scottish-born physician and paleontologist who lived in South Africa. Among other things, he was noted for digging in all weather wearing a formal business suit complete with tie and high starched collar. Broom immediately recognized the significance of Dart's specimen. In 1936 he came to have a look at Sterkfontein, where, as at Taung, baboon fossils had recently been discovered. (As fellow ground dwellers, the ancestors

of humans and baboons shared life on the savanna.) It was the start of a **58**
second career for the 69-year-old investigator. Within two weeks he
found pieces of the skull of an adult *Australopithecus,* and he decided to
concentrate on the search for early hominids.

During the succeeding years, Broom and his young assistant John
Robinson of the University of Wisconsin conducted excavations at Sterkfontein and two nearby sites. It was slow work. The deposits of sand,
earth, bone, and shattered rock containing fossils were cemented together
by lime salts and as hard as concrete. The only practical way to get at the
material was to drill holes in it and blast it into chunks with sticks of
dynamite and later in the laboratory to pick away at the chunks or treat
them with mild acid.

This procedure yielded several dozen new specimens, including
the remains of another kind of *Australopithecus*, which also walked upright and had a somewhat larger brain but was considerably more rugged. It was heavier (weighing about 100 or more pounds as compared
with perhaps 75 pounds for *Australopithecus africanus*), taller (about 4½
to 5 feet as against 4 feet), and had a more massive skull. This is the
species that has been classified as *Australopithecus robustus.*

Meanwhile, Dart sent students to another rich site he had heard
about during the 1920s located about 150 miles away in the Makapan
Valley. At one end were red cliffs and a waterfall. It was the valley of a
lost world, as wild in appearance today as it was when our ancestors
wandered there more than 20,000 centuries ago. Makapan included a
network of caves under a domed roof larger than a football field and
some ten stories high.

Familiarly, Dart was led to the ruins of this huge cave system in
1945 by a limestone quarry, abandoned long ago, and the finding of a
fossil baboon. Two years later, one of his students recovered the back
part of an *Australopithecus* skull from the quarry dump. A year after
that, it was a lower jaw and, within another four months, part of a face
and several other pieces, including parts of a skullcap, upper jaw, and
pelvis. The evidence was piling up, and none of it checked with the notion that humans had a big brain from the beginning or with Dawson's
increasingly puzzling Piltdown remains.

Finally things reached a point where it had to occur to someone
that the chances of the Piltdown find's being genuine were somewhat
less than the chances of its being a fake. The someone was Joseph Weiner, now at the London School of Hygiene and Tropical Medicine and
then at Oxford University. Driving from work one afternoon in 1953
and mulling over the peculiar remains, he suddenly considered deception as a serious possibility. Special studies conducted at Oxford and
the British Museum of Natural History removed all doubts. The Piltdown skull fragments belonged to a modern human, the jawbone and
teeth to a modern ape. The material had been filed down, chemically

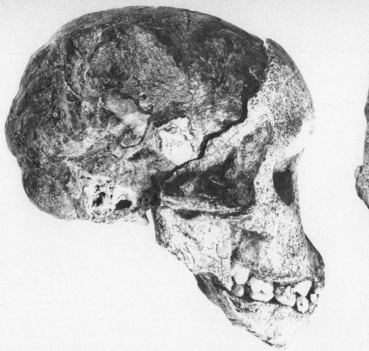

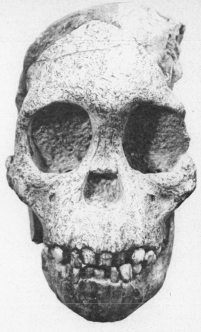

Dart's ''Taung baby'':
the original
Australopithecus
discovery

*Australopithecus
robustus:* artist's
conception of head
(right)
*Australopithecus
africanus:* lower
jawbone and teeth
(*left*)

Man's ancestors,
Australopithecus, as
they may have looked
five or six million
years ago

treated, and otherwise tampered with to make it appear ancient and authentic. Then someone had planted the doctored specimens in the gravel pit.

The job was done quite skillfully. But that is not what fooled the experts, who, like all scientists, had been trained to take the evidence as it came. They were taken in mainly because they had absolutely no reason to suspect a deliberate fraud. The truth became evident as soon as the possibility of fraud was seriously considered. The culprit was probably Dawson himself who, it recently turned out, had participated in at least one other fraud, the discovery of inscribed bricks supposedly dating back to Roman times but actually fired in the twentieth century. His motive seems to have been a compulsive drive to fool and make fools of experts.

In any case, because exposure of the skulduggery at Piltdown alerted anthropologists to the possibility of deception, the odds against their succumbing to another major hoax are enormous. Furthermore, discrediting once and for all the theory that people were created big-brained and fully human cleared the way for more plausible insights based on a wealth of new evidence.

Investigations still under way in the Rift Valley are revolutionizing ideas about the human past, which turns out to be far more remote than most experts suspected. In 1964 Leakey, who had a feeling for the remoteness, going on the basis of skull fragments unearthed in

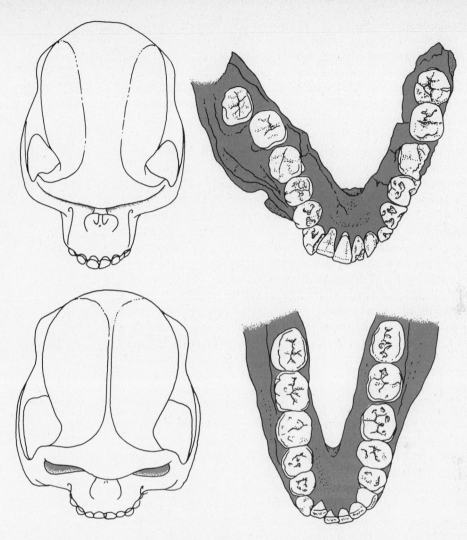

Australopithecus skulls, top view, and jaws: *africanus* (top) and *robustus* (bottom)

Tanzania's Olduvai Gorge, identified a new species. His announcement of *Homo habilis* (which means handy or skillful man), dating true human beings back nearly 2 million years, or more than double the previously accepted figure, was widely disbelieved, as Dart's had been. Colleagues acknowledged that the fossils were indeed unusual, representing creatures with brains half again as large as other hominids of the period, but still not large enough to rate as full-fledged members of the genus *Homo.* The consensus was that they represented an advanced form of *Australopithecus.*

Subsequent studies tend to support Leakey's original interpretation, some of the most important conducted by members of his own family. Nine years later, during a survey of a desert area in Kenya east of Lake Turkana, his son Richard, director of the National Museums of Kenya, found a shattered skull about as old as the Olduvai specimens and with a larger brain capacity. Also of interest are Mary Leakey's finds at Laetolil, a site near Olduvai. In the fall of 1975, she reported a collection including the jaws and teeth of at least 11 individuals, perhaps members of the genus *Homo* and, according to potassium-argon dating, between 3.35 and 3.75 million years old, the earliest traces of human beings.

At about the same time in another part of the Rift Valley, in Ethiopia near the southern end of the Red Sea, Donald Johanson of the Cleveland Museum of Natural History and Maurice Taieb of the National Center of Scientific Research in Paris were recovering traces of a first family in an ancient stream bed. They found more than 150 bones representing two children about 3 to 5 years old and three to five adults, who may have been members of the genus *Homo*. According to Johanson, "these people could have been sleeping or resting together in a dry wash and been caught and drowned in a catastrophic event like a flash flood." The event probably occurred some 3 million years ago.

Johanson has only begun to explore one of the richest regions for traces of early hominids and other extinct species. Perhaps his most widely publicized find took place just before lunch one day in November 1974, with the temperature at about 110 degrees. Walking over a rise in the ground, he saw a small hominid arm bone, enough of a discovery in itself. But the area also included fragments of skull, vertebrae, and a bit of lower jaw. It turned out to be the most complete *Australopithecus* specimen ever discovered, about 40 percent of a female, 3 million years old, and nicknamed Lucy.

These are only a few of the most notable discoveries made during the past few years. Hundreds of new specimens have been collected, and the list grows with every season. A French-American expedition has been exploring Ethiopia's Omo River Valley north of Lake Turkana. Clark Howell of the University of California in Berkeley, director of the American participants, reports the finding of more than 200 *Australopithecus* teeth, half a dozen lower jawbones, parts of two skulls, fragments of leg bones, an exceptionally well-preserved forearm bone (the first complete specimen found in Africa), and even fossil footprints.

Work is going on at old as well as new sites. Present-day investigators have revisited the scenes of some of the most important discoveries of a generation ago, and have come up with new material and new interpretations of old material. To cite only one example, Charles Brain of the Transvaal Museum in Pretoria, South Africa, has done further excavating at a site previously excavated by Broom and Robinson, the Swartkrans Cave, located less than a mile from Sterkfontein, and has yielded remains of at least 60 hominid individuals.

The cave is also rich in fossil animal bones, some 15,000 of them

Hominid fossils from
Ethiopia: Donald
Johanson holding skull
fragment; legbone
fragments on table.

having been collected to date (3,000 by previous workers, 12,000 by Brain), representing the leftovers of meals eaten by some prehistoric carnivore. It has been suggested that the killer was *Australopithecus robustus*, whose remains have also been found in the cave. But Brain believes that this theory overrates our early ancestors, that they contributed very little to the total debris, mainly because only a small proportion of the bones are shattered to bits, the typical hominid practice.

A careful investigation of the habits of other carnivores convinces Brain that the actual culprits were leopards. He has even reconstructed the scene of the action. The Swartkrans Cave had a vertical shaft leading down into its underground chambers, the sort of location where trees often grow today. Combining this observation with the observation that contemporary leopards often drag their prey into trees where they can eat undisturbed by scavengers such as hyenas, Brain suggests that prehistoric leopards did the same and that the discarded bones fell into the chambers below.

He also has an explanation for the presence of most of the hominid remains among the cave's animal fossils. Our ancestors were hunted as well as hunters, victims of leopards along with antelopes, zebras, baboons, and other species. As part of his proof, he offers a piece of the skull of a young *robustus* individual. The skull has two puncture holes in it, 33 millimeters or about an inch and a third apart, which is about the distance between the lower canine teeth of an adult leopard.

There was another hominid in the cave. One July day, Brain, Howell, and Ronald Clarke of the Center for Prehistory and Palaeontology were in the Transvaal Museum examining a collection of Swartkrans fossils classified as *Australopithecus robustus* remains. Suddenly, Clarke noticed that a number of skull fragments, including an upper jawbone fragment, a cheekbone and part of an eye socket found more than 20 years before, did not seem to fit into the *robustus* category, and that led to a fruitful jigsaw-puzzle session.

The investigators managed to fit the fragments together to produce most of the left side of a skull. The result was a newly reconstructed face from the past—a hominid which seems to be more advanced than other Swartkrans *robustus* individuals, may have lived later, and in certain respects resembles *Homo* specimens from Kenya and Ethiopia. Incidentally, this work confirms the insights of one of the original Swartkrans investigators, John Robinson, who reached the same conclusion long ago and had difficulty convincing many of his colleagues.

It will take time to analyze all the new findings. A major problem, for instance, is to determine the relationship between *Australopithecus robustus* and *Australopithecus africanus*. As already indicated, *robustus* individuals had massive back teeth and impressive machinery to go with the teeth. Their cheek bones had flaring projections, special

Who killed the
Swartkrans ape-men?

places for the attachment of huge muscles, especially thick cables to work heavy-duty teeth and jaws. A bony crest or ridge running along the top of the skull served the same purpose.

Africanus and *robustus* were clearly adapted to different living conditions. According to one recent theory, *robustus* was a highlander and, like present-day gorillas, lived on a diet that may have included wild celery, bamboo, and a variety of other tough fibrous plants requiring powerful grinding and mashing tooth action, while *africanus* specialized in a more chimpanzeelike diet of softer fare, such as fruit from the lowlands. But the search continues for evidence to support this or any other theory.

The general situation is confusing. At least one investigator close to the evidence feels that this is an appropriate state of mind considering the abundance and complexity of accumulating fossil material: "Anyone who isn't confused by the hominid story just doesn't under-

65

stand the situation." A tentative family tree, one of a number of possibilities, might start 15 million years ago with a small biped not unlike *Ramapithecus*. The most advanced hominid of perhaps 8 million years ago may have been an early form of *Australopithecus africanus*, a species that gave rise to two separate lines 3 or 4 million years later—one line including three or more *Australopithecus* species and dying out about a million years ago, and the other branching off to *Homo habilis* and eventually to modern humans. It should be noted that the two lines co-existed for several million years.

Among the many problems remaining to be solved is the relationship between the two kinds of hominids. The first true human beings were presumably more adaptable than their smaller-brained relatives, evolved more effective social organizations and defenses against predators, and ultimately may have helped speed the passing of *Australopithecus* as their numbers mounted and competition for food became increasingly intense. Another problem involves human origins. So far all the earliest traces of *Homo* have come from Africa, but some investigators believe that still earlier remains may turn up in southern Asia, somewhere between Turkey and India.

Perhaps the most impressive and challenging thing about the current state of affairs is the variety of specimens being gathered. If this represents a corresponding variety in the forms and adaptations of early hominids, life in times long past was probably more complicated than anything yet contemplated in present-day theories. Certainly, the facts confirm that our ancestors, starting out with relatively small brains, played a central role in making themselves more human.

Olduvai Gorge, one of the world's richest sources of knowledge about human beginnings; discovery of stone tools a million years too soon; painstaking excavation and mapping of living floors; study of living baboons as a guide to the human past; baboon troops and their responses to emergencies; early diseases

CHAPTER 4 FOSSILS AND TOOLS AS CLUES TO HUMAN BEGINNINGS

Our remote ancestors left more than their bones behind, more than the broken and scattered remains of individuals preserved ages before the invention of burial and burial rites. Their living patterns endure in the places where bands came and settled down for a time, in the open, near trees and lakes and streams. Some left forever to exploit new territory and some stayed and died where they were. Before passing on, they rearranged things a bit to make themselves safer and more comfortable, brought in stones from other areas and shaped some of them into tools, put up barriers to keep animals away at night, and left a variety of camping debris. They changed the environment only slightly, but enough so that signs of the changes have endured for more than 20,000 centuries.

One of the places is the Olduvai Gorge, where the Leakeys found remains of *Homo habilis* and a great deal more, and it deserves special attention as an unusually rich source of information about the social life of early hominids. It is located about 350 miles from Nairobi, past Mount Kilimanjaro and fever trees and herds of antelopes, giraffes, and zebras; past cliffs as high and steep as the Hudson River Palisades; past an extinct Rift Valley volcano, Ngorongoro, with a 12-mile crater; and down the other side into the Serengeti Plain, one of Africa's great game reserves.

Buried deep beneath the Serengeti is another plain. Runoff streams flowing from mountains to the south and east fed a brackish lake 5 to 8 miles across, whose fossil shorelines are visible today as rippled margins of black sand and whose central portion is marked by clays, transformed muds that are still soft. Many generations of hominids lived near the lake and the streams in a region that had already seen some spectacular geological displays. About half a million years before the coming of our ancestors, the entire top of Ngorongoro, some 2 miles of mountain, had collapsed to form the present crater. Later, **67**

during hominid occupation times, a peak in the south, probably Mount **68**
Olmoti, became violent and expelled a *nuee ardente*, or glowing cloud, a
huge mushroom of red-hot particles rising thousands of feet high. Then
the particles started falling back to earth, rolled down the sides of the
mountains at speeds of more than a mile a minute, and buried part of
the lake and probably all the lakeside dwellers beneath 15 feet of ash
and molten fragments. (In 1902, a similar volcanic avalanche on Marti-
nique Island killed 28,000 persons in the town of Saint-Pierre, the sole
survivor being a prisoner locked in an underground dungeon.)

This was the first of a series of major events. Another glowing
cloud burst out of the mountain, or perhaps a flow of hot volcanic mud.
Then things became relatively peaceful for a time, only to stir up again
with the onset of Rift movements in the region and a dramatic change
in climate. Before the change, the lake was extensive, as indicated not
only by the black-sand shorelines but also by the remains of crocodiles,
which require an abundance of fish and deep waters. After Rift-
produced dislocations and cracks formed in the earth's crust, traces of
the lake disappeared and 20-foot deposits of wind-blown sand and volcanic ash marked the prevalence of desert conditions. Then there were
alternating wet times, when the lake reappeared, and dry dust-bowl
times, when sand dunes dominated the landscape and the lakes shrank
or turned into a system of ponds and swamps or vanished entirely.

As a result of all this activity the original plain, thousands of
square miles of fossil wilderness where populations of hominids lived
and died, is inaccessible. It lies under some 300 feet of volcanic ash and
sand and lake sediments, except for one area in which nature has carried out a large-scale excavation. About 50,000 years ago, rifting produced a series of cliffs over which swift rivers cascaded, gouging down
through accumulated deposits and exposing part of the old plain. The
torrents created a miniature Grand Canyon, the 25-mile-long Olduvai
Gorge.

The gorge has been explored largely through the efforts of Louis
Leakey, who was born in Kenya and grew up with his two sisters and
brothers as the only white children in a Kikuyu village (his parents
were English missionaries). He devoted his life to the discovery and excavation of African sites. From the beginning, he felt there was something special about Olduvai, even before it yielded anything extraordinary. Within a few hours after arriving there for the first time, he found
stone tools on the slope of a side gully less than a hundred yards from
his tent, and determined on the spot to start a continuing search for remains of the toolmakers.

That was in 1931, a generation after a German entomologist discovered Olduvai, when the trip from Nairobi took the better part of a
week. Leakey returned again and again over the years, accompanied by
Mary Leakey. Season after season, they camped not far from the edge of

the gorge, walked down into canyons to explore areas as much as ten miles away, and shared a water hole with rhinoceroses and other big game. ("We could never get rid of the taste of rhino urine," Leakey recalled, "even after filtering the water through charcoal and boiling it and using it in tea with lemon.")

They found many concentrations of tools and animal bones and sites to be excavated some time in the future, if sufficient funds and help became available, but few hominid fossils—until one July morning in 1959. The Leakeys were digging on borrowed time, having exhausted current research funds and drawn on the next year's budget. Prehistorians in the field never stop looking, and Mary happened to be walking along the same slopes where her husband had first found tools nearly three decades before. Only this time a recent rock slide had exposed previously buried deposits. Mary noticed a bit of skull and, stuck firmly in the face of a nearby cliff, two very large and shining brownblack premolar teeth whose size and cusp pattern indicated a primate more advanced than a monkey or ape.

It took the Leakeys 19 days to free the teeth and parts of a fossil palate from the soft rock, sift tons of rubble and dirt, and gather a total of more than 400 bone fragments. Some months later at a scientific meeting, Leakey, whose flair for showmanship matched his flair for anthropology, invited a few privileged colleagues to an advance hotelroom preview of a new find. He opened a black box and removed the beautifully reconstructed skull of an 18-year-old *Australopithecus*. Not long afterward, the National Geographic Society began supporting his work, providing funds for workers and equipment. During the next 13 months, about 7000 tons of dirt and rock were moved, more than twice as much as had been moved during all the previous digging seasons.

Since then, Olduvai has yielded a number of important and surprising discoveries, including the first absolute date for such early sites. The South African sites have not been dated because the only sufficiently accurate radioactive clock currently available, the potassium-argon technique, depends on the analysis of volcanic materials, and volcanoes were not erupting in South Africa during hominid times. But there are such minerals at Olduvai, and the deposits containing the 1959 skull turned out to be about 1.75 million years old, nearly twice as old as had previously been estimated on the basis of geological studies. The new date has done a great deal to increase respect for the hominids of the times, since their relatively advanced development appears more striking the earlier they lived. In an analogous way, adults may not be particularly impressed with a painting until they learn that the painter is a child.

So far, remains representing more than 20 individuals have been found in older and more recent deposits, including the specimens Leakey identified as *Homo habilis*. There were also a number of rarely preserved foot and hand bones. The feet of the Olduvai hominids are re-markable because they are so much like ours. They are smaller, about 7 inches long, or about the foot size of an 8-year-old child today, and show a few other minor differences. But they show that *Australopithecus* individuals and their contemporaries walked upright, a conclusion supported by studies of the pelvis, particularly the upper part of the hip-bone blade, which is shortened and tilted toward the vertical position. As a rule, apes bend forward when they walk on two feet, because their hipbone blade is long and bent forward. Also they cannot stride as we do, because their main thigh and buttock muscles tend to flex the leg so that walking must be done in a weak, bent-kneed fashion.

How well Australopithecus walked is a matter of debate. But intensive studies of walking patterns in chimpanzees and nonhuman primates and modern *Homo*, as well as the relevant fossil material, suggest to Owen Lovejoy of Kent State University that these hominids may have walked rather better than we do. He believes that their pelvic region was in better balance as they shifted their weight from foot to foot, that they swayed less and used less energy in striding. For a number of reasons, including the widening of the birth canal to permit the delivery of larger-brained infants (see Chapter 7), we walk somewhat less efficiently and must upon occasion endure low back pain and childbirth difficulties.

Adrienne Zihlman of the University of California in Santa Cruz has studied much the same material and is not so sure: "*Australopithecus* would have required more muscle energy than modern man to perform the same actions. He probably walked with toes turned out and might have carried his weight more on the outside of the foot." Further refinements were yet to come regarding internal rotation, the more efficient hip-joint action which would reduce fatigue during long trips in search of food and new places to live. Zihlman emphasizes that these and related developments also favored the coordination and balance required to aim and throw accurately and to stand still for long periods during the stalking of game.

In any case, the hands of *Australopithecus* were apparently less advanced than the feet. According to the anatomist John Napier of the Royal Free Hospital in London, their structure is "strangely nonhuman," chiefly because the fingers are robust and curved like those of a young gorilla rather than straight and slender as in the human hand. Furthermore, although most of the thumb is missing from the Olduvai specimen, indirect evidence shows that this important digit was apparently shorter and somewhat less mobile, indicating a hand less well developed for precision work than for sheer power. It had one distinctly human feature, however. In contrast to the narrow, rounded fingertips of apes, its tip was broad and flattish like ours. The fingertips provided not only good cushions for a firm grip, but also room for a rich supply of nerve pathways to coordinate intricate hand-wrist-finger movements and for special sense organs designed to respond to pressure, pain, temperature, and textural differences. An estimated 5 million such sensory detectors are located in the skin of the body, about a third of them concentrated in the hands, mostly in the fingertips and palms.

There is another, more direct way of assessing the manual skills of African hominids. Their stone tools reveal that they were not as backward or primitive as was once believed. For a long time no stone tools were announced from any of the South African sites, which was hardly a surprise. Most investigators were looking for fossils and expected no tools. They assumed that toolmaking was beyond the capacities of relatively small-brained hominids, although the use of ready-made unworked objects as tools was considered a possibility.

This position had to be abandoned later when clearly shaped tools were found together with hominid remains. But the tenor of the times was still a reluctance, as if the objective at every stage of discovery was to concede as little as possible. Granted that the hominids actually made tools, the general opinion or expectation seemed to be that they must have been extremely crude tools, and at first only extremely crude tools were recognized and reported. As a matter of fact, the tools found were so crude that it would be impossible to identify anything much cruder as an artifact. Scientists as well as other committed persons often see what they want to believe, and their findings and interpretations tend to confirm their expectations.

The older sites of Olduvai, those located in deposits not far from the bottom of the gorge, have yielded interesting collections of stone materials. In the first place the great majority of pieces look like nothing in particular and would be gathered by specialists only. They may not be tools at all and are simply rubble, natural chunks of rock which have not been shaped or altered in any way. Yet even unworked material has something to tell us about prehistoric activities and purposes. The stones consist mainly of lava and quartz which do not come from the immediate vicinity of the site itself. They were carried in from places at least 3 miles away, perhaps to hurl at marauding animals or to hold down animal skins. If the hominids slept on the ground, as Leakey believed, stones could have been placed on damp surfaces under straw and grasses to make a dry bedding, or above the straw and grasses to keep the material from blowing away during the day.

One of the most common worked tools found among the rubble is the chopper, a cobblestone with a rough cutting or bashing edge made by knocking flakes off both sides. Such pieces must be studied on a statistical basis to be identified positively as artifacts. If they make up an appreciable proportion of the total stone assemblage, then one can be reasonably sure that they were made by human hands. But the finding of a few flaked stones that could be tools means nothing at all because they could also have been produced by nature rather than man.

Desmond Clark has walked along English beaches at Dover and elsewhere, examining stones chipped and broken by pounding surf. Many stones showed the removal of a single flake from one side, and some had flakes removed from both sides or both ends. Revil Mason of the University of the Witwatersrand in Johannesburg once examined 20,000 stones collected at Makapan. A number of them looked as if they were worked tools, but after considering the assemblage as a whole he realized that there was no solid evidence for the presence of artifacts. Nature had done the shaping, such as it was. So categories grade off into one another, and at the most rudimentary level it is not easy to distinguish accidents from artifacts. The late Abbé Henri Breuil, one of France's foremost prehistorians, expressed the problem as follows: "Man made one, God made ten thousand—God help the man who tries to see the one in ten thousand."

Most of the choppers among the earliest Olduvai collections are about the size of a tennis ball or perhaps a bit smaller. But there is another kind of chopper, which I first saw in Napier's London office. He has two walnut-sized choppers made of greenish lava, and although the hand of early hominids was smaller than ours, it was not so small that such miniature tools would fit it comfortably. They must have been held with the thumb and ring and index fingers and used for some purpose such as preparing small pieces of plant or animal food. Olduvai sites also include bone tools such as a flattened and highly polished rib of a zebra or some other horselike species, which was possibly rubbed against hides to make them smooth and pliable. A similar tool has been found at Sterkfontein.

The most unusual discoveries, however, have been made recently and show that the hominids were not only versatile toolmakers but that they engaged in fairly complex activities. For example, a site at the bottom of the gorge contains 11 different kinds of stone implements, such as engraving-gouging tools, quadrilateral chisels, large and small scrapers, and other special-purpose tools generally made of difficult-to-work lavas and quartz. Incidentally, these materials have rough, irregular surfaces which are coarsely grained and do not show clearly where flakes and chips have been knocked off, one reason why the tools were not recognized immediately. The same kinds of tools were made by later generations of hominids that had access to more finely grained materials. Their work is easier to appreciate.

These tools seem highly individualistic in the sense that they cannot be classified readily and are not shaped according to a few standardized traditional patterns. But they are not crude. In fact, they represent a complete surprise to prehistorians who had previously found related tools only in sites a million years more recent. In this sense, the tools come a million years too soon, and it is almost as if one opened up a musty vault in the Great Pyramid of Egypt and found vacuum cleaners and television sets. "At first the tools were a great shock to us," Mary Leakey comments, "and we had a hard time believing it. After this, it should be easy to believe anything."

Some of the oldest known tools turned up east of Lake Turkana near a low hill called Fever Tree Ridge, where Glynn Isaac of the University of California in Berkeley excavated an area about 20 feet across which included half a dozen choppers and other artifacts among shattered hippopotamus bones. This butchering site is probably about 1.8 million years old, while the artifacts at some other sites in Africa may be considerably older. Olduvai sites are roughly the same age, and many have intact living floors, areas with tools and other objects in their original context in practically the same positions they occupied when hominids lived near the ancient lake and streams. It is nothing new that evidence of this sort may be preserved at more recent sites representing the days of early civilizations with elaborate purposes and elaborate structures to match—palaces, courtyards, and battlements. The ashes of Vesuvius which buried Pompeii only yesterday, A.D. 79, left houses and floors and furniture and bodies in place. But few investigators suspected that there were living patterns of any sort 2 or more million years before Pompeii, much less that they could possibly have survived ancient eruptions and subsequent geological changes.

Yet such patterns do exist. Objects covered gently by volcanic ash or fine lake sediments may be moved little or not at all, and such living floors survive almost in mint condition like intricate three-dimensional mosaics. Archeologists are always on the lookout for intact sites like the one Clark discovered at Kalambo Falls (see Prologue), places where erosion has laid bare the remains of prehistoric people. Or they may inspect miniature mesas, flat elevated areas surrounded by steep erosion gullies. If tools and fossils are abundant in the gullies, it is possible that the uneroded highlands may include sealed-in layers containing undisturbed traces of the distant past.

Once a living-floor site has been found, the work really starts, and it is slow and demanding work. It calls for the application of new digging methods, or rather methods developed chiefly during the past 75 years by archeologists in Germany, Denmark, England, and other countries at farm and village sites of the past 4000 or 5000 years. A site is approached with almost surgical care and precision. First the outer cover of very recent rock and soil must be removed, taking pains to expose but not cut into underlying occupation layers. Then the job is to obtain as complete a picture as possible of the patterns in the layers.

Every item, every piece of bone and rock, worked or unworked, and chips and flakes as well as tools, must be exposed but not moved.

Every object is part of the pattern of objects; it means nothing by itself. Its position is all important. The digging rate varies depending on how much material lies on the living floor. But in a reasonably good spot, it may take one person an entire eight-hour day squatting in the dust under a hot sun to excavate 2 or 3 inches deep in an area the size of the top of a bridge table.

Much of the time is spent doing paperwork. Using a steel rule or a yardstick, one measures the position of every single one of several hundred pieces of material, their location on the living floor, and the depth beneath the surface of the site where they were found. One may also record the direction in which the piece is pointing because, among other things, that may help check on whether or not the site has actually been disturbed. If a large proportion of the pieces are pointing in the same general direction, it may mean that they have been moved by flowing water; while unmoved pieces tend to be oriented at random. All this information is written in a notebook together with the number of each piece and its type, that is, whether it is a tool and if so what sort of tool. Later the pieces are washed and numbered for identification, using a fine pen and India ink.

Louis and Mary Leakey examining early Olduvai living floor

As far as the nonspecialist is concerned, the older the site, the less interesting or impressive the objects uncovered. A classical site can yield pottery, necklaces of gold, teacups of iridescent glass, bronze statuettes. Figurines and animals carved out of ivory and delicate engravings on stone may date back 25,000 years or more, and beautifully worked tools of flint and obsidian come from sites many millennia older than that. But to the nonspecialist, pieces collected at the Olduvai sites usually appear to be hardly worth collecting. Archeologists who have brought such material to show to their nonscientific friends are familiar with the disappointment lay people try to conceal by polite interest.

So at the root of discovery, in archeology as well as in every other branch of science, there is tedium—the painstaking and sometimes grim accumulation of data, often under the loneliest of conditions. Tedium is and must be the guts of scientific endeavor because nothing worth coming by comes easily. In a sense no one person sees anything as he or she excavates the earliest living floors, brushing the dirt off individual pieces and measuring their positions and marking them day after day. Each excavator is part of a group that moves thousands of

tons of dirt and rock. The full story may not be revealed until months or
even years later, when the data have been analyzed and all the maps
and charts drawn.

At that stage, when one sees the whole picture or a major part of
the picture, the results may be spectacular. Reading the map of a living
floor is something like trying to decipher a code or translate a manuscript in a strange language, the symbols being patterns in the positions
of the objects. For example, the site at the bottom of the gorge which
yielded surprisingly varied tools also included another unexpected feature. The work called for the marking of many chunks of unworked and
individually undistinguished stone, and only gradually did it become
apparent that the stones were arranged in a definite pattern. The pattern shows up clearly in a map prepared by Mary Leakey, who learned
precise digging techniques at a hill-fort site in Devon, England. It consists of piles of rock placed in a rough semicircle around a saucer-
shaped area, perhaps a crude wall which may have served as a windbreak.

Incidentally, this site has been dated by the potassium-argon
method and also by a new radioactive-clock method which depends on
the analysis of bits of volcanic glass scattered over the area. The glass
contains traces of U-238, the radioactive form of uranium used in early
atomic weapons, whose atoms split at a regular rate and leave fission
tracks in the glass. The tracks look like tiny grooves under the microscope, and can be counted to provide a measure of time elapsed since
the glass cooled. According to results reported by General Electric investigators, the stone semicircle is 2.03 million years old, plus or minus
280,000 years, which makes it the oldest man-made structure known.

Mary Leakey has also drawn a large map of the 3400-square-foot
living floor where she and her husband found the *Australopithecus* skull
in 1959. The map shows the precise positions of more than 4000 artifacts and fossils, and includes an area about 15 feet in diameter which
is thick with shattered pieces of rock and bone and choppers, where
"everything is bash, bash, bash." Outside this area the concentration of
material drops off sharply until one comes to another area off to one
side, a few feet from the main concentration, a place containing larger
bone fragments and unshattered bones.

This pattern has been interpreted as a dining-room complex. The
tools, chips, flakes, and bone splinters mark a part of the site set aside
for the job of smashing bones to get at the marrow. Practically every
bone that could yield marrow has been smashed. The nearby concentration of bones, including jaws and skulls which do not contain marrow,
is believed to be a kind of garbage heap. Between the heap and the
main concentration is an almost bare arc-shaped area, which may have
been a windbreak of branches because it lies directly in the path of prevailing winds in the region today. Another possibility is that the barrier

helped protect hominids from predators, a strategy still used today not **77** only by native tribes, but in the Leakey's camp itself. (Leopards, rhinoceroses, and lions wander in from time to time and must be discouraged.)

The Olduvai site as a whole represents a distinctively human pattern. It served as a home base, a camping place where some members of the band remained, including infants, children, and elderly persons, while others went out to gather plant foods and hunt. The notion of leaving a group of individuals behind is totally foreign to monkeys and apes, whose troops generally move about as single units. Although we cannot tell how long the home base at Olduvai was occupied, the bones and other materials must have accumulated over a period of years, during which hominid bands left their lakeside camp and returned many times. They were in the process of forming new kinds of associations and familiarities centered about one relatively small area, the sort of place where increasingly complex traditions and taboos would develop.

Remains of the oldest known structure, possibly a windbreak, uncovered at foot of Olduvai Gorge

Revil Mason, University of the Witwatersrand archeologist, trying to identify man-made tools among chipped and broken stones at Makapan *Australopithecus* site

Olduvai also includes a factory site, which illustrates the importance of saving every excavated item however uninteresting it may be in itself. Studies of more than 30,000 pieces of fractured and flaked chert, a form of quartz, show that at least as early as 1.6 million years ago hominids were bringing the stone to the site from sources in the neighborhood, and making flakes with sharp cutting edges. Furthermore, whatever their purposes, they preferred small flakes from 15 to 35 millimeters long and from 2 to 12 millimeters thick.

The sites at Olduvai were probably not occupied all year round. John Speth of the University of Michigan and David Davis of Brandeis University compared the kills of present-day Bushman hunter-gatherers in southern Africa with kills made up to nearly 2 million years ago at **79** Olduvai (as deduced from the identification of more than 10,000 fossil bones). They found that modern and ancient hominids tended to concentrate on the same prey. Their analysis also indicates that most early sites were occupied during the dry season, when herds of wildebeest and other prey animals come together at permanent lakes and waterholes. During the rainy season prey dispersed, probably moving outside the gorge, to be followed by dispersing predators, including hominids.

A great deal more can be learned in the future from living floors. Different patterns, different systems of bone and stone concentrations, and crude structures can be compared to hieroglyphics whose meanings may become increasingly clear as they are repeated in different contexts. The patterns so far uncovered are so few that their interpretation relies to a large extent on clever guesswork. But the discovery of related patterns and new details will transform the guesswork into highly probable hypotheses. At Olduvai alone there are some 50 sites which have not yet been excavated and represent enough work to keep excavators and prehistorians busy for another generation or two.

Studies of existing primates supplement deductions based on material recovered from the earth. Baboons supply clues to early life on dry, wide African savannas. For all the differences between them and early hominids, highly probable and striking similarities exist. The large monkeys have been studied intensively in the wild by Irven De-Vore of Harvard, Jean and Stuart Altmann of the University of Chicago, Thelma Rowell of the University of California in Berkeley, and John Crook and the late Ronald Hall of the University of Bristol, England. (Hall died in the summer of 1965, probably of a virus infection, after a laboratory monkey had bitten him on the hand.)

Baboons of Nairobi Park and the Amboseli Game Reserve move in diurnal cycles, locked in as it were to the clockwork rhythm of sunrises and sunsets. They sleep in the trees, halfway out on the branches, and begin to stir with the first light of day, generally around five in the morning, and often in a groggy half-trance state somewhat reminiscent of more advanced primates like ourselves. "They tend to awaken very sluggishly," according to DeVore, "and you get the impression that what they need most is a cup of coffee." The next two hours are spent in waking up and grooming one another, always near the sleeping tree or trees.

Then the time comes for leaving the trees, and it is at this point that one begins to feel the difference between forest and savanna. The forest offers many hiding places and escape routes and refuges in the trees, and life can be relatively relaxed. But there is more fear and danger in the open savanna. Tourists today are forbidden to get out of their cars, and investigators do so at their own risk and generally make a

Pebble tool and a chopper, first stone tools made by man's ancestors

practice of coughing softly so that any predators in the vicinity may hear and not be surprised. (A startled predator is more likely to attack.)

The boldest troop members leave the trees first, adult males who are not at the top of the social hierarchy and juveniles corresponding roughly to older teenagers in a human group. They move rapidly in a beeline as if they know exactly where they are going, and they do not look back. Other older juveniles and adult females follow; next comes the central nucleus of the troop—mothers with their infants and the youngest juveniles and the most dominant and generally the biggest and oldest males. The back part of the troop is a mirror image of the front with more older juveniles and adult females following the nucleus group and more adult males bringing up the rear. This convoy pattern has been observed in terrain where lions, hyenas, and other predators are abroad. It rarely occurs among troops living in settings free from predators.

A baboon troop on the move makes a formidable array and is attacked only rarely and only by lions. Its early-morning trek is from a few hundred yards to a few miles to reach the day's main feeding place, where intensive eating may go on for as much as two or three hours after the area has been surveyed for possible predators. Often you come across a troop feeding together with a herd of impalas in a natural and effective association, since baboons have fine eyesight and impalas have a fine sense of smell. Between them they can detect practically any predator and give the alarm in the form of warning barks. As a rule, it seems that baboons recognize and respond to the alarm cries of many other species.

Sometimes, particularly during the dry season, it is amazing how much food they can obtain from apparently barren areas. They pull up everything in plain sight, and then scan the ground for withered stalks and other signs of succulent plant runners that extend like tiny pipes just beneath the surface. They can also detect almost invisible wisps, hairlike filaments which mark the location of deeper-lying tubers, bulbs, and roots. At midday they rest, usually not far from the feeding place in a shady spot where grooming clusters form, juveniles and infants play, and adults may take a siesta or sit quietly and keep watch.

Later the baboons move in formation toward another feeding place, again after making sure the coast is clear. On one occasion Altmann and I observed a dramatic example of courage and caution in the Amboseli Game Reserve at the foot of Mount Kilimanjaro. Something had frightened a troop when it was about to move into the plains from the shade of a fever tree. The leader, a sleek husky male with a magnificent mane, was sitting on a rock looking ahead. Then, apparently deciding that it was safe to advance, he got up and started moving past a bush toward tall grasses.

All at once something we could neither see nor hear made him change his mind. He hesitated, turned his head, and retreated to the rock as the rest of the troop, which had started to follow, scampered back into the tree. He peered around once more in such a human fashion and so intensely that I expected him to shade his eyes with his hand like a lookout aboard ship. Finally he started again, with a firm and confident this-is-it stride, and led his troop out into the savanna.

After resting, the troop does not go any farther from the trees where it will spend the night. In fact, the second feeding place generally lies on the way back, because tensions rise as the afternoon wears on and the sun sinks. Several years ago DeVore observed an encounter between predators and a troop which was already within sight of its sleeping place in a shallow valley. One baboon stopped eating and turned to look in the direction of a clump of trees about a hundred yards away; gradually, over a period of a minute or so, every monkey was sitting and looking in the same direction, that is, all but two infants that started playing and were promptly slapped down.

Suddenly an old male baboon grunted twice and walked toward the trees. Almost immediately, he was joined by about half a dozen other males, big adults and juveniles that advanced with him side by side in a tight line. At this stage DeVore first saw what was upsetting the baboons, the heads of two cheetahs sticking up out of the grass near the trees and only a hundred feet or so ahead of the line. The line advanced until it was only about 60 feet away, when several of the baboons broke out of formation and made a lunging charge directly at the cheetahs. The big cats turned and ran off, and the baboons behind the line started eating again.

Defensive tactics are not always so successful; lions do not run under similar circumstances. Baboons are safe or comparatively safe only when they have reached sleeping trees near rivers and permanent water holes, and even there they may occasionally fall prey to leopards. Shortly after sunset, they are dozing off and the day has come full circle. The troop moves about 3 miles a day on the average, often returning to the same trees which it left early in the morning. Normally every member of this tightly organized little cluster of monkeys is constantly in sight of the other members, and many baboons spend their entire lives within a few miles of the places where they were born.

Our ancestors may have lived comparable lives on similar savannas millions of years ago. They had little choice about it, since there are certain fundamental ways of dealing with such environments which would have to be used by practically any primate and practically any mammal. They had to face the same dangers, the same predators, and they had to evolve some type of social hierarchy. A high degree of organization is essential on the savanna. It is not that emergencies occasionally arise, but life is a continual emergency and the odds in favor of survival are greater if each individual knows what to do in case of trouble. Man's ancestors also took cues from the alarm cries of other creatures, and moved across open areas with rear guards and vanguards and side riders in the same basic formation used more recently in covered-wagon trains and naval convoys.

There were other dangers besides predators. The teeth of the 18-year-old *Australopithecus* found at Olduvai in 1959, for example, suggest that he may have been sickly as a child. The enamel of permanent teeth is built up layer by layer during a child's development, and periods of illness show up as tiny hollows resulting from retarded growth in the layers. An illness like measles or chicken pox which usually runs a brief course may leave shallow hollows. But the hollows in the teeth of this hominid are deep and suggest that he had a disease that lasted for many months, probably gastroenteritis due to malnutrition. Furthermore, he suffered three major attacks of the disease—at the ages of 2, 4, and 4½.

In general, Olduvai hominids and their contemporaries harbored two types of disease-producing organisms, those shared with other primates and those restricted to members of the human family. From a study of primate infections Aidan Cockburn of the Mayor's Committee for Human Resources Development in Detroit believes that among the diseases which may date back more than 25 million years to the ape ancestors of modern apes and people are amoebic dysentery, yellow fever, pinworm infections, malaria, syphilis, and yaws. Diseases which may have appeared and evolved with humans include typhoid and leprosy. (Certain modern diseases, such as measles, mumps, cholera, and the common cold, which require large concentrated populations to support them, probably could not for this reason have existed in prehistoric times.)

Baboon at leisure: mothers and infants resting and playing; male juveniles chasing one another while an adult male watches

Early hominids, like their fellow primates, lived mainly exposed to the elements. Sometimes on stormy nights, however, they may have been driven to seek cover under overhanging cliffs, where they huddled together wet and cold in the dark in a world still dominated by other animals. Bad weather may even have driven them into caves. Early one morning in southwest Africa during a very cold, harsh season, Hall saw a troop of baboons emerging from a cave high in a cliff overlooking a river bed, and on another occasion he took motion pictures of a troop leaving a cave by the edge of the sea.

But habitual cave dwelling came later. Caves were occupied by more efficient killers, that had to be driven out and kept out, and had to await the widespread use of fire. (There is no evidence that early African hominids used fire.) On the other hand, brief visits may have been common, a possibility suggested by the finding of hominid remains and bones presumably shattered by hominids at Swartkrans and other Transvaal caves. According to Kenneth Oakley of the British Museum of Natural History, hominids may have entered rock shelters near the entrances to these caves in the daytime to obtain water or get out of the noonday sun rather than for extended period of shelter.

Of course, emphasizing the similarities between baboons and

hominids can take us just so far. There were also great differences just **84** on the verge of making their impact and, more significantly, a potential for even greater differences. Some hominids seem to have hunted regularly. Furthermore, they were already beginning to change nature in a new way, to fight back by refusing to take things as they found them. They were modifying things, however slightly, and evolving toward an increasing measure of independence. Signs of the trend may be seen in the existence of home bases and a crude wall-like structure which shows that, although they lived in the open, they may have been learning to protect themselves from savanna winds.

Their surprisingly advanced tools imply a variety of activities, a brain already capable of some sort of language, and the possibility of social organizations considerably more elaborate than those of other primates. New kinds of ties created solidarity even among scattered populations. Troops and bands tend to break into small groups when rainfall declines and the land turns to semidesert and when dwindling sources of food and water are few and widely dispersed. Many individuals coming en masse upon one of these sources would soon exhaust it without satisfying their needs, and some might perish before reaching the next source perhaps miles away. Limited resources are best exploited by small groups, as is the case today among Bushman hunter-gatherers of the Kalahari Desert in southern Africa. But strong forces bring them together from time to time, even during the driest times, kinship ties that evolved in the remote past.

As more is learned about the hominids who appeared 3 or 4 million years ago, they seem less and less like apes and more and more like humans. Some investigators are still reluctant to credit them with traditions or rudimentary language or with relatively sophisticated cooperation and social organization, although the evidence points increasingly in that direction. The trend is definitely toward assigning a higher status to our remote ancestors and recognizing that the gap between them and subsequent species is not as great as once believed.

Discovery of Poor George in Africa and a relative, a Lantian individual, in China; discovery of Java man; Peking man on Dragon's Hill; Vallonet and Escale caves; quantum evolution and increase in brain size and its relation to meat eating

CHAPTER 5   EARLY MIGRATIONS OF HUMAN ANCESTORS

A major surprise of the 1963 digging season at the Olduvai Gorge occurred one January morning when an African worker announced he was going to find a fossil man and then did precisely that—turning up some time later with a matchbox containing a few badly broken hominid teeth. He had picked them up in the middle of a track made by cattle belonging to local Masai tribesmen, which meant that a valuable specimen had probably been trampled to bits. In fact, hundreds of further fragments were recovered after some two months of scraping, sweeping, and sifting mud.

One result of this episode was a top-level meeting of Masai elders, government officials, and the Leakeys, who agreed to build dams and establish watering places for the cattle, provided that the Masai would keep their herds out of the gorge. Another result was a specimen known unofficially as Poor George (or, at the suggestion of an anonymous punster, as Olduvai George from Olduvai Gorge). I saw the specimen one Sunday at the Leakeys' home outside Nairobi. Mary removed it from a safe in her office and placed it as carefully as an antique dealer with a fragile vase on a folded blanket. It was a skull about the size of a softball, with prominent brow ridges, representing some 200 fragments glued and plastered together by Mary "on odd Sundays" over a period of more than eight months.

Poor George in his prime may have been more of a man than *Homo habilis*. Among other things, his brain was bigger and his teeth were smaller, more like ours. His remains were found just below sterile wind-blown deposits of sand and volcanic ash, which indicates that he lived more than a million years ago. He and individuals like him represent true humans, descendants of *Homo habilis*, and belong to the widespread species known as *Homo erectus*. The species includes a number of highly publicized representatives that stirred up some debate during the early days of research in human evolution and whose **85**

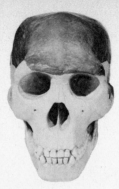

Homo erectus:
reconstructed skull
and artist's
conception

significance is just beginning to be appreciated in light of recent studies. A notable story, according to one anthropologist "the greatest story
of serene confidence I have ever heard," concerns the first *erectus* remains to be discovered.

About 90 years ago, Eugene Dubois, a young Dutch anatomist,
performed the highly unlikely feat of deducing where hominid remains
should be found, and then going out and finding them. His argument
was that one should look in the tropics, specifically in the East Indies,
where apes still lived and where no glaciers had come to disturb possible sites. By 1892, he had extracted part of the jaw, skull, and other
fossil bones of a "missing link" from the bank of a river in central Java,
a creature which he regarded as more advanced than an ape and not
quite a human.

Dubois found a reasonably respectful audience for his ideas, especially considering the tradition of heated disbelief which still prevails

among prehistorians. (For some reason, when investigators in this field disagree, they disagree rather more violently and bitterly than investigators in other branches of science.) Certainly the Java remains received far more support than Dart's Taung baby was to receive three decades or so later. But some anthropologists were skeptical and suggested that the remains might be those of a small-brained relatively modern man, perhaps a microcephalic idiot. Others believed it was a giant gibbon; still others refused to commit themselves.

The situation became clearer following excavations in China, which started during the 1920s as the result of a strange series of events. For centuries, expeditions had gone out into the remote mountain gorges and caves of Mongolia, China, and Indonesia and brought back tons of fossils annually, but not in the name of science. The expeditions were led by traders supplying the enormous demand for dragons' teeth which, according to Far Eastern folklore, had potent medicinal effects. Chemists and apothecaries ground the bones into a fine sour-tasting powder and used it in a variety of elixirs and tonics probably no more ineffective than many over-the-counter preparations currently for sale in the drugstores of the Western world.

Paleontologists aware of these practices had long been shopping for fossils at local apothecary stores and inquiring about the locations of promising sites. One such inquiry led from a human tooth purchased at a Peking store to a large debris-filled limestone cave in Dragon Bone Hill, about 30 miles from the city, where excavations were carried out between 1923 and 1937. By the time digging stopped, workers had reached a depth of some 160 feet without hitting bedrock and had unearthed 14 Peking type of skulls, about 150 teeth, and other remains representing more than 40 individuals who resembled the Java individual.

Hearths and tools were found in the deposits, and also signs of a long struggle between Peking individuals and other cave dwellers. Some of the deepest and oldest layers contained animal bones of large carnivores, such as sabertooth tigers and giant hyenas, together with bones of their prey. Other layers sandwiched between the animal layers contained only human remains, indicating that the carnivores had been driven out of the caves for a time. There were no animal layers in the uppermost deposits. Peking individuals seem eventually to have won in the struggle.

These discoveries more than vindicated Dubois. In fact, they showed that he had been too conservative and that his Java find was not a prehuman but a full-fledged human. But by that time Dubois had become a secretive, conservative, and eccentric old man. He went into virtual hiding, belittled the significance of the Chinese excavations, felt his colleagues were plotting against him, and buried his fossils in a chest in the ground beneath his dining-room floor. It happens that all the material on Peking individuals, which had taken so long to find,

was lost without trace during World War II. According to a recent version of what occurred, the remains had been packed in crates and were en route to the United States for the duration of the war as part of the personal luggage of a young doctor in the U.S. Marines heading for home in 1941. Intercepted by the Japanese, he managed to leave the crates with Chinese friends and Swiss and French officials before being imprisoned until the end of the war. Despite recent efforts to trace the material, a search that involved many leads and a $150,000 reward, chances of recovery now seem slim.

Fortunately, the record remains and includes fine plaster casts of the skulls, although the original specimens would be much more useful in continuing studies. During the past decade, digging has resumed on Dragon Bone Hill. Workers have found tools, animal bones, and some further fragments of Peking individuals in deeper levels of the large cave as well as in nearby caves. Digging has continued in Java, and two other skulls and skull fragments have recently been found in the central part of the island, not far from the site where Dubois made his original discovery.

The oldest *Homo erectus* specimen may be a skull announced in 1976 by Richard Leakey which was found on the eastern shore of Lake Turkana. Its estimated age is 1.5 million years. Java and Peking man are probably about 750,000 years old, and most other *Homo erectus* remains **89** date back at least 400,000 to 500,000 years. The earliest specimen in Europe is a lower jawbone uncovered in 1907 in a sandpit near Heidelberg, Germany. In 1963, the year when Poor George was found, an expedition led by Woo Ju-kang of the Chinese Academy of Sciences discovered the lower jawbone of an individual named Lantian man, after Lantian County in northwest China. The specimen was embedded deep in a hundred-foot deposit of red clay and, judging by its size, Lantian man was probably a woman. The following year, Ju-kang and his associates unearthed the skull of another Lantian specimen, also probably a woman and more than 30 years old.

Other *erectus* traces have been found during the past three decades, among other places near a Mohammedan cemetery on top of a sand dune in Algeria and on an ancient shoreline of Lake Chad in the Sahara. Further remains come from a Hungarian limestone quarry in the village of Vertesszöllös about 30 miles from Budapest. In a valley where a tributary of the Danube once flowed, investigators are excavating an important sealed-in site where hearths, burned bones and charcoal, many tools, several teeth, and part of a skull representing what is probably an advanced *erectus* individual have been found.

Evidence accumulates to give a fuller picture of the rise and spread of human beings throughout the Old World. Africa is their probable homeland, the place where their oldest known remains and sites are located. It was in Africa that they established themselves as toolmakers and hunters and advanced social animals learning to live in millions of square miles of open country, with no winters, among ocean-wide grasslands, and with herds among the grasses. But as time passed, their future involved the rest of the world to a greater and greater extent.

Outside Africa, the earliest traces of human camping sites and tools dated at about a million years later, turned up more than 3500 miles from the Olduvai Gorge, in southeastern France. They were collected in Vallonet cave, found some time ago by a young schoolgirl, among frost-shattered rocks and deposits sealed in by stalagmites. The cave extends deep into a 300-foot limestone promontory overlooking the Mediterranean. The evidence obtained to date is scanty but as clear-cut as the unearthing of an entire settlement. It consists of five pebbles chipped on one side, two of them choppers like those found at Olduvai; four flakes, two of which show use or working on the edges; and the fossil bones of rhinoceroses, elephants, horses, and whales, several of which seem to have been broken deliberately. According to estimates based on animal remains and the geology of the site, this material may be more than a million years old.

Another site, the Escale cave, contains traces of about the same age or perhaps somewhat younger. In 1960, workers dynamiting a road through the valley of the Durance River not far from Marseilles exposed the back chambers of the buried cave and noted old bones among the limestone debris. Excavations conducted since then have furnished the earliest evidence for the use of fire, traces of charcoal and ash, fire-cracked stones, and five reddened hearth areas up to a yard in diameter. Escale is believed to include relatively undisturbed living floors; it promises to be one of the most important sites ever discovered in Europe.

Important questions, and we have no answers for them, are why our ancestors left Africa at all and why specifically during this period—1 to 2 million years ago—and not sooner. After all, they had been around for at least 4 to 5 million years before that without entering the

Vallonet cave near Monte Carlo, oldest known campsite in Europe

vast Eurasian continent, as far as currently available evidence indicates. A complete theory would take account of such problems and might relate them to the sort of restlessness that moves people today.

Geological changes certainly affected the movements of hominids and other animals, and the last 2 million years or so mark not only the rise of our kind but also one of the most unstable climatic periods in the earth's history. As already indicated, large-scale northward migrations may have become possible for the first time after the formation of the African Rift Valley removed water barriers by shifting the courses of major rivers from a general east-west to a north-south direction.

The coming of glaciers also had at least an indirect effect on the timing and course of migrations from Africa into other continents. Prehistory features what Karl Butzer of the University of Chicago calls "one of the rare spasms of extensive and recurrent glaciation affecting the planet." Indeed, no human being has yet lived under conditions which, considering the prevailing climates of the past, can be regarded as normal. The previous spasm had come and gone more than 200 million years ago. The latest one was preceded by a relatively quiet period, a long calm before the storm.

More than 60 million years ago, in prosimian times, long before the appearance of modern monkeys and apes, the earth consisted mainly of tropics. Vast forests and grasslands were widespread; alligators and other reptiles splashed about in streamy swamps as far north as Montana and Wyoming. The average year-round temperature of Central Europe was about 70 degrees Fahrenheit. Temperatures held fairly steady for about 20 million years and then started falling, and this is believed to be related to a comparatively late event in the breaking up of the supercontinent Pangea. South America and Australia split off from the southern part of the land mass, isolating Antarctica at the South Pole, creating a swift and icy circumpolar current, and producing a sudden drop in ocean temperatures. Gradually the world became much cooler, average temperatures in Europe dropping some 20 degrees Fahrenheit.

The stage was set for a spectacular phenomenon. About 2 to 3 million years ago, climates started to oscillate, temperatures falling to subfreezing levels and rising and falling again in a series of cold spasms. Snows in the north and on the highest mountains no longer melted away during summer thaws, but piled up layer by layer season after season to form great ice masses or glaciers. During cold periods, ocean levels fell as more and more water was locked up in the glaciers, which advanced from the poles and covered large portions of the earth. The process reversed during warmer periods, ocean levels rising again as the glaciers melted and retreated.

We do not know why these oscillations occurred. In fact, James Kennett of the University of Rhode Island believes that they represent

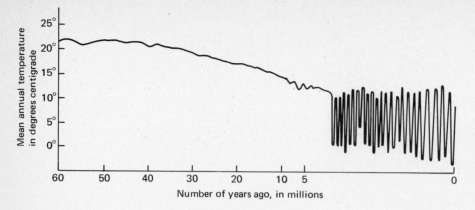

Schematic curve showing slow temperature decline and recent oscillations in Central Europe during past sixty million years. Time scale greatly exaggerated for the past five million years

"one of the major unsolved scientific problems of the century." It is a double problem. First, investigators are seeking periodic processes which could trigger periodic worldwide temperature changes, such as long-term changes in solar radiation and long-term cycles of upheavals from still-active volcanoes that are perhaps related to colliding continental plates which created the Himalayas, Alps, and Rockies. Beyond that, there is the problem of accounting for the existence of cycles, because we know of no obvious reason why solar radiation, volcanoes, or any other contributing factors should vary in a periodic way.

Questions of how many oscillations there were and how many glacial stages and warmer interglacial periods are still wide open. The traditional number of four, based on older observations, is still cited in widely read texts. But new research, most of it conducted within the past decade, has changed the picture entirely. Studies of fossil pollen, sea-floor sediments and sedimentation rates, and changing concentrations of oxygen isotopes in microscopic marine shells point toward more than 20 major advances and retreats of great ice sheets, 8 during the last 700,000 years alone and, according to many experts, the next to come within 2,000 years or so.

Africa was far from the steep fronts of mile-high ice masses that moved like giant bulldozers down from polar regions. But its highest mountains felt the cold, and during glacial times, the snow line on the slopes of Mount Kenya extended some 5000 feet lower than it does today. More widespread effects are suggested by pollen studies which indicate that the Ice Age influenced climates all over the world, conditions being cooler and wetter in Africa when glaciation was most extensive in polar regions.

The new work draws attention to possible relationships between such changes and barriers to free migration. For example, increased rainfall during the first glacial stage may have created steppes and savannas and lakes in the Sahara and opened up routes across previously impassable desert. On the other hand, the Kalahari to the south may have advanced as the glaciers retreated in drier times during the subsequent interglacial stage, while the sand and ash deposits which cover some of the hominid remains and traces of a broad deep lake at Olduvai are more than 40 feet thick, indicating a long stretch of extremely arid conditions. So climate produced at the poles influenced the movements of our ancestors in and out of traditional living zones.

Social forces, critical changes in evolving human behavior patterns, may have been at least as important as geological forces in early migrations from Africa. For example, home bases were established where members of prehistoric bands could rest if necessary in comparative safety. As indicated in Chapter 4, such bases are unknown among lesser primates. All members of a baboon troop, for example, move together when leaving the trees in which they slept in the morning and return together at night. Weak or sick or injured members must try to keep up, and if they cannot they are left behind. Within hours after the troop has gone, and probably before its heart stops beating, the deserted baboon may be devoured by a predator. (Lions and other carnivores prey primarily on incapacitated animals.)

Washburn emphasizes the importance of the home base: "The whole evolutionary impact of disease and accident on the human species was changed when it became possible for an individual to stay in one place and not have to take part in the daily round of the troop. Certainly one of the reasons why it has been possible for man to migrate without building immunity to local diseases is that his way of life allows him to be far sicker than a baboon and still recover. Injuries to the legs are common and are far more serious, of course, for a biped than for a quadruped. It is the home base that changes sprained ankles and fevers from fatal diseases to minor ailments."

Although home bases may have helped make migrations possible, they do not explain why or when migrations actually occurred. Although crowding can be a relative thing, as we are learning today, perhaps crowding or the feeling of being crowded has remote prehistoric origins. Perhaps small groups of younger individuals felt an urge to live well away from the old folks at home and moved on to the next valley, and their children or their children's children kept moving on until hunter-gatherers had spread throughout Africa and beyond. Or it could have been an urge to wander and explore, to go somewhere simply for the sake of going, and preferably to a place where no one had been before.

But why during a particular period, and not before or after? There is no shortage of possibilities or bright ideas; there rarely is. The problem remains to figure out what sort of evidence could prove or disprove a particular theory, and then to go out and find the evidence. In general, such work has not been done. So we continue to speculate about forces which sent our ancestors across the Sahara and out of Africa. The hominids who reached Java nearly a million years ago presumably took many generations to pass through northeastern Africa, Israel, Iran and southern India on their way to tropical climates in the Far East.

The wanderers who settled in places like the Vallonet and Escale caves had to deal with harsher conditions in glacial lands. Their probable route into Europe was also through northeastern Africa and Israel, and then perhaps across the Dardanelles in Turkey, where there was either a land bridge or else very narrow straits with slow tides. The most direct route, across Gibraltar, had tremendous tides associated with a deep submarine canyon and was a formidable barrier to early hominids. Based on estimates of prehistoric migration rates in more recent times, and the estimates are very rough, it might have taken them about 3000 to 4000 years to spread from Olduvai to southeastern France, moving and settling down and moving again, generation after generation, at an average rate of about a mile a year.

Who made the crossing is not known for certain, since no hominid remains have been found in the earliest living sites such as those at Vallonet and Escale. It was probably *Homo erectus*, who had an appreciably larger brain and presumably an enhanced ability to adapt to new environments. In fact, the expansion of the brain is one of the most spectacular developments in human prehistory. It is a good example of what George Gaylord Simpson of Harvard calls quantum evolution, an explosive burst of new adaptations. Of course, explosiveness is relative, and Simpson warns that "considerable imagination must be used to conceive of an explosion that makes no noise and goes on for several million years." A process which lasts that long is fast only on a time scale involving many hundreds of millions of years.

Quantum evolution occurred among horses some 25 million years ago. Horses had lived mainly on succulent leaves, which are easy to chew up; but their survival was threatened when forests became sparse and they had to survive on a diet of tough, gritty grasses. Many species failed to adapt to the new conditions because their short teeth were worn away at an early age, but populations that included a relatively high proportion of longer-toothed individuals proved more successful. The shift from browsing to grazing, which brought about changes in tooth shape, to provide more efficient grinding surfaces, and the appearance of a special tough cement as well as longer teeth was extremely rapid in evolutionary terms, requiring about 8 to 10 million years.

More rapid changes took place among early hominids. There are a number of ways of looking at the phenomenon. According to one study, the average cranial capacity of *Australopithecus africanus*, dating back more than 5 million years, was about 450 cubic centimeters, as

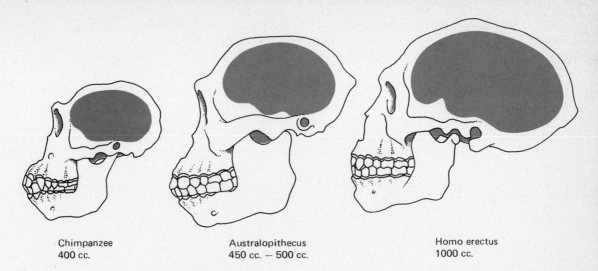

Chimpanzee
400 cc.

Australopithecus
450 cc. — 500 cc.

Homo erectus
1000 cc.

Average cranial
capacities, indicating
more than doubling
of brain size from
Australopithecus to
Homo erectus
(chimpanzee cranial
capacity included for
comparison)

compared with 650 cubic centimeters for *Homo habilis*. The cranial capacity of *Homo erectus* averaged about 1000 cubic centimeters, although some specimens reached the 1300 level, which overlaps the range for modern man, which is less than 1000 to about 2000 cubic centimeters. In other words, some members of *Homo erectus*, had brains larger than many people living today. The brain had increased two to three times in some 5 million years.

Powerful evolutionary forces were at work selecting for larger brains, particularly during the stage of development from *Australopithecus* to *Homo habilis*. The pressure was on for survival. Something happened to step up the pace of change or, to put it another way, something interrupted the naturally slow course of evolution. As usual a significant factor was the basic quest for food. The big change was a widening of food horizons, a diet including practically everything edible, with a special emphasis on meat.

The problem is why our ancestors turned increasingly to meat eating. An old tradition exists that meat eating is corrupt, something to be guilty about, a sign of how far we have fallen from a state of original innocence. A seventeenth-century theologian, looking back to a fictitious past, described "those artless Ages, when Mortals lived by plain Nature . . . Men were not carnivores . . . and did not feed upon Flesh, but only upon Fruit and Herbs." More recently William Golding in *The Inheritors,* a novel about prehistoric life, writes of the guilt which primitive people felt as they tore into a doe and of "the rich smell of meat and wickedness."

The origins of beliefs and of taboos observed and violated are always difficult to trace. But there was certainly a time when hominids ate less meat than we do now. Most primates live chiefly on fruit, grasses, leaves, and other plant foods. But probably many primates and many mammals could become meat eaters under certain circumstances. For example, if a baboon happens to come across a nest of fledgling birds or newborn rodents, it may on rare occasions scoop up the contents casually, without breaking stride. In other words, meat eating may be an act performed in passing.

It may also be considerably more than that, however. A male baboon was observed pursuing a hare in a zigzag dodging course for about 70 yards in a chase that lasted more than a minute. The hare finally jumped over a log and froze motionless on the other side, only to be picked up and devoured by its pursuer. Such a tactic may fool many predators with poor color vision, and baboons may use it themselves,

Carnivorous primate: baboon eating young gazelle

but in general it plays into the hands of primates, whose highly developed color vision helps them detect motionless objects.

Baboons may become regular meat eaters, a fact reported recently by Robert Harding of the University of Pennsylvania and Shirley Strum of the University of California in San Diego. Harding discovered the practice while observing a troop foraging on cattle ranches in Kenya's Rift Valley, about 75 miles northwest of Nairobi. In more than a thousand hours of observing he saw the baboons kill 47 animals, mainly the infants of Thomson's gazelles (or Tommies) and other antelopes as well as hares and birds. Killing was predominantly a male activity. There were only 3 to 5 adult males in the 50-member troop, and they accounted for 44 of the 47 victims. Adult females accounted for the other 3 victims. Often the killers walked into a field where gazelles were grazing and deliberately criss-crossed the area in search of helpless infants.

Later observations by Strum revealed important changes in predatory patterns. The number of kills by adult males and females more than doubled, and younger troop members participated in the killing for the first time. Even more significant were the first steps in the development of cooperative hunting, which Strum witnessed one day. An adult male, Rad, went after a herd of Tommies, succeeding only in scattering the group while grabbing at a dodging baby, which he missed. Just as Rad was tiring, Sumner, the troop's oldest male, took over the pursuit, joined by Big Sam, a younger male, and Brutus, a newcomer from another troop. "The chase turned into a relay," Strum reports, "one male running after the baby and another taking over when the first tired. Finally, Big Sam chased the young antelope into Brutus' grasp. The baboons obviously learned from the experience. More and more frequently I witnessed hunting in which one or more baboons chased a Tommy toward another hunter. The success rate climbed sharply."

More elaborate hunting patterns have been observed among chimpanzees at the Gombe Stream Research Center (see Chapter 6). The central point is that among nonhuman primates hunting is and apparently has always been a welcome method of obtaining food—but not an essential one. Baboons and chimpanzees, like human vegetarians of the twentieth century, can get along very well without meat. That may not have been the case for the hominids of remote prehistory; for them meat eating may have been a matter of survival, as a supplement to diets consisting mainly of plant food.

In the beginning they may have ventured out of the forests mainly during times of temporary and relatively mild shortages of fruits and other preferred foods. Today in the Budongo Forest of Uganda, for example, intermittent periods of scarcity last for a total of about three months a year. It would be interesting to learn whether chimpanzees living there move into surrounding open woodlands or grasslands dur-

ing such periods. The earliest hominids may have gone into the savanna in search of new food sources and returned to an almost exclusive forest existence as soon as the shortages passed.

Later on, during prolonged dry periods, when they came into the
savanna to stay, they had to find an evolutionary zone for themselves
and exploit the natural resources of the savanna to the fullest possible
extent. They began competing in earnest with other species—with herbivores and their fellow primates for plant foods and perhaps with other
primates, including giant baboons, for trees in which to sleep. Perhaps
the conflicts and occasional killings that resulted from competitive encounters had something to do with promoting an increased awareness
of other species as potential prey.

The fossil traces of animals found at Taung in South Africa and
the older Olduvai sites suggest that our ancestors consumed a wide variety of meats, ducks, geese, and many other birds, as well as lizards,
rats, hares, tortoises, and the young of antelopes. Their prey consisted
mainly of small game, a pattern which generally continues today among
hunter-gatherers, nonhuman as well as human. Now and then, however, when the opportunity arose they undoubtedly dined on bigger
game, as indicated by the hippopotamus-butchering site near Fever
Tree Ridge (see Chapter 4) and the remains of giant pigs, sheep, horses,
medium-sized antelopes, various pachyderms, and other species at
Olduvai. They were the only primates to go after animals larger than
themselves.

Certainly meat might have been especially important in providing a well-balanced diet. As far as plant foods are concerned, grassy
savanna lands may offer less protein to primates than a forest or woodland environment; and, in addition, the work of foraging over wider
areas in a less abundant environment could have contributed to an increased need for protein. Furthermore, there may have been an expanding need for more protein to nourish an expanding brain.

There are many signs of hunting in early sites outside Africa. At
Vertesszollos the bones of large animals such as bears, bison, and deer
(broken and split, presumably for the marrow) tend to be concentrated
in those deposits which also contain tools and other traces of human
beings. Peking individuals showed a marked preference for venison,
about three quarters of the bones found at the Dragon Bone Hill cave
being those of two species of wild deer. They also appear to have been
cannibals, judging by charred and split human bones found in their
hearth. Although plant remains tend to disintegrate faster than bone,
hackberry seeds and other plant fragments serve as a reminder that
vegetarian fare made up an appreciable part of their diet.

Running down small game may have been one of the early methods of obtaining meat. Many animals are swift runners, in relatively
short spurts. But then they tend to slow down and stop as if they were

going on the assumption that the spurts would be enough to shake off or discourage pursuers. Even larger animals, such as kangaroos, zebras, and wildebeests, can be run down by species that do not give up after the first dash but follow persistently, for example, wolves, wild dogs, and humans.

One archeologist observed a chase of this sort a few years ago while he was looking for artifacts on a rock-covered hill in Zambia. An African was running at top speed over and around the rocks, chasing a young antelope about the size of a collie dog and losing ground as the antelope darted over a slope and disappeared. But the African kept running and came back a while later with the live animal in his arms. (He took it home, fed it, and later killed it.)

Members of the Poka tribe on the Nyika Plateau of northern Malawi use similar tactics to catch elands and the francolin or spur fowl, a kind of partridge. This bird operates on a built-in almost automatic schedule consisting of three flights, each flight being shorter than the one before it. When first startled, the francolin flies away swiftly for a hundred yards or so before coming to earth; then if it is still pursued it soars off for perhaps half that distance. But a third approach will send it flying only a few yards away, and that is the final stage. At this point the bird is through escaping. It freezes, huddling close to the earth wherever it happens to land, in the grass or fully exposed on bare ground—an easy catch for anyone in the vicinity. *Australopithecus* individuals may have been clever enough to figure all this out. At any rate, quantities of francolin bones are found among their leavings at Olduvai sites.

Leakey studied primitive hunting techniques and tried many of them himself in an effort to understand better and perhaps reconstruct prehistoric strategies. He actually learned an effective way of running down hares: "When you see a hare, it runs straight away, and you run after it. It has its ears back as it goes, but not all the way back. The ears move all the way back when it's about to dodge, a sharp right or a sharp left.

"Now if you're right-handed you always dash to the right anticipating a dodge to the right. That means the odds are fifty-fifty, and you should catch half the hares you chase right off. If you've guessed correctly, the hare runs by instinct directly at you and you can scoop it up like fielding a fast grounder. Even if it happens to get past you, you haven't necessarily lost it. Stop and watch. It will probably dart under a bush and freeze there, assuming it has gotten rid of you. Then you can go over and simply pick it up."

Hares are among the animals that can be killed and dismembered in a few moments with teeth and bare hands. But this direct method will not work for other small game. The skins of young antelopes which must have been a significant source of meat, are so tough that they can be penetrated only with sharp cutting tools, and efforts to get at the meat may well have led to the regular use of such tools. Hominids probably first turned to naturally sharp rocks or rocks split as a consequence of bashing bones or rocks that were hurled at escaping prey and missed and broke as they ricocheted off cliff walls.

The increasingly frequent use of deliberately shaped stone tools in preference to the ready-made variety, the imitation of accidental chipping and flaking, could have come about in a relatively straightforward manner. It could have been discovered several times before being accepted as a tradition to be passed along from generation to generation, like meat eating itself. Certainly the result was a new and efficient pattern of behavior, as Leakey demonstrated on a number of occasions. One Christmas Eve at his Olduvai camp, an audience of attentive Masai tribesmen watched him spend half a minute making a chopper out of a handy rock, and 20 minutes skinning and cutting up the carcass of a freshly killed antelope.

A widespread tendency among certain primates, the casual and episodic eating of meat, had been transformed into something habitual and part of a way of life. The transformation involved a complex combination of circumstances in the continuing transition from primitive pre-human forms to human beings—the use and shaping of stone tools, migrations out of Africa, the spread of savannas, the availability of prey, and undoubtedly other factors. Meat eating and hunting were two of the factors which led to the full-scale development of evolution by culture and tradition.

CHAPTER 6   FOOD QUEST AND BIG-GAME HUNTING

The world became a more complicated place for evolving hominids largely because of the nature of the food quest. Meals and meal times had not yet been invented. There were no set times for eating separated by long intervals of doing other things. Judging by the activities of baboons and other present-day savanna-dwelling primates, obtaining food must have been practically a full-time occupation. Except for rest periods, a baboon troop's entire day is a steady round of eating and keeping on the move in search of more to eat.

Hominids probably lived a similar life in the beginning, but their own evolutionary development created new and persisting pressures and demands for continual change and new adaptations. As they became bigger, for example, they were better able to defend themselves against the big cats and other predators (see Chapter 1). Every change has its price, however, and that change had a far-reaching impact on subsistence strategies. Bigger bodies required more food, which meant ranging more widely over the savanna and burning up more energy—which, in turn, called for still more food.

One way out of this circular situation was to get more out of the same territory, to exploit the land more intensively and use as many different foods as possible. Increased meat eating and what one investigator has called "an extremely rich and probably readily available source of protein and animal fats—insects," became part of that pattern. Details about the behavior of potential prey became increasingly important, their feeding habits and escape tactics, where they hid and when, and, above all, the things they did automatically, which often led to their undoing. (See, for example, the three reflex flights of Malawi francolins and the telltale flattening of the ears in the hares trying to avoid Leakey's clutches in Chapter 5.)

Kalahari Bushmen are intimately acquainted with the way of life of more than 50 animals. They can follow a herd of antelope, even over **101** hard dry ground which holds only the very faintest impressions of hoofprints, and can detect the subtle differences in hoofprint patterns that distinguish a wounded animal from its fellows in the herd. They know the great unmarked areas of their home territories in far greater detail than postal delivery people know the streets and houses of the villages they have lived in all their lives.

The places where plants grow are observed with special care. Elizabeth Marshall Thomas points out that in an area of hundreds of square miles the Bushmen know "every bush and stone, every convolution of the ground, and have usually named every place in it where a certain kind of veld food may be even if that place is only a few yards in diameter, or where there is only a patch of tall arrow grass or a bee tree." They do not read or write, but they learn and remember. If all their knowledge about their land and its resources were recorded and published, it would make up a library of many many volumes.

They can tell from tiny, hair-fine shoots when succulent plants will appear (and be there on the spot before competing species); from the tiniest buds whether next season's fruits will be scarce or abundant; from the shape of a leaf or the color of a berry which species are poisonous. They use sharp-edged tools to cut and shred fibers, pointed sticks to pry out roots and tubers, stone hammers to crack nuts, and containers of skin to carry food back to camp. Early hominids developed similar techniques. Nuts, incidentally, not only satisfied immediate needs, but also represented nourishment for the future. These packets of naturally stored protein and fat could be gathered in large quantities and shared and eaten later on.

The environment became richer when many species were tried and added to the list of possible foods. The world of specialized eaters, carnivores or herbivores, tends to be somewhat limited; in general, they concentrate on relatively few species. Omnivores, creatures that go after everything edible, animal or vegetable, live in a fuller and more varied world. They are aware of more, because more species are important to them. Our omnivorous ancestors foraged under powerful pressures. There is always a premium on conserving energy by getting as much food as possible from a given territory. But the stakes were particularly high for them—species adapting to new evolutionary niches, and growing bigger and probably more numerous in the process.

There is another way of saving energy in the food quest. As emphasized recently by Speth, information can be shared as well as food. One factor in the expansion of the brain was the increasing amount of knowledge necessary to meet subsistence requirements. Memory capacity increased along with the ability to communicate. Language, like everything else, evolved in the interests of survival. George Silberbauer of Monash University in Australia, who has spent more time among the

Kalahari Bushmen than any other investigator, stresses the importance of communicating about plants:

"As most food plants are distributed rather thinly, there is an unavoidable waste of time and energy in searching for them and in moving from one patch to another. This wastage is minimized by the expertise in field botany which is . . . passed on to girls while they are out gathering with their mothers and the other women of the band. Any individual moving about the band's territory, whether a man on a hunting trip or a band member migrating to a new campsite, takes note of the state of growth of food plants and passes this information on to others in the band. This constant updating of intelligence more narrowly defines the possible areas in which food plants might be found."

Once the abundant areas had been located, a further premium existed in developing more efficient ways of collecting food. Because bones endure longer than plant remains, there is considerably more evidence bearing on hunting techniques than on the gathering of plants. No one knows when meat eating became a regular practice. It was well established 2 million years ago, and may have started several million years earlier. Although small game probably provided most of the meat, early hominids exploited big game on occasion.

They could hardly avoid it. Within the boundaries of the shrinking reserves of the twentieth century some evidence exists for prehistoric abundances. In 1959, Francois Bourliere of the University of Paris counted some 21,000 ungulates, or hooved animals, in the short grass of 230 square miles of savanna in Uganda's Albert National Park. The total included more than 7,400 buffaloes, 4,800 hippopotamuses, and 1,026 elephants, an estimated density of about 130,000 pounds of big game per square mile. Assuming that animals were as plentiful on all the plains of Africa in prehistoric times as they are now in a few areas, and they were probably rather more plentiful, early hominids lived within the sight and sound and smell of huge herds.

They may have consumed carrion upon occasion, perhaps more in the beginning than later. As they rose with the first light of sunrise and scanned the horizon from their trees or from the top of a nearby kopje, they must have seen vultures circling in the distance and heard the alarm sounds of other birds. They had to move swiftly for the carrion to outrace the vultures, which, swarming like maggots over a carcass in a commotion of wings and darting beaks, can strip the good meat away in minutes.

This is exactly what human and nonhuman scavengers do today. In the Ngorongoro Crater of Tanzania, jackals and hyenas frequently go where the vultures are, and so do the Gond tribesmen of north-central India, who are always ready to scavenge off the prey of tigers. They watch for vultures and listen for the food calls of crows, and as soon as they detect signs of a kill, they race over to the spot. If the tiger is still there, they stand at a safe distance and shout and toss stones and wave sticks. Generally the killer leaves within a few minutes, and the tribesmen move in to devour every scrap of meat and break up every bone, leaving only the stomach contents.

Early hominids almost certainly did some scavenging, which put them in direct competition with other species. They would have been compelled to beat off other scavengers, such as jackals and hyenas as well as vultures, and presumably to carry chunks of meat into trees or rock shelters high on the sides of rocky slopes where they could eat in peace. They had many reasons to fear lions and other large predators; but, if they were indeed successful scavengers, they also benefited from the killing prowess of their competitors.

George Schaller and Gordon Lowther of York University, Toronto, once spent a week camping by a river bank in the woodlands of the Serengeti Plain, about 70 miles west of the Olduvai Gorge. The investigators did some experimental scavenging, five days on foot and two days by car, with reasonable success. They came across four freshly abandoned lion kills which would have provided prehistoric people with brains and bone marrow. One day, guided to a thicket by circling vultures, they found a bull buffalo that had died of disease or old age; the vultures and hyenas had been at work, but more than 500 pounds of meat and skin still remained. Another source of scavenged meat would be the prey of wild dogs, highly effective hunters that are surprisingly easy to chase away from their kills.

As far as doing their own killing was concerned, the investigators counted it a kill if they could run down or stalk an animal and come close enough to hold on to its tail. This happened on two occasions. Once Schaller saw a zebra foal standing alone, gave chase, and after a brief sprint, caught up with it and grasped it firmly by mane and tail. Judging by its awkward gait while trying to escape, and by the fact that it had been abandoned, the foal was suffering from some disease; it was released, but undoubtedly fell prey not long afterward to carnivores who were playing for keeps.

Later on the same day Schaller stalked a young giraffe until he was directly in front of it, looking into its eyes. It was blind, and dashed off after he grabbed its tail. During another meat-gathering experiment, this one carried out on the open grassy plains instead of in woodlands, a hare and a number of crouching gazelle fauns were encountered and could have been killed without much trouble. Dismembering any prey could readily have been accomplished with the aid of sharp-edged rocks conveniently lying about.

Notice that in all cases the animals were very young, small, sick, old, or dead. Capturing a large, live, healthy individual presents an entirely different problem. On one occasion Schaller ran full speed at a

Schaller on the
Serengeti: zebra foal
"kill"

group of wildebeests with a stick in his hand, and succeeded in corner-
ing an adult male. It was a fleeting triumph. The animal promptly
turned and lunged at Schaller, who wisely stopped in his tracks and decided to leave well enough alone. A hunter ready to risk his life, and
perhaps working with a companion or two, might have outmaneuvered
and eventually killed the angry bull, but then again he might not have.

Schaller and Lowther conclude: "The means by which scavenging
and hunting hominids might fit into the ecological community without
competing too extensively with other predators pose a number of questions. Their primate heritage suggests that they were diurnal, and selection pressure from their primate and carnivore way of life undoubtedly
favored a social existence. The only other diurnal social carnivore is the
wild dog, which hunts at dawn and dusk, and favors prey weighing 60
kilograms or less (about 130 pounds). An ecological opening exists for a
social predator hunting large animals and scavenging during the day,
an opening some early hominid may well have filled, assuming that
none of the saber-toothed cats did so."

Our ancestors found a place among seasoned predators. Schaller
reports that if a herd of gazelles is grazing on the bank of a stream, lions
may attempt a pincer movement, one lion circling around to the left,

another circling to the right, and perhaps two or three others advancing at a very slow pace frontally, that is, directly toward the stream and herd. Recent studies of African hunting dogs on the Serengeti Plain show, surprisingly, that gazelles have not yet learned to flee soon enough. They start running away only when a dog approaches within 600 to 800 yards, at which distance the dog can generally overtake them. A gazelle has a reasonably good chance of escaping from a single dog by zigzagging tactics, but it rarely escapes from a pack which can attack from several directions at once.

Packs have also evolved ways of hunting wildebeest calves. The objective is to separate a calf from the herd, which means first of all snarling and snapping and coming as close as possible to the edge of the herd until the bulls charge. The dogs avoid the charge of the large antelopes, and then dart in to harass the mothers and calves in the core of the herd. As long as the core group remains together, the pack can do nothing. But the instant a calf becomes panicky and breaks away, the entire pack goes after it. The mother may try to defend the calf for a while, but she soon runs off to join the stampeding herd.

Survival on the savanna favored group hunting. As advanced primates, early hominids certainly had the capacity for acting together, a practice demonstrated in the cooperative chases of meat-eating baboons in Kenya's Rift Valley (see Chapter 5). Jane Goodall reports a successful maneuver by Gombe chimpanzees: "The prey, a red colobus monkey, was sitting in a tree when an adolescent male chimpanzee climbed a neighboring tree and remained very still as the monkey looked toward it. A second adolescent male chimpanzee then climbed the tree in which the colobus was sitting, ran quickly along the branch, leapt at the colobus, and caught it . . . presumably breaking its neck, as it did not struggle or call out." The other chimpanzee, a confederate, then jumped into the tree to share the kill.

She notes what seem to be meat-eating crazes, periods when hunting and killing are notably more frequent than usual. One incident may be enough to serve as a trigger. Perhaps there is a brief and bloody encounter with a bush pig or some other small animal, and other members of the troop see and become excited and increasingly aware of meat and potential victims, in a kind of blood-lust episode. A chimpanzee craze may last for a month or more, during which time dominant males generally get the lion's share of the meat, and then the excitement generally peters out until the next episode.

In a recent study Geza Teleki of Pennsylvania State University reports 167 "predatory episodes" involving Gombe chimpanzees over a ten-year period, with an estimated success rate of about two kills out of every five tries. Meat-eating is not seen often among chimpanzees. But it takes place often enough to show not only that the apes can acquire a taste for meat, but also that they have the imagination and intelligence

Chimpanzees eating
meat: note hand
outstretched in
begging gesture

to become regular hunters should the pressure become sufficiently
strong — as it did among our ancestors.

By *Homo erectus* times humans had become the most formidable
of predators. They were killing elephants systematically, among other
animals, and not even the big cats did that. Direct evidence of such
feats comes from a site 400,000 years old on top of the arid plateau of
Old Castile in north-central Spain, near the village of Torralba. Like
many prehistoric sites discovered by people excavating for nonscientific
reasons, this one was discovered in 1888 by railroad workers digging a
trench for a water main. They found fossil bones and stone tools. Starting in 1907, a Spanish nobleman who was an amateur archeologist
spent about five years excavating not far from the now-abandoned railroad station. Although his findings indicated that the site was one of

107

the most important in Europe, no one thought of digging there again for more than half a century, when Clark Howell spent a day at Torralba.

Howell located the overgrown trenches and back dirt of the old excavation, collected a few tools and bone fragments in adjoining fields, and decided that further digging was called for. He and his associates and crew, including Leslie Freeman of the University of Chicago and some 30 local farmers, worked in the region for three summers, 34 weeks in all. They excavated a total of 20,000 square feet to an average depth of about 8 feet; collected more than 500 pollen samples, 2,000 stone tools and waste pieces, and uncounted fossil bones; and mapped more than 20 living floors. A recently completed analysis of the evidence indicates that Torralba served as a prehistoric abattoir, a place for butchering and meat processing. Concentrated in a relatively small region are the remains of at least 30 elephants, 25 horses, 25 red deer, 10 wild oxen, and half a dozen rhinoceroses. The remains lie where they were abandoned long ago.

In one 270-square-foot area, much of the left side of a large adult elephant was found, with tusks and bones unbroken and in place as if put together for an exhibit. The pelvis was missing and so was the skull, although the lower jaw was left intact. Four flake tools that might have been used for cutting were also found. In another somewhat larger area nearby, some of the bones of this same elephant were found, most of them shattered. There was a broken right leg bone, some vertebrae, and fragments of ribs, upper jaw, and collar bone as well as two stone cleavers and more flakes.

This evidence suggests that the two areas were used for different purposes. What seems to have happened is that the elephant was killed and dismembered in the area containing its left side and the unbroken bones, and that large pieces of meat were carried to the nearby area for further butchering and processing. In two other areas, finer splinters and fragments were found, together with a cleaver and a number of heavy side scrapers. It is more difficult to deduce what was going on here, but people may have been eating their share of the spoils—perhaps cleaning all the meat off the bones with the aid of the scrapers and then, as their ancestors at Olduvai had done more than a million years previously, smashing the bones for the marrow inside.

A great deal more can be learned from these remains. What is the significance of the arrangement of the large elephant's left-side bones? At first, the theory was that the animal had been caught in a swamp, struggled to pull itself out, and finally fallen on its left side. According to this notion, it sank so deeply that only its right side was exposed and accessible to butchery, so prehistoric hunters took what they could and did not try to get at the buried left side. But the theory has not survived a more detailed analysis.

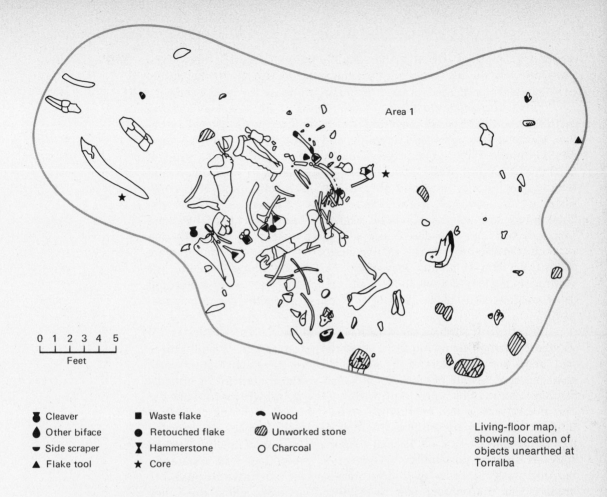

Area 1

Cleaver
Other biface
Side scraper
▲ **Flake tool**

■ **Waste flake**
● **Retouched flake**
✗ **Hammerstone**
★ **Core**

⌒ **Wood**
▨ **Unworked stone**
○ **Charcoal**

0 1 2 3 4 5
Feet

Living-floor map, showing location of objects unearthed at Torralba

The elephant may indeed have become stuck in the mud; its remains are preserved in clay silt deposits, signs of a fossil swampland. The left-side bones, however, were not left in place. Freeman points out, among other things, that the bones are not completely articulated, that is, they are not all fitted neatly joint in joint. Also, they have all been turned over. It seems that the animal was completely butchered, and after the butchering, someone took some of the big left bones and vertebrae and laid them down side by side to produce a partially reconstructed skeleton. Why anyone would have done this is another question. It may have been a game, joke, or ritual, but there are no clues to support these or any other guesses.

The next question is how the elephant became bogged down in the first place. Torralba lies in a steep-sided little valley which includes the headwaters of a principal tributary of the Ebro River; even today, under generally dry conditions, places exist in the region where the water level rises to within a few inches of the surface and where a heavy animal would break through and sink. The terrain was wetter in the time of the

109

elephant killers. Fossil pollen gathered at the site indicates that there was a
pine forest on the plateau, a sluggish meandering stream in the poorly drained valley, and seasonal swamplands with dense reeds and sedges.

Prehistoric man must have stood often on high ledges and slopes and followed the leisurely movements of herds grazing in the valley below. Perhaps now and then a young and unwary elephant wandered away from the herd and suddenly found itself sinking in thick mud. If so, hunters would hardly have missed the chance to race down and close in for the kill; indeed, a surprisingly high proportion of the elephant bones unearthed at Torralba are those of juveniles. Perhaps the large adult, the elephant whose skeleton had been partially reassembled, had also wandered into a swamp and was promptly dispatched. On the other hand, people might have played a rather more active role, and elephants may not have simply blundered into the swamp, an explanation which after all implies that they were too stupid to avoid dangerous places during the course of their everyday movements.

That many animals seem to have been driven to disaster is indicated by certain items found in surrounding areas and carefully mapped, items that excavators of the past would not have considered worth charting, such as bits of charcoal and carbon distributed in an unusual fashion. Instead of being concentrated in a few spots, which would be the case if they represented hearths where fires burned over long periods of time, the materials are thinly and widely scattered. Perhaps the charcoal represents the remains of hearths dispersed by the wind, but Howell suggests another possibility: "Whoever lit these fires was apparently burning grass and brush over large areas and for a definite purpose. My guess is that the purpose was to drive the elephants along the valley into the swamp."

In a recent reconstruction, Freeman expands on the collective-drive theme. He speculates that a number of charred pieces of wood served as torches wielded to drive fire-fearing elephants and other game into the swamp and that heavy stones found in the butchering area were used to stone the mired prey to death. The people, probably well over a hundred of them in four or five bands, were "purely opportunistic" big-game hunters who lived in the region and joined together for mass killing. Men, women, and older children may have participated in drives, which demanded the organizing and exchange of considerable information, "a highly developed communication system, as complex as articulate speech." In other words, Freeman believes that human beings may have had fairly sophisticated language at least 400,000 years ago.

Howell discovered another major site in the region, or rather rediscovered a site where, according to old records, preliminary excavations had been carried out half a century ago. The records merely stated that the work was done "in Ambrona," a village in the same valley as Torralba and less than 2 miles away, but that was not enough information to locate the site. Then one day in 1962, when Howell asked his workers whether they knew of any places with fossil bones, a man answered: "Yes, in my field," and it turned out to be the missing site. Subsequent investigations uncovered a kill and butchering site with deposits of about the same age as the Torralba deposits, remains of the same kinds of animals, with elephants again predominant (perhaps 40 to 50 being represented), and a number of most important living floors.

One area included most of the skeleton of an enormous bull elephant, an old animal judging by his very worn molar teeth, together with a few isolated bones of an infant and a young female. The bones, left in place just as they were excavated, are now housed in a museum built on the spot. The area also contained bones of other elephants as well as of horses, red deer, and wild oxen, all in deposits which had once been deep swamplands; scattered clusters of charcoal and carbon, suggesting the deliberate use of fire; and cleavers and many other tools which served to dispatch and dismember the prey. The same techniques were used here as at Torralba, perhaps by the same people.

Freeman conducted a statistical analysis of material excavated at Ambrona which suggests that different kinds of meat-processing methods were used in different places. One set of remains includes concentrations of chopping tools and the vertebrae, pelvic fragments, and other parts of elephants as well as of horses. Such areas may have been used for "rough primary butchering," the first general dismembering. Other sets of remains seem to mark areas devoted to finer operations, such as processing selected parts of smaller animals and getting at the brains in elephant and oxen skulls.

Some of the most intriguing and enigmatic patterns were found on another Ambrona living floor—three long elephant bones, two thigh bones, and a large tusk, arranged in a line and forming a kind of boundary some 20 feet long. Other large bones were lying perpendicular to the line, one of them the only complete elephant skull found during the excavations at Torralba and Ambrona. One of the mysteries at these sites is where the hunters took the heads of the elephants they killed; all but one of the heads was missing. Examination of the lone, almost perfect Ambrona specimen shows one of the things they did with the heads. The top of the cranial vault has been smashed open, exposing the brain, which weighed ten pounds or so and was probably extracted and eaten.

One has a peculiar feeling while studying the living-floor diagram of the aligned bones and associated material. Pictured before one's eyes in plain black and white are patterns whose total meaning would be so clear if there were only a little more information. Not far away is another puzzling feature. For some unknown reason some pre-

Elephant remains, including large tusk (front) and boundary of long bones (rear), excavated at Ambrona

historic worker whittled a pencil-sharp point on the tip of an elephant tusk over four feet long.

Perhaps the tusk had something to do with the aligned bones. Specifically, it might have been driven into the ground and, together with other sharpened tusks, have served to support hides as part of a temporary shelter. The hides might have been slung over the tusk-posts in a kind of tent formation and anchored in place where they reached the ground by the line of large bones. Even a crude shelter would have provided at least some protection, but whether or not it actually existed can be determined only by extensive excavations of living floors at other sites representing the same period of prehistory and comparable activities.

Clear-cut signs of more elaborate shelters, the oldest dwelling structures known, come from another site, also about 400,000 years old. The hillside site is located in Nice on the French Riviera, on a dead-end street called Terra Amata overlooking the Mediterranean, and luxury apartments stand there today. But in 1966, when the apartments were

Excavators at
Torralba hunting and
butchering site

being built, bulldozers uncovered some prehistoric tools, and work stopped for five months while Henry de Lumley of the University of Aix-Marseilles, his associates, other investigators, and student volunteers spent 40,000 man-hours excavating an area of about 1,100 square feet. The Mediterranean was higher several hundred thousand years ago, and 80 feet of water covered the site of today's boulevards and hotels and beaches. Surf broke high among the hills on the shores of other beaches, and a band of hunter-gatherers camped on one of them at Terra Amata, on a bay near the mouth of a small river where animals came to drink.

On the slopes of an ancient sand dune, de Lumley found remains of a number of oval huts 20 to 50 feet long and 12 to 18 feet wide—postholes, hearths, a wall of stones, probably to protect the hearths from prevailing northwest winds, and the bones of deer, elephants, wild boars, and other animals. He believes that the huts were made of sturdy branches, bent so as to interlock at the top, with an entrance at one end and a hole at the center to let smoke escape. The branches were supported by posts and by large and small rocks placed against the posts. There are 11 fairly thin and undisturbed occupation layers near the dune, suggesting that people, probably the same group throughout, visited and revisited the site for perhaps only a few days during 11 con-

113

secutive seasons. We know that they came in the spring because their
coprolites, or fossilized feces, contain the pollen of plants which blos-
som in the late spring and early summer.

The huts may have housed 10 to 20 persons. The areas closest to
the firesides are clear of debris, indicating that the people slept there, a
practice still observed today among the Australian aborigines. A number of domestic furnishings were also found, including flat limestone
blocks, which may have provided convenient surfaces for sitting or
breaking bones (similar to some found at Torralba and Ambrona), as
well as traces of the earliest container yet discovered, a wooden bowl
with a rough bottom. In a corner near the bowl, excavators found lumps
of the natural pigment red ocher, pointed like pencils at one end and
possibly used to color the body in preparation for some sort of ceremony.

Findings at Terra Amata supplement those at Torralba and Ambrona, specifically, in helping to reconstruct some details of life in early
shelters. The Spanish sites have also yielded a rich and varied collection
of tools, implying a correspondingly rich and varied range of activities.
Cleavers, wedge-shaped objects with a straight cutting edge at one end
generally made by knocking flakes off both sides of a flattish piece of
quartzite, flint, or limestone, served for heavy-duty chopping and hacking. Similar techniques were used to make hand axes, almond-shaped
or pointed implements often with thick heavy butts at one end and cutting edges along the sides. They were widely used over a period of
more than half a million years, probably, despite their name, for skinning and slicing meat and for woodworking rather than for chopping.

In addition to these tools, Howell and Freeman collected many
others, which, since they were smaller and often less obviously worked,
tended to be discarded along with the back dirt of past excavations—
borers, scrapers, backed blades, burins (or engravers), pointed flakes,
and various kinds of notched tools. What is important and exciting
about tools such as these and the ones found by Mary Leakey in the
Olduvai Gorge is that they appear far earlier in the record than anyone
had expected. They signify the very early appearance of relatively advanced purposes since they are the tools needed to carry out such purposes.

The tools do not seem to have changed much over exceedingly
long periods. Crude choppers occupied a prominent place in prehistoric
tool kits for more than 2 million years, hand axes may have lasted a
million years or more, and Neanderthal people were using notched and
toothed tools nearly 2 million years after their first appearance in
Olduvai deposits. To be sure, the passage of time brought some significant refinements, notably the use of bone, hardwood, or antler to put
the finishing touches on tools already roughed out with hammerstones.
(The softer materials have more give, produce thin flakes, and permit

Reconstructions of Terra Amata: (top) actual hearth as excavated; (middle) reconstruction of the hearth being used 400,000 years ago; (bottom) reconstruction of the hut exterior, showing chimney and entrance

more controlled and delicate shaping.) But the basic ideas, the basic tool types, were there from the beginning. Such evidence implies a degree of stability or conservatism inconceivable to modern people.

We measure tradition in shorter terms, a few decades or a few centuries. For us the good old days are not really so old. There are people who remember when and how things were different. But in a world without remembrances of different times, where life and myths have remained much the same for thousands upon thousands of years, innovation would be bizarre and alien and dangerous, something to be resisted as a matter of sheer instinct. In times past, far-reaching changes seem to have come almost despite the nature of people. Chronic change as a policy—the rising tradition of modern people—is something new.

There are tools of bone as well as stone at Torralba. This is one of the very few sites at which an appreciable number of undoubtedly bone tools have been found in living-floor contexts. (Olduvai is another such site.) Some of the more than 100 implements appear to be versions of familiar stone types—scrapers, blades, cleavers, and hand axes, and were often made from specially split elephant tusks. Others were used to finish stone tools, to trim and retouch edges; still others, including scoops and spatulalike objects, have no known stone counterparts and served purposes as yet undetermined.

Perhaps the most unique items found at Torralba are pieces of waterlogged wood which have somehow survived through the ages in clayey, boggy deposits. Marks of use and working have also survived— polishing, whittling and cutting scars, and hollowed-out sections. A few of the pieces may be parts of spears, which would make them the oldest known examples of a weapon invented early in the prehistory of hunt- ing, although the oldest definite evidence at present is a 15-inch yew spear point found at Clacton-on-Sea, a site located on the eastern coast of England believed to be at least 250,000 years old. But such remains are so rare and so fragmentary that unless very rich sources of pre- served wood turn up, a remote possibility, we cannot expect to learn precisely how this material was used.

Another problem is the location of the home sites of the Torralba and Ambrona people. The sites we know are only temporary places where they gathered for perhaps a few days and nights to kill and butcher their prey. Most of the excavated bones are the debris of meals eaten on the spot, and the hunters must have carried off the biggest, meatiest chunks. They must have had established camps in the valley, home bases not very far from the swamplands and the sluggish stream, protected from the bitter cold of those glacial times, and almost cer- tainly high on the slopes, where they could follow the movements of game down below.

Howell and Freeman have explored the valley thoroughly without finding such sites, which is not surprising. Slope locations are particularly vulnerable to erosion, and all traces of home bases were probably washed away millennia ago. Living floors at a permanent campsite would not only add greatly to knowledge about early hunting life, but might also yield an important type of evidence that is still missing regarding the remains of the hunters themselves. As previously indicated, they may have been members of the species *Homo erectus*, relatives of Peking individuals, but this is only a guess.

The high proportion of elephant remains at the Spanish sites also raises certain questions. Assuming that Howell's interpretation is correct and the animals were deliberately stampeded to their death, why did the hunters do it? The answer is not obvious. Land with sufficient plant foods to support elephants can generally support ample herds of other animals as well. Indeed buffaloes, horses, wild cattle, and various species of antelope are likely to be several hundred times more numerous than elephants. So concentrating on elephants may have been more than a straightforward matter of getting meat. Perhaps something ritualistic was involved in the sense that hunters killed the large animals mainly to prove their courage and skill.

Whatever the motives, findings at other sites also suggest cooperative hunting. A site in the Olduvai Gorge, a clay bed once part of a swamp, contains signs of an organized drive that may have taken place more than half a million years ago—the fossilized bones of a number of large animals, including a horse-sized, sheeplike creature. Some sort of roundup or surrounding maneuver may account for the shattered remains of more than 60 giant baboons concentrated at a Rift Valley site outside Nairobi.

Analysis of tools found at various early hunting sites reveals some intriguing patterns. Comparing the Torralba and Ambrona tool assemblages as a whole with assemblages from other sites poses some new and subtle problems. There seem to have been two broad types of tools, the Oldowan, named after sites in the Olduvai Gorge where it was first identified, and the Acheulian, which also exists at Olduvai but is named after the French site of Saint-Acheul in the Somme Valley where it was originally found. The tools of the Spanish sites fit into the latter category.

Oldowan tools trace back nearly 2 million years to the earliest sites at the bottom of the gorge. The living-floor site includes what may be a crude wall or windbreak as well as a chopper—a heavy tool generally made on a cobblestone or oblong block (see Chapter 3)—and lighter tools such as scrapers, engravers, notched implements, and so on. This basic tool kit is found at Olduvai in higher and more recent deposits, up to the bottom of the thick layer of wind-blown sand and ash, indicating a time span of about a million years.

No traces of humans and their works appear in this sterile layer. But above the layer, after an interval of many thousands of years, the

Oldowan assemblage is found again with some additions. It not only includes choppers and other familiar tools found at earlier sites but also some new or rarely found items, the most characteristic of which are rough and battered spheroidal tools, purpose unknown. Presumably, people had abandoned Olduvai during arid times, and their descendants had returned, bringing with them implements invented and refined elsewhere.

But there is an intriguing complication. Another tool kit, the Acheulian, appears for the first time just above the sterile sand and ash layers at sites contemporary with those containing Oldowan assemblages. Together with some choppers and other older items, the tool kit contains the earliest unmistakable hand axes reported to date, hand axes believed to be between 1.0 and 1.5 million years old. It does not contain battered spheroids and other items more characteristic of the Oldowan industry.

The big question is what the two assemblages mean, what can be deduced from the fact that two different tool kits were being used at the same time in the same general region. It may have had something to do with where people lived. Olduvai Gorge camps containing Oldowan tools were located on flatlands next to lakes, at the mouths of streams fed by runoff from nearby mountains. On the other hand, African camps containing early Acheulian tools tend to be found away from lake shores along seasonal streams. These upstream sites have an abundance of large stones washed down from the mountainsides, and tools, notably hand axes and cleavers, made from correspondingly large flakes are common in Acheulian assemblages. Such stones are rarer at lakeside sites, however, and Oldowan assemblages rarely include tools made from large flakes.

In other words, people tended to use what they had in the neighborhood to do their hunting and food processing. Thus, one reason for the difference between the two kinds of tool kits would be different kinds of local resources. Different occupational patterns may also be involved. According to Desmond Clark, the battered spheroids in Oldowan tool kits may not have been implements deliberately made for some special purpose, but simply stones which acquired their shape from being used time after time over prolonged periods. Actual experiments and observations among recent hunter-gatherers show that repeated use of a stone for bashing and pounding tends to wear away protruding parts and eventually produce a rough spheroid. If this is what happened, then Oldowan sites which include such artifacts may have been occupied for longer periods or visited more regularly than Acheulian sites.

There is certainly more to the problem. One view is that two traditions are involved, two different groups of people or tribes each with their own customs and way of life, in other words an Oldowan culture and an Acheulian culture. The problem widens when other sites are considered. Oldowan tool kits, featuring a variety of choppers and lacking cleavers as well as hand axes, predominate in the eastern part of the Old World—in northwest India, Burma, China, and Southeast Asia—until about 100,000 years ago. Acheulian tool kits, including those uncovered at Torralba and Ambrona, predominate throughout the rest of the Old World, in Africa, Europe, the Near East, and peninsular India. They lasted until about 75,000 years ago.

Such facts suggest a number of possible explanations. For example, hunter-gatherers may have migrated from Africa to Europe between 1 and 2 million years ago, before the development of Acheulian tool kits. If so, they may not have done very well. Their traces exist at only two sites, at the Vertesszöllös limestone quarry in Hungary and at Clacton in England, both of which have tool kits clearly derived from the Oldowan. The two oldest known European sites, the Vallonet and Escale caves of southern France, have not yet been thoroughly excavated; but if this theory is correct, they should also contain Oldowan tool assemblages. A second wave of influence from Africa may have come 300,000 or 400,000 years later when people with Acheulian tools entered Europe and took over the vast majority of available sites, including the Torralba and Ambrona sites. These people may have settled in the west and either wiped out or assimilated the descendants of earlier immigrants from Africa, or else driven them east.

The theory will stand or fall on the basis of findings yet to be made. But it does seem that the Oldowan type of people who turned up in China and Java and other parts of Southeast Asia evolved little, if at all, while important changes were under way among Acheulian type peoples in the west. Hallam Movius of Harvard University has pioneered in studies of Southeast Asia, and concludes: "It seems very unlikely that this vast area could ever have played a vital and dynamic

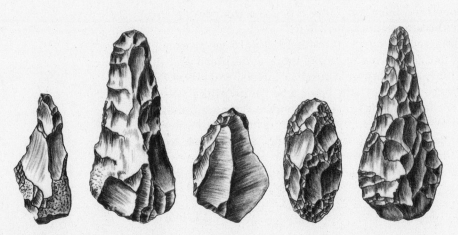

Acheulian tool kit showing flake tool (middle) and various forms of hand ax

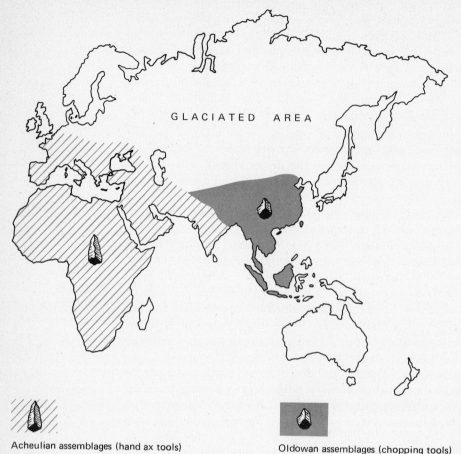

GLACIATED AREA

Acheulian assemblages (hand ax tools)

Oldowan assemblages (chopping tools)

Location of Oldowan and Acheulian assemblages: Africa and Eurasia

role in early human evolution, although very primitive forms of early man apparently persisted there long after types at a comparable stage of physical evolution became extinct elsewhere."

One possible reason for the relatively slow pace of change in Southeast Asia is that forests tended to be more widespread and denser there and, since huge herds are not found in forests, game was far less abundant than in the savannas and open woodlands of the west. In a sense, Movius' conclusion lends further support to the notion that hunting represents an important factor in accounting for the uniqueness of human beings. It also emphasizes the importance of Southeast Asia as a rich and largely untapped source of information about the nature of our early ancestors, and about the role of environment in shaping human evolution.

The widening gap between hominids and other species; larger brains and prolonged infant dependency; females as gatherers and the invention of carrying devices; males as hunters and the increase of meat eating; female sexual receptivity and the prehistory of love; alliances, exogamy, incest taboos; fire as a force for change

CHAPTER 7 ORGANIZING FOR SURVIVAL: THE RISE OF TRADITION AND TABOOS

By this time humans had almost completed their evolutionary journey. It was only half a million years away from the twentieth century, out of some 15 million years of hominid development—the equivalent of the last 15 minutes or so of a jet flight from New York to Paris. Their brain, the brain of *Homo erectus*, was already well within the size of modern people. But the hominid way of life was far from modern. The future had hardly begun.

The wonderfully complex process of human evolution had accelerated and was building on tendencies rooted in times long past, before the coming of our kind, before *Ramapithecus*. The process started 15 million years ago when small near-apes, prehumans, left the dense primeval forests and moved out into sparser woodlands and savanna lands. Other animals were making the same transition at about the same time. The small ancestors of today's antelopes and ox-family species, such as the wildebeest and buffalo, also came out of the forests into savannas, developing a herd instinct, a tendency to mass together, that was so powerful that a mother would leave her offspring to keep up with the group. Our ancestors were part of it all, part of a great movement into open plains, where there were fewer places to hide and the premium was on social organization and troops, herds, and prides that would stick together in emergencies. For many species, increased body size was part of the adaptation to new evolutionary niches, and that meant wider ranging.

Regarding ranging differences among primates, some small monkeys may spend a large part of their lives in half a square mile of forest, while gorillas have a range of 15 to 20 square miles. Although our ancestors were no gorillas in stature, the search for food sent them roaming more widely than any other primate. In fact, judging by the extent of their range, they were more like wolves and wild dogs. Wolf packs may cover from 500 to 1500 square miles, and rough estimates based on

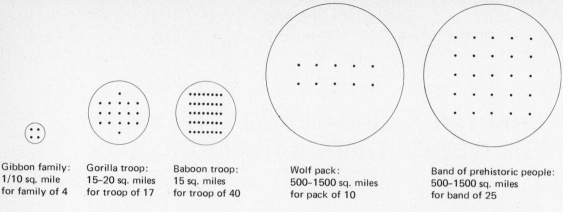

Gibbon family:
1/10 sq. mile
for family of 4

Gorilla troop:
15–20 sq. miles
for troop of 17

Baboon troop:
15 sq. miles
for troop of 40

Wolf pack:
500–1500 sq. miles
for pack of 10

Band of prehistoric people:
500–1500 sq. miles
for band of 25

Home ranges

the recent practices of primitive tribes suggest that early humans may have had territories of comparable size. According to Sherwood Washburn, "the most minor hunting expedition covers an area larger than most nonhuman primates cover in a lifetime."

Wider roving exposed humans to a wider variety of experiences, thus increasing their chances of encountering novelty throughout life. In effect, that extended their youth as compared with that of nonhuman primates, whose chances of encountering novelty or being surprised presumably decreased much faster after childhood because of their restricted ranges. Humans had every incentive to know their wider world and know it well. Getting food was the most important thing in life, and they could not afford to miss anything. As omnivores, they were competing with many other species, with other plant eaters as well as other meat eaters. Getting there first, whether to a grove of just-ripened fruit, a stand of seed-bearing grasses, or a herd of grazing antelopes, became part of the business of survival.

Early hominids were more and more on their own and became increasingly alienated from the rest of the animal kingdom, although they had once lived among other species with considerably more than mutual tolerance. As already indicated, baboons and impalas often feed together on African savannas, enjoying the protection of a doubly effective early-warning system. The baboons' visual powers supplement the impalas' acute sense of smell. Each species is alert on its own, but together they are almost invulnerable to the attacks of lions and other predators.

Our remote ancestors probably once lived on similar terms with the ancestors of present-day antelopes in a symbiotic if not always idyllic relationship. But hunting widened the gap between humans and other species, in effect creating two worlds where one world had existed before. If there was ever a loss of innocence in the human past, a feeling of original sin or guilt about killing and eating creatures that had once been equals or superiors, it would have dated back to the transition times when early hominids were developing their taste for meat.

Of course, there is very little likelihood that any species, pre-human or otherwise, has ever felt qualms about the process of adapting for survival. Prehistoric hunters learned predation so well that they probably helped kill off a number of species, perhaps including one of their most formidable competitors, the saber-toothed tiger. People, in short, were beginning to live in opposition to as well as in concert with other animals.

Other differences were becoming sharper, for example, the differences between the sexes. Body structure was affected, as an indirect result of all the forces which brought about larger brains. A fundamental problem in the design of the female body involved the optimum dimensions of the female pelvis. From a strictly engineering point of view, the obvious way of allowing for the delivery of bigger-brained infants is to enlarge the pelvic opening or birth canal and widen the hips, and evolutionary pressures were at work which favored this solution. The difficulty is that individuals with wider hips and related modifications lose a measure of mobility. As far as speed is concerned, the ideal pelvis is a male pelvis. Women cannot generally run as fast as men, a disadvantage in prehistoric times when flight was called for frequently.

Another theoretical way of meeting the problem is to go to the other extreme and avoid the necessity for widening the hips. If the infant is born sufficiently early in its development so that its brain is still small, delivery difficulties can be minimized or eliminated. The limitation in this direction, however, concerns the danger of being brought too immature into the world; the earlier the infant is born, the smaller its chances for survival. The death rates for premature infants, weighing 5.5 pounds or less, are about three times higher than for full-term infants.

Confronted with these alternatives, nature in effect did a little bit of both, achieving a not altogther happy compromise. Natural selection arrived at a solution in which the hips were indeed widened sufficiently to permit delivery of an infant with a brain somewhat larger and sufficiently developed to ensure a reasonable chance of survival. On the other hand, the brain was by no means fully developed. It was still immature and small enough so that the hip widening did not reduce the mother's mobility to a dangerous extent. So the brain had to do most of its growing after birth. A rhesus monkey is born with a brain that has already reached nearly three-quarters of its adult size, but the brain of a newborn *Homo erectus* infant had probably completed only about a third of its growth.

Delayed maturity, of course, means extending the state of infancy, and that had crucial repercussions. Most mammals are ready to fend for themselves only a few months after birth, but a unique type of growth was established among primates and accelerated among hominids. Monkeys remain helpless for about a year, apes for two to three years; *Homo erectus* was in a similar condition for perhaps four to five years (as compared with six to eight years for modern humans). Indeed, the first human infants were not only helpless longer than the infants of other primates, but they were also additionally helpless since they could not cling to their mothers.

Another trend in primate evolution is away from large litters and toward single births, or at least litters consisting of no more than two or three offspring. This development, like the development of stereoscopic vision and other features, is mainly a consequence of life in the trees, where it is considerably more difficult to care for infants than on the ground or in dens and burrows. One result is that prenatal growth can proceed at a more leisurely pace. Among species with large litters there is competition for nourishment and space within the uterus, a condition favoring relatively rapid growth and a short gestation period. Since higher primates typically give birth to only one infant, however, such competition does not exist and a slower rate of growth is possible. The focus has been increasingly on the infant as an individual, in a way that can never be the case among species with large litters. A single birth is more special, and can receive more care and attention.

Perfect solutions are rare in evolution. Prolonged infant dependency certainly increased the chances of suffering early psychic traumas, a fact which psychoanalysts have interpreted as highly significant, even regarding dependency itself as an inevitable and therefore universal trauma. But elementary biological considerations suggest that this may possibly have been a price worth paying, that in us as in other species something of value was gained as well as lost. It is at least arguable that selection was taking place for something rather more directly advantageous to the species than an increased susceptibility to neurosis.

Prolonged infancy is only part of an evolutionary process which has brought prolonged childhood, prolonged adolescence, and prolonged life, part of the slower pacing of things in a species which relies more than any other species on learning. It is difficult to imagine the young of a rapidly maturing species learning to behave appropriately in a highly organized band. An individual that could run, fight, and feed itself within six months or less after birth would probably not excel at the art of learning complex and flexible social responses. It would find itself too busy being a vigorous animal.

Growing up, human style, demands a delay in such activities. It is well served by early immobility and dependency which permit observations, listening, and contemplation of a sort, before full-time commitment to active doing. For example, although the circumstances under which language arose are unknown, it was probably evolving in important ways during early hominid times—and a connection may have existed between slow maturation and the ability to acquire new linguistic skills. A docile infant and an experienced adult must have made an effective combination for the establishment of social communications.

Evidence is accumulating to indicate that culture was already of some importance in *Australopithecus*, a notion originally proposed by Dart more than a generation ago. In a key investigation of molar-tooth development, Alan Mann of the University of Pennsylvania points out that the first, second, and third permanent molars erupt at about 6, 12, and 18 years respectively, in both *Australopithecus* and modern humans. On the basis of this observation, he suggests that "the growth stages of *Australopithecus* are comparable to those of *Homo sapiens* and [that] childhood development is similar in both groups." The implication is clear that hominids have long depended on "a large complex of learned behavior, or culture."

Marks of the new societies involved the food quest and the division of labor between the sexes. Going after the biggest game in collective drives as at Torralba and Ambrona was certainly an exciting and glamorous challenge. It required planning and courage to take on elephants, rhinoceroses, and other massive animals capable of fighting back, maiming, and killing. But the odds are that it rarely provided a steady, dependable source of food. As far as day-to-day subsistence is concerned, people relied on small and medium-sized game and, of course, on abundant supplies of plants.

Among today's hunter-gatherers all members of the band contribute what they can, animal or vegetable. Women may kill small game and birds when the opportunity arises, and they are at all times on the alert for tracks and other signs of bigger game; men may do their share of the picking and carrying when the time comes to collect large quantities of nuts and fruit. As a general rule, however, hunting is mainly a male activity and gathering a female activity.

This arrangement is dictated mainly by the fact that human beings are born helpless and remain helpless for years. There can be no gambling on the care and feeding of offspring. That is primarily the mother's job, and she naturally exploits those resources which are most reliable and tend to be closest to home base, namely, plant foods. One result in remote prehistoric times may have been the development of an effective carrying technology. Sally Linton of the University of Colorado speculates that "two of the earliest and most important cultural inventions were containers to hold the products of gathering, and some sort of sling or net to carry babies." She also speculates that the in-

vention of baby-carrying devices came first, and led to food-carrying **126**
devices and perhaps, still later, to the development of chopping and
grinding tools for preparing food.

The evolution of the foot supports this notion, a point stressed
by Adrienne Zihlman and Nancy Tanner of the University of California
in Santa Cruz. Infant monkeys and apes have gripping feet that are
half-hands and have mobile and opposable big toes designed to bend
around and cling to the mother's hair as she moves along with the
troop. *Australopithecus* infants did not have that option. Their feet were
already so specialized for walking that clinging was no longer possible.
As a result, there was considerable pressure on mothers to invent devices so they could simultaneously carry offspring and engage in gathering food.

The hunting activities of males made it possible for hominids to
exploit the savanna to the fullest extent. They were free to leave home
base for long periods, and they learned from and improved on stalking
strategies of lions and other rival competitors. Lions, for example, apparently do not know that their scent will not be detected if they approach
prey from the upwind side, a fact which our ancestors were probably
intelligent enough to deduce. Experience gained during hunts may also
have enhanced the male's role as defender of the home base against the
attacks of the big cats and other predators. Zihlman and Tanner estimate that meat may have made up about 1 percent of the diet among
the earliest hominids, and perhaps 5 percent for the earliest representatives of *Australopithecus*. By *Homo erectus* times the proportion may
have risen to a third or more.

Lionel Tiger of Rutgers University suggests that as hunters went
after more game and a wider variety of game, they developed closer ties
with one another. Men went away in groups, ranged widely and stayed
away perhaps all night and perhaps on occasion for several nights. They
began forming the all-male associations which more recently have led to
such things as clubs, lodges, athletic competition, secret initiations, and
an assortment of stag institutions.

Differences and stresses intensified within the male community
between younger and older males. This was nothing new among primates. Goodall observes that among chimpanzees the young male has
hard lessons to learn. Early in adolescence, which starts between the
ages of 7 and 8, he becomes independent of his mother and increasingly capable of dominating the females, who used to dominate him.
But this is also the time when larger, dominant males become increasingly aggressive toward him, and tend to keep him away from females.
His frustration may be expressed by charging through the troop dragging branches and throwing rocks, but even here he must learn to be
careful because all the hubbub may get on the nerves of the dominant
males. Or he may wander off alone into the forest.

Making it, getting into the club of dominant males, was as important to hominid as to chimpanzee adolescents, only rather more complicated. The institution of hunting probably provided new ways for adolescents to take out their frustrations—to prove themselves. It was one further step in the accelerating development of symbols as hunting and the eating of meat acquired new values and meanings.

Such developments dramatize the very special position of hominids in evolution. They provide an example of species being put to the severest of tests. All species survive by adapting, but the adaptations of hominids were far more elaborate, and have become increasingly so. The divisive forces of the past, which tended to create new and conflicting groups within groups, is only part of the story. The existence of society is possible because such conflicts served to accelerate the building up of powerful counterforces in a continuing interplay of tensions and the relaxation of tensions. Our ancestors became the only primates to kill regularly for a living, and the only primates to share regularly on a day-to-day basis involving the entire group.

Evolution worked to establish a secure, stable social framework in a milieu of potentially disruptive forces. The new framework had to be strong and flexible enough to include male-male as well as male-female associations. The problem has not yet been solved to the complete satisfaction of either sex, but early steps toward a solution included changes in patterns of sexual behavior that were designed to reduce new tensions and anxieties.

The typical pattern among mammals involves regular bursts of sexual frenzy which take precedence over all other activities. At every ovulation or immediately after, all nonhuman females, including occasional nursing females, come into estrus or heat. Sexual activity is so concentrated and intense during such periods that it tends to interrupt the care of the young and all other forms of behavior. This sort of all-inclusive estrus ensures effective reproduction among most mammals which have rapidly maturing offspring; but not among primates. If all the females in a primate troop were subject to three days of sexual mania every month or so, it would probably be to the detriment of their slow-maturing infants. Natural selection brought about a modification in monkeys and apes, to the extent that estrus ceases during the later part of pregnancy and the early part of nursing.

A modified form of estrus is fully compatible with the primate way of life, that is, with the way of life of nonhuman primates. Man is the only mammal in which estrus has disappeared entirely. Ralph Holloway of Columbia University suggests that this development may have started with the appearance of *Australopithecus,* which occurred more than 5 million years ago. It was probably established among the hunting-gathering bands of *Homo erectus.* Estrus cycles may simply have made less and less sense in a species with single births spaced further and further apart as the period of infant dependency lengthened. A new reproductive rhythm was being established; estrus no longer served an evolutionary purpose, and it went by default, as it were.

More positive forces may have been at work to speed the departure of estrus. The female of the species became sexually receptive at practically any time rather than during estrus only, eliminating periods during which male competition and aggressiveness reached a peak and contributing further to the stability of life. Extended sexual receptivity on the part of females served also to extend the period of their attractiveness to males and may have helped counterbalance the new appeal of male-male associations. The changing pattern of female behavior helped to tie males more securely into the group.

The increased possibility of choice in the timing of sexual relations had long-range repercussions. Estrus, even as modified among nonhuman primates, is essentially beyond the individual's control. Its presence and absence are determined by the automatic turning on and turning off of sex-hormone secretions, presumably by a kind of biological clock in the brain which keeps track of the passage of time and periodically triggers the activity of centers concerned with the arousal of sexual urges. Under such conditions, the sexual act among early hominids tended to be relatively impersonal and mechanical, as it is among contemporary monkeys and apes.

When sexual urges came under a measure of voluntary control, it became possible to select not only the time and place for mating, but also the mate. According to Zihlman and Tanner, it may have been another step in the continuing socialization, domestication, or taming of the male: "A male could attract a female's attention by disruptive displays or through friendly interaction, including greetings, grooming, playing with her offspring, food sharing, protecting, or simple proximity. Females preferred to associate and have sex with males exhibiting friendly behavior, rather than those who were comparatively disruptive, a danger to themselves or offspring. The picture then is one of the bipedal, food-sharing and sociable mothers choosing to copulate with males also possessing these traits."

Personal preference acquired a new meaning. For the first time more enduring male-female-offspring relationships became possible, which ultimately led to the family as we know it. These were the opening phases in the prehistory of love, at least love in the human sense, which includes homosexual love, a by-product of the male-male associations in hunting bands, as well as heterosexual love. Of course, both were by-products of the replacement of automatic hormonal control of social behavior by a measure of free selection of partners.

Changing sexual patterns brought new orders of social complexity, new things to be learned and remembered, new inhibitions and prohibitions, and wider relationships. Nonhuman primates may be highly organized, but the organization is primarily internal, within the troop; their social systems tend to be closed, most matings taking place among established troop members. Their foreign affairs, however, are rather less well ordered than their domestic affairs. Troops generally either ignore one another or fight. Human beings alone attempt to form organizations, tribal unions, confederations. Alliances among bands or tribes may have been created as a form of life insurance. Subsistence has always been uncertain. Even in normally fertile regions, unpredictable droughts or plant and animal diseases produce local food shortages and the threat of famine. In emergencies, survival depends on being able to pack up and move into more abundant lands occupied by other bands. That, in turn, depends on being welcome, and one way of assuring a warm welcome is to have relatives in many places, to set up networks of kinship ties.

Such networks may be established by encouraging individuals to mate outside their own band. Out-marriage, exogamy, a characteristic of primitive tribes, may be traced back to the need for widespread alliances in prehistoric times. "The exclusive control of a hunting territory can be efficiently maintained only with the mutual consent of neighboring bands," Washburn notes. "Excessive fighting over territorial borders both disturbs game and dissipates the energy of the hunters. The exchange of mates between neighboring groups helps to insure friendly relations . . . because it disperses persons with close emotional ties among many groups and over a large area."

This development inevitably involved the control of mating patterns within the group. Incest taboos may have served to promote out-mating and alliances, and also to keep the peace at the home base. The fact that human males mature sexually years before they mature socially probably created as many problems in prehistoric times as it does today. Contemporary hunting and gathering groups have devised a variety of marriage customs and rituals to ensure that the production of children is delayed until the male has learned the ways of hunting and is fully prepared to provide for a family. Incest, like premarital sexual intercourse, is incompatible with these objectives, and incest taboos may have helped reduce conflict, jealousies, and rivalries within families or protofamilies.

Such restrictions might also have reduced rivalries between families, counteracting any tendency of the group to break up into competing units—just as exogamy counteracted any tendency of the tribe to break up into competing bands. The effect would be to produce a more integrated group and tighter communal bonds. Gregory Bateson of the University of Hawaii has pointed out that when the objective is just the opposite, when it is desired to create an exclusive rather than an inclusive situation, incest may be permitted and even enforced. Thus brother-sister marriages were the rule among the royal families of dynastic Egypt.

Natural selection also put a premium on the development of a moral sense. Hominids who cried out to warn the other members of their group about the approach of a predator may have drawn attention to themselves and run the risk of being killed. But a mathematical analysis shows that such behavior may actually increase reproductive success if close relatives are aided or if the individuals benefited return the favor. In other words, individual members of a group act so as to preserve and pass on their genes to succeeding generations.

This is one result of an important study by Robert Trivers of Harvard. The system depends on doing unto others as they did unto you, reciprocal altruism. Trivers shows that such behavior is likely to be favored among groups of relatively long-lived individuals who live together over long periods and depend on one another for food and defense, precisely the sort of groups formed by early hominids. He indicates that selection favors a capacity for gratitude, sympathy, friendship, and other qualities useful in playing the game of reciprocal altruism. Selection also favors such feelings as guilt, shame, and moral indignation which tend to discourage individuals from cheating at the game by giving less than they receive or by dodging their responsibilities entirely.

Underlying all these changes is an enormous increase in complexity. Individuals were observing more, doing more different things, learning more, developing a wider range of emotions, participating in more and more complex social systems. The hominids' view of the world was expanding at an unprecedented rate—and so was the hominid brain. The brain expresses in its actual tissue, its biological structure, the state of the world outside. Somehow it includes in the interconnections among its billions of nerve cells a small-scale model of the world and its processes, of reality as it appears to the species at a particular stage of evolution. As our ancestors learned sharing and caring and other rules of evolving social systems, they had more to remember and analyze—all of which put a premium on a large brain with a larger memory capacity, and there was a multiplication of memory units.

Research such as that conducted by John Young at University College London indicates the possible nature of such a memory unit or mnemon, which can be thought of as a small cerebral circuit consisting of perhaps half a dozen interconnected nerve cells. Its main component is a classifying cell which receives nerve impulses from a sense organ and has two extending fibers which transmit messages to appropriate muscles. Impulses transmitted along an "advance" fiber cause the animal to approach, while the "retreat" fiber carries avoidance messages only.

We are designed to expect the best, at least to start with, and, in **131** general, the mnemon has a built-in positive bias so that an object seen for the first time is apt to be attractive and stimulate the sending of signals along the advance fiber of the classifying cell to the muscles. If the object turns out to be dangerous or forbidden, however, the advance fiber is blocked chemically and all subsequent signals from the classifying cell pass along the retreat fiber. Actual behavior is based on the interplay of many mnemons, but generally this seems to be how we learn that discretion is the better part of valor.

So evolution added more mnemons, more nerve cells, and the brain grew like a benign tumor at the head end of the spinal cord. Of course, it was far more than a mere increase in gross size. Subtle changes were taking place in internal organization—especially in the nerve circuitry required to inhibit or control the not-doing of things, continuing a long-established trend in primate evolution (see Chapter 1). The mnemon with its advance and retreat fibers is the anatomical expression of an elementary choice between alternatives; depending on experience, one of the two fibers will be blocked. The multiplication of mnemons is the anatomical expression of the increasing complexity of hominid society, the multiplication of alternative behavior patterns.

Restraint did not come automatically. Every choice, every course of action selected for the future benefit of the group rather than for the immediate satisfaction of the individual, had to be learned and remembered. Events weeded out those with an inferior capacity for learning and remembering. The hunt demanded patience and waiting—waiting for prey at water holes or salt licks, waiting for an animal to look away as you stalk it, waiting after the kill so that you do not devour all the meat on the spot but save most of it for others waiting at the home base.

There was also waiting for the fulfillment of sexual urges. Younger males who could bide their time and control themselves in the presence of aggressive dominant males outlived those who could not. In anatomical terms, selection favored a rewiring of the brain so that increasing numbers of inhibitory retreat fibers ran from the highest control center, the cerebral cortex, to subcortical centers which released sex hormones and aroused sexual urges. The controls did not work perfectly. Robin Fox, a colleague of Tiger at Rutgers University, indicates that the flare-up of sexual urges during adolescence demanded intensive initiation ceremonies and other social controls. Inhibition is also at the root of incest taboos and reciprocal altruism.

The entire process of human evolution was complicated and enriched by the greatest technological advance of the times, the use of fire. The first force of nature to be domesticated, fire gave human beings a new degree of independence. By bringing fire to the places where they lived, they created zones of warmth and light in the darkness, halo spaces, caves of light. The wide wilderness became a little less wild and less lonely. They achieved a way of keeping the night and nighttime prowlers at bay and the freedom to explore new lands with harsh climates.

Judging by the evidence at hand, still largely negative, our ancestors first put fire to work on a regular basis to keep themselves warm somewhere along the route out of Africa across the Sahara and into Europe. Hominids must have been familiar with fire in Africa. They lived with it, and perhaps died by it, during volcanic upheavals associated with the formation of the African Rift Valley. They probably moved away when volcanoes were active, and returned when the earth became quiet again, being no less persistent than people today who keep returning to areas devastated by floods, earthquakes, and other natural disasters.

But no early hominid hearths have yet been found in Africa. Of course, most African sites may have been located in the open rather than in caves, and ashes and charcoal may have been scattered by winds blowing across savannas. On the other hand, early hominids presumably had no great need for fire in generally mild subtropical climates. In any case, ample evidence for fire exists in colder times and colder places, and as pointed out in Chapter 5, the earliest known hearths burned some million years ago in the Escale cave of southeastern France. Humans had wandered about as far north as they could at the time without starving and freezing to death. They were living where no normal primate should be, nearly within the shadows of alpine glaciers.

Fire was probably first obtained ready-made from natural sources. (The first sign of artificial fire making is an iron-pyrites ball with a deep groove produced by repeated striking to create tinder-igniting sparks; it comes from a Belgian site only about 15,000 years old.) The notion that Prometheus stole fire from the heights of Mount Olympus is not as widely believed as it once was. But Prometheus has a certain relevance if, as seems likely, volcanoes were a major source of fire in early prehistory. According to Kenneth Oakley of the British Museum of Natural History, other sources were available in less turbulent areas: "Man could also have relied on accidental fires started by lightning in dry brush or grassland or where there were seepages of mineral oil and gas. Occasionally in damp environments coal or shale-oil deposits might be ignited by spontaneous combustion, and during the last century one such fire burned for four years in Dorset."

Perhaps people camped near fire, a natural resource like game, water, and shelter. They may sometimes have left otherwise favorable areas when fires began petering out. If so, they had to take it with them when they moved away. It had to be kept burning like the Olympic flame, fed and nursed like a newborn infant. Each band may have had a fire bearer; perhaps one of its older members was responsible for carrying and guarding embers in a cup of clay covered with green leaves and breathed the embers into flame when the band found a new place to live.

Fire provided more than warmth. It soon became another factor in setting man apart from other species. With it he could move more freely, and instead of having to avoid other predators, they got out of his way. Fire must have kept cold weather as well as predators at a safe distance. On icy wilderness nights, big cats and other predators, attracted by the smell of meat and light, stayed outside the protective circle of the fireside. Perhaps people observed that on occasion the animals scrambled even further away when sparks flew at them out of the flames. They may have learned to produce the same effect by hurling glowing pieces of wood at animals' heads. In any case, they eventually began using fire more aggressively, in a shift from defense to offense.

The earliest known hearths were located in caves, originally occupied by stronger and longer-established killers. Before fire people often had to be content with second-best sites, rock shelters, and overhangs and less effective protection. Fire, however, could help them drive other killers out. Bears, hyenas, and many other cave-dwelling animals shared the Durance Valley with early humans but stayed out of their caves.

Fire probably enabled Peking individuals to take permanent possession of Dragon Bone Hill cave. It is no coincidence that the first layers which provide evidence that people had moved into the cave also happen to be the layers which contain charcoal fragments, burned bones, and other traces of fire. Only after they had learned to tame fire could they become regular cave dwellers whenever conditions demanded it.

They also used fire to become more and more effective predators themselves, to stampede animals as they did in the Torralba Valley, and to produce more effective spears. The Australian aborigines charred the tips of their digging sticks lightly, a treatment which hardens the core of the wood and makes the outer part more crumbly and easier to sharpen. People were acquainted with this technique at least 80,000 years ago, as indicated by a yew spear with a fire-hardened point found at a site in north Germany. Some investigators feel that equally advanced treatments had been developed as far back as the days of Peking individuals.

Cooking is also believed to date back to these times, mainly on the basis of indirect but convincing evidence involving teeth, sensitive indicators of evolutionary change. As described in Chapter 2, one argument for dietary changes among the earliest hominids is that they had small canine teeth instead of the large canines characteristic of many other primates. But molar teeth, which serve chiefly for grinding and heavy-duty chewing, tended to remain large until *Homo erectus* times, when they began to become smaller, perhaps because people were eating softer, cooked foods.

Regular cooking may have helped reshape the contours of the human face, in a kind of chain-reaction process. According to one theory, softer foods put less of a strain on the jaws and jaw muscles, which became smaller along with the molar teeth. This in turn had an effect on the design of the rest of the skull. Thick bony protuberances on the side of the skull had evolved largely as platforms to which powerful jaw muscles could be attached, and massive overhanging brow ridges may have served as shock absorbers to take up stresses transmitted upward through jaws and cheeks from incisor and canine teeth. These structures were reduced as jaw muscles dwindled in size. Furthermore, the skull itself became thinner, perhaps one of the changes involved in expanding the cranium to house a bigger brain.

As for the origin of cooking, no one has yet been able to improve on the basic point of Charles Lamb's story about the suckling pig that was done to a turn when a house burned down. There were no houses half a million years ago, but a forest fire could have done the job just as effectively. Or perhaps a careless hunter dropped his share of the day's kill into a blazing fire and relished the meat when it was recovered. Such accidents must have happened many times before man finally made a practice of roasting tough foods.

There were psychological as well as physical changes. Cooking played a part in promoting more restraint. With the advent of cookery people tended to spend less time devouring freshly killed game on the spot and more time back at the cave eating with the rest of the band around a hearth. The domestication of fire was one more step in human domestication. Inhibition is as much a mark of evolutionary advance as action itself.

And above all, fire was light. It increased the length of the day, created a new kind of day, independent of the movements of the sun. Life became less routine. People no longer rose and slept with the rising and setting of the sun. They had become independent of one great natural rhythm, the internal rhythm of estrus, so now they were independent of the external rhythm of day and night. The hours after dark were hours of relative leisure, which they could use to plan activities that were more and more complex (often because of the new uses of fire, as during the Torralba elephant hunt, which may have required the cooperation of several bands).

The existence of elaborate plans implies the evolution of more sophisticated ways of communicating. Language, the most human form of human behavior, must have taken a tremendous spurt when hunting was on the rise and fires burned brightly past sunset. There was so much to share—the day's adventures, a herd or a band sighted at a distance while out gathering, tall tales about the big one that got away during the hunt, tomorrow's food quest, story telling, and the elaboration of myths, legends, and beliefs.

The fireside became an institution, a cohesive force bringing members of the band closer together, old as well as young. Other primates also had their patriarchs and matriarchs, but now age acquired a new importance. Now individuals too old to fight, carry heavy things, or walk long distances became important because they remembered things beyond the memories of others—particularly things that happened rarely, such as floods and other catastrophes, and things that required special knowlege, such as the settling of territorial disputes and the treatment of illnesses. The elders took their places at the fireside and were consulted and listened to.

Finally, fire presumably played a role in early religious experiences. A tendency to engage in rituals can be seen in our closest living relatives. Goodall has observed chimpanzees engaging in elaborate rain dances during tropical storms. On one occasion seven adult males performed before an audience of appreciative females and juveniles that climbed into the trees to watch. The males moved to the top of a grassy slope, divided themselves into two groups of three and four members, and took turns making sudden charges down the slope and springing into a tree, tearing off branches, hurtling themselves to the ground, and dragging the branches along while barking and hooting.

They were responding to the elements. The entire ceremony, which lasted about half an hour, was carried out in the midst of a heavy rain to the accompaniment of thunderclaps and bolts of lightning. According to the British observer, "against the green grass they looked black and very large, like primitive men displaying their strength." It requires no great stretch of the imagination to think of early hominids responding with their own varieties of ritual to the forces of nature.

We know that prehistoric people carrying torches and lamps penetrated deep into the remotest chambers of caves, covered the walls with paintings and engravings of animals, and met by firelight to practice rituals, whose purposes we can only speculate about. Their underground meetings took place during the past 30,000 years or so. But many investigators are convinced that they engaged in similar activities hundreds of thousands of years before the coming of art, and that fire served a double purpose, to arouse excitement as well as to provide light.

Such effects may have very ancient origins. Kenneth Oakley emphasizes "the deep subconscious or sensual appeal" of fire, noting that the appeal may be traced back to the earliest days of primate evolution: "The fact that the Philippine tarsier has been named *Tarsius carbonarius* on account of its propensity for picking up hot embers from camp-fire sites suggested to me that man's prehuman ancestors may have been attracted to natural fires and toyed with burning matter." Fire may be a stimulant as potent as drugs in arousing visions and previsions, and as such it would have served the purposes of priests and priestesses, the cultural descendants of the fire bearers of *Homo erectus* times.

Fire, like tools, had a double impact. It kept predators and the cold away and at the same time drew people closer together. It served material needs and at the same time helped create a new way of life and a new kind of evolution. Tracing cause-and-effect patterns in such a context becomes exceedingly difficult. Though we make inferences which go beyond the evidence, the effort is always to speculate along lines compatible with the evidence.

Many elements went into the shaping of *Homo erectus*—the widening food quest, the invention of carrying devices and tools, big-game hunting, fire, selection for bigger brains, prolonged infant dependency, loss of estrus, the coming of taboos and traditions. Each element contributed in an important way to hominid development. But the fundamental problem is to see things as a whole, as parts of the network of increasingly complex interrelationships which is human evolution.

Three lucky finds in Swanscombe village; a possible contemporary of Swanscombe people; the use of computers in investigating human origins; another gap in the record; the discovery of Neanderthal people and their rejection by outraged Victorians; the persistence of prejudice; the Le Moustier and Shanidar caves; burial and religious ritual

CHAPTER 8   THE SEARCH FOR REMAINS OF THE EARLIEST MODERN-TYPE PEOPLE

Now for the first time we can begin to describe our ancestors in words which do not really apply to other animals, which make sense only in a human context. Human development was no longer a matter of dealing only with the outside world, with climates and other species and prey and predators. An entirely new class of problems had come into being, uniquely human problems, which seem to be chronically associated with cultural as contrasted to genetic or organic evolution. Dealing with the full impact of this sort of evolution demanded a new breed of people, our immediate ancestors and the direct descendants of people like those who camped at Torralba and Ambrona.

Human populations and living conditions varied widely in those days, although not as widely perhaps as they do today. According to one estimate, some 40,000 bands of hunter-gatherers occupied as many home bases scattered like outposts through the wildernesses of Africa, Asia, and Europe, an average of 1 million acres per band. The earth was hardly a crowded place, but crowding can be a relative thing, and certain regions were far more densely populated than others. So then as now some environments must have been especially favorable for hunting and for the elaboration of social systems.

The population centers of *Homo erectus* times were the richest grasslands, which attracted the largest herds and the greatest number of predators, including humans. Hunting bands on the track of game crossed paths from time to time and exchanged wary glances or silent greetings as they proceeded on their ways. Planned as well as unplanned meetings probably took place, not only the joining of forces for group hunts and stampedes as at Torralba, but also seasonal get-togethers involving several hundred individuals, the foreshadowings of county fairs. Some people may have found things too crowded for comfort and moved on to get away from it all.

There were also isolated backwood regions, where the land and   **137** the living were less abundant. A band of hunter-gatherers could have wandered for years or a lifetime in these wildernesses without coming across another band or even such traces of another band as a burned-out hearth, worked flints and flint debris, a hollow sheltered place where people had slept, or an almost overgrown trail leading from a fireside to the edge of the nearest stream or lake. In many cases members of such inbred, marginal bands subsisted on foods inferior to those exploited by bands in richer territories, and they lived less interesting, less healthy, and shorter lives.

Populations varied in many other ways. Some individuals may have had brains nearly twice as large as their smallest-brained contemporaries, as is the case today. Equally striking differences existed in the degree of sloping of the forehead, tooth size and cusp patterns, chin structure, the size of overhanging brow ridges, and so on. There may have been a number of subspecies or races of *Homo erectus*. Perhaps one of these, a subspecies, with a larger than average brain, living in a territory where life was neither so easy that it posed no major challenges nor so harsh as to crush initiative, developed into *Homo sapiens*.

We do not know where or when the transition took place, but a gravel pit in the English village of Swanscombe not far from London has yielded important fossil clues, as usual through a combination of searching and luck, in this case luck triply compounded. The Thames Valley site is a well-known collectors' paradise, possibly a place where hunters camped to kill big game coming to drink from the river. Several hundred thousand stone tools must have been found there during the past century or so. But no human remains had appeared until one Saturday noon in June, 1935, when local cement workers who had stopped digging for the day noticed a piece of bone protruding from a gravel bank. It turned out to be part of the skull of a prehistoric individual, probably a female who had died in her early twenties.

A second lucky find occurred the following March near the original find, another bone fragment which was not only human but also happened to be part of the same skull. The two pieces fitted neatly. The final discovery, representing something of an anthropological miracle, occurred one moonlit evening during World War II. A fleet of trucks came to the Swanscombe pit and removed hundreds of tons of gravel as part of the top-secret Mulberry harbor project to make concrete caissons, or floating docks, for the Allied invasion of Normandy. How many prehistoric remains were ground up for the concrete will never be known, but at least one important object was left behind and found after the war in 1955—a third skull fragment. This specimen turned up about 75 feet from the original find and, by remarkable coincidence, belongs to the same individual as the other two specimens; furthermore, it fits together with them to form the entire back half of a skull.

The relative age of these remains has been fairly well established.

As pointed out in Chapter 5, after some 60 million years of comparatively mild and stable climates, Europe experienced a number of climatic oscillations when mean annual temperatures varied from 50 degrees Fahrenheit to below freezing levels. Geological studies show that the gravels which contained the Swanscombe remains were laid down during a period of glacial retreat, a so-called interglacial stage which dates back perhaps 250,000 years.

Swanscombe people enjoyed a comfortable climate. In fact, as far as the weather is concerned, that was the time to be in England. Elephants and rhinoceroses, which had come from Africa over the Dardanelles land bridge, browsed in warm Thames Valley forests along with wild boar, deer, and other woodland species. But cooler times were on the way. A decrease in the number of these species and an increase in the number of open-grassland species, such as giant oxen and horses, indicate that the forests were beginning to recede, a prelude to the coming of another glaciation.

Swanscombe people represent a distinct advantage over their fossil predecessors, although the extent of the advance has been debated. Examination of the three fragments and reconstructions based on them indicate that they had large brains; their cranial capacity is estimated at about 1300 cubic centimeters, which, as pointed out in Chapter 5, lies well within the modern range. Furthermore, there is a general suggestion of rounded and expanded skull contours, somewhat like the modern shape. These features have been interpreted as evidence for an apparent evolutionary leap, the sudden appearance of a human being who was nearly fully modern. On the other hand, the relatively low brain case and certain other characteristics suggest that the specimen may be a less advanced form, intermediate between *Homo erectus* and modern people.

Supporting the latter viewpoint is another fossil skull found in 1933 in another gravel pit, near the village of Steinheim in western Germany. This specimen includes the face and upper jaw, which are lacking in the English specimen, and it may have something to tell us about Swanscombe people, assuming, of course, that the two were contemporaries (both skulls were found in interglacial deposits) and were members of the same species or subspecies. In any case, Steinheim people were modern in back but not in front. They had sloping foreheads and very large brow ridges; it was argued that Swanscombe people may have been at the same stage of development.

These impressions have been put to the test by Weiner, the man who exploded the Piltdown hoax, and Bernard Campbell of Cambridge. They turned to statistical techniques, which depend on carefully selected measurements of corresponding areas and curvatures of different skulls. For example, one problem was to ascertain as precisely as possible the area of the neck region at the back of the skull, an area which

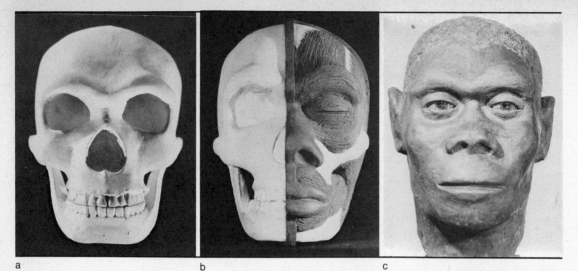

a   b   c

Stages in reconstruction of Steinheim man, one version of early *Homo sapiens*,. front view: (left) skull in plaster; (center) building up muscles and skin with clay; (right) completed bust

tends to become smaller and smoother during the course of human evolution, reflecting the expansion of the brain and a decrease in the size of face and jaws.

In all, 17 measurements were made between points on the Swanscombe skull. For purposes of comparison, similar measurements were made of some 500 male and female skulls excavated from a 4,000-year-old communal tomb in southern Israel, about 60 skulls of contemporary races and 10 fossil specimens, representing finds from 250,000 years ago (the Steinheim specimen) to 35,000 years ago. This information was used to calculate the so-called distance functions, numbers which indicate how closely the different fossil skulls are related to modern skulls. The task required millions of calculations and would have taken years using desk-type adding machines, but it took only a few minutes using an electronic computer at Oxford University.

Judging by the results, the Swanscombe individual meets the general specifications for a transitional species, a species on its way but not yet arrived. Like the Steinheim specimen, it is definitely *Homo sapiens*, but very early *Homo sapiens*, embodying certain relatively primitive as well as modern features. In short, the individuals are just about right for their time, the products of a gradual and continuing process rather than a sudden spurt. The same thing goes for an individual about 20 years old, part of whose skull was excavated recently by de Lumley at a cave in the eastern Pyrenees region of France. That such specimens may represent early precursors of modern humans is by no means a new notion; some investigators had already arrived at it without benefit of statistics. But the main point is that other investigators had arrived at quite different interpretations on the basis of the identical evidence; the study provides a relatively objective evaluation of the evidence.

Even more important, the study establishes an approach which reduces personal bias to a minimum. It can be applied whenever experts disagree, and experts disagree with impressive frequency and intensity in the study of prehistory. For example, it showed that a big-toe bone found at Olduvai resembled the big-toe bone of modern people much more closely than it resembled that of the gorilla or chimpanzee, indicating that the individual walked with a human type of gait. A similar approach has also demonstrated the modern features of an *Australopithecus* upper-arm bone found near Lake Turkana and may be used to help determine the status of important specimens from Olduvai and other sites which may represent transitional forms between *Australopithecus* and *Homo erectus.*

Advanced statistical methods are being used increasingly as anthropology becomes more and more quantitative and as high-speed computers take care of the prodigious number of calculations involved. Among those exploring new methods is Charles Oxnard of the University of Chicago, who has made a number of three-dimensional models analyzing the evolutionary position of early hominids. One model presents "similarity" distances indicating the relative positions, with respect to African apes, Neanderthal people, and modern people, of *Australopithecus robustus* and *Homo habilis,* from Kromdraai (a site near Sterkfontein in South Africa) and Olduvai respectively, as far as foot-bone structure is concerned.

Statistics alone cannot solve all problems. For example, more needs to be known about the origin of our species than the Weiner-Campbell analysis can possibly reveal. It concerns early but not earliest *Homo sapiens.* It indicates that such individuals existed at least 250,000 years ago, but leaves open the question of when the first members of the species arose. They may have appeared 50, 100, or several hundred millennia before Swanscombe and Steinheim times, depending on which current point of view strikes one as most plausible.

But the answer, if it is ever found, will come at excavations of sites yet to be discovered, and the same thing holds for the question of where our species arose. In certain respects the simplest and most direct theory is that it happened in Europe; that the men of Swanscombe and Steinheim were descendants of hunters who, judging by the remains at the Hungarian site of Vertesszöllös, may have been well on the way toward attaining *Homo sapiens* status as much as 400,000 or 500,000 years ago. According to another theory, however, they were immigrants rather than native Europeans and evolved either in the Far East, perhaps from an ancestral stock such as that of Peking people, or else in Central Asia. Still a third theory, and the one which certain investigators favor in absence of solid evidence to the contrary, involves widespread rather than specific regions, the idea being that the transition occurred in many places during roughly the same period.

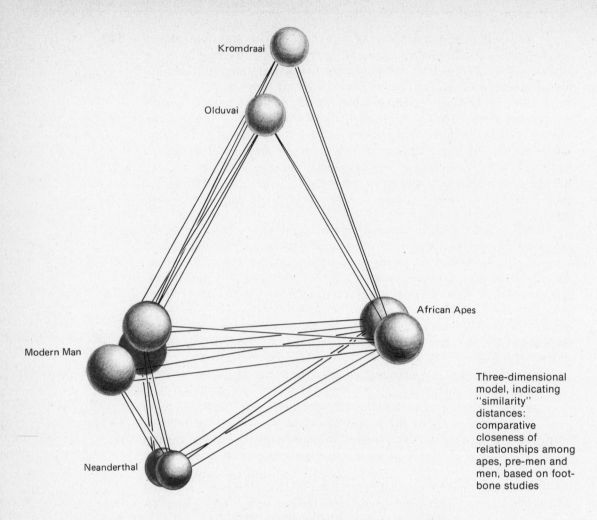

Kromdraai

Olduvai

African Apes

Modern Man

Neanderthal

Three-dimensional
model, indicating
"similarity"
distances:
comparative
closeness of
relationships among
apes, pre-men and
men, based on foot-
bone studies

Wherever they came from, the early forerunners of modern
people probably lived pretty much the same as late representatives of
Homo erectus lived. At least, stone tools and other excavated materials
suggest no obvious differences. Although their workmanship was
somewhat superior, Swanscombe people were not radical innovators
and they made the same basic Acheulian-type tools that had been made
for hundreds of thousands of years—hand axes, notched and saw-
toothed implements, scrapers, engravers, and so on. There are characteristics, however, which might represent differences in behavior if we
only knew enough to interpret them. Why did the Swanscombe tool kit
include nearly twice as many hand axes as the tool kits of Torralba and
Ambrona predecessors? Why did Swanscombe people use an unusually
high proportion of hand axes with a wide base, tapered to a point at

the apex, and an unusually low proportion of ovate or egg-shaped hand axes? Current opinion is that these different tool kits may reflect different activities (Chapter IX), but evidence for the specific nature of those activities is still lacking.

Another English site at Hoxne about 65 miles northeast of Swanscombe and of about the same age or slightly more recent provides further evidence. It contains rich deposits of clay, which mark the place where a huge mass of ice broke off a retreating glacier perhaps 300,000 years ago and melted slowly to form a small lake. (At another site near Birmingham, England, a block of ice about 50 feet across took more than 30,000 years to melt.) Ever since the eighteenth century the clays have been used to make bricks and terra-cotta pipes. In 1797, the English antiquarian John Frere visited the site and made a remarkable observation.

People do not see what they are not prepared to see, and since the notion of a remote prehistoric past simply did not exist in those days, a variety of involved theories were invented to explain away traces of this past. Flint tools, some of them beautifully shaped, were considered natural accidents like shapes seen in drifting clouds or in the gnarled branches of trees—things that had been formed either by thunder in the clouds and then fallen to earth or by lightning as it struck and shattered flint lying on the ground. Frere knew better. He found hand axes and other tools in the Hoxne clay deposits and recognized them as man-made implements dating back "to a very remote period indeed, even beyond that of the present world." (Frere, by the way, has the added distinction of being Mary Leakey's great-great-grandfather.)

Modern excavations at the site reveal a Swanscombe type of Acheulian tool kit, including the same unexplained high proportion of pointed hand axes with wide bases. Another finding emerges from fossil-pollen studies conducted by Richard West of the University of Cambridge. Pollens recovered from gray clays and muds deposited before the coming of man show that thick oak and elm forests surrounded the lake. But signs of a different environment are found in overlying brown-green clay layers containing tools and other human traces. A decline of oak and elm pollens and a sharp rise of grass pollens indicates that open grasslands replaced the forests.

Geological research rules out the most obvious explanation for this change, a change in climate, for the climate was generally mild throughout. Another possibility exists, however. Charcoal has been found in the occupation layers, suggesting that the deforestation was caused by fires which were originally set during a dry summer, perhaps to stampede animals as in the valley of Torralba, and then raged out of control. In any case, the forests returned soon after the people left, first

temperate oak and elm forests and later forests of dwarf willows and other trees found in arctic environments. Another major glaciation had begun.

Little evidence exists for the course of human evolution during this period, which lasted more than 150,000 years. This is a particularly tantalizing state of affairs, since other information, such as the fact that surprising anatomical changes appeared later following the retreat of the glaciers, suggests that important developments were taking place. A number of French sites provide evidence of human activity. One workshop area in the archeologically rich Somme Valley region near Amiens, no larger than a living room, has yielded thousands of flint tools and associated pieces, including various types of hand axes and cleavers as well as an assortment of scrapers and knives.

There is another interesting site in England at High Lodge not far from Cambridge where people camped by a lake during a time of temporary relief from arctic conditions. (The climate was not stable in glacial periods, fluctuating from very cold below-zero temperatures to cool conditions rather like those encountered in mild winters today.) Many of the tools recovered from clay deposits marking the location of the lake are remarkably similar to tools found at the Somme Valley site.

Some clues about the people who made the tools comes from the Lazaret cave, a site excavated by de Lumley and located in Nice on the French Riviera. An ingenious reconstruction of one living floor indicates that about 125,000 years ago people may have built a tentlike structure inside the cave. Piles of stone may have held up posts supporting a roof of skins, and two hearths inside the area suggest it was occupied by two families, a total of ten or so individuals. The area also included concentrations of small marine shells, a variety found only attached to seaweed; de Lumley believes this may mean that seaweed was used as padding beneath skins to make more comfortable sleeping **145**

places. He also believes that a wolf skull found at the cave entrance may have served as a kind of Keep Out sign to warn off intruders when the occupants were away.

The next glimpse of humans comes from the next interglacial stage in Europe, the period from about 125,000 to 75,000 years ago. England and Ireland were part of the Continent then. Broad valleys existed where the English Channel and Irish and North seas are now, and great rivers flowed through the valleys, rivers which included the Seine, Thames, and Rhine as tributaries.

The people living among lions, hyenas, elephants, and other European animals of the times were not what one might expect of our evolving ancestors. They were definitely *Homo sapiens*, but they belonged to new subspecies or races, and in certain respects a strikingly more primitive subspecies. Although their brains were about as large as the brain of Swanscombe and Steinheim people, their massive receding jaws and faces were actually closer to *Homo erectus* than to *Homo sapiens*. Their remains have been found in a limestone crevice in central Germany, in deposits on the left bank of a tributary of the Tiber near Rome, and at several other sites in Europe, the Soviet Union, and Palestine.

Even stranger breeds of humans arose later. The bands hunting in western Europe during most of the subsequent cold period, the next-to-last glaciation, were made up of individuals anatomically more remote from modern people than were their predecessors from some 6000 or 7000 generations before. They had appreciably larger brains, one of the features by which they are ranked as *Homo sapiens*. But their primitive features included lower cranial vaults, which tended to be flat at the top and bulged at the sides, heavier bone ridges over the eyes and at the back of the neck, and more sharply receding chins. Large, heavy, long bones—heavily reinforced where muscles were attached and with huge joints—indicate that their bodies were stocky, short, and heavy-limbed.

These were the classic Neanderthal people. Every anatomical sign points to their extraordinary muscularity. They must have been extremely powerful individuals, performing on a habitual day-to-day basis physical work of the most strenuous sort—probably including walks of 20 miles or more through snow and over ice and rough terrain, and coming back with loads of meat, plant foods, and firewood. Even allowing for their exceptional strength, it is still difficult to understand how they survived, moving long distances through deep snows, apparently without snowshoes or any other specialized equipment. They provide perhaps the most impressive example of the adaptability of the human species, the human physique, even in the absence of a sophisticated technology.

The Neanderthals come to mind whenever cave dwellers are

mentioned, and they inevitably serve as models for artists depicting our early ancestors. They have become symbols—for good reason. As the first fossil people to be discovered, they made a powerful impression on a world that was not ready to accept the notion of evolution or its implications. The discovery and the reaction to it mark one of the most significant and revealing episodes in the annals of science. It was the beginning of the study of prehistory and the atmosphere was one of bitter debate and intense emotional involvement, bordering at times on a hysteria from which it has not yet completely recovered.

In 1856, when human bones were found in a small limestone-quarry cave in the Neanderthal, a valley near Dusseldorf, Germany, practically everything discussed in this book was unknown and the rest was ignored. Some investigators recognized the importance of the remains from the beginning, but they were a very small minority. The predominant opinion, which people were ready to accept, was that the bones represented not an extinct breed of humans, but a modern, freakish, and sick individual. A prominent anatomist reported that the fossils were those of an idiot who had suffered from rickets and other bone diseases and had a violent disposition. The flat forehead and heavy brows, he explained, had been caused by blows on the head.

According to other authorities, the bones were those of a Cossack who had perished during Napoleon's retreat from Moscow, a victim of water on the brain, "an old Dutchman," "a member of the Celtic race." Everyone wanted to disown this human specimen. An English scholar was responsible for one of the most melodramatic diagnoses: "It may have been one of those wild men, half-crazed, half-idiotic, cruel and strong, who are always more or less to be found living on the outskirts of barbarous tribes, and who now and then appear in civilized communities to be consigned perhaps to the penitentiary or the gallows, when their murderous propensities manifest themselves."

These and other reactions amounted above all to a violent rejection of the Neanderthals as legitimate human ancestors and, at a more basic level, a violent rejection of the notion that we have arisen from less-human species. Evolution, biological change, was an alien and heretical concept. It had long been taken for granted that species were immutable, that all living things had been created in their final perfect form in the beginning, and that nothing important had happened since. In the sixteenth century, for example, this belief was so firmly established that people simply refused to concede the existence of fossils of any sort.

Fossils implied extinctions, and extinctions, in turn, implied that the creator had designed species so poorly that they failed to endure. So the general attitude was to regard the objects which kept turning up, objects that looked very much like skulls and teeth and vertebrae and the imprints of ferns and seashells, as mere illusions produced by the action of thunder and other forces. In other words, fossils, like flint tools, were believed to be natural accidents. A less widely supported and slightly more realistic theory allowed that fossil bones were actually the remains of dead animals. On the other hand, the animals were not believed to be extinct; they still lived in unexplored parts of the world or in mammoth caverns deep beneath the earth's surface.

The theories had changed somewhat by the mid-nineteenth century. Extinction was recognized as a fact of nature, but the notion of perfect and unchanging species was preserved. According to prevailing ideas, fossils were the remains of creatures wiped out during the Flood (not having been passengers on the Ark) and not related to existing forms. Indeed, the whole past was a Biblical past. Genesis, Eden, the Flood, were not myths but familiar historical events, and very recent events at that. Different interpretations of the Scriptures gave different dates for the creation of the earth, 3700, 4004, or 5199 B.C., but authorities generally agreed on a past so brief as to allow little time for evolution of any sort.

Furthermore, the world was in many ways a simpler and cozier place than it is today. There were no eons, no vast stretches of geological time to make the past remote and evoke a feeling of infinity and other worlds. The past was close at hand and had a special aura to it, a glow like that surrounding a long-lost childhood. Although there were vague notions of barbarian times, the emphasis was on golden ages, knights, and chivalry. Modern living seemed shoddy by comparison.

In such times and against such a background of beliefs, the discovery of Neanderthal people came as a terrible shock. It might have created less of a scandal if other discoveries had been made in the proper evolutionary sequence, if the way had been prepared during preceding generations by finding *Ramapithecus* first and then *Australopithecus* and finally *Homo erectus*. The discoveries came in precisely the reverse order, however, which was partly to be expected by the nature of things. The laws of chance favored the possibility that fossil humans would be found first in western Europe, where population densities were highest and quarries most numerous, and that the first people found would be Neanderthals because Neanderthal remains seem to outnumber all other human fossil remains in this region.

Neanderthals came into the world of the Victorians like naked savages into a ladies' sewing circle. In the eyes of the Victorians, Neanderthals were beasts. Neanderthals suggested not only that the past may have been less golden than the Scriptures implied, but also that disturbing forces were at work in the present. They reminded people of the Jekyll-and-Hyde qualities and the animal side of human nature. We who live with our knowledge of fire bombs and Hiroshima and gas chambers and napalm can afford to be tolerant of the Victorians' horrified response to the sort of self-understanding that evolution offers. We **149** are much closer to them than we like to think.

Attitudes began changing somewhat not long after the original 1856 discovery. The publication of Darwin's *On the Origin of Species* three years later provided a biological basis for evolution in general, and the discovery of more fossils provided new evidence for the evolution of humans. Between 1866 and 1910, half a dozen sites in France and Belgium yielded Neanderthal remains associated with flint tools and the remains of woolly rhinoceroses, mammoths, cave bears, and other extinct species. There was no longer good reason to regard the Neanderthals as mad or diseased moderns. It was widely agreed that they had vanished tens of thousands of years ago.

But most investigators were slower to recognize the Neanderthal breed as advanced human beings, and much less as *Homo sapiens*, than they were to recognize its fossil status. As recently as the 1920s Neanderthal people were considered far more remote from modern people and far closer to the anthropoid apes than a reasonably sophisticated analysis of the evidence could possibly justify, half-monsters of a kind, ungainly, ugly, and brutish. This picture was based to a large extent on a highly respected and highly misleading study of a skeleton found in 1908 near the village of La Chapelle-aux-Saints in southern France.

The study is one of the most amazing phenomena in the history of man's efforts to downgrade his ancestors. On the basis of casts of the inner surface of the skull, the study concluded that the convolutions of the brain had been simple and "coarse" and resembled the convolutions of the "great anthropoid apes or microencephalic man" more closely than those of modern people. Furthermore, it presented an outlandish view of Neanderthal posture and gait. It not only pointed to a supposed "simian arrangement" of certain spinal vertebrae and stated that the Neanderthals walked slumped over and with bent knees, but suggested that their feet may have been grasping organs like the feet of gorillas and chimpanzees.

As recently as 1957, this study was still being cited as a major source of information about the nature of Neanderthal people. In that year, however, the La Chapelle-aux-Saints skeleton was reexamined by William Straus of Johns Hopkins University and Alec Cave of St. Bartholomew's Hospital Medical College in London. They found that it was hardly typical, belonging to an *old* man between 40 and 50 suffering from arthritis of the jaws, spine, and perhaps lower limbs, and concluded with the following somewhat ambiguous statement: "There is thus no valid reason for the assumption that the posture of Neanderthal man . . . differed significantly from that of present-day man. . . . If he could be reincarnated and placed in a New York subway—provided that he were bathed, shaved, and dressed in modern clothing—it is

doubtful whether he would attract any more attention than some of its
other denizens."

Anatomical evidence does not support the stereotype of Neanderthal people as semihuman brutes. The trouble is that myths die hard, especially myths in the area of human origins, and it may take decades before the popular image coincides with the scientific image. The latest edition of a standard text still presents certain major conclusions of the La Chapelle-aux-Saints study as if they had never been discredited. Apparently some anthropologists still accept these conclusions. It is little wonder that the old prejudices and cliches also persist among laymen.

Not all questions about the Neanderthals have been answered. They were one of the subspecies of *Homo sapiens* which lived in the Old World from about 70,000 to 35,000 years ago, and it should be no surprise that they walked fully erect. After all, their ancestors had been walking that way for several million years. Furthermore, it should be no surprise that they and other subspecies of the times differed widely in physical characteristics since this was the case for *Homo erectus*, as it is for us and other species. What calls for an explanation, however, is that their distinctive set of characteristics should reappear, in the sense that this was reminiscent of earlier human forms, and that they seem to have confined themselves largely if not entirely to western Europe.

One possibility is that they were cut off from their contemporaries. The longer and more completely breeding populations of a single species are separated from one another, the more widely they differ. Brief and partial isolation, such as that imposed by the institution of royal families, may produce such characteristics as the well-known protruding lower lip of the Hapsburgs. These characteristics, of course, are not sufficient to create new races. Longer periods of isolation, occasioned perhaps by geographical as well as social factors, may eventually produce differences so great that the result is distinct species such as *Australopithecus africanus* and *Australopithecus robustus*.

The conditions which gave rise to the Neanderthal subspecies may have been somewhere between these extremes. Howell has suggested that they may have been caught in a kind of ice trap in western Europe, a glacial pincers movement. During the coldest periods, glaciers crept southwest from the great Scandinavian ice sheet into central Poland, and at the same time glaciers from the Alps moved northeast toward the Carpathians and the Danube. It was by no means a complete trap. The ice masses never met, and there was always a corridor several hundred miles wide between them. But routes through the corridor may have been few and hazardous enough during periods of severe cold to isolate many Neanderthal populations and bring about the appearance of a new subspecies.

Moreover, there are traps more effective than the geographical variety. The Neanderthals were fully adapted to their environment,

which may be reflected in the very shape of their bodies, since there is physiological evidence that people with short stocky builds conserve body heat better than lean and lanky individuals and hence are better suited to survive in Arctic and sub-Arctic climates. Their massive jaws may have evolved as adaptations to a diet of tough meat, that is, raw or lightly cooked meat. They probably felt no greater urge to pack up and leave than Eskimo tribes feel today. People still tend to remain in their homelands, even where it is an unending struggle merely to keep alive, and bonds at least as strong may have formed among prehistoric hunters.

One can only wonder at the ability of the Neanderthals to endure the intense cold of western Europe during the next-to-last glaciation. Their loneliness, for example, is something difficult to imagine. In today's densely populated world, news travels fast and there are always rescue parties on the way. But there were no rescues in that world, and every band was alone and on its own. As already emphasized, moving through the snow must have been a major problem since people probably had to get along without snowshoes and sleds and no one moved during blizzards when snows were highest.

Survival would have been impossible without reserves of food and fuel. The chief hunting grounds must have been snow meadows, wide flat areas swept by icy prevailing winds, where the snow may be

151

only a foot deep and edible grasses grow under it. Today, in Canadian sub-Arctic regions, such places are a major source of food for herds of caribou and caribou hunters, and similar regions helped feed reindeer and Neanderthal reindeer hunters some 50,000 years ago. Small game also provided meat; many traps must have been set along snow trails, the habitual routes of animals on the move.

But winter hunting could never have provided enough food by itself. According to one estimate, it takes about 800 to 900 pounds of lean meat to feed ten people for a month, and Neanderthal winters may have lasted four to five months. Such conditions demanded stockpiling, and extensive stockpiling. The people may have used underground cellars, pits hacked out of permanently frozen ground known as permafrost, as Eskimos use today, or "blue ice caves," or ice-cliff formations, could have served as deep-freeze lockers.

Prehistoric natural refrigerators of this sort have not yet been found, although a study of where Eskimo hunters locate their storage places today might furnish clues for archeologists in search of evidence of prehistoric practices. The record suggests that at least one family had a special larder for its winter food. A pit in a Neanderthal cave on the island of Jersey off the western coast of France apparently contained a liberal supply of large chunks of meat ready for cooking. It had been dug through deposits next to a cave wall, and three rhinoceros skulls and the remains of at least five mammoths had been found.

Fuel was another problem, to collect as well as to store. When wood was scarce, the Neanderthals burned bones, and they may even have learned to use fat. They and earlier people also had ways of promoting efficient burning. Soviet investigators have discovered "tailed" hearths, basins with a narrow trench or furrow extending out from one side. Actual tests indicate the reason for the trench. Apparently it provided a kind of flue or draft through which air was drawn to produce more complete burning.

Archeological excavations rarely provide direct information about the feelings of our remote ancestors; usually we are reduced to guesses, shrewd or otherwise. But now and then the past leaves patterns whose significance cannot be mistaken. During the early 1900s such evidence was uncovered at Le Moustier, about 30 miles west of La Chapelle-aux-Saints, which shows that these people had developed a new way of thinking, a new attitude toward life and death. A boy about 15 or 16 years old had been buried in a cave. He had been lowered into a trench, placed on his right side with knees slightly drawn and head resting on his forearm in a sleeping position. A pile of flints lay under his head to form a sort of stone pillow, and near his hand was a beautifully worked stone ax. Around the remains were wild-cattle bones, many of them charred, the remnants of roasted meat which may have been provided to serve as sustenance in the world of the dead. (The old man of La Chapelle-aux-Saints was also buried in a trench and surrounded by stone tools.)

Not far from the Le Moustier site is a cave which was discovered by a road-building crew and probably served as a family cemetery. The number of people buried there is unknown. Some 21 mounds and pits have been found in the cave, 6 of them containing skeletons representing four children and two adults. The other 15 may also have contained skeletons which were looted or disintegrated over the years. Or they may have held meat and other perishable material for the use of the dead in other worlds. One mound, part of a pattern of 9 neatly arranged mounds, included the skeleton of a very small infant, perhaps a stillborn infant, and three flint tools. A nearby pit was covered by a triangular limestone slab and included the bones of a 6-year-old child and, again, three flint tools.

The record is rich in symbols which we cannot decipher. Near Monte Circeo, on the Mediterranean coast between Rome and Naples, is a deep cave whose innermost chamber contained a circle of stones, at the center of which was a human skull with a hole bored into it. There are also signs that animal rituals were practiced along with burials. A

Artist's conception of Neanderthal burial at Le Moustier

cave in a steep ravine in the mountains of Uzbek in Central Asia held the shallow grave of a young boy; half a dozen pairs of ibex horns were stuck in the earth around the head end of the grave, indicating that an ibex cult existed here among Neanderthals more than 50,000 years ago, as it does today among people living in the same region.

Other rituals involved cave bears, which often had to be driven out of caves before people could move in and which were killed by the hundreds. They were respected and worshiped as well as eaten. A

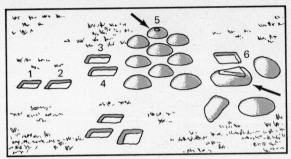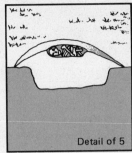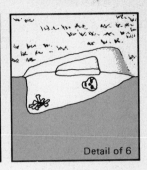

Detail of 5   Detail of 6

Multiple Neanderthal burial, possibly a family cemetery (Numbers indicate places where skeletons were found)

mountain cave in eastern Austria contained a rectangular vault holding 7 bear skulls all facing the cave's entrance; while material excavated from Regourdou, another site in southern France, represents perhaps the most elaborate bear-cult burial known. It included a skeleton complete except for the skull (which had probably been taken by an amateur collector), stone drains, a rectangular pit covered by a flat stone slab weighing almost a ton, and the remains of more than 20 cave bears.

One of the most revealing of recent discoveries comes from a site in the Near East, the Shanidar Cave in the Zagros Mountain highlands of Iraq, about 250 miles due north of Baghdad. Kurdish goatherds still live here, as they have for generations, making fire with steel and flint in brush huts under a vaulting roof which encloses an area about the size of four tennis courts. The site was excavated by Ralph Solecki of Columbia University. He hit bedrock at a depth of 45 feet and, in deposits up to 100,000 years old, found skeletons of 8 Neanderthal individuals, one apparently recovering from a spear or knife wound in the ribs.

A man with a badly crushed skull was buried deep in the cave with special ceremony. One spring day about 60,000 years ago members of his family went out into the hills, picked masses of wild flowers, and made a bed of them on the ground, a resting place for the deceased. Other flowers were probably laid on top of his grave; still others seem to have been woven together with the branches of a pinelike shrub to form a wreath. Traces of that offering endure in the form of fossil pollen collected from the burial site, the remains of the ancestors of present-day grape hyacinths, bachelor's buttons, hollyhocks, and yellow-flowering groundsels. The man was probably buried between late May and early July, which is when these flowers are in bloom today. (There are no signs of radical climatic changes in the region since prehistoric times.)

These findings, the graves, and the patterns around them, mark a great change in human evolution. Death, and presumably life, had become something special. No comparable evidence appears in earlier records, and as far as we know, before Neanderthal times, humans and

155

Find at Shanidar: ribs
and pelvic region of a
Neanderthal man of
about forty years who
lived at least 44,000
years ago (top); skull,
as unearthed, of
same individual,
probably killed in a
rock fall (bottom)

the ancestors of humans had always died as other animals did, being abandoned when they were too weak to keep up with the band or wandering off to wait alone for the end to come. Burial implies a new kind of concern for the individual and, according to one theory, it arose as part of a response to bitter glacial conditions when people needed one another even more than in less demanding times and formed more intimate ties and cared more intensely when death came.

Severe climates may have had something to do with the new spirit. Certainly considerable evidence exists in our own times to suggest that people living under the most depressing circumstances often have the highest hopes for the future, in another world if not in this one. But there had been hard times before, and death must always have been a mysterious phenomenon. The new element was the evolution of a brain capable of framing questions, arriving at answers, and establishing rituals—which, by the very fact that they were practiced regularly, reinforced the validity of the answers. Ritual expresses the belief or hope that a connection exists between repetition and truth, the notion that if a possibility is stated often enough it becomes a certainty.

There may have been another reason for an emphasis on burial. Perhaps the Neanderthals, like many hunter-gatherers in recent times, believed in ghosts and in the haunting of places where people have died and preferred to move away or dispose of their dead at some distance. If so, these practices might not have been possible during glacial winters. They could not move far through deep snows, and besides, their home bases probably included large stockpiles of food and fuel. So perhaps they had to stay put, bury their dead nearby or even inside their caves, and devise special ceremonies to appease ancestral spirits.

Neanderthal people invented, or at least formalized, illusion when they invented burial. The belief in an afterlife says in effect that death is not what it seems; that it represents an apparent ending only, an ending only as far as the evidence of the senses is concerned; and that in this case, the crude evidence of the senses is wrong. Reality involves not observed and observable facts, but an abstraction, the idea that death is actually a passage from one world to another. In this respect the burial ceremonies of prehistoric hunters expressed the kind of thinking used today to develop theories about the structure of the atomic nucleus or the expanding universe.

Another new phenomenon, another aspect of the new way of thinking, makes an appearance during Neanderthal times. Traces of violence, in the sense of person killing person, become more common. Some sort of mayhem took place in a sandstone rock shelter overlooking a river in northern Yugoslavia, where at the turn of the century investigators recovered more than 500 bones and bone fragments representing at least a dozen individuals. A number of the bones are charred, suggesting that cannibalism may have been practiced, while other bones show definite signs of having been cut. Similar evidence has been unearthed more recently in a French cave not far from the Mediterranean.

Unfortunately, excavators did not work as painstakingly then as they do now, and no living-floor patterns were reported. But the mass killings hint at organized fighting among neighboring bands, a possibility strengthened by the findings at other Old World sites of a flint projectile point in a rib cage, a pelvis with a spear hole in it, and skulls bashed and penetrated in various ways. Is this another sign of the *Homo sapiens* status of the Neanderthals? They not only believed in an afterlife, but they may also have taken the initiative in evolving effective ways of speeding the departure of their fellow beings to the other world. They may have invented warfare as well as religion.

CHAPTER 9 DEVELOPMENTS IN THE SCIENTIFIC STUDY OF NEANDERTHAL PEOPLE

One of the most beautiful parts of France is the region surrounding the village of Les Eyzies more than 300 miles southwest of Paris. Rivers have gouged the countryside out of a great limestone plateau. There are remote gorges and side valleys, wide-open valleys bounded by steep cliffs several hundred feet high, and in the cliffs, scooped-out places under massive overhangs and caves, many small ones and others that extend deep into the rock.

This is an ideal land to live in, and has been for a long time. Much of the local activity takes place near the cliffs which dominate the landscape. Farmers plow to the edges of the cliffs, and some of their

Le Moustier cave, Les Eyzies region, early burial site

159

farmhouses are fitted so snugly into the hollows of overhangs that they
seem to be growing out of the limestone. Indeed, cliff dwelling is an old
tradition in these parts. In medieval times the nobility built castles on
and into the cliffs, using natural caves for arsenals, storehouses, and
wine cellars. Roman legions came before farmers and feudal lords; remnants of the walls they made have been found underneath ruined
stables and towers.

But the Les Eyzies area is primarily a center of prehistory. For all
that has happened since, for all the conquests and pageantry, its richest
records and deepest mysteries involve people who flourished a thousand centuries before the Romans, Neanderthal people and their ancestors and descendants. Walking where they walked, one feels their presence everywhere, like ghosts. In good weather, they camped and lived
outdoors; their flints can be picked up by the dozen in plowed fields
near rivers and in the shadows of the cliffs and on the plateaus above
the cliffs. Traces of hearths as well as flints are found in the mouths of
caves and under the overhangs used for homes in glacial climates.

The record in this region demonstrates the human's extraordinary
ability to adapt, to live practically anywhere. Here, people probably encountered glacial climates more rigorous and demanding than their ancestors had ever encountered, and yet they managed to cope with icy
temperatures and blizzards and accumulating snows. Certainly they
could never have endured without making the most of natural resources, and the land around Les Eyzies offered a unique combination
of advantages.

Shelter, of course, was provided by the cliffs, eroded structures
formed by the lime-containing remains of tiny animals deposited and
consolidated more than 100 million years ago in the warm shallow sea
that covered most of Europe. The cliffs provided raw material as well as
shelter. Embedded in the limestone were large quantities of fine-
grained flint in the form of nodules which, like the limestone, consist of
the remains of microorganisms (in this case, colonies of single-celled
animals with shells containing silica). Water was also available, runoff
from mountains in the Massif Central, where the Dordogne and Vézère
rivers rose and joined a few miles below Les Eyzies and passed through
on their way to the Bay of Biscay, as they do today.

Above all, there was an abundance of game during the coldest
times, chiefly reindeer, which seem to have been created in large measure for the nourishment of man and other large carnivores. Wild
horses, for example, will not stay long in areas where they are being
heavily hunted. But reindeer such as the caribou of the Canadian Arctic
are creatures of habit, and vast herds tend to return to the same general
regions year after year, often along the same well-rutted trails, across
the same mountain passes, lakes, fords, rivers, and high gravel ridges.
Judging by the quantities of reindeer bones found at numerous sites in

Les Eyzies, center of prehistory

the Les Eyzies region, prehistoric reindeer were equally predictable and equally vulnerable. Groups of Neanderthal hunters, working together rather like wolf packs, must have waited at strategic crossing points and stalked and killed individual animals.

So people found many resources they could use in the glacial climates of southern France. They must also have had a feeling for the beauty of the land and for the hard-won security of standing with a solid wall at their backs and looking out over a river valley. Some 200 prehistoric sites have been reported within a radius of about 20 miles of Les Eyzies, including Le Moustier and Regourdou and other burial sites mentioned in the last chapter. Many more sites are known but unreported, since every investigator familiar with the area has a private list of places he or she hopes to excavate some day.

Most archeologists feel reasonably certain that several hundred undiscovered sites exist in the area. The great majority of reported caves, rock shelters, and open-air locations with prehistoric remains have been found within a mile or two of well-traveled routes, modern roads which often follow the original courses of old carriage roads. No one really knows what lies beyond. From the tops of the highest cliffs one looks into the distance and sees inviting backcountry valleys and other cliffs which have not yet been thoroughly explored and which almost surely contain the living places of prehistoric people.

A relatively straightforward approach would very likely lead to the discovery of further sites. The plan would be to start with a large-scale map of the region and detailed aerial photographs, concentrating first on valleys where no sites have been reported to date, and marking all cliffs and other uncovered limestone deposits which, like most presently known sites, have southern or western exposures. Archeologists believe that a trip into these valleys would reveal that an appreciable **161**

proportion of the locations had served as the occupation sites of pre- **162**
historic people. The only difficulty is that there has been little support
for such a search because enough sites are known already to keep excavators busy for four to five decades.

One exceptionally interesting site lies in the little valley of
Combe Grenal, about 14 miles from Les Eyzies, on the side of a hill not
far from the Dordogne River. A dirt road leads there, or rather a pair of
ruts marking the remains of a dirt road; and off to the left, along a rising path hidden by trees and bushes, lies the site, a gouged-out place
resembling an abandoned quarry. Higher up on the cliff and within
sight of the excavations is a mine which provided flint in prehistoric
times. Medieval stone workers also came there to obtain huge flint slabs
for millstones.

François Bordes, director of the Laboratory of Quaternary Geology and Prehistory of the University of Bordeaux and archeologist in
charge of all investigations in the Les Eyzies region, began digging at
the Combe Grenal cave in June, 1953. He expected to complete the
project in short order, probably by the end of the summer, because a
colleague told him that since bedrock had already been reached, only a
small area remained to be exposed. But it soon turned out that the bedrock sloped sharply downhill, and he and his associates followed the
dipping rock line deeper and deeper season after season without hitting
bottom in the form of a level floor. When the work finally came to an
end in 1964, they had made a huge hole in the ground, digging to a
maximum depth of some 40 feet and uncovering 65 separate layers of
geological and archeological deposits.

The oldest and deepest layers can be dated approximately, by geological methods. They include a clayey red soil, the clay representing
muds formed during thaws of the next-to-last glaciation. (The red color
is rust resulting from chemical reactions between iron-containing minerals and oxygen, reactions which are limited in cold climates and took
place during the subsequent interglacial stage.) These deposits are estimated to have been laid down 125,000 to 150,000 years ago, about the
time when prehistoric pioneers explored the area, looked over the cave,
and decided to move in.

The first occupants left no fossil remains. But they may have
been people rather like those represented by the skull fragments found
at the Swanscombe and Steinheim sites, definitely on the way to being
modern people. They had Acheulian-type tools like some of those
unearthed at Swanscombe, including hand axes designed according to
the same basic pattern used by their remote Olduvai ancestors hundreds of thousands of years before. Judging by the fact that about 80
percent of the bones found among their tools were reindeer bones, their
diet included ample supplies of venison.

Combe Grenal's richest and most important deposits lie directly

163

above the red Acheulian deposits, furnishing an almost continuous record of Neanderthal occupation from about 40,000 to 90,000 years ago. There are a few sterile layers without artifacts or any traces of human beings; the climate may have become too severe, even for the Neanderthals, and chunks of rock from the roof remained where they fell since probably no one was around to clear away the debris. In at least one case, people abandoned the site during favorable climatic conditions, possibly to follow game other than reindeer, animals with sufficient good sense to move out when hunters moved in. One or two layers contain very little material, indicating that hunters had a home base elsewhere and used the cave only occasionally for brief stopovers.

Combe Grenal was a center of activity most of the time, however, for groups of about 35 or 40 individuals, at any one time, who lived and died there over periods of many generations. Archeologists are continually on the alert for any unusual features, which inexperienced excavators often miss entirely. One day, Bordes uncovered a flat stone of about 4 inches across; nothing much in itself, it turned out to be one of a series of flat stones arranged as if to cover something. The soil under the stones was finer and looser than the soil surrounding the stones, the sort of pattern which may indicate that a hole had been dug and refilled. Careful removal of the fine soil revealed a basin-shaped pit, probably the funeral pit for a very young child. The presumed grave was empty, a fact difficult to explain since it had not been disturbed by looters or scavenging animals. Most likely the skeleton was destroyed by the bone-dissolving action of waters seeping through layers containing sand and ashes and rock; also, young bones are not fully calcified and may tend to disintegrate faster than adult bones. Three smaller pits near the grave, also empty, may have held meat and clothing for the dead child.

Another unusual feature was exposed in a higher, more recent layer. One of Bordes' co-workers noticed a dark circular patch of fine soil in an ashy layer. He scooped out the soil, taking care to leave the ashy material intact, and ended with a hole about 2 inches in diameter and 8 inches deep. Then he poured plaster into the hole, obtaining a cast which resembled the pointed end of a stake. This may have been one of several postholes at the mouth of the cave, where stakes were driven into the ground to support skins or woven branches which provided shelter from wind, rain, and snow. It may have supported a meat-drying rack (this is discussed later).

But Combe Grenal is especially important for the richness of its tool assemblages and for the analysis of those assemblages by a statistical approach, which Bordes himself pioneered. Since excavating his first site at the age of 14 in a valley not far from Les Eyzies, he has examined more than a million tools, most of them by the Neanderthals. This experience is the basis for his widely used system of classify-

Plaster cast of posthole, Combe Grenal

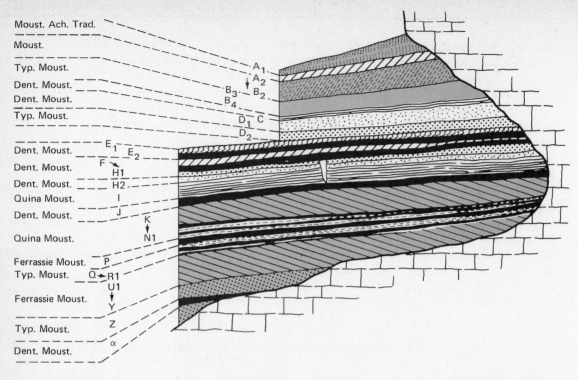

Moust. Ach. Trad.
Moust.
Typ. Moust. — A₁
                 A₂
Dent. Moust. — B₃ — B₂
Dent. Moust. — B₄
Typ. Moust. — D₁ — C
                 D₂
Dent. Moust. — E₁
                 E₂
Dent. Moust. — F
                 H1
Dent. Moust. — H2
Quina Moust. — I
Dent. Moust. — J
                 K
Quina Moust. — N1
Ferrassie Moust. — P
Typ. Moust. — Q — R1
                 U1
Ferrassie Moust. — Y
                 Z
Typ. Moust. — α
Dent. Moust.

Cross section at
Combe Grenal:
location of posthole

ing tools. He has published a list of tool types, each type being identified clearly and objectively enough so that other investigators can make
the same identifications on their own. The list includes a total of more
than 60 different kinds of points, scrapers, knives, burins, and so on—
tools also made by much more ancient peoples, although in smaller proportions and not in such variety.

The variety of tool types itself is enough to indicate what may be
deduced from other evidence, such as the burial practices of the Neanderthals and their ability to live in rigorous climates, namely, that they
were advanced and complicated human beings. But further analysis reveals another sort of variety, and more about the people. In the process
of identifying and counting the tools in Neanderthal layers, Bordes discovered the existence of a number of unique and characteristic patterns.
Different layers contain different proportions of tools, different tool kits,
which hints at basic differences in prehistoric living.

The patterns occur among the 19,000 Neanderthal tools collected
at Combe Grenal. One pattern appears in the layer where the posthole
mentioned above was found. The layer contained 766 tools and a great
many tool types, including an assortment of scrapers and even 3 hand
axes. But nearly 600 items in the assemblage belong to the single broad
class of flints with one or more notches struck on the edges. Most of the
pieces are denticulate, or toothed tools, having three or four notches in
a row which form teeth, and these look much like saw blades. There are

also single-notched tools which might be used, among other purposes, **165** to help scrape the bark off narrow branches in making stakes and spear shafts. The site includes nine other denticulate layers.

A second kind of tool kit is found in 14 other layers. It also includes a variety of different tools and, again, one class of tool predominates. Nearly two out of every three pieces is a scraper, a high proportion being Quina scrapers, named after La Quina shelter, a site about 70 miles northwest of Combe Grenal where many were found. The large thick tools are often delicately chipped along their curved working edges to produce a characteristic overlapping fish-scale appearance; they may have served as heavy-duty implements to clean hides for clothing.

The discovery of these and two other tool kits has changed ways of looking at tool assemblages everywhere. Tools uncovered in Neanderthal layers generally fit into one of Bordes' four categories wherever the layers are found—not only at Combe Grenal and in the Les Eyzies region but also in Spain, Syria, Germany, Israel, and other countries. The problem is what to make of such widespread and persistent patterns. Apparently they have little to do with evolution among the Neanderthals since the tool kits do not appear in any regular sequence from the oldest to the most recent layers at various sites, and there is no conclusive evidence of simple seasonal or climatic influences.

Bordes believes that the four tool kits belong to four tribes or traditions. Different Neanderthal groups had different ways of doing things, customs handed down from much earlier times and represented by the tool kits they left behind. For example, the Quina Neanderthals may be traced to a tradition that existed nearly 100,000 years before them at the High Lodge site in England, where people were using similar tools, including finely worked Quina-type scrapers. Another Neanderthal tool kit may stem from Acheulian industries which first appeared more than a million years ago (see Chapter 6), a line passing through intermediate stages such as those observed in the remains at Torralba and Ambrona and, more recently, in the lowest layers at Combe Grenal itself.

Cultural evolution proceeded very slowly compared to its current pace. Bordes believes that contacts between Neanderthal bands with different traditions were few and far between: "A man may well have lived all his life without more than a rare meeting with anyone from another tribe . . . and it is very possible that these contacts, when they did take place, were not always peaceful and fruitful." After all, it was a relatively empty world, the entire population of France probably numbering less than 20,000 persons.

Combe Grenal provides a record of successive wanderings in and out of the little Dordogne Valley by people who had developed different ways of doing things, different habits and beliefs. Groups settled in the cave and eventually died out or left in search of better living conditions or new hunting grounds or simply because they wanted a change of scene. (There were always more than enough caves and shelters to go around.) They would be replaced by other groups in a series of occupations that took place over a period of 500 centuries.

The approach upon which Bordes' ideas are based, the statistical approach, has opened the way for still more extensive and more refined studies. Some of his conclusions are being challenged as a direct result of work stimulated by his own research. The challenge calls for a major shift of emphasis, a different way of looking at and analyzing Neanderthal tool kits. Instead of interpreting them as the products of different tribes or traditions, they can be interpreted as signs that different sorts of activity were going on.

According to this viewpoint, different tool kits do not represent people with different traditions doing essentially the same things, such as hunting, gathering, preparing foods, making tools and fires, and so on. They represent people who shared many important cultural characteristics and were simply doing different things at different times and places. For example, the existence of Quina-type and denticulate tool kits might simply indicate that one group was engaged chiefly in scraping hides, while the other group was concentrating on woodworking. In other words, people were using Combe Grenal for different purposes. The focus is less on things that prehistoric people did because their forefathers did them, and more on things people did as part of the practical day-to-day business of staying alive.

The most articulate and influential spokesman for this functional point of view is Lewis Binford of the University of New Mexico, who evolved his approach and philosophy during the course of work on American Indian sites. His increasing concern with the more remote prehistory of the Old World is due in large part to his former wife Sally, who has specialized in Neanderthal problems and worked closely with Bordes. There have been some friendly but heated arguments over the interpretation of Neanderthal data with Bordes and his wife Denise, also an archeologist.

Binford's approach, like Bordes', is a statistical one involving a refinement of the tool-kit concept. Any group of people, prehistoric, primitive, or modern, has a large set of tools for carrying out all its activities. Investigators interested in comparing different cultures can obtain information from an unsorted collection of items representing the entire assemblage. But the information is likely to be very limited without further analysis. There must be some way of isolating from the total set the subsets of tools or specialized tool kits which naturally go together because they are used together in performing specific activities. One must identify these subsets and activities if one is to understand in detail the lives of prehistoric people.

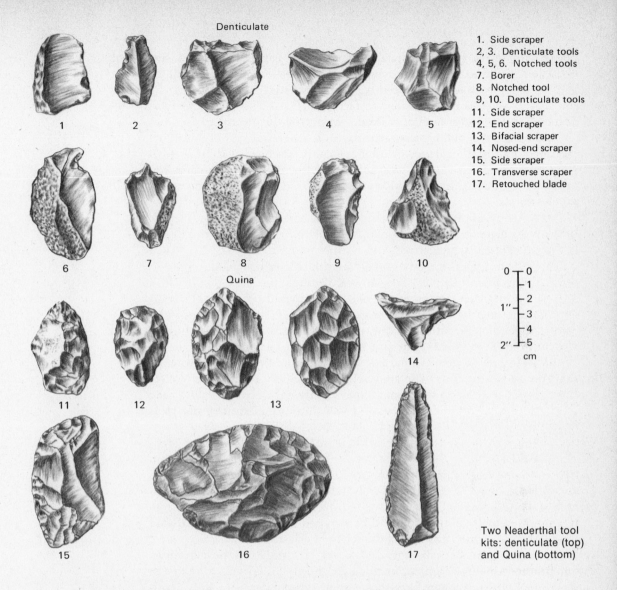

Denticulate

1. Side scraper
2, 3. Denticulate tools
4, 5, 6. Notched tools
7. Borer
8. Notched tool
9, 10. Denticulate tools
11. Side scraper
12. End scraper
13. Bifacial scraper
14. Nosed-end scraper
15. Side scraper
16. Transverse scraper
17. Retouched blade

Quina

Two Neaderthal tool kits: denticulate (top) and Quina (bottom)

Similarly, an individual completely ignorant of modern life would have a problem trying to analyze an unsorted collection of the implements we use today. The collection might consist of more than a hundred different types of objects, including a mixture of items used in grooming, cooking, writing, and sewing—for example, razor blades, pots, paper clips, thimbles, hair curlers, bread knives, ballpoint pens, safety pins, combs, frying pans, letter openers, needles, nail files, funnels, paperweights, and scissors. The problem would involve finding out which tools were used together and for what tasks.

In the study of prehistoric people, a single collection from a single living place means nothing by itself. The search for subsets of ar-

167

tifacts as clues to repeated practices and living habits requires a sufficiently large and representative sample of collections—and Binford and his students have introduced a special statistical technique for the analysis of such samples known as factor analysis. The technique was developed as an outgrowth of research conducted during the early 1900s by American psychologists concerned with discovering sets of questions that were effective measures of intelligence. It has been widely used in studies of executive morale, weather trends, accident-proneness, urban development, the voting behavior of Supreme Court justices, and many other projects.

An early application of factor analysis to research on prehistoric tool kits involves evidence obtained from a site in Israel near the Sea of Galilee. The area, which marks the northernmost part of the Great Rift Valley system, includes many caves where Neanderthal people lived in times when a now extinct river flowed through the area to the Dead Sea. Sally Binford excavated one of the caves, a large two-chamber affair located in a steep limestone cliff more than 100 feet above the floor of a river canyon. It was a difficult dig, not only because of the early morning climb up the cliffside, but also because most artifacts and other remains were buried deep in narrow crevices or embedded in hardened sand-limestone deposits. The site yielded a sample of eight tool collections, suitable for analysis, from as many different deposits in the cave area, and a total of about 2000 tools. Sally Binford identified the tools according to Bordes' list of types.

The size of the sample was increased by the addition of eight other tool collections, seven from levels in a shelter near Damascus in Syria and one from a French open-air site near Rouen. These collections also yielded about 2000 tools—closely related to those found at the Israeli site and presumably manufactured during the same period of prehistory. Moreover, all the tools had been typed by Bordes (he had listed over 60 types), which ensured consistency of classification.

Factor analysis calls for a detailed investigation of variations among the items of a sample. In this case the first step was to take one of the tool types, compare it with a second type for each of the 16 collections, and then evaluate the result. A rating of +1 would indicate that the two types varied in exactly the same way—that both types increased by, say, 10 percent from collection A to collection B, decreased by 25 percent from B to C, maintained the same proportions in D, and so on. If the rating was −1, that would indicate that the two tool types were exactly out of phase, varying in exactly the opposite way. A rating of 0 would indicate no relationship at all. Intermediate values on the scale from +1 to −1 represented different degrees of correlation or association.

The process was repeated over and over again in the Neanderthal study. Each tool type was compared successively to every one of the **169** other 39 tool types (this particular sample included 40 of the 60-odd types listed by Bordes), and every one of the relationships was evaluated. These and many subsequent steps required considerable calculating but took only about two minutes of the time of a high-speed computer. The analysis produced five factors, five sets of tools that varied together as independent clusters with high degrees of correlation. The following is a list of the specialized tool kits together with some suggestions as to how they might have been used:

1. Tool kit I: twelve tool types, including two kinds of borer, a beak-shaped engraver (or bec), and other tools which may have been used to make out of wood and bone such objects as shafts, handles (or hafts), tent pegs, and cordage from hides. Used for maintenance activities.
2. Tool kit II: ten tool types, including three kinds of spear points and many kinds of scrapers. Used for killing and butchering.
3. Tool kit III: seven tool types, including three kinds of knives for heavy cutting and three kinds of flakes for delicate cutting. Used for food processing mainly of prepared meat.
4. Tool kit IV: four tool types, including denticulates for sawing and shredding and two special types of scrapers for fine work. Used for shredding and cutting, perhaps of wood and other plant materials.
5. Tool kit V: six tool types including points, simple scrapers, and the rabot (or push plane). Used for killing and butchering activities possibly more specialized than those requiring tool kit II.

The main tool kits at the Israeli site are I, II, and III. Tool kit I predominates, which indicates that the cave was used chiefly for maintenance work such as repairing old tools and weapons and making new ones, tasks most likely to be carried out at a base camp. Tool kit III suggests food processing, another domestic activity, while the presence of tool kit II indicates that a small amount of killing and butchering may have been done at the site. The idea of a base camp is supported by the fact that the cave is a large one, enclosing a naturally lighted area of about 2700 square feet, which is enough floor space for 25 to 30 individuals according to studies indicating a requirement in such settlements of at least 100 square feet per person.

The analysis permits further deductions about how the cave was used. Most of the deposits contain tool assemblages that are remarkably alike in numbers, types, and proportions of tools. This observation fits in with the notion, hinted at by other evidence, that the same group of people used the cave intensively to perform the same general tasks for a relatively short period, say, a few years. Their cooking area may have been located just outside the cave entrance. It is marked by a deposit that includes three small fire layers and an unusually high proportion of knives, and flakes, and tools from tool kit III, which could do an effective job of meat carving.

A different living pattern existed at the Syrian site, a shelter containing only about 1600 square feet of floor space. Tool kits II and V, the killing and butchering factors, tend to predominate here. There is also evidence suggesting that tool kit V may represent the hunting of a type of game which demands that the hunters spend relatively long periods away from the base camp. The general impression is that the site served as a temporary work camp, where hunters stopped to do their butchering and, perhaps, to make plans for the next day's activities. Only one of its occupation levels contains traces of fire and, as at the Israeli site, this is also the only place where food-processing tool kit III is represented.

After completing the Near Eastern studies, the Binfords carried out a more extensive analysis of evidence from Combe Grenal—with its 50-odd Neanderthal layers, 19,000 Neanderthal tools, abundant bone and pollen remains, and a 50,000-year record of Neanderthal occupations. In the Near Eastern study, hunting items (spear points) and scrapers were included in a single tool kit, tool kit II. But in the Combe Grenal analysis, this unit breaks into its major components and becomes two distinct tool kits. The same effect was noted for maintenance and food processing, which were represented by several different tool kits. In all, the analysis yielded some 14 different tool kits, believed to be fairly close to a complete listing for the Neanderthals, although future studies may reveal 2 or 3 more. The statistically determined factors or clusters are elements of a most important kind. Comparable to small pieces of glass and stone used in making mosaics, they can be used in recreating the human pattern of the Neanderthal way of life. Some major features of the pattern have already been discovered.

Combe Grenal has 55 Neanderthal occupation layers, 40 containing enough tools for statistical analysis. Of the analyzed layers, 25 include one or more of the three kinds of tool kits associated with maintenance activities and were probably camps. The implication is that these camps were either home bases for all members of the groups or else places away from the home site reserved primarily for intensive activities associated with hunting or food processing. The rest of the layers did not contain maintenance tool kits and are thought to be stations for temporary occupations connected with more specialized activities. A few of these layers do not fit in with this preliminary hypothesis since they include abundant traces of fire, generally characteristic of intensive settlements rather than of temporary stations.

Other associations stimulate new ideas about what was being done and by whom. One of the Binfords' arguments leads from a consideration of the kinds of flint used for different types of tools to new interpretations of some old and puzzling observations. They asked themselves what sort of archeological evidence might help indicate which tasks were done by women, and speculated that since women generally stay near the group's camp or station to care for the children, they might tend to make their tools out of readily available raw material near the site.

This notion immediately raised a simple question which had never been asked before: What sort of tools were made of local materials? The most readily available sources of flint available to the Neanderthals at Combe Grenal were dull grayish or blackish nodules embedded in the walls of their own cave, and the Binfords spent many hours at Bordes' laboratory in Bordeaux going through drawer after drawer jammed with tools, classifying every item by tool type, material, and the layer in which it was found. They found that tools made of Combe Grenal flint are likely to be primarily denticulate or notched tools, items commonly associated with the processing of foods—which might well have been predominantly woman's work as it is in hunting-gathering tribes today.

Reinforcing and complementing the theory is evidence bearing on men's work. Spear points, certain types of scrapers, and other tools made of certain raw materials, generally from remote sources, were most often used in hunting—for example, tools made of opalescent white flint from a site more than a mile away on the plateau above Combe Grenal and of brown flint from Dordogne River gravels. One implication is that the variety of materials represents a mark of the hunting life, of men away from their base camp and ready to use whatever suitable material happened to be at hand.

Hunting tools seem to be associated with a special way of working flint, the purpose of which has never been fully clear. The Levallois technique (named after a site in Levallois-Perret, a suburb of Paris) appeared in Africa and western Europe some 150,000 years ago and required a high order of finesse, the careful preparation of a flint nodule by trimming the top and edges before striking off a flake for shaping into a finished tool. There has been a great deal of speculating about the significance of such flaking since, for no obvious reasons, it is common at some sites and rare or absent at others.

For many years the technique was believed to be a cultural trait, a matter mainly of tradition and style. Later, Bordes and others emphasized the fact that it generally occurred at sites where flint was plentiful and easily accessible. Now the technique may be given a new significance as regards its advantages in connection with the hunt. In contrast to denticulate tools, generally on the small side and made of flakes of widely varying shapes since the important thing apparently was the cutting edge, hunting tools often require large and relatively standardized flakes. It has been noted for some time that the Levallois technique permits the manufacture of such flakes.

Broader and more complex problems remain to be discovered and solved regarding the data from Combe Grenal, problems involving the further application of factor analysis and the relationship of tool assemblages to other traces of the past. Bordes collected fossil pollens from many layers at the site, and the Binfords have subjected this material to statistical study, again with the aid of a high-speed computer. The result is eight clusters of pollen types which tend to occur together, and which tell a story of prevailing climates in the area.

One cluster includes oak, poplar, alder, elm, ivy, ferns, and other plants characteristic of low, damp, shaded places such as are found in the upland meadows of the Dordogne region today. Other clusters suggest a typical very dry, very warm forest-margin terrain (blackberry, raspberry, roses, nettles), steppe grasslands (cool-climate grasses and sedges), and cold, seasonally wet conditions (hazel, willow, Queen Anne's lace). As might be expected, a clear-cut relationship exists between climate and the activities indicated by tool kits. In general, the

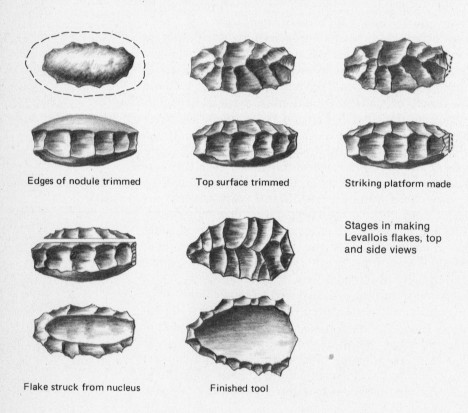

Edges of nodule trimmed

Top surface trimmed

Striking platform made

Stages in making
Levallois flakes, top
and side views

Flake struck from nucleus

Finished tool

pattern of ongoing activities does not change much as long as climate remains relatively stable.

There are also six animal clusters. Ibex, wolf, and a northern species of horse are typical of cold steppes; deer, Irish elk, and an extinct species of rhinoceros indicate open forest; and so on. The greatest variety of animal remains is usually found together with tool kits characteristic of base-camp layers, which suggests that the people chose to settle here precisely because the area contained many kinds of game. On the other hand, the fewest species are found at more temporary and specialized stations.

Combe Grenal includes three types of so-called shredding stations, settlements characterized among other things by a high proportion of denticulates and other notched tools. The animal remains associated with one of the station types are predominantly those of horses and reindeers, and Lewis Binford has a hunch about what was going on. The sawtooth tools may have been used by Neanderthals to cut chunks of already butchered meat into little strips that could be hung on racks to dry in the sun or over fires. American Indians used this technique for preserving meat, and French traders sold them special metal shredders for the cutting operations, tools designed along the same lines as small denticulate flints.

If this technique was practiced by Neanderthals, one might expect to find in the appropriate layers clues such as the remains of smoke fires, postholes, or even pieces of preserved wood from the drying racks. Unless a speculation suggests what excavators can possibly find by way of evidence, unless it suggests specific procedures for its own proof or disproof, it has very little value in stimulating new studies. Some confirmatory evidence exists at Combe Grenal in one of the denticulate layers—a posthole as well as traces of fire.

Continuing analysis reveals patterns or fragments of patterns which are beginning to fit together. Small tools such as engravers, borers, and end scrapers tend to be found together with the remains of salmon, marmots (a bushy-tailed rodent somewhat resembling a woodchuck), mountain sheep, and other rarely killed animals. The association makes sense when you realize that these tools are used for maintenance activities such as woodworking and preparing hides, activities generally carried out at base camps occupied for relatively long periods—and the longer the occupation, the greater the chances of finding some rare animals.

These and a great many other statistical patterns, the output of high-speed computers, provide clues to behavior among prehistoric people. Another source of clues to the past is the actual behavior of people who still live primarily by hunting. Primitive people are by no means living in a pristine, untouched state; their world has been changed irrevocably by waves of foreign explorers and settlers. Yet even allowing for all that, certain practices endure, and some striking parallels exist between the present and the remote past.

Chapters 15 and 16 consider such observations in some detail, but one example here will demonstrate a direct application to the understanding of Neanderthal times. As part of an effort to learn more about what happened at Combe Grenal and elsewhere, Binford has completed a series of intensive studies among Eskimos living in the Brooks Range region of north-central Alaska, about 250 miles from Fairbanks. In one of his recent archeology projects, he excavated the site of a house occupied by Eskimos 80 to 90 years ago.

Among other things, he found caribou lower jawbones, all of which had been cracked open, a practice explained to him by Eskimos who remembered what their fathers and grandfathers had done. The jawbones contained patik, a fibrous tissue eaten as a starvation food in times of near-famine. The Neanderthals may have faced similar emergencies, since all but one of several hundred reindeer, horse, and ox-cattle jawbones found in Combe Grenal layers were also cracked open. Furthermore, it seems that Eskimos and Neanderthals shared related superstitions. The Alaskan hunters had a taboo against eating material from the jawbones of bears, foxes, wolves, and other meat-eating animals—and not a single one of the two dozen or so bear, wolf, cave lion, and hyena jawbones found at Combe Grenal had been shattered.

So observations of contemporary hunters enrich the understanding of prehistory, mainly by suggesting things to look for during archeological excavations and providing evidence relevant to the question of whether different tool kits represent different traditions or different activities. Further support for the latter viewpoint comes from new work conducted during the last few years. Leslie Freeman, digging Neanderthal layers in the Morin Cave in northern Spain, found separate concentrations of three different tool kits on the same living floors, indicating a functional rather than a traditional context. People were simply doing different things in different parts of the cave. Freeman's statistical studies of animal remains at the 400,000-year-old Spanish site of Ambrona (see Chapter 6) were also based on factor analysis.

Desmond Clark, who has long suspected that different tool kits found at different places reflect different activities, reports a number of persisting patterns which turn up at a variety of sites occupied during the past 2 million years or so. One pattern is the general predominance of small tools, mainly cutting flakes and scrapers, at sites where one animal or only a few animals had been butchered. Another pattern involves the presence of large numbers of large cutting tools, hand axes, and cleavers, at sites containing very little bone and no signs of butchering.

Clark's observations are confirmed and extended in a recent factor-analysis study by Binford, who makes a number of further inferences. For one thing, he suggests that the large cutting tools may not have been used in hunting at all. They may have been used primarily to dig for and process plant foods, and their prominence at a site may indicate a heavy reliance on such foods, a state of affairs which prevails among primitive people currently living in southern Africa and other warm regions.

This possibility has some provocative implications. It may help in understanding the unexplained east-west division of Oldowan and Acheulian industries, as described in Chapter 6. The idea is that Acheulian hand-ax industries—concentrated in Africa, Europe, the Near East, and peninsular India—may reflect an emphasis on plant foods, while the Oldowan industries of southeastern Asia which include chopping and lighter flake tools represent the tool kits of people consuming higher proportions of meat. An intriguing question is the possible connection between this notion and the notion proposed by some prehistorians that modern type of people and large-scale cooperative hunting first appeared in Asia.

Such studies will have to be extended considerably to arrive at truly scientific theories about the lives of our prehistoric ancestors. A staggering amount of material has already been collected, including skeletal remains of more than 150 Neanderthal individuals from about 70 sites throughout the world. An important site is located in northeast China near the Great Wall. Soviet investigators have dug extensively at rich Neanderthal sites along river banks in the Crimea and elsewhere and have found traces of elaborate burials and semipermanent dwellings. One of the dwelling sites, Molodova in the eastern Soviet Union more than 250 miles from Kiev, includes a large ring of mammoth tusks, perhaps used for supporting posts; inside the ring are bones of horses, rhinoceroses, bison, and brown bears, 29,000 pieces of flint, and 15 hearths.

There has even been increased activity in Greece and Italy, where archeological interest has hitherto focused almost exclusively on classical sites. Eric Higgs of Cambridge University has located more than 50 prehistoric sites in red erosion gullies among the mountains of northwest Greece (as compared to less than half a dozen such sites reported previously for the entire country). His work at one site yielded a number of living floors as well as some unusual remains such as tool assemblages with a high proportion of microliths—points, bladelets, scrapers, and other miniature implements usually from half an inch to an inch long.

Other sites have been excavated in Africa, where, in certain regions at least, the pace of evolution seems to have been slower than in Europe, perhaps because life was so abundant and things came so easily that survival represented far less of a challenge. The world's richest hunting grounds existed in Africa throughout prehistory, and most of the world's hunters lived there. According to one study, during Neanderthal times there may have been two to four times more people in southern Africa alone than in all of Europe.

Factor analysis and other statistical techniques will be required increasingly for comparative studies of material from many sites. A new approach is being developed, a new way of looking at things. Results are not yet completely consistent and cannot serve as the basis for hard-and-fast conclusions. On the other hand, there is no choice but to use analytical techniques. The data must be organized, and that does not happen automatically. One of the most futile pursuits in research is to accumulate facts and keep accumulating them in the hope that sooner or later they will make sense and the truth will out.

Bare facts are neither particularly interesting nor particularly informative. They do not speak for themselves in archeology or in any other branch of science. But they will speak if they are treated properly, if they are marshaled and organized. That means using statistics to help get the most out of the evidence, a process which generally requires the aid of a high-speed computer. The relationships involved are too complicated for even the most imaginative investigators to deal with on their own.

Imagination comes into its own most effectively, most powerfully, after the analysis. Computers simply present information organized according to the instructions prepared for them. They indicate that certain types of tools tend to vary together and form statistical clusters, but they say nothing about the uses of individual tools or the activities represented by individual tool kits. It is up to the investigator to frame hypotheses that can be checked, like the notion that the Neanderthals may have used Levallois flakes to hunt large open-plain animals such as horses and wild cattle. And imagination and intuition will have to lead the way in interpreting tendencies involving subtler things than activities, things such as attitudes and beliefs.

Bordes has definite feelings about the men and women whose artifacts he is uncovering. They are still alive for him. As he digs in a rich Quina layer and finds one beautifully worked scraper after another, he is impressed not only with the craftsmanship but also with the fact that the craftsmen were working in an almost automatic fashion, as if they had perfected their techniques and had stopped inventing: "They made beautiful things stupidly. Digging Quina layers can be very boring. For the first week you are impressed with the tools, but after that you see scrapers and more scrapers and still more scrapers until you are sick of them!"

These people seem to have done most of the burying of the dead. At least, most Neanderthal graves in France are associated with Quina-type tool kits, a finding suggesting that ritual may have played a particularly important part in their lives. So one may ask whether a relationship exists between this quality and the stereotyped, repetitive aspect of their flint technology—and, if so, what special stresses and fears might have fostered the intensive development of their rituals.

One possible clue comes from Binford's most recent analyses of Bordes' Combe Grenal findings. According to Binford, layers of the Quina type generally indicate summertime use of the site because the 4-month-old calves, yearlings, and cows make up most of the animal remains and it is during the summer that herds disperse into small nursing groups. He believes that the central purpose of hunting expeditions was to prepare for long hard winters and obtain hides for winter clothing. Perhaps the rigors of glacial climates resulted not only in a high death rate, but also in a vision of a happier and easier afterlife.

Layers related to earlier Acheulian industries hint at an entirely different attitude toward the world. They include some hand axes and a relatively high proportion of knives, especially backed knives, blunted on one side for a firm and comfortable grip. Bordes believes that Neanderthals using such tools were far more inventive than those using tools of the Quina type. "They had some imagination. They made all sorts of backed blades and offbeat tools which you can't classify, including some combination tools, prehistoric versions of today's Swiss pocket knives with scissors and screwdrivers and nail files as well as regular blades. They experimented a great deal, and their experiments worked."

The continuing cooperation and arguments between Bordes and Binford indicate that investigators whose basic viewpoints differ can nevertheless achieve productive results. The problems at issue demand a tribal or cultural approach and a functional approach as well. Archeologists concerned primarily with cultural factors tend to dig deep, to go back as far as possible into time, and to obtain a long record of successive changes. Functionally minded archeologists, on the other hand, tend to dig wide and to excavate broad areas at sites which cover more space and can reveal more about the organization of camping places and the variety of activities under way.

This difference of emphasis itself may express a cultural difference. After all, it is natural for Bordes and other investigators of Old World nations with long histories and established traditions to approach prehistory in cultural terms, and it is natural for the Binfords, as members of a nation whose history is brief and whose pioneers and prehistory are recent, to stress the practical aspects of how things are done and for what purposes. Prehistory is sufficiently complex to benefit from both approaches. The best excavations are both deep and wide.

New people and new institutions; the coming of art, organized predation on a large scale, tribal society; the mystery and controversy about the passing of the Neanderthals; the discovery of Cro-Magnon people; new tools and toolmaking techniques; a possible relationship between an early population explosion and the retreat of the glaciers; humans enter Australia and the New World

CHAPTER 10 THE DISAPPEARANCE OF NEANDERTHALS AND THE APPEARANCE OF MODERN PEOPLE

One summer evening a number of years ago Francois Bordes played a recording for me in an old farmhouse not far from Combe Grenal, his home during the excavating season. He called the recording "The Song of the Neanderthals." It was a New Caledonian war chant, sung loud and deep and partly shouted to the beating of drums; sung with feeling but strangely without pattern. There was no sustained rhythm, only occasional and random intervals of rhythm which came like interruptions. For a few moments the chanters would sing in unison, and their voices and the drumbeating seemed to gain in power and purpose, and then the rhythm would break again. The song, with its flashes of harmony and style and its feeling of limitations and aspirations unfulfilled, symbolizes the situation of people who somehow could not quite make it.

A new breed of *Homo sapiens* appeared on the scene 35,000 to 40,000 years ago, and with it major changes representing the first signs of a worldwide cultural revolution. The revolution was reflected anatomically in a new brain. It was no larger overall than that of the Neanderthals, but it incorporated within a more rounded cranium expanded areas at the front and sides that apparently included the required nerve circuitry for wider, more complex associations, advanced planning, and other varieties of more abstract thinking. The new people were our direct ancestors in the sense that their brains were essentially the same as ours. They developed art, perhaps their most impressive achievement. The first paintings and engravings appeared on the walls of caves, often deep inside and far from natural lights, in places that suggest secrecy and ceremonies whose nature can only be guessed at. Critics can be as obscure about the significance of the world's earliest art as about today's art, but we do know that cave art (discussed more fully in the next chapter) was the product of powerful, confident, and imaginative individuals.

Another innovation can be attributed to the new people. Apparently, they were the first to concentrate heavily on the hunting of herd animals. The general practice during Neanderthal times seems to have been the killing of single animals by single bands, the killing of one animal at a time. The idea was to stalk a herd and go after a particular individual, often an individual weakened by injury or disease or advanced age. Lions, wild dogs, and other carnivores use similar tactics to good advantage. For a long time, at least since Torralba and Ambrona 400,000 years ago, people and herds had moved together, locked together in a natural rhythm set by the seasons, the herds moving instinctively along familiar trails, the people following and learning and preparing more ingenious ambushes. For a long time, however, there were very small groups of hunters and very large groups of animals, and that part of the pattern changed with the coming of the modern type of human beings.

People were being shaped more intensively by the creatures they hunted. To kill herd animals more efficiently, people became herd animals. With all the space in the world to live in, they formed more densely settled communities. They invented crowds to become better predators. More than that, there is increasing evidence that they took the first steps toward domestication in the form of herd management. Developing such techniques called for increasingly sophisticated thinking. It was not enough merely to remember where and when herds had appeared and to be there ready and waiting on the spot. The stakes were too high. Sometimes herds changed their routes or came earlier or later, and that might mean mass starvation for hunters and their families. They had to analyze their past experiences, deduce general principles of herd behavior, and make more reliable predictions.

People developed new social structures. They still lived in bands of perhaps half a dozen to two dozen families, from about 30 to as many as 100 or so individuals. But in certain places the band was on the way out. In the Les Eyzies region, for example, people probably took the first steps toward the full-fledged tribe, an association of many bands held together not only by marriage but by shared traditions and shared problems, large-scale hunting and herd management, and perhaps warfare. They evolved rituals for coming together and remaining together, accentuating traditions that might have arisen in the remote past. Incest taboos and kinship rules created more intricate and cohesive relationships among larger number of individuals.

It should be pointed out that these developments may represent what happened in western Europe, during cold winters and in tundra regions where large herds were the main source of meat. The food quest was rather different in other environments, for example, among hunter-gatherers in southern Africa. Richard Klein of the University of Chicago has excavated at Nelson Bay Cave and other sites east of Cape Town and reports, as one might expect, that where a variety of foods was

available, people in harsh environments adapted accordingly and did
less specializing.

Fossil evidence for the new human beings, for the transition from Neanderthals to individuals of the modern type is sparse in Europe, but relatively abundant at a number of sites in the Near East. For example, there is a cave in Israel, on the slopes of Mount Carmel overlooking the Mediterranean near Haifa, where excavators found the skeleton of a short, stocky individual with heavy limbs and bony brow ridges, definitely a Neanderthal but apparently not the kind that was living in western Europe. The brow ridges were less massive, the skull somewhat more rounded. Furthermore, near the cave is a rock shelter which served as a cemetery for people who lived in the region several thousand years later, and who were even closer to modern people. The ten skeletons recovered there had longer and straighter limbs than the Neanderthals, more prominent chins, and smaller faces.

Why did such changes occur at that particular time, 40,000 to 50,000 years ago, and why in the Near East? A basic reason, then as throughout the course of human evolution, probably had something to do with obtaining food, specifically with large-scale exploitation of herds. Conditions were ripe for such developments in the Near East. More specifically, conditions were ripe within a particular region which includes the cave on Mount Carmel as well as a number of other sites. The full-scale hunting of big game may have originated in lands along the coastline of what is now Israel, Lebanon, and Syria—in the corridor formed by the Mediterranean to the west, and to the east by the Lebanon Mountains and other ranges running parallel to the coast and walling the corridor off from the Syrian and Arabian deserts. This is the central idea of a study by Sally Binford, a synthesis of information from many sources, which suggests a new model or hypothesis to explain why the Near Eastern corridor became an evolutionary focal area.

Many factors helped bring large groups of people together in this area. Wild cattle, fallow deer, and other herd animals grazed in green wooded valleys which rose from the coastal plains and extended into the foothills of the mountains. When leaves and grasses became scarce they moved on, in the spring to pasturelands on the plains and in the fall to highland meadows tucked away in the foothills. Small bands of hunters naturally concentrated where the game was, in the valleys and the narrowest places along seasonal migration routes, and a number of further circumstances encouraged increasing cooperation among them.

For one thing, pollen analysis and other studies indicate that a shift to somewhat drier climates occcurred about 40,000 to 45,000 years ago which probably helped step up the pace of evolution. It may have intensified the search for food among humans and animals. Herds became larger, and their movements through the valleys became more and more mass movements. For the hunters, risks increased as well as opportunities. A single band could go after wild cattle, for example. But it was a dangerous business, more suitable for a number of cooperating bands. These extinct animals should not be pictured as the docile cud-chewers of today's farmyards. They were fierce, fast on their feet, big (some of the bulls measuring 6½ feet high at the shoulder), and quite capable of fighting back.

Certain basic observations support the notion that major changes were under way in the Mediterranean corridor. The richest and deepest sites have been found where vegetation and game were most abundant, in the valleys on the western slopes of the coastal ranges. The Mount Carmel cave and rock shelter lie in such a valley, and so do other important sites. For example, farther inland, about 50 miles from Haifa and not far from Nazareth at the narrowest part of a pass to the mountains of Lebanon, is the enormous Qafzeh Cave where the remains of at least seven individuals were found more than 30 years ago, transitional people resembling those found at the Mount Carmel shelter.

Investigators recently revisited this site, which had been blown up by British troops as a suspected Israeli ammunition depot. After spending about six weeks removing the debris of the explosion, tons of fallen rock, they found two beautifully preserved skeletons, enclosed them in blocks of plaster, and flew them back to Jerusalem by helicopter. Since then about half a dozen more individuals have been recovered. Although a full report has yet to be published, the skeletons have already been identified as the remains of people who were very closely related to individuals of the modern type—and they were still using Neanderthal tools.

Western valley sites have deposits up to about 75 feet deep where lower layers contain Neanderthal tool kits and, in most cases, layers above contain later tool kits with high proportions of blades, tool kits characteristic of a modern type of people and representing long periods of occupation. There are also signs that wild cattle were hunted intensively. At two sites, the Mount Carmel shelter and a shelter located in a bluff north of Beirut in Lebanon, quantities of cattle bones increase sharply in late Neanderthal levels. One level at the Lebanese shelter contains the bones of only about a dozen individual animals, while the level immediately above it contains more than 500 individuals.

These and other observations make a good case that the evolution of people of the modern type occurred in the Near East. As far as their appearance in Europe and elsewhere is concerned, there are two theories. The migration theory states that they arose in the Near East, moved northwest as well as in other directions, and dominated and eventually replaced the Neanderthals, who had not evolved sufficiently to hold on to their ancestral lands. Perhaps Neanderthals had adapted too well to glacial conditions in the sense that when their world changed they could not change with it. This is hardly an unusual state

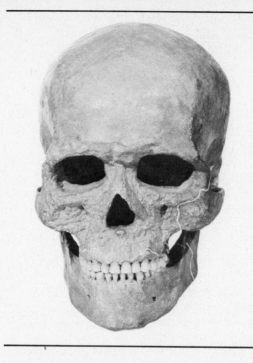

Reconstructed skull
of Cro-Magnon man

of affairs. Groups exist today, such as the Kalahari Bushmen and the Afrikaaners of South Africa, which face extinction because they find it difficult to adjust to a changing world.

People like ourselves were first recognized at the famous Cro-Magnon shelter located in the limestone cliffs of Les Eyzies. In 1868, workers building a railroad through the Vezere Valley discovered five skeletons deep in the rock at the back of the shelter, the remains of individuals with small faces, high foreheads, protruding chins, and other physical features typical of today's populations. (Incidentally, the cliff that includes the site is still inhabited and provides a ready-made rear wall for one of the village's most popular tourist hotels.)

According to the migration theory, Cro-Magnon people came from the Near East and appeared in Europe more than 35,000 years ago during a period of relatively mild, moist climates. They brought a new way of life with them. The change can be observed in their artifacts, among other things. They had mastered the art of shaping flints to a degree difficult to appreciate unless you actually try it yourself. Many archeologists are skillful flint workers, and Bordes is one of the best. The most beautiful hand ax in my own collection is one he made for me in a few minutes during a luncheon break at the Combe Grenal dig. But generally it takes several attempts to make one good tool, and the odds are that Cro-Magnon people achieved better results.

They developed a special technique to obtain the blades—the long slender flakes out of which most of their tools were made. The first step was to prepare a roughly cylindrical flint core, a nucleus perhaps 4 to 6 inches long, and then to rest a bone or antler punch on the top of the core near the edge and strike the punch sharply with a hammerstone. The blow chipped a narrow sliver off the side of the core, and many more slivers were detached by successive blows along the edge in an inward-spiraling path. The peeling operation was very efficient. Payton Sheets of California State University in Fresno and Guy Muto of Idaho State University used it to remove 83 blades from a prepared obsidian core weighing 1.8 pounds, a total length of more than 55 feet of acute cutting edge. According to one estimate, only about 6 feet of cutting edge would have resulted if the same core had been worked by earlier methods. Incidentally, full-scale cooperative hunting probably favored the development of this technique, stressing the need for cutting tools which could be manufactured rapidly and in large quantities.

New tools and new varieties of old tools were developed during the period from about 13,000 to 35,000 years ago—a wide selection of burins to make differently shaped grooves and slots, composite tools consisting of several barbs, other flint elements set into grooved hafts, spear throwers, harpoons, lamps, and so on. Tools made of bone, antler, and ivory as well as flint turn up in increasing proportions in excavated tool collections. The first invented material was clay mixed with powdered bone as a binder; it was molded into female figurines and other items. People also engaged in such specialized activities as reindeer hunting, mammoth hunting, and fishing.

The Neanderthals of western Europe had no chance against Cro-Magnon people and their institutions. In any competition for the best living places and hunting grounds, which must have occurred on many occasions, Neanderthals came out second best. All fossil traces of the heavy-browed, heavy-limbed "natives" vanish from the record, together with their toolmaking techniques and tool kits and most of their characteristic tools. Bordes reports signs of cultural decline in some of the upper layers at Combe Grenal, fewer tools, made crudely out of poorly prepared flint nodules. The end seems to have come with dramatic abruptness at certain sites where layers containing Cro-Magnon tools lie directly above Neanderthal layers.

Impressed by such evidence, a number of investigators have suggested that the Neanderthals were wiped out in a relatively short time, almost as if by plan. This theory is not in good standing today. It is doubtful that the capacity for systematic mass extermination evolved so early. Other evidence suggests a more gradual and complicated process. Conflicts and catastrophes probably took place here and there. Some of the new people may have regarded their less advanced contemporaries in the way that some early American settlers regarded the Indians, as

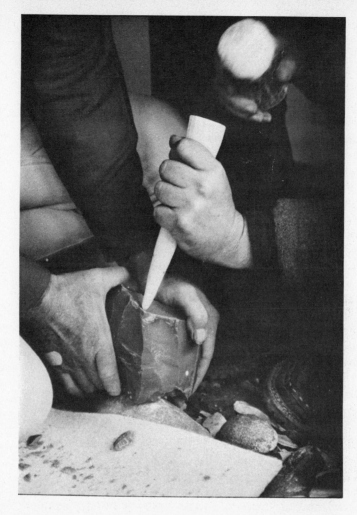

Punched blade technique: bone punch, as probably used in Cro-Magnon times

creatures so brutish and inferior that they could be hunted and killed for the fun of it.

But things happened somewhat more gradually in other places. One cave in the Les Eyzies area includes a layer that is probably Neanderthal; but it contains a tool kit with a relatively high proportion of knives, some of them made on long narrow flakes in a manner closely resembling later techniques developed to an advanced stage by Cro-Magnon flint workers. As a matter of fact, the resemblance is so close that at one time the layer was believed to represent a Cro-Magnon rather than a Neanderthal occupation. Perhaps Neanderthals, having already experimented with new toolmaking techniques, learned quickly from the newcomers and joined their tribes in certain localities and eventually became assimilated. All of us have some Neanderthal genes.

Stages in making
punched blade tool

In other places, Neanderthal bands may have retreated and hidden themselves in a last effort to endure. In fact, some prehistorians believe that they may not have died out yet, and several Soviet-led expeditions are reported to have gone into the Himalayas to check the theory that the Abominable Snowman is a surviving Neanderthal. Although this very slender possibility is not widely entertained, some evidence exists for less extreme theories. The last surviving wild Indian in North America, a member of a tribe from northern California, died in 1916 after having spent years living undetected with a few people of his tribe in forests and canyons near densely settled areas. Similarly, pockets of Neanderthals may have survived for centuries before the breed died out entirely.

This is the story of what happened, according to the migration theory. Investigators who do not go along with the theory agree that Neanderthals were replaced by Cro-Magnons, but they doubt that Cro-Magnons came from the Near East. Their argument rests on the notion of independent origins, the notion that evolution can proceed along parallel lines in different parts of the world. The transition from Neanderthal to modern-type people took place in the Near East, to be sure, but not only in the Near East. It may also have taken place in a number of other places during the same general period, in Europe, for example. Consider the Les Eyzies cave containing the layer made up of Neanderthal as well as Cro-Magnon tools. That can be interpreted as indicating that the Neanderthals learned from and joined the visitors from the Near East. It can also be interpreted as a sign that the Neanderthals were developing on their own, and that in the process of developing they evolved into modern-type people.

Furthermore, fossil remains excavated in Czechoslovakia and other parts of eastern Europe, although fragmentary, suggest the existence of transitional Neanderthals, while David Frayer of the University of Kansas reports certain Neanderthal-like traits in remains of early Cro-Magnon people. There are hints that similar developments occurred some 4000 miles away in southern Africa, and also in the Far East. A mixed tool kit has been found at the Chinese site mentioned in the last **185** chapter, the one near the Great Wall. The site includes a high proportion of denticulates and other typical Neanderthal tools—but nearly a third of the tools are the sort found predominantly in Cro-Magnon sites. It is clearly a transitional type of tool kit, and may have been used by a transitional type of man.

We do not know enough to choose between the two theories. The migration theory finds support in the fact that as far as the fossil record is concerned, the best evidence for people in transition comes from the Near East. Certainly the change might also have taken place elsewhere, but in general, direct fossil evidence is limited. Furthermore, the notion of independent origins sometimes seems to lean too heavily on coincidence, on accepting that people in different places can make the same sort of tools without communicating with one another. There is something more direct and appealing about the idea of technologies spreading out from central regions of origin.

On the other hand, considering that people are far more alike than they are different and that they faced very similar problems in the prehistoric past, it should hardly be surprising that they generally arrived at very similar solutions. Then as now, people may well have developed inventions independently in different places. Also, the very appeal of the migration theory and a central region is something to be wary of. It has the dangerous attraction of any Garden of Eden theory— namely, that it tends to oversimplify a highly complex situation.

In any case, the Neanderthals were definitely on the way out. They had learned to cope with glacial conditions, and their ability to endure is all the more impressive considering that as far as we know they had neither snowshoes nor sleds for getting about during subzero winters. But from about 35,000 years ago on, all the action and new ideas and new inventions would be the work of modern people; and for the next 25,000 years or so we know them best from the record they left in France, especially in the Les Eyzies area. The record includes four major types of tool kits, dated by a method which depends, as does the potassium-argon clock, on the steady rate of decay of a radioactive element, in this case a radioactive form of carbon known as carbon 14. The technique, which involves chemical analyses of charcoal samples, works best for material less than 40,000 years old. It has provided the following approximate durations for the following tool kits:

Perigordian: Named after the region which includes Les Eyzies; about 23,000 years to more than 35,000 years old

Aurignacian: Named after the Aurignac site in the Pyrenees; 20,000 years to about 35,000 old

Solutrean: Named after the extensive open-air site near the village of Solutre in east central France; about 17,000 years to 20,000 years old

Magdalenian: Named after the La Madeleine shelter about 3 miles from Les Eyzies; 12,000 to 17,000 years old

Recent investigations emphasize the complexity that lies behind this deceptively straightforward sequence. An interesting early Perigordian occupation layer has been found in a cave in the village of Arcy-sur-Cure about 100 miles southeast of Paris, one of the few caves which happens to have been discovered by design rather than by accident. About 20 years ago, André Leroi-Gourhan of the University of Paris was surveying the village for prehistoric camping places and noticed, high on a hillside, a little shelter formed by a peculiarly curved section of rock.

He suspected that the shelter might be the top of a buried cave, a possibility reinforced by two further clues. Badgers in the area are good cave locaters. They seem to sense the location of hidden chambers that will make cozy nests, and, sure enough, there was a badger hole in the hillside with some flint tools in it. Also, a large oak tree was growing in the rich loosened soil near the foot of the hill, another local mark of caved-in places. The first season of digging revealed a thick layer of red earth, rich in prehistoric remains. Excavating has been going on at the site periodically ever since.

The layer above Neanderthal layers contains an early Perigordian tool kit, including characteristic knives with a curved back blunted by the removal of tiny parallel flakes as well as denticulates and other tools commonly found in Neanderthal deposits. A tentlike structure apparently existed inside the cave entrance. There are a dozen postholes arranged in a semicircle around several hearths; the posts were probably mammoth tusks. In one of the holes was an intact tusk with a piece of limestone wedged against it for support. Leroi-Gourhan estimates that a family unit of no more than 15 persons lived here about 32,000 years ago.

Indications of how their descendants lived some 10,000 years later come from a site just off the main street of Les Eyzies, the Abri Pataud. (*Abri* is French for "shelter" and Pataud is the family name of the farmers who owned the site in the nineteenth century.) The site lies directly against the limestone cliff that dominates the town, a few minutes' walk from the hotel built into the old Cro-Magnon shelter. It has been excavated by Hallam Movius of Harvard University. Bedrock was reached at a depth of more than 30 feet after six seasons of digging which uncovered 14 occupation layers. In all, more than 50,000 worked pieces of flint have been cataloged.

The third layer from the top contains a tool kit typical of those generally found at more recent sites. It is the evolved or final Perigordian of about 23,000 years ago. Its outstanding feature is a row of hearths more than 30 feet long under the rocky overhang of the shelter. Lying around the hearths are smooth river pebbles, most of them broken and colored red or black by the action of heat. These stones were very probably pot boilers that had been heated in a fire and then dropped into water to bring it to a boil for cooking. American Indians used the technique not long ago, and Basque shepherds in the Cantabrian Mountains of northern Spain still use it occasionally to boil milk and water.

Movius has tested this hypothesis by direct experiment. He heated some river pebbles, tossed them into a pail, and observed that they boiled water effectively. He also observed that after being used three or four times the stones split in two, and split into smaller and smaller pieces during subsequent plunges. When the pieces reached a certain size they no longer split but burst into fragments, a phenomenon which undoubtedly startled prehistoric man as much as it did Movius. This experiment produced shattered stones and fragments closely resembling debris in the Perigordian layer, implying the existence of some kind of skin containers or, more probably, of wooden vessels.

The row of hearths is only part of a large complex. In front of the row and also roughly parallel to the rear of the shelter is a row of large limestone blocks, some weighing half a ton or more. They form a solid barrier, except for a gap at one end which may have served as the doorway into a long house built for a community of several families. The entire arrangement and the tool assemblage found with it suggest that the people who lived here huddled around their fires during glacial winters, organized themselves into larger groups, and engaged in a wider variety of activities than the Perigordians of earlier times. Sites with Aurignacian tool kits are quite different, and some of them include the first known cave art. Also found were special kinds of scrapers and burins and a variety of elaborate bone tools such as points with split bases for firm hafting, presumably used at the ends of spear or javelin shafts.

The deepest nine Abri Pataud layers, ending at bedrock and covering a period of about 4000 to 5000 years, contain Aurignacian tool kits. Signs of change during that period include sharp reductions in the proportions of some bone and flint tools and the appearance of new types, notably new bone points. Also, while later Aurignacians burned wood in their hearths, earlier generations of perhaps 33,000 or more years ago burned bone predominantly, probably because they lived under cold and relatively barren conditions when wood was scarce. Bone must have served as a last-resort fuel then as it did in even earlier times, the practice having been observed at a number of Neanderthal sites, for example, at Combe Grenal.

Movius found an unusual pattern in one of the early Aurignacian layers, a complex made up of two shallow pits and seven hearths. The pits are located near the front of the shelter, measure 4 to 5 feet across, and served some purpose which is still obscure. One possibility is that they may represent the floors of small conical huts made of hides supported by a central pole, something like American Indian tepees. (Pits of this sort have been found at Indian sites.) Eskimos make similar huts in the Canadian Arctic today, using large stones at the base to hold the hides down, and large stones were also placed around the Abri Pataud pits.

Another noteworthy site is the Morin Cave in northern Spain which was probably occupied on and off over a span of some 50,000 years. It includes, besides the Neanderthal layers mentioned in the preceding chapter, a number of Aurignacian living floors. One of them is of special interest since it has yielded evidence of intensive occupation and a unique burial complex. According to Leslie Freeman's reconstruction, its past began about 30,000 years ago when a family of about half a dozen members moved in, cleared off and leveled the floor, and proceeded to make themselves at home for 10 to 25 years.

They dug a roughly rectangular depression about 15 feet from the cave mouth, built stone walls, and set up a row of posts to support a windbreak or roof. Five postholes were detected because the soil filling them was softer and darker than the surrounding soil, and finer in texture. Also, in two cases the dark circular area included a still darker central area, suggesting that a post had rotted away and been replaced. Careful excavating uncovered marks made by a digging stick when the posts were being replaced, curved grooves whose shape and location indicate that they were made by a right-handed person kneeling as he dug. The result of this construction was a shelter within a shelter, a partly subterranean hut inside the cave.

The most striking find came from a deeper part of the cave. More than 40 feet from the entrance were two burial mounds, and one of them contained a remarkable object—a kind of natural earth model, a rounded three-dimensional mold of a person and associated grave goods. What had happened over the years was that as the body decomposed, the soft parts were replaced by fine sediments which filled the cavities and ultimately produced a replica of the body, a pseudomorph.

A study of the mold reveals that the buried person had been more than 6 feet tall. He had been decapitated and laid on his side with arms flexed in front. The mold also shows traces of what may have been thongs or rope used to bind the arms, as well as another pseudomorph representing a small animal, perhaps a kid or deer, which had been placed over the dead person's head. Freeman spent more than a month digging in this area and preparing the earth around the burial so that with the aid of winches and a home-built railroad it could be removed in a solid 2-ton clay block. A model of the Aurignacian pseudomorph is on exhibit at the Smithsonian Institution in Washington.

The coexistence of Perigordian and Aurignacian tool kits in France raises the same sort of problems that have arisen in the case of Bordes' four Neanderthal tool kits (see Chapter 9). Do the tool kits rep-

Freeman Aurignacian
"pseudomorph"
model on exhibit at
Smithsonian Institute

resent different cultures, people with different backgrounds and traditions, or different functions, the same people doing different things?
Proponents of the culture theory believe that the Aurignacians came
from some area outside western Europe. But it is difficult to understand
how these hunter-gatherers and the Perigordians could have lived as
contemporaries for thousands of years in the same region without influencing one another appreciably, a surprising state of affairs considering people's capacity for minding their neighbor's business.

Another point may be taken as evidence against the cultural view
and in favor of the functional view. Denise Bordes observes that as a
rule Perigordian tool kits are found in sites with relatively thin layers,
which suggests brief or intermittent occupations. Also, the sites are
generally scattered throughout the Les Eyzies region and located in dif-

ferent kinds of terrain. Aurignacian tool kits, on the other hand, tend to be concentrated in narrow valleys or against cliff walls which contain clusters of neighboring shelters. The archeological layers are usually on the thick side, implying that there were more people or longer occupations or both.

The different site locations support the view that there were functional differences, that special activities were required to cope with different environments. So do new findings reported recently by Jean-Philippe Rigaud of the University of Bordeaux. Excavating in the Flageolet rock shelter not far from Combe Grenal, he has found three Perigordian tool kits, previously interpreted as representing three cultures, on separate areas of the same living floor. This strongly suggests that members of the band were conducting different kinds of work at the site.

The Solutrean tool kits which appeared about 20,000 years ago with the passing of the Perigordian and Aurignacian, arose during a period of intense cold. In fact, conditions were probably colder then than at any previous time during the past million years or more. The Scandinavian ice sheet covered Scotland and most of Ireland and, together with other glacial systems, held so much water that sea levels fell sharply. As in previous glacial periods, there was no English Channel and no North Sea; a plain connected England and France, and the Baltic Sea was a vast fresh-water lake. People living in southern France had to contend with severe climates, with winters which may have lasted nine months and brought average temperatures as low as 10 degrees Fahrenheit below zero.

Philip Smith of the University of Montreal, suggests that the Solutreans may have originated in the southeast corner of France—in the lower valley of the Rhone River, not far from the edges of the Alpine glaciers. Occupation layers at a number of sites in this region include tools closely resembling those found in early Solutrean tool kits. The same layers also include Neanderthal tools such as thick Quina-type scrapers which, as far as we know, had disappeared from Europe and from the rest of the Old World some 10,000 years before.

The possibility exists that the ancestors of the Solutreans were Neanderthals living past their time in a kind of lost-world environment, or else they were people using Neanderthal toolmaking techniques to cope with the same glacial conditions Neanderthals had to cope with. The discovery of skeletal remains in the precisely dated deposits would help decide between these two possibilities. But the terrain would certainly have made a good retreat. The lower Rhone valley is a rugged mountainous land, a backwater with caves and shelters located in remote canyons and ravines. In such a region, people might not only have preserved old toolmaking traditions but also have developed unusual techniques.

The Solutreans endured for 2000 or 3000 years. During that relatively brief span they introduced significant changes. Along with scrapers and burins and quantities of other ordinary items, their tool kits included some of the most beautifully shaped tools ever made. To cite only one example, they produced laurel leaf blades, slender, symmetrical, flat pieces tapering to a point. Dozens of different kinds, long blades and short blades, thin and thick ones, were produced, all variations on the same basic theme. Some sites contained so many laurel leaves and other finely shaped tools that they may have been special workshops organized for a flourishing export trade.

In its extreme form, such craftsmanship is the earliest sign of the can-you-top-this quality of human nature, the tendency to exhaust the possibilities of a technique or idea. The same spirit that impels modern people to race engines to the breaking point or engrave as many Lord's Prayers as possible on the head of a pin or create the most elaborate op-art effects was working at full force in Solutrean individuals. Like most virtuosos, they were upon occasion carried away by their own abilities.

Many laurel leaves, for instance, are far too delicate for any practical purpose. The longest one known to date, found in part of a cache of blades uncovered at a site near the Loire River in southeastern France in 1873, was nearly 14 inches long, about 4 inches across at its widest point, and only about ¼ inch thick. The blade could never have been applied with any force. It would have snapped in two if someone had tried to cut meat with it or use it as a spear point.

Tools like this one represent a new stage in the development of abstract thinking. Hunters had spent extra time producing finely worked hand axes and other implements 200,000 or more years before, but not with such skill and in such large quantities. As far as the archeological record reveals, the Solutreans were the first people to engage on a regular basis in making tools as symbols. They doubtless used the tools for some special function, in rituals or as showpieces, a form of art for art's sake or for some purpose combining art and utility. They may have been items for trading, a kind of prehistoric money.

The Solutreans may have invented the bow and arrow. Not long ago Eduardo Ripoll-Perello of Barcelona University dug in a cave in the mountains of southeast Spain, the Cueva de Ambrosio, and found an assortment of points closely resembling arrowheads found by the thousands at American Indian sites. Indeed, if the same points had been uncovered at one of these sites, they would have been identified without question as arrowheads. Similar points have been found in other Spanish caves, and they provide the earliest indirect evidence for the invention of the bow and arrow. (The earliest direct evidence, from a 10,000-year-old open site in Denmark, consists of two arrow shafts preserved in water-logged deposits with tanged arrowheads still in place.)

Lawrence Straus of the University of New Mexico recently studied

36 Solutrean sites in the Asturian and Basque provinces of northern Spain. He reports two basic tool kits. One includes many projectile points, endscrapers, sidescrapers, and denticulate or notched pieces; it is associated with Asturian sites located on the coastal plain or in wide mountain valleys, and with the remains of red deer, horses, cattle, and bison. The other tool kit, found at sites in "the steep broken terrain" of rugged Basque hill country, includes few points, many burins, backed blades, and bladelets; it is associated with ibex and fox remains. People were obviously doing different things in different settings, perhaps the same people moving seasonally between coastal plain and uplands, a point which only further research can determine.

The Solutreans vanished abruptly; it was "like the puffing-out of a candle," according to one investigator. Their passing set the stage for perhaps the most spectacular development of the period, the rise and rapid expansion of the Magdalenian tradition. Part of the record has been found at the site for which the tradition is named. It lies on the banks of the Vézère River, in the hollow of a massive limestone cliff overhang. To reach it one climbs up one side of a ridge rising above the river valley, passes a ruined medieval abbey at the top, and then goes down the other side of the ridge along the long face of a cliff to a place surrounded by a high wire fence with a sign that says "Abri de la Madeleine—Fouilles Interdites (Digging Prohibited).

The setting is remote, hidden in the trees on a hairpin loop of the river with water rushing past and meadows nearby. But things hummed here during prehistoric times, perhaps 13,000 to 14,000 years ago. This was predominantly reindeer country, and there were also herds of bison and wild horses in the valley and salmon in the rapids of the river. Collections from this site feature tools made of bone and antler and ivory, often decorated with engravings of reindeer, horses, bison, mammoths, abstract spiral designs, fish and stylized fish motifs, and, more rarely, crude human figures.

Magdalenian tool kits include shaft straighteners, spear points, wands of unknown purpose and, above all, the first harpoons—a rich variety of them, long and short, with single and double rows of differently shaped barbs. There are also bone needles, first seen in Solutrean deposits but by now developed and used in quantity, generally containing eyes which must have required piercing with tiny flint awls. The needles imply the wearing on a large scale of fitted clothing made of hides sewn together, presumably with sinews.

Another prominent item is the spear thrower, a device designed essentially to amplify muscle power and still used today by the Australian aborigines. It consisted of a thin flat piece of wood about 2 or 3 feet long with a barb at one end that hooks into a hole in the end of a spear shaft. Held over the shoulder with shaft in place, the thrower is snapped forward by a sharp twist of the wrist in a motion that propels the spear several times faster and farther than would be possible with the unaided hand. Prehistoric hunters probably also had wooden spear throwers, although the only surviving specimens are made of antler or ivory. These devices disappear toward the end of Magdalenian times in France, perhaps because bows and arrows were beginning to be used on a widespread basis.

Excavations have been resumed at the La Madeleine shelter after years of archeological inactivity, except for the efforts of enthusiastic amateurs digging for discarded flints in the dirt outside the wire fence, dirt excavated decades ago. Jean-Marc Bouvier, one of Bordes' associates, has found large numbers of artifacts including narrow little blades which are less than half an inch long and were made as cutting elements to be hafted in composite tools. His main objective is to obtain a clearer picture of the origin and evolution of the toolmakers, and so far he has dug to a depth of more than 12 feet and identified several Magdalenian layers representing different stages of development.

The shelter itself is only part of a larger living complex. It marks the first in a line of prehistoric row houses, occupied shelters strung out side by side for several hundred feet along the cliff. About 20 miles farther downstream along a 2-mile stretch of the Dordogne River is another row of shelters which housed an estimated 400 to 600 persons. This sort of housing pattern is often associated with the Magdalenians, particularly during their later stages. They tended increasingly to establish large concentrated settlements along low-lying river banks.

Such settlements were not confined to shelters and cliff edges. Rich and thick occupation layers, as yet unexcavated, extend out to the Vézère River at La Madeleine, and it seems that the people lived and worked in the open here and elsewhere, perhaps using the shelters only in the worst weather. As archeologists became more and more aware of this tendency, they began paying serious attention to reports of extensive open-air sites in areas containing no caves or shelters. Flints kept turning up during the plowing season on highland farms on the plateaus above the cliffs.

Most digging has been done in caves and shelters containing deep protected deposits with many occupation layers, which offered the opportunity to go far back in time and reconstruct cultural changes. Current interest in sites on the open plains is in line with the renewed emphasis on wide excavations and the search for evidence of what people did, their full range of activities. A number of sites, known for some time in a broad area extending from western Europe to Siberia, were home bases for hunters of the woolly mammoth. (These are the creatures which in recent times have been found deep-frozen and almost perfectly preserved in Arctic ice crevasses where they fell millennia ago.)

For example, extensive traces of the hunters and their prey have been uncovered along the Don River in the southwestern Soviet Union. A cluster of rich sites is located near Kostenki, Russian for "bone village," where mammoth fossils were found in medieval times and regarded as the remains of half-human giants who lived in underground caverns. This area includes a row of eight hearths in which bone was burned, almost certainly because wood was scarce on the plains; the hearths may have been located inside a long house with a gabled wooden roof and clay-supported walls. Similar settlements have also been found in open stretches near the Ural and Caucasus Mountains, Czechoslovakia, and northern Germany.

Another interesting site, Pincevent, is a 25-acre Magdalenian settlement about 35 miles southeast of Paris, not far from the palace of Fontainebleau. After more than three years and 300,000 man-hours of digging, Leroi-Gourhan and his associates uncovered about 5 acres of what seems to have been a summer and fall camp for reindeer hunting.

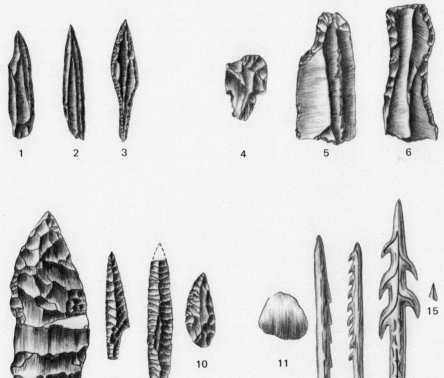

Major tool kits of modern-type prehistoric men in Europe

Perigordian
more than 35,000 to 23,000 years ago

1, 2, 3. Typical Perigordian points

Aurignacian
about 35,000 to 20,000 years ago

4. Nosed scraper
5. Nosed scraper
6. Blade

Solutrean
about 20,000 to 17,000 years ago

7. Laurel leaf
8. Shouldered point
9. Willow leaf
10. Unifacial point (worked on one side only)

Magdalenian
17,000 to 12,000 years ago

11. Scraper
12, 13. Harpoon with single row of barbs
14. Harpoon with double row of barbs
15. Triangle

One of half a dozen living floors consists of three hearths and three sleeping areas, all of which may have been enclosed by a large tent made of skins. The entire site is in a remarkable state of preservation and includes considerable pollen and animal remains as well as hearths. Things have been so little disturbed over the centuries that tiny chips have been found and fitted to the blades from which they were removed, and the source of the blades, the original flint core, has also been recovered nearby. An open-air museum established at the Pincevent site promises to become as great a tourist attraction as the Fontainbleau palace itself.

All the evidence tells of a powerful people who could live where they wanted to live, where the big herd animals were. And there is more than that in the record. Life was changing in response to factors beyond the control and knowledge of the people and as the result of a complex chain of events which involved geological forces and caused a major population explosion. Surviving signs of the change are everywhere. The most recent Magdalenians, people who lived 14,000 to

Artist's conception of camouflaged Magdalenian hunters stalking reindeer

Artist's conception of Cro-Magnon home, showing tents in rock shelter

12,000 years ago, occupied three to four times more sites than their predecessors, and occupied a large number of sites that had never been used before.

The change can also be seen at individual sites. At La Madeleine, for example, most occupation layers extended out from the cliffside toward the river. But the most recent layers happened to be by far the most extensive. They are also the widest and thickest and richest, including the most tools and the greatest variety of tools. The same pattern emerges at other sites, and it has been estimated that the total population of France alone increased from 15,000 to 50,000 during this period (in a world containing perhaps 10 million persons).

New studies, particularly those of Lewis Binford, indicate that the population explosion may have been one result of widespread geographical and biological changes accompanying the retreat of the Scandinavian ice sheet and other glaciers. The changes depended on the shape of the ocean basins, the contours of lands beneath the sea. In general the bottom does not dip sharply from the shoreline on out. There is a long gradual slope, a very gentle downhill grade, forming the continental shelf, which may extend as much as 800 miles off the Siberian coast in the Arctic Ocean. The shelf ends rather abruptly, with a precipitous drop at the edge to ocean floors more than 2 miles deep.

197

If sea levels started dropping today, and dropped at a steady rate of a foot per day, the slope of the continental shelf is such that in ten days the waves of the earth's oceans would recede about a mile on the average, adding that much dry land to national coasts. In a year or so sea levels would fall enough to expose some 11.5 million square miles of land that had once been submerged, a total area about the size of Africa. Most of the great harbors of the world would become lesser inland cities with a wide coastal plain separating them from the sea. New York City, for example, would lie stranded more than 100 miles from the Atlantic Ocean.

This is the way things stood about 20,000 years ago during early Solutrean times when the glaciers had completed one of their major advances. Masses of ice more than a mile high covered vast areas and captured enough water from the oceans to lower sea levels by 250 to 500 feet, exposing most of the continental shelf throughout the world.

Other changes affected the course of evolution. The coasts were more turbulent places than they are now and considerably less hospitable to life, human and otherwise. Since the land generally extended to the steep edge of the continental shelf, the waters along the shores were deep and cold. The contained relatively small quantities of plankton and other species, which provide food for schools of larger fish. Furthermore, most major rivers tended to flow swiftly into the seas, often cascading with a roar over the edge of the shelf—and such conditions are not particularly attractive to organisms which prefer quieter environments. According to Binford, only a few species of mollusk, mussel-like organisms, clung in clusters to rocks near the cascades, as compared to more than 40 species found in the sluggish flat delta regions of today's rivers.

More abundant times came with the melting and retreat of the glaciers. Ocean levels rose and waters crept back across the plains of the exposed continental shelf, covering them with a wide sunlit and sun-warmed shallow sea, a natural marine farmland where many forms of life flourished. And the cascades vanished as rivers, instead of spilling over the edge of the shelf, flowed into the shallows and merged less violently with the seas. The sheer bulk of marine life along the world's seacoasts is estimated to have increased more than a hundred times during the period from 16,000 to 20,000 years ago, and it is no coincidence that people seem to have begun eating seafood on a large scale during this period.

Life changed in the interior as well as along the coasts. Salmon and other fish that migrate upstream to spawn could not negotiate high coastal cascades; but when the cascades disappeared, they began using the rivers increasingly as waterways. And they turned up in southern France, among other places, in the Dordogne River and its tributaries and in the waters rushing past the fields and trees outside the La

Madeleine shelter. The region was also a stopping place for flocks of **199**
migratory birds on their way to new breeding grounds created by the
retreating glaciers.

The development of harpoons was part of the new technology
created to take advantage of these food sources. The existence of other
equipment made of less durable material can only be inferred. American Indians living on the northwest coast of the Pacific camp at salmon
runs suspend basket traps in the falls and remove the heads of the fish
on the spot before bringing their catch back to the village for drying.
Prehistoric people were capable of developing similar techniques. Sites
exist along the Dordogne River, near rapids where the banks are practically solid with fish scales, and salmon vertebrae are found in many
sites occupied by the Magdalenians.

But the population explosion was not due simply to a larger food
supply and the development of large-scale food preservation and storage. The chief difference was a more steady and reliable food supply.
Migratory fish and birds came at a most convenient season, during the
spring when food yields from reindeer and other migratory animals declined because herds dispersed to take care of their young. Binford suggests that one result was a reduced need to pack up and move to new
hunting grounds, an increased trend toward all-year-round settlements.
Why settling down should lead to population growth is still a matter of
debate and continuing research. But better nutrition had something to
do with it, especially the building up of adequate body-fat reserves in
women, a condition which seems to favor fertility. Also, as long as
mothers had to keep on the move, they were limited to one child every
three or four years, because that was all they could carry. Nomadic peoples have always resorted to abortion, infanticide, and taboos against
becoming pregnant during lactation, practices which could be relaxed in
more settled times.

According to this reconstruction of the past, many of the conditions favoring expansion and population growth had existed before,
during former glacial retreats. More ancient times had seen floodings of
the great coastal plains, the vanishing of cascades beneath rising waters,
and migrations of previous generations of fish and birds. The new elements this time were more people; the world's population had been increasing steadily from an estimated 125,000 about 2 million years ago to
10 million persons by 10,000 B.C. People with the brains, technology,
and capacity for social organization needed to exploit the changing environment.

The record is rich in western Europe, not only because the region was densely occupied in prehistoric times, but also because so
many archeologists have lived and excavated there. But human beings
were evolving all over the world, multiplying and expanding into a
great many other regions. For example, hunter-gatherers reached Aus-

Mass slaughter site:
fossil bison remains
from Olsen Chubbuck
site, eastern Colorado

tralia about 40,000 years ago, five millennia before Aurignacian families were camping in the Abri Pataud and Morin Cave, an outstanding achievement considering that the crossing required island hopping and boats seaworthy enough to negotiate some 50 miles of open water. Finds in Australia include the world's oldest ground-stone axes, reliably dated back at least 20,000 years, which is so much earlier than anything comparable found in Europe or the Near East that one British investigator came, saw, and simply refused to accept the evidence.

People probably entered the New World about 25,000 years ago or perhaps, according to new dating techniques, as much as 50,000 years ago. Apparently they did not have to make a water crossing. The glaciers had begun to melt, but sea levels were still low and hunter-gatherers followed mammoths, mastodons, bison, and other immigrants over a plain more than a thousand miles wide connecting northern Asia and Alaska. North America has a number of spectacular mass-slaughter sites, generally located in marshy areas or stream beds, often at sharp bends or meanders which form deep-cut natural walls and keep animals from escaping. The remains of about 200 bison have been found at one

Mass slaughter: reconstruction of bison being stampeded over cliff

such site in Colorado. But it should be reemphasized that although killing big game has always been a glamorous thing, most bands subsisted
on a day-to-day diet which also included ample quantities of small
game and plant foods.

Social and psychological changes were under way at an accelerating rate and on a worldwide basis. Some of them can be inferred from
studies of flint artifacts. If assemblages of Neanderthal tools from two
widely separated sites in western Europe were thoroughly mixed, even
an expert would find it extremely difficult to sort them out again. But in
a similar experiment involving tool kits from the period that started
only a few millennia later, the job of unmixing two Solutrean tool kits,
for example, would be much easier.

The difference represents a change in outlook. Neanderthal
groups did not make tools according to strictly controlled and distinctive regional patterns. But later as populations increased and people
lived closer to one another geographically, they unconsciously developed ways of increasing what Edwin Wilmsen of the University of
Michigan calls their social distance. They developed a new quality of
self-awareness and group awareness, a way of making themselves distinct from others; an enhanced sense of style, which is reflected in the
making of their artifacts. And with all this came a new breed of human
being and modern races and a new brain, the same brain that shapes
our activities today.

Death rituals and personal adornment as factors in the origin of art; the earliest known "art galleries" discovered in caves of France and Spain; ridicule of the Spanish nobleman who first recognized the cave paintings as the works of prehistoric people; speculations about the role of caves and cave art in prehistoric times; the relationship between retreating glaciers and the decline of cave art in Europe; the invention of agriculture and the end of prehistory

CHAPTER 11   THE GOLDEN AGE OF PREHISTORY

In the archeological record of *Homo sapiens*, religion occurs with the appearance of the Neanderthals and art with Cro-Magnon or modern-type people. The oldest known paintings have been found in association with occupation layers deposited more than 30,000 years ago, at least 40,000 years after the earliest known burial ceremonies. It seems that some 40 millennia of evolution were required before descendants of the first "philosophers" to think about death and an afterlife found reasons to portray things that were important to them.

Art came with a burst in the sense that from the very beginning the record includes works performed in a mature and established style. Of course, previous cruder efforts existed, but until further evidence turns up, we face the possibility that art indeed appeared full-blown, and we must try to explain why. The earliest hint of an aesthetic sense in our forerunners comes from the Olduvai Gorge. Near the bottom of the gorge, in places where *Australopithecus* foraged more than 1.5 million years ago, are lumps of translucent, pale pink quartzite, all of them unworked and obtained from a single mineral deposit, and all apparently picked up and carried around.

Later, during Acheulian times, we find crude designs engraved on bone and occasional hand axes shaped far more beautifully than required for strictly utilitarian purposes. Such pieces may represent pride of craftsmanship more than art, but they show that people were expressing feelings for proportion and symmetry several hundred thousand years ago. Many factors were undoubtedly involved in the origin of art itself, for example, in the use of symbols connected with death rituals. The notion that death is an apparent ending only and that part of a person lives on demands external signs of some sort—something that will remain intact after the rituals are done.

One of the earliest symbols known from excavations is a hand ax found in southern Tanzania and about 250,000 years old. More than 2 **203** feet long and weighing about 25 pounds, it is much too massive to use and, like certain Solutrean blades mentioned in Chapter 10, may have been designed for ceremonial purposes. The wolf skull at Lazaret also served as a symbol (see Chapter 8) and so did the stones, ibex horns, and cave-bear skulls, which Neanderthal people arranged in patterns around their graves. Judging by an unusual piece of bone found in the Morin Cave, a piece with a vaguely defined animal-like form engraved on it, they wanted to preserve certain images. It would be surprising to learn that they had not produced other patterns and symbols of permanence, designs and figures may have vanished long ago.

Personal adornment was another precursor of art. There was a time before people cared enough about themselves, before they were sufficiently aware of themselves, to want to appear more attractive or add to themselves. Then something happened to bring an increasing self-consciousness, perhaps the presence of more people in larger groups and the threat of a loss of identity. Part of the response was to color one's face and body, to use the personal pronoun more, and say, in effect: "I am an individual; look at me; pay attention to me. I am different, something special."

Identity problems may also have arisen in a wider social context. Populations were on the rise. There were more bands abroad, more meetings of bands, more individuals than one could recognize and remember. It became increasingly important to make oneself known as a member of the group. Recent studies by Martin Wobst of the University of Massachusetts suggest that certain kinds of personal adornment served to distinguish friend from foe, especially items visible at a distance (say, beyond spear or bow-and-arrow range).

The earliest sign of such changes comes from the Neanderthals. The flowers at the grave in Shanidar, for instance, indicate a new feeling for the importance of individuals. Also, Neanderthal sites commonly include natural pigments, probably to serve as cosmetics for the dead in "viewings" and burial ceremonies as well as for the living. The pigments are lumps of black manganese and red ocher, some sharpened like pencils and others scratched presumably to make powder.

The new spirit flowered among Cro-Magnon people, who not only used cosmetics, but made the earliest known jewelry. They wore ivory bracelets, necklaces of pierced teeth and fish vertebrae, and clothes decorated with rows of colored beads. Their more elaborate decorations were related to a general increase in the complexity of communal living, to the rise of more advanced hunting methods. Jewelry did a great deal more than beautify. It was the first sign of a new way of organizing people, foreshadowing radical changes which were to appear in full force in the earliest towns and cities and states. It served not only to identify members of different tribes, marking off one group from another, but also to identify special individuals within tribes, the first elites or proto-elites.

Judging by today's hunter-gatherers, small bands living in back-country areas of Australia and Africa, among other places (see Chapters 15 and 16), the hunter-gatherers of times past lived mainly as equals among equals, without the benefit of big men or chiefs. But equality had to go by the boards with the coming together of larger and larger populations in the Les Eyzies region and elsewhere. People had to devise new ways of controlling society, controlling themselves, and one result may have been the emergence of the first leaders and exchange systems.

Evidence bearing on this possibility is being gathered by Olga Soffer of the City University of New York in studies of Magdalenian-type sites on the Russian plains. Archeological remains include amber for beads and perhaps amulets obtained from sources up to 5 days or about 60 to 90 miles away, and marine shells for bracelets and necklaces from the Black Sea some 25 days or more than 500 miles away. Soffer believes that there may have been organized networks involving the exchange of furs, meat, and other utilitarian products for rare and exotic material to mark people of high status.

This is the framework, the social context, in which art had its beginnings. The world's first great "art movement" lasted more than 20,000 years, from Aurignacian to Magdalenian times. Some if its most spectacular products are found in underground galleries, away from natural light, in the passages and chambers and niches of limestone caves; they indicate in a most vivid fashion how completely hunting dominated the attention and imagination of prehistoric people. They rarely drew people, and never anything that would be recognized as a landscape, and there are a wide variety of signs which have no obvious meaning to us. The overwhelming concern was with game animals seen as individuals, clearly defined and detached, and isolated from their natural settings.

It is difficult to conceive of a reason that explains why most of the earliest art known should have been produced in lands which are still among the centers of artistic endeavor in modern times. But such happens to be the case; the great majority of art caves are located in France and Spain. According to one count, France has 65 sites and Spain 30. About half of all known sites are concentrated in three regions: along a 99-mile stretch of the northern coast of Spain; in the French Pyrenees, 50 miles south of Toulouse; and in the countryside around Les Eyzies.

The Les Eyzies region includes the largest cluster of art sites as well as the most striking of the lot, the famous Lascaux cave located in the woods on a plateau above the valley of the Vézère. Four boys and a

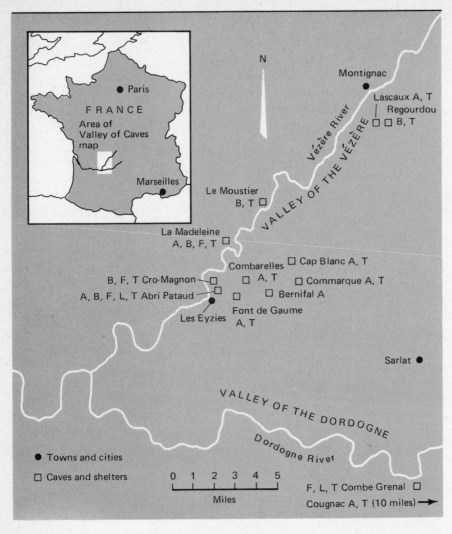

"Valley of Caves"
Homo sapiens Sites,
in Les Eyzies Region,
France

Things found:

A Art   F Fire   T Tools
B Bones of primates   L Living floors

dog discovered it during a walk early one September afternoon in 1940, the dog disappearing down a hole half-concealed by roots and moss and the boys scrambling after. (Such neighborhood boys are officially credited with the discovery of about a dozen art caves, but the unofficial count would be considerably higher since archeologists often receive sole credit for caves they originally learned about from these discoverers.)

What the boys were the first to see by the wavering light of their homemade oil lamp, thousands of visitors, tourists as well as archeologists and artists, have seen many times since. There is no prelude to the splendor of the Lascaux gallery. The entrance leads down a short flight of stairs directly into the main hall, into a world of huge horned animals painted in red and black. In a way, the first moment is the high point of the visit. You stand silent in the dark; lights are turned on, and images appear as if projected on a screen, a kind of three-dimensional panorama since the wall curves in front of you and around at the sides. For that moment, almost before the eye has a chance to look and before the ideas and questions start flowing, you take it all in at once.

Then the experience breaks into parts. The animals become individuals in a frieze along the upper wall of the hall, along an overhanging ledge formed by the scooping-out action of an ancient river. Four bulls in black outline with black curving horns dominate the assemblage; one of them, the largest cave painting yet discovered, measures 18 feet long. Two of the bulls face one another, and five red stags fill the space between them. The frieze also includes six black horses, a large red horse, three cows, a so-called unicorn which is actually a two-horned creature resembling no known species, and a number of other animals which are difficult to distinguish because they are partly covered by more recently painted figures.

Below the frieze, two dark holes mark passages which branch off from the main hall and lead to places underground which have not yet been thoroughly explored. The left-hand passage slopes downhill, far into the rock. It contains more than 40 pictures, including depictions of a group of six large horses and three cows which covers part of the wall and the entire ceiling near the entrance; a menacing black bull with head and horns lowered; and a brown horse falling over backward, which is at the end of the part of the passage that is easily navigable. From here on the passage narrows to a twisting tunnel that runs still deeper into parts of the cave not yet investigated.

The other passage is even more intriguing. A small chamber, which looks like a rather uninteresting dead end until one comes closer, lies off to the side. One must step carefully at this point because there is a pit here under a domed ceiling covered with a tangle of engraved lines and crisscross patterns and unidentifiable remnants of some red and black paintings. The edge of the hole is worn smooth as if many persons had lowered themselves to the bottom in times past, perhaps by rope. (A fragment of three-ply rope has been found in the cave.)

Today an iron ladder extends into the pit. It leads to a ledge where there is a work unique in the records of cave art. It shows a buffalo disemboweled by a spear through its hindquarters; a stick-figure man whose head is that of a bird and who is falling backward in front of the buffalo; a pole with a bird on it below the man; and to the left,

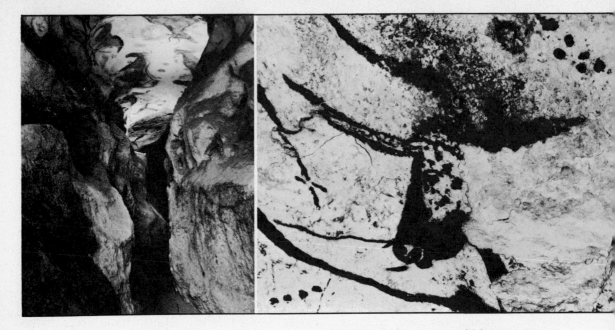

behind the man, a two-horned rhinoceros. This enigmatic scene has been interpreted often and variously. François Bordes has an explanation that he will impart if pressed, and if you do not take him too seriously: "Let me tell you my story of this painting, a science-fiction story. Once upon a time a hunter who belonged to the bird totem was killed by a bison. One of his companions, a member of the rhinoceros totem, came into the cave and drew the scene of his friend's death—and of his revenge. The bison has spears or arrows in it and is disemboweled, probably by the horn of the rhinoceros. This is how it was."

The most remote part of the cave, which lies more than 200 feet past the pit, is known as the Shaft of the Dead Man. The way in becomes lower and lower, until one must crawl along, winding past little alcoves containing engravings of lions and other animals. Then it crosses a shallow pit, and ends at a cleft blocked with clay.

Lascaux has been closed to the public ever since 1963, and most prehistorians believe it should never have been opened to them in the first place. The more popular a cave, the faster its art deteriorates, mainly because exhaled carbon dioxide reacts with limestone and accelerates the erosion of rock surfaces and the formation of calcium films that obscure paintings. This happened at Lascaux. In addition, little patches, colonies of green algae, began spreading over the walls. Things have now been brought under a measure of control. For one thing, *le mal vert* has been conquered with the aid of an antibiotic spray including penicillin and streptomycin. There has been some talk about a grand reopening, perhaps with a built-in glass tunnel which would help protect the art from the effects of exhaled air.

Since the risk of continued deterioration is still great, however, the cave will probably never again be open to the general public, although a limited number, including anthropologists, can obtain special permits. Tourists will find an artificial art cave, a faithful and impressive replica of Lascaux, in the Les Eyzies region. The family that owns the land on which Lascaux was found has sold the paintings to the French government for 700,000 francs (about $140,000); but the family retains copyright and royalties on all reproductions, an arrangement which inspired an observer to remark, "Little did Cro-Magnon man know for whom he was working."

Two major art caves are located some 15 miles downriver from

209

Lascaux Cave: enigmatic scene in the Shaft of the Dead Man

Lascaux, at Font-de-Gaume and Les Combarelles. Font-de-Gaume has about 200 paintings and engravings, many of which have also deteriorated; but after several visits, one learns to follow the sweep of the visible lines, imagine the missing lines, and recreate the paintings, which in their original condition may have surpassed those of Lascaux. After the closing of Lascaux, tourists turned to Font-de-Gaume in increasing numbers, causing the paintings there to fade faster than ever. At one time, it seemed this cave would also have to be closed, but that has not yet been necessary. The walls received a careful washing, and some of the paintings are brighter and clearer than they have been for years.

Les Combarelles consists of a long narrow passage containing more than 300 engravings, many of which cannot be seen unless they are lighted from the side and at just the right angle. The region includes many other sites: the Cap Blanc shelter with a frieze of six sculptured horses; Bernifal and its engraved mammoths, one of them hidden in a narrow fissure; and the Cougnac cave, supposedly found by divining-rod methods, which includes a large elk in black outline and, drawn inside the elk just above its foreleg, a human figure with three spears or darts stuck in it.

The little cave of Commarque, at the foot of a cliff under a ruined medieval castle, is noted for a magnificent horse's head, which has been engraved at about eye level in a narrow side gallery and may be extremely difficult to find. The engraving is about 2 feet long and one cannot see it unless the light of one's lamp strikes the limestone surface at just the right angle. (I explored the cave with three other searchers, and it took us about 45 minutes to locate the engraving.)

The art of prehistoric men and women has inspired some strange and wonderful responses in us, their latter-day descendants. In the beginning, the main response was violent disbelief and ridicule, no doubt the traditional tendency to underrate people who lived so long ago. Although it seems reasonable to suppose that the lower their status, the higher our own is by comparison, it does not work out thay way, because modern people are so close to them that efforts to belittle the past always belittle the present as well.

The first man to present a good case for the antiquity of cave art was laughed out of court. In 1875 Don Marcelino de Sautuola, a nobleman and amateur archeologist, started investigating a cave called Altamira discovered near his estate in the village of Santillana del Mar on the northern coast of Spain—again, as at Lascaux, after a dog had disappeared down a hole in the earth. He worked on and off for four years, often with his young daughter Maria for company, collecting bones and artifacts not far from the mouth of the cave and not far from a side chamber with a very low ceiling. He had gone into this chamber a number of times on his hands and knees, always looking down in an unsuccessful search for a place to dig.

One day Maria, who was 12 years old at the time and did not have to crawl, wandered into the chamber and looked up and saw paintings by candlelight. It must have been a breathtaking sight. Even today, after appreciable fading, it is perhaps the most impressive cave-art exhibit, now that Lascaux is closed to the public. The ceiling looks something like an upside-down relief map of low hilly country, and animals up to 7 feet long have been engraved and painted on its bulges and hollows, producing an almost sculptured three-dimensional appearance. About 20 of the paintings are in good condition, including some 15 bison drawn in red, yellow, and black with delicate line and shading.

The events which followed that day at Altamira demonstrate how, given a certain set of prevailing beliefs, one could avoid discovering practically anything. Caves have always been exciting places—surprises and dangers underground, shapes high in the rocks, colors and moving shadows, miles of winding galleries in which to get lost, water dripping into pools so black they seem solid, chambers so large that lamps do not reveal the ceilings, and winds rushing past as on a mountainside. The urge to explore this unexpected world runs as deep in us as it did in our prehistoric ancestors.

Local people and tourists, who had been going into art caves for generations, often saw the paintings and engravings, but the experience simply did not register. Only the mildest sort of curiosity was aroused. During the early 1800s, a guide to the Niaux cave in the French Pyrenees, which contains many beautifully executed pictures, told museum officials in the area about the art. As far as we know, nothing ever came of it. In 1864, an archeologist visited the cave and entered the following comment in his diary: "There are some paintings on the wall. What on earth can they be?" And nothing came of that either.

De Sautuola had no trouble answering this question; he was convinced on the spot. The figures on the ceiling at Altamira were very much like those he had seen the year before at the Paris World's Fair, figures engraved on pieces of bone and antler and already identified as the work of prehistoric people. (One engraving found at La Madeleine not only depicted an extinct animal, a woolly mammoth, but was done on a fragment of mammoth tusk which had been fresh at the time it was worked.)

Most authorities found this line of reasoning too direct. They were ready to accept engravings on bone, but not engravings or paintings on cave walls. They balked at the notion that people who wore skins and used stone tools went deep into underground places

equipped with pigments, brushes, lamps, and other artist's supplies— **212**
and with the purposes and imagination required to create fine polychrome paintings. A Spanish artist offered the following argument to
prove that such work must have been done by one of his contemporaries:

> There are perhaps twenty figures, some life size, in profile on the vault
> of the roof, attempting to imitate antediluvian quadrupeds. Their execution
> shows no sign of primitive art. . . . By their composition, strength of line and
> proportions they show that their author was not uneducated. And though he
> was not a Raphael he must have studied Nature at least in pictures or well-
> made drawings. As is seen by the abandoned mannerism of their execution,
> such paintings have none of the character of either Stone Age, Archaic,
> Assyrian or Phoenician art. They are simply the expression of a mediocre
> student of the modern school.

Within a year of the Altamira find, prehistorians attending an international congress in Lisbon challenged the claims of de Sautuola for a
number of reasons, most of them quite plausible. The paintings seemed
far too sophisticated to jibe with current ideas about the sophistication
of Cro-Magnon people; the pigments were amazingly fresh; the limestone crumbled so readily that it was difficult to understand how the
painted surfaces had remained intact; and so on. A Spanish professor
administered the finishing touch by dismissing the paintings as forg-
eries and revealing to his assembled colleagues the identity of the presumed forger, an artist who had been living at de Sautuola's estate for a
number of years.

That dampened official interest in cave art until just before the
turn of the century, when resistance began to crumble under the pressure of new evidence. In 1895, a local archeologist reported paintings
and engravings in a Les Eyzies cave, and although the find was greeted
with the old cry of forgery, it encouraged another archeologist to report
the existence in a cave near Bordeaux of art he had first seen more than
ten years before. This news in turn attracted the attention of one of de
Sautuola's bitterest opponents, who changed his mind after visiting the
French caves and unearthing one painting himself.

Soon reports were coming from many quarters. In 1901, a group
of prehistorians guided by a local farmer found pictures at Les Combarelles and at Font-de-Gaume. One of the group, the young priest
Henri Breuil, was to spend the next six decades reproducing and studying cave art. In 1902, 14 years following the death of de Sautuola, he
visited Altamira and helped establish the authenticity of its paintings.
Not long afterward half a dozen further art caves were found within a
few miles of Altamira.

Some 125 caves with 15,000 paintings and engravings have been
discovered to date. The list continues to grow at a rate of about a new

cave every one or two years in France and Italy, and especially in less intensively explored parts of Spain. The Belgian husband and wife team of Marcel and Lya Dams, the most widely traveled present-day investigators of cave art, have visited about a hundred of the caves. They have reported on recent finds, including a cave in northern Spain which has a river running through it, a gallery with wall paintings of a dozen stags and horses and as many black triangles whose meaning is unknown, and, half a mile deeper through passages leading to a dead end, a number of other abstract designs. Another new cave, exposed by an explosion in a quarry in southern Portugal, is important not only for a bird-man figure reminiscent of the one in the Shaft of the Dead Man pit at Lascaux, but also for its location. Known as Escoural, it contains the first art cave found in Portugal; it lies in limestone country where many more underground paintings and engravings probably remain to be discovered.

Lya Dams emphasizes "the very curious tendency of decorated caves to form clusters around a central nucleus." In addition to clusters of a dozen or more caves in the neighborhood of Les Eyzies and Santillana del Mar, she reports one new nucleus on the Bay of Biscay coast round the town of Ribadesella, and a probable nucleus centered about the La Pileta cave in southern Spain some 40 miles northeast of Gibraltar. The clustering is still unexplained. "Abundance of food may be one explanation," Dams suggests, "Another could be the abundance of ac-

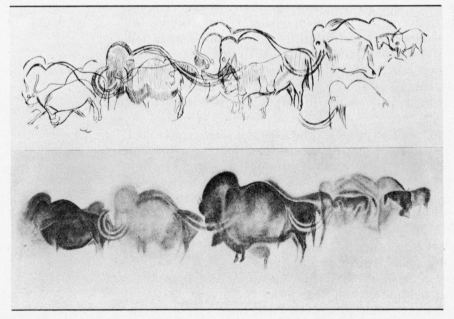

Font-de-Gaume cave: frieze of mammoths, deer, horses, bison

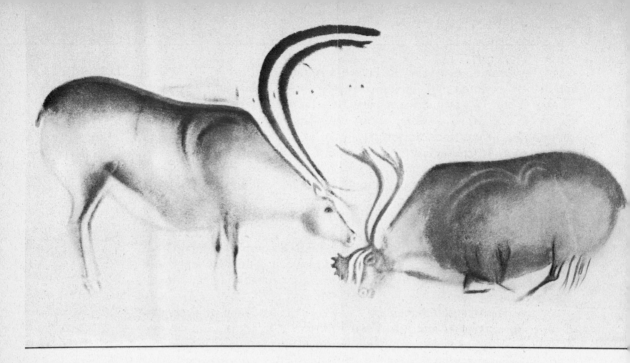

cessible caves. Why not an annual or seasonal gathering area for cult reasons, about which we know less than nothing?"

Artists had more immediate and wider responsibilities in earlier times than they do now. Today, writing serves to pass on knowledge, facts, processes, and concepts from generation to generation. Prehistoric people had only memory and symbols such as spoken words, cave art, and probably music, chants, and the dance, judging by Aurignacian pipes made of hollow bone with clearly cut fingerholes and a suspected castenet bracelet found not long ago in the Soviet Ukraine. Ceremonies repeated time after time and words repeated over and over again in settings of rhythmic beats, masks, and painted images played a predominant role then as they do today in impressing traditions upon memory and preserving them.

Art served a number of purposes, perhaps the least complicated being to bring color and form into the home. Most paintings and engravings in living spaces at cave mouths or in rock shelters have disintegrated because they were exposed to weather. Some complete figures survive, however, and remnants often turn up during excavations. Among debris found in occupation layers at Abri Pataud are fragments of rock broken off nearby walls; they are colored red and black and were once part of large paintings. At another site, Bordes has seen a painted foot on a large piece of fallen rock.

A decade ago, in the first really critical analysis of cave art, Andrée Rosenfeld of the British Museum and Peter Ucko of University College London considered it likely that such work "was intended to enliven

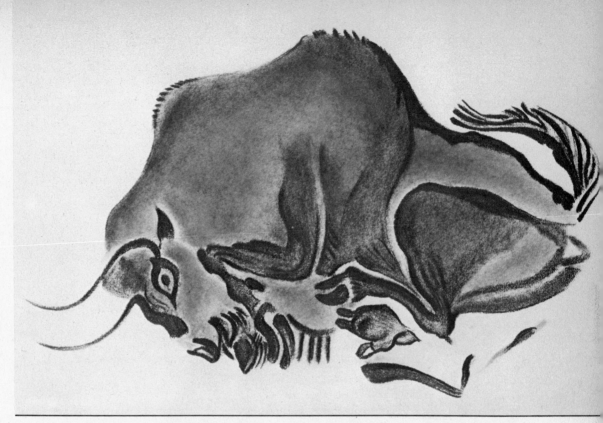

and brighten domestic activities.'' Some of the art was also furniture, pieces that could be moved in to make Cro-Magnon chambers more attractive, sculpted and painted limestone blocks that were probably propped up against convenient walls. Small statues of women, so-called Venus figurines, most commonly found in southern Russia and other eastern European sites, may have had some special family significance since they tend to be associated with houses such as those constructed at Kostenki; they were often placed in special storage pits under the floor.

Other purposes are more elusive and involve a shift from open living quarters to hidden chambers and passages, from light to darkness. Most cave art is located deep underground, and some works are extremely difficult to get at. In Arcy-sur-Cure, André Leroi-Gourhan once guided me through a small cave which extends only about a hundred yards into a cliffside, but it was a long hundred yards. The entrance was a torpedo tube, a horizontal tunnel just about big enough for a man to squeeze into. He went in headfirst, wriggling along in salamander fashion and pushing a lamp in front of him over the muddy floor, and I followed.

Crawling is hard work with solid rock all around and one's face usually an inch or so above the mud and sometimes in it. At one point

215

Cast of Venus
figurine found at
Willendorf, Austria

the tunnel becomes even more constricted, and I had to hunch my shoulders and inhale deeply to force myself through. (I learned later that Henri Breuil became stuck in this part of the tunnel at the age of 69 and had to be pulled and shoved through; it was one of the last caves he ever explored.) Further hazards existed on the way to a chamber with engravings in it, including a place where one had to skirt the slippery edge of a pit leading to still deeper passages.

Even after negotiating such passages, additional problems may be encountered in finding the art. For motives which remain obscure

Les Trois Freres cave, French Pyrenees: the "sorcerer," one of the most famous expressions of prehistoric art

but which certainly involved the deliberate creation and overcoming of obstacles, the artists often chose surfaces difficult of access where they would have to work in cramped and awkward positions—in crawl spaces and alcoves, close to the floor, crammed into corners, above and at the bottom of pits like the one at Lascaux. Near the end of the main gallery at Font-de-Gaume is a narrow damp place where the rock has split. You climb a ladder built into the fissure for the convenience of visitors, lean backward, and twist your head sharply to the left, and see engraved at eye level ten feet or so above the floor a group of horses and a lion nearby, apparently ready to pounce.

There are many such places, and also many exceptions. Some art-cave entrances are wide enough to house factories, and one in the Pyrenees was actually used as an airplane factory during World War II. The majority of paintings and engravings are located so that they can be seen readily by lamplight, provided, of course, that one knows where to look. But the significant element in practically all cases is the trip underground, often by long and tortuous routes, to out-of-the-way but not necessarily secret or private places; accounting for this phenomenon is one of the most challenging long-range problems in the study of prehistory.

An important clue involves Cro-Magnons' concern with their effectiveness as providers. Half the battle in hunting and fighting is confidence; and if they were anything like modern people, they used ritual on numerous occasions to help replenish and increase their powers. Perhaps they cast spells on their prey. Certain places in the depths of caves are covered with superimposed figures drawn one on top of the other and overlapping, as if the artists paid little attention to the work of their predecessors but considerable attention to where the art was located. They also represented some animals with darts or spears sticking into their sides, for example, the bison in the Shaft of the Dead Man, which may have been killed ritually in revenge for the death of a hunter.

Similar practices have been observed in modern times. As recently as a decade or two ago, for example, aborigines living in the stony tablelands and mountains of northern Australia prepared themselves for a successful hunt by painting pictures of the animals they wanted to kill on sacred spots in rock shelters and ravines. The prehistoric use of hunting magic might explain why people are seldom depicted in cave art, the idea being that drawing the human figure could bring death or injury to other members of the group. It may be significant that cave art reached a peak toward the close of the Magdalenian period when herds were becoming smaller. Most of the great polychrome paintings seem to have been done during this period, which also saw an apparent increase in depictions of slain animals, suggesting one last ritual effort to restore past abundances. Generally, ceremony and the intensity of belief tend to increase in times of crisis.

219

Another possible use of art was in initiation ceremonies. In many primitive tribes coming of age is a time of ordeals and revelations. For an adolescent male to prove himself as a man and a hunter, he may suffer mutilation and inflicted pain, starve himself, go without sleep, take hallucinogenic drugs and emetics—and then go out alone to sites in the wilderness to have visions, communicate with some sort of guardian spirit, and perform a feat, such as catching an eagle and killing it with his bare hands, an old Blackfoot Indian custom. A cave would be an ideal place for such experiences. The darkness and shadows and eerie settings, enhanced by figures of animals and mystical signs, might well encourage a person to see and hear things during long vigils even without the suffering and fatigue and drugs. The feat might be to find hidden art, and leave your own work or mark to prove you had found it.

A hint of prehistoric initiations was discovered more than 60 years ago when a man and his son rowed a boat into the Tuc d'Audoubert cave in the French Pyrenees. A stream, the remnant of a swift river that had originally formed the cave, took them to a gravel beach and a passage leading to a hall, where they found a pond, white stalagmites, and stalactites. At the end of the hall they climbed a steep slope, or chimney. Breaking through a sheet of stalagmite at the top, they followed a tunnel several hundred yards through chambers and a torpedo-tube section, and found not far from the end of the cave a large circular room with two clay statues of bison propped up against a rock at the center. Near the statues is a clay area with small heelprints in a circle, as if children had danced there, perhaps preparing for a vigil or ordeal. As mentioned earlier in connection with dance, Aurignacian pipes made of hollow bone and containing well-cut fingerholes have been found in at least one French cave.

Several theories involve what may have been meeting rooms.

Tuc d'Audoubert cave: bison modeled in clay

There are several such places, including one in the Trois Freres cave, near Tuc d'Audoubert and probably part of the same underground system, and another in a Spanish cave, where one climbs to the top of a natural platform and looks down on a chamber and can practically see the audience looking up. Engraved on a wall of the French chamber is a large figure of a man dressed in an antler headgear and reindeer skin, which may represent a sorcerer or a shaman. Some of the art found on cave walls, as well as on bone and antler, hints at a kind of score-keeping or counting. Alexander Marshack of Harvard, in a continuing study involving intensive microscopic examinations of many signs and symbols, suggests that certain sets of dots and parallel lines are calendars based on phases of the moon and that seasonal rituals and a mythology may be represented in associations of plants, animals, fish, fishing and wading birds, and other figures.

These theories all have a measure of plausibility and should make one thing clear: no single notion, however ingenious, can account for even a major proportion of the observed facts. People were doing many things with their art and with their caves. The caves represent the prototypes of institutional sites before the coming of separate specialized institutions; from time to time they probably served as prehistoric archives, shrines, playgrounds, offices, schools, vigil places, theaters. Indeed, for limited periods at least, some of them may have been as bustling for those times as downtown business and cultural centers are today. Generally speaking, the more we learn about settled communities in open-air sites like those near Kostenki and Fontainebleau, the more carefully we must reexamine our notions about how people used caves.

It should also be clear that investigators are long on guesswork and short on evidence. All they have to go on is a mass of unanalyzed observation and imagination, and that is not enough. In the past, the tendency has been to present a theory as the last word, with a this-is-how-it-was attitude that discourages inquiry, rather than as a preliminary statement to be proved or disproved by fresh studies. This tendency was largely a result of the personality of the great prehistorian Breuil, who died in 1961 after dominating cave-art research as completely and almost as long as Louis XIV dominated France.

The priest was a jealous leader. At meetings he would shout down younger investigators who disagreed with him, and after a while they learned to keep their thoughts to themselves. One of his former students and a close friend for 30 years once dared to suggest in the mildest terms that Breuil might not have been entirely correct about the authenticity of the art in a certain cave, and he never spoke to her again. Another close friend summed things up as follows, after Breuil's death, of course: "As he got older and perhaps less sure of touch in his intuitions . . . he did not become less pontifical and it became more personally difficult to disagree with him."

Ideas have started to flow more freely during the past few years. **221**
The studies of Ucko and Rosenfeld and the Damses are outstanding examples of the new spirit, and so is a detailed study of more than 65 art
caves by Leroi-Gourhan. He has made the first systematic large-scale effort to classify cave paintings and engravings, to find out what animals
and signs are found most often in certain parts of caves, in different localities, and at different times. For example, bison and horses appear
more frequently than other animals in large chambers and passages,
while such dangerous animals as bears and lions are usually found in
hidden recesses and isolated places containing few other figures;
barbed signs and dots are found more frequently inside chambers and
galleries off the main passage. Also, Leroi-Gourhan believes that the
artists of 25,000 to 30,000 years ago tended to work near cave entrances,
and that their descendants went deeper and deeper underground during the next ten millennia or so.

The French prehistorian, in short, is beginning to do for prehistoric art what Bordes has done for prehistoric technology. He is seeking significant associations, and at this stage that is more important
than interpretations. (His notion that most cave art consists of sex symbols and deals almost entirely with sexual themes may reflect twentieth-
century rather than prehistoric preoccupations.) Eventually the time will
come for more sophisticated statistical techniques like the factor analysis which was used to analyze the Neanderthal tool data from Combe
Grenal, and it may be possible to obtain more precise answers to some
old unanswered questions.

The problem is to devise subhypotheses which, if proved, might
lend weight to major hypotheses. For example, if superimposed figures
included a high proportion of wounded animals, one would have more
confidence in the hunting-magic theory. The initiation theory implies,
among other things, that unusual objects might be found in vigil places.
In primitive tribes, persons undergoing such experiences generally
bring good-luck pieces with them—polished or painted pebbles, clear
quartz crystals, parts of animals, such as rabbit feet, and so on. Such
items have been found in art caves, but they have never been looked
for systematically. In fact, no major art cave has ever been excavated using modern techniques.

Another area of scholarship that has not been brought to bear
directly on the origins of cave art is the study and analysis of myth.
Caves continue to be regarded with awe as openings deep into the
earth's crust where gods dwell. For example, the Maya Indians of Mexico believe that lightning comes from the mouths of caves located high
on mountain sides, and they come to worship at shrines housed in
caves. Comparisons between today's symbols and yesterday's may un-
cover similar beliefs among our ancestors. They may also help explain
the existence of holy places, where prehistoric paintings were super-

imposed one on top of the other, but, in Dams' words, "not to achieve **222** visual effects. . . . The act of painting must have been the chief purpose."

Some of the most promising research on prehistoric art involves fragments of bone, antler, and ivory rather than cave walls, so-called "portable art" consisting of engravings made to be kept in dwelling places and perhaps carried about. Such objects, which more than a century ago convinced de Sautuola that our ancestors were fully capable of executing the Altamira paintings, may represent messages of a sort, identifying people the way jewelry may have done—but expressing something over and above identification.

Margaret Conkey Fritz of the State University of New York in Binghamton has studied the abstract designs on more than 1200 decorated pieces found in northern Spain, and notes a number of significant developments. For example, pieces produced 15,000 to 13,000 years ago include a wide variety of styles and motifs, as if many individual artists were going separate ways and expressing their own ideas and feelings. A change took place during the next 2000 years. The trend was toward standardization, fewer styles and fewer motifs, suggesting a new kind of coming together, the emergence of a community of interests and ideas, in Fritz's words "a cultural integrating mechanism." It may have been the beginnings of a formal religion or system of beliefs.

Research can take us only so far. We will never know what was in the mind of the artist who some 15,000 years ago forced himself into a space the size of a rat hole in the side of the cliff near Les Eyzies, slid into the pit, squeezed his way around two sharp turns, and, when he came to a dead end, rolled over on his back to paint a little red and black horse on a surface only a few inches from his face. And what was the private mission of the other lone artist who walked nearly three-quarters of a mile through mud in a huge cave near Altamira and drew two horses in black outline, the only animal figures found in miles of chambers and galleries? There will always be such awe and mystery, if that is what we want; but it is also exciting to consider what may yet be discovered.

The shifts from intuition alone to intuition plus analysis and from speculations not designed for checking to scientific hypotheses will bring us a great deal closer to prehistoric artists and to the roles they played in their communities. Perhaps, as a bonus, the new knowledge may affect our understanding and current insights regarding experiments. It may even bring us closer to the artists of our own times and to a genuine awareness that they too are engaged in serious business.

The first great period of prehistoric art came to an end with the end of the Magdalenian culture about 12,000 years ago. Cultures had come and gone before, but this one had risen higher than any previous culture, and therefore subsequent events somehow seem like more of a letdown. What happened is plain in the record. Occupation layers at major Magdalenian sites are thick, extend far out beyond the area immediately in front of caves and rock shelters, and contain many tools and many varieties of tools. They represent the remains of a stable, powerful and prosperous people.

By contrast, the layers on top of the most recent Magdalenian deposits are meager. They are thin, so thin at certain sites that early excavators frequently missed them, and they contain far fewer tools and more limited tool kits, which include characteristically flat harpoons and many microlith, miniature tools like those which Higgs found in northwest Greece (see Chapter 9) and which other investigators have found throughout the world. (A steady decrease in the size of tools was a widespread tendency in prehistoric times.) These meager layers mark a kind of retreat confined generally to areas under sheltering rock and toward the face of the cliff. These are the remains of a shrinking and unsure people, the so-called Azilians (named after the Mas d'Azil cave in the French Pyrenees), who lived literally with their backs to the wall.

The Azilians hunted in the same regions where the Magdalenians had hunted and occupied many of the same sites. Like most dwindling people, they probably lived to a large extent in the past and told nostalgic legends about their ancestors, the mighty hunters of another age. On occasion they may have visited Lascaux and Altamira and other art caves, and wondered at the pictures on the walls. They left no art of their own, or at least no art worthy of the name. All we find at their sites are geometric designs painted on pebbles.

A world had passed, and for a surprising reason. The climate improved. There is always a danger in becoming too well adjusted and in developing practices and institutions that are too firmly established. The Magdalenians had mastered, and flourished in, bitter glacial conditions, but they were not ready for better times. Animal bones in an occupation layer at La Madeleine tell a familiar story of successful hunting, predominantly the hunting of reindeer, snow partridge, chamois, and other sub-Arctic species. But in the layer immediately above this one, the uppermost Magdalenian layer, reindeer are less abundant; it is especially significant that certain forest species such as the red deer and wild boar appear for the first time.

This change, also observed at many other sites, foreshadows the beginning of the end for the Magdalenian culture. The continuing retreat of the glaciers brought milder climates to the region and produced a series of further retreats. Species of grass which had adapted to glacial conditions and provided food for reindeer followed the glaciers north, the reindeer followed the grasses, and most hunters followed the reindeer or moved to coastlines and lived on other herd animals and seafood. The Azilians were descendants of those who stayed behind to

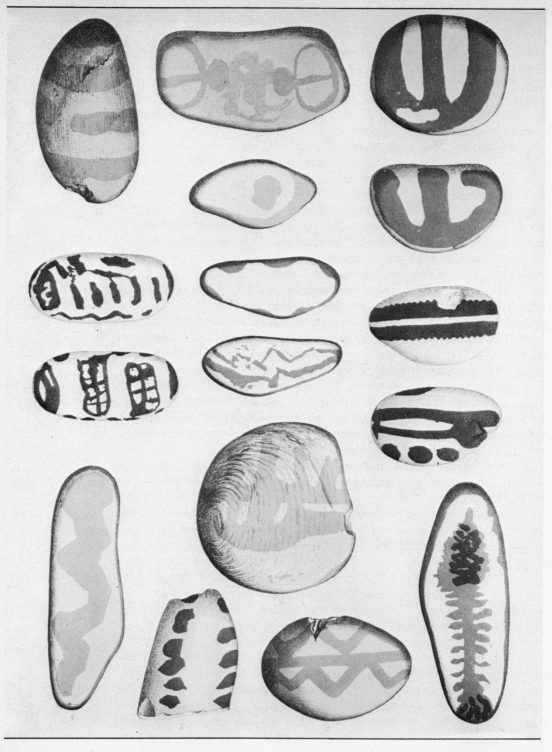

Painted Azilian
pebbles

carry on in the new environment as best they could, and, all things con- **225** sidered, they did well.

The world's earliest art died out locally, but other works turned up elsewhere. For example, art flourished between 5,000 and 12,000 years ago in eastern Spain in the so-called Spanish Levant, where some hundred sites have been found on cliff and rock-shelter walls, most of them unmarked by signposts and tucked away in back country far from roads. Dams notes that the artists went several steps beyond their pred- ecessors and cultural ancestors, the Magdalenians. They introduced scenes and a feel for composition where previously there had been iso- lated individual animals almost exclusively. Motion, pursuit, and action are also featured for the first time in the art of the Spanish Levant. (Ef- forts to depict motion are confined to only a few of the thousands of earlier paintings and engravings.)

Although climatic changes in the Les Eyzies region brought about a defeat of a sort compared with what had been, one very posi- tive result was the development of a new and ingenious way of life. Vast herds of game on the hoof were no longer around to be killed en masse by hunters lying in wait along traditional migration routes. The problem was to deal with more elusive forest animals which moved about in small groups and were agile, swift, and camouflaged. Snaring, trapping, and other techniques that had played secondary roles in rein- deer times were refined and used more intensively; the bow and arrow may have evolved into a major weapon. The Azilians also leaned more heavily on fishing and acquired new food tastes, for snails, for example, which must have taken some doing after a diet of venison; presumably snails became delicacies at a later date. (Stone picks similar to those found at Azilian sites are still used on the northern coast of Spain to pry open mussels.)

Up to this point people had lived chiefly on what food the good earth happened to offer in the form of wild plants and wild animals. The story of the Magdalenians shows how much could be achieved when conditions were right and remained that way for long periods. But it also shows how vulnerable people were to changes beyond their control, as long as they depended on natural abundances for survival. If they had not "cheated" by tinkering with the natural orders of things, by producing food instead of collecting food ready-made, the world would be a much simpler place. We would probably all be hunters and gatherers still.

The outcome of the tinkering was the invention of agriculture. That step took place independently, far from the river valleys of south- western France, in such "underdeveloped" areas as the Near East, Southeast Asia, and Mesoamerica. Many explanations have been for- warded for the rise of domestication. One of the most frequently cited theories, one which Darwin subscribed to, suggests that it happened as the result of a lucky accident. Perhaps a perceptive individual noticed wild seeds left over from winter storage sprouting in a "magic spot" where nothing had grown before, say, on a dump pile where earth had been disturbed. The idea of planting seeds on purpose was supposedly born then and there. Eventually the practice brought surpluses of food, some of which could be used to nourish easily tamed animals.

This notion is in line with the "Eureka!" theory of human advancement, the idea that all discoveries come in flashes to geniuses sitting in bathtubs or under apple trees. It is certainly not in line with what we know about the evolution of *Homo sapiens*. It hardly flatters our forebears to suppose that they used plant foods for ages without realizing why plants sprouted near living places in the spring. The odds are that the Neanderthals, and perhaps their predecessors, knew very well what happens when seeds are planted; and they may even have tried planting from time to time for the sheer fun and interest of it.

Evidence is also accumulating which indicates that people were controlling herds long before keeping animals on farms became a large-scale practice. Earl Saxon of the University of Durham in England has found sites in Israel that are 15,000 to 18,000 years old where gazelle bones predominate and high proportions of the bones represent young animals. Apparently people were no longer gambling on obtaining meat. They were not hunting in the sense of going out in search of game. They knew very well where the game was. Herds already accustomed to the sight of people were permitted to roam freely within their natural ranges and were "harvested" from time to time much as Greenlanders do today with reindeer herds. Saxon believes that herd management in Israel and elsewhere may date back at least 30,000 years.

People knew a good deal about agriculture many thousands of years before they started giving up the hunting-gathering life-style some 10,000 years ago. They changed, not because they wanted to, since hunting-gathering was generally an easier and more reliable way of obtaining food. They changed, because they had to. The full explanation remains to be worked out, but one major factor was overpopulation and the threat of famine. The world contained an estimated 10 million persons 10,000 years ago, which is hardly crowded in terms of twentieth-century populations. But considering that it took about a square mile to feed a person by hunting and gathering, and that most of the best territories were already occupied, the pressure was mounting. Furthermore, as mentioned in Chapter 10, rising seas were submerging large areas of the continental shelves, so that land was scarcer.

At present the evidence indicates that the world's first farmers appeared in the Near East. Agriculture associated with farming villages seems to have arisen around 7500 B.C. in the so-called Fertile Crescent along a 2000-mile arc starting in Israel and Jordan, extending up the eastern Mediterranean coast, swinging around through southern Turkey and then southeast, and following the Zagros Mountains of Iran to lands bordering the Persian Gulf. A side branch of the arc runs 500 miles due west along the coast of Turkey. The region included wild goats, sheep, pigs, and cattle as well as massive stands of such wild grasses as wheat and barley. During the next five or six millennia farming villages also appeared in China, the Indus Valley, Egypt, Mesoamerica, South America, and other regions. People had created artificial abundances. The land was now producing more than 50 times the amount of food that nature had provided in the form of wild species. Populations soared.

From this period on changes came one after the other at an accelerating pace. Villages grew large and split into clusters of villages, and still larger centers took shape among the clusters. In most parts of the world early cities arose within three or four millennia after the first farming villages. The first cities were small by modern standards, numbering perhaps 10,000 to 30,000 inhabitants; but that was enough to create enormous new complexities and new problems. Above all, people had to be organized to work long hours, not only for their own subsistence as in hunter-gatherer days, but for the subsistence of others—notably to provide emerging elites with the best of everything.

Such demands were made in the name of serving the gods. Great temples and plazas were built for ceremonies on a grander and grander scale. One result was what Fritz calls "an explosion of symbolic behavior." Another result was the invention of writing, the coming of records and archives and myths preserved word for word. This was the end of prehistory and the beginning of a race between rising populations and food supplies, a race against famine, which continues in our own times.

The study of primates in zoos instead of in the wild as the cause of misconceptions about aggression; minimizing violence, a prerequisite for survival; varieties of animal societies; baboons, contemporary savanna dwellers; the collective wisdom of the troop; the importance of hierarchies; infant protection, grooming, affection

CHAPTER 12 PRIMATE STUDIES AND REVISED BELIEFS ABOUT ANIMAL BEHAVIOR

The story of human evolution, the rise over a period of some 15 million years of our kind from breeds of bygone primates, has been based chiefly on dead material dug out of the earth. Most of the evidence involves analyses of remains and artifacts of creatures that have long since perished. It comes from fossil bones, soils, pollen, worked flints, paintings, engravings, burial sites, living-floors—in a "mint" state as people abandoned them ages ago. Studies of living material—baboons, chimpanzees, and the hunter-gatherers of the twentieth century—have been cited to help interpret archeological findings, to support arguments bearing on the development of erect posture, tool use, meat eating, and social organization.

But living prehistory, information from living rather than extinct species, is of major importance in its own right. The preceding chapters have drawn on only a fraction of the research being conducted on nonhuman primates and on the entire spectrum of human primates from the Australian aborigines and Kalahari Bushmen and other primitive tribes to families living in high-rise apartments. A fuller account of such findings is essential in the effort to understand our origins and possible futures.

When it comes to animal studies in general, the problem is to see them as objectively as possible. Attitudes depend on whom you read; they may be seen as cute, charming, and a bit bumbling and foolish (the Br'er Rabbit or Disney approach); or as noble, wise, and pure; or as brutes and innate killers; and so on. Such attitudes are poorly disguised messages, preconceptions rather than principles deduced from the evidence. Writers use animals to make a point, to tell you what they think they know, not about animals but about people. For example, the odds are that if a writer belongs to the pure-and-noble school of animal behavior, he or she is commenting, implicitly or explicitly, on the Fall of Adam and the corruption of the human species. The temptation to moralize is strongest when discussing primates, humans' closest relatives, the species which have most to teach us.

Studies of primates in the wild have increased enormously during the past 15 years, after a long and almost exclusive concentration on captive animals. Biologists reacted strangely to Darwin's discoveries. In effect, they turned away from Darwin and turned their backs on the wilderness, investigating monkeys and apes in laboratories and zoos instead of in savannas and forests. In other words, instead of venturing into the great outdoors where the facts were, where they could observe primates living freely, they went indoors to observe primates locked in cages.

Such behavior, of course, was in part a matter of playing safe, because in some areas the danger of yellow fever and other diseases was greater then than it is now, at least until about half a century ago. Looking back, however, it appears to have been more than that. It amounted to a flight from reality, an evasion of nature, and it produced some spectacular results. Captive primates engaged in numerous and bloody fights, often to the death, killed their infants, and indulged in a variety of bizarre sexual activity, all of which might have been predicted, if only by analogy with the actions of people subjected to prison conditions. Biologists had mistaken social pathology for normal behavior. Arguing from caged to free-ranging primates, they assumed violence to be an innate primate characteristic, part of the basic heritage of monkeys and apes and, unfortunately, of people.

These findings were definitely in line with the Puritan and Victorian views of people as Jekyll-Hyde creatures, part disheveled, lustful, and violent animals and part well-groomed and restrained gentlefolk. The discovery of Neanderthals scandalized the Victorians because they saw them as Mr. Hydes built into the human past. The moral, of course, was that if only the beast in us could be curbed, life would proceed in a lawful and orderly fashion. But putting animals in cages had practically guaranteed that they would exhibit a high level of aberrant behavior, the "bestial" behavior generally expected of nonhuman people. It was almost as if observers were deliberately creating conditions under which the gap between humans and other primates would appear as wide as possible.

The first systematic study of wild primates came in 1931, when Ray Carpenter of Pennsylvania State University began observing howler monkeys in Panama. But extensive research did not start until the decades following World War II, a conflict which gave rise to second thoughts about the quality of human primates and brought about a new and harder look at human origins. Powerful observation techniques were developed by investigators studying fish and birds, notably by Niko Tinbergen of Oxford, who made a special point of the value of animal research in the analysis of motives and purposes: "The fact that animals cannot tell us what urges them to behave as they do might well be a blessing in disguise; at least they cannot tell us conscious or unconscious lies. They just behave." Tinbergen focused attention on repertoires of behavior patterns, repeated actions and reactions, and their interpretation in evolutionary terms.

These and other developments encouraged a new interest in primates, and for the first time observations in the wild became a major research activity. Early work created a certain amount of confusion since primates failed to behave as expected. Anthropologists and zoologists entered wildernesses expecting mayhem, and found peace. As a matter of fact, fighting was so rare that in the beginning observers made a special point of reexamining their own results—perhaps the species they were studying represented an exception to the rule of violence, or the animals were members of unusually amicable troops.

Later the observers compared notes and realized that they had not been dealing with exceptions, but with a common state of affairs. Their findings have since been confirmed by continuing field studies involving some 150 investigators in 20 or so countries, including Japan,

World Distribution of Contemporary Nonhuman Primates

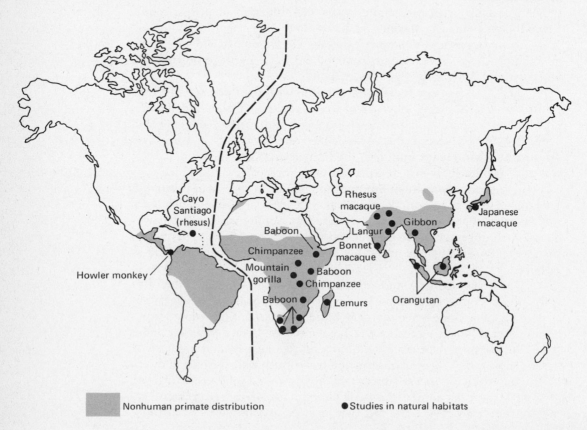

Nonhuman primate distribution   ● Studies in natural habitats

India, Kenya, Uganda, and Borneo. Wild primates and most wild animals tend to avoid fighting with one another. Survival is too serious a business to allow for the luxury of violent dissension within the ranks. If primates behaved as aggressively in the wild as they do in cages, they would have become extinct long ago.

The striking point about primates is not the existence of aggression, but the uses and control of aggression. In them, evolution has produced new orders of unity. The members of a troop of primates depend on one another as intimately and directly as if they were all physically connected by tough nerve fibers, which, in effect, is the way things are. The group is the adaptive unit, and the more that is learned about groups, the more notions about individuals and individualism will have to be revised. The evolutionary trend not only among primates but among mammals in general has been toward increasingly complex and close-knit groups.

The broad features of this trend have been analyzed by John Eisenberg of the Smithsonian Institution in a survey of nearly 500 studies. He describes four grades or levels of mammalian social organization:

Grade 1—female-young unit: A mother caring for her offspring is the most elementary of all mammalian social units, a bare minimum in the sense that no species could endure with anything less. The wood rats of North America, for example, live alone in nests of twigs and come together only for mating. The female provides shelter and food and protection for her litter, and attacks and drives away males which come too close.

Grade 2—mother-family group: Here again mothers and offspring make up the basic units, but they may aggregate into large groups, a situation found among red deer. Fifteen or more hinds, each with two or three young, live together throughout the year under the leadership of an older female. A hind goes off alone to give birth, rejoining her group after a few days when the calf can walk and follow. The stags live separate lives, wandering more widely and foraging in loose all-male herds; during the breeding season a stag will associate himself with a female group and defend it against other stags. Stags and hinds may come together in good feeding grounds during the winter.

Grade 3—male-female pair bond: This rare situation includes a wide variety of specialized living arrangements, the common element being that the male is part of the basic family social unit, and that both male and female provide food and care for the young. Among wolves, for example, the male not only shares in protecting the litter but he is also the provider and may join with other males in hunting. At the kill site, he will swallow chunks of meat without chewing them, and disgorge the food back at the den for family consumption.

Grade 4—permanent male-female group: More than one male is generally associating with a number of females. Certain primate societies represent this grade of organization, living in troops that may include more than a hundred individuals and that are generally closed to outsiders. The males may act collectively in defending females and offspring. In such groups conflicts involving the individual and the organization may arise in acute form and demand new and complex control mechanisms.

Eisenberg points out that relatively unspecialized or low-grade social structures are typical for representatives of new orders among mammals, populations engaged in finding places for themselves in a world of established species. The newcomers were often small and inconspicuous, lived in the shelter of forests rather than in open terrain, and did their foraging at night—all characteristics which favor grade 1, female-young units. Developments which appear later in evolution may have the opposite characteristics. Species frequently became larger in the process of adapting successfully, acquired greater freedom of movement, and foraged actively during daylight hours. There is also a trend toward larger brains and more complex sense organs. Such changes favor the formation of more and more elaborate social organizations.

Similar patterns may be seen in the evolution of primates. The first prosimians, forerunners of monkeys and apes, were small forest dwellers, probably nocturnal. They depended largely on the sense of smell for communicating with one another and for detecting danger. Like some surviving prosimians, they probably lived solitary lives and were dispersed over wide areas. The trend has been in the opposite direction ever since, toward increasing brain and body size, increasing importance of sight and hearing in communications, and the formation of permanent troops. As far as human evolution is concerned, life in open country accentuated the need for tight group organization as a protection against big cats and other predators.

Detailed studies of nonhuman primates provide a more precise and dynamic picture of our own origins. In the words of Paul Bohannon of Northwestern University, "Whether we like it or not, anthropology is a branch of primatology." It is particularly important to learn as much as possible about monkeys and apes in a variety of different environments. The more we know about the range of adaptations to open woodlands, for example, the better we will understand the behavior of the first hominids who depended increasingly on their ability to cope with such terrain. Going one step further, our ancestors gradually moved out of open woodlands into still more open grassy savanna lands, and the impact of that change can be appreciated more fully by considering how other primates have adapted to similar conditions.

This point has been emphasized by Woodrow Denham of the University of California in Berkeley. After a systematic analysis of possible environments and adaptations, he indicates that the earliest hominids, like other primates living in open woodlands, generally lived in large groups because food, although ample, tended to be concentrated in a number of separate areas. Extreme territoriality among large groups, fighting to the death to defend feeding and living places from other troops, would hardly promote survival, and it is uncommon; within limits, troops may move in and out of one another's home ranges. Also, direct confrontation and fighting against predators is rela-

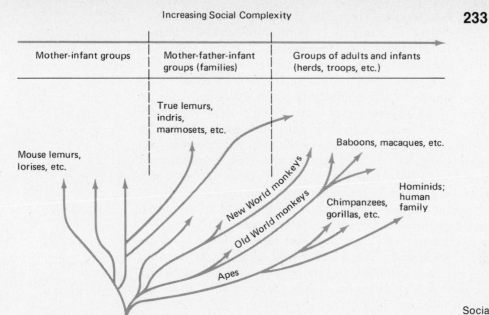

Increasing Social Complexity

| Mother-infant groups | Mother-father-infant groups (families) | Groups of adults and infants (herds, troops, etc.) |

Mouse lemurs, lorises, etc.

True lemurs, indris, marmosets, etc.

New World monkeys

Old World monkeys

Apes

Baboons, macaques, etc.

Chimpanzees, gorillas, etc.

Hominids; human family

Social evolution among primates

tively rare because it is usually possible to escape into trees, which means that the male is not often called on to defend the troop and, hence, is not likely to be much bigger than the female.

Early hominids lived in a comparable setting until they moved into grassy savannas. At that point, life became less relaxed and more highly organized. Denham suggests that compared with what happens in open woodlands, in grasslands food is more uniformly distributed, and this encourages foraging by many small groups rather than a few large ones, the multiplication of home ranges, and a readiness to defend territories more vigorously. The male's role changes correspondingly, not only in keeping fellow primates out of his home territory, but also in confronting predators; escape is more difficult since trees are few and far between. The tendency under these conditions is for males to be appreciably larger and more formidable than females, and our remote ancestors may have gone through some such stage.

Something about the past may be deduced from the behavior of primates currently at large in grassy savannas—African baboons in particular. Baboons have received special attention from a number of investigators because they provide a dramatic example of adaptation to an exposed environment. The rest of this chapter is devoted chiefly to baboon troops observed by myself and studied by Jean and Stuart Altmann, Irven DeVore and others in Nairobi Park and the Amboseli Game Reserve of Kenya. The baboons' world demands a degree of alertness analogous to that demanded in baseball or cricket, in which nothing happens most of the time and most plays are routine. The challenge is always to be ready for swift and sudden action.

The difference between playing fields and savannas, of course, is that in savannas emergencies tend to be fatal. Under such conditions a lone baboon does not have much of a chance. Individuals living almost constantly within sight and sound of one another must experience shock when they find themselves isolated on a wide plain. It must be something like falling overboard and seeing the ship disappearing over the horizon. One young Nairobi Park baboon that was unusually bold as long as the rest of the troop remained reasonably close (it had earned the name Brash for leaping onto the hood of a fast-moving car and begging for food) lost its courage whenever the troop moved too far away, scampering back and emitting alarm barks all the way.

A sick or crippled individual does not survive long. It cannot keep up with the troop. Nor will the troop wait, although adult males sometimes drop back to accompany lagging females with infants. A sick baboon tries so hard to keep up that it does not take time to get enough food. It becomes weaker and falls farther and farther behind. Finally, it no longer moves. I once saw a sick female lying paralyzed in short grass, crouching as low as possible, fitting its body into every depression in the earth in a last effort to become invisible. Next morning she was missing, and presumably devoured.

Baboons in open country endure by moving together in patterns that depend on the lay of the land, food resources and the ways of predators. But the patterns are by no means self-evident. Following a large troop of baboons for the first time is likely to be frustrating if you expect to find clear-cut signs of organized behavior. A troop implies some sort of coordinated structure, but what you generally see from a distance is baboons scattered over several acres of savanna, apparently paying little attention to one another, or to you. There are no neat rank-and-file formations and no mass movements in a particular direction, only baboons wandering about in small groups and baboons off by themselves, some sitting on branches and rocks as if surveying the terrain. (On closer inspection it turns out that a few of the sitters are asleep.)

Everything seems casual until observations can be made close up and for long periods, and that does not happen until troops grow accustomed to people. Some troops never learn to trust people and keep their distance. Others permit closer and closer approaches, and after several weeks they accept the investigator as a familiar part of the landscape, even to the point of falling asleep when a person is only a few yards away.

A number of years ago DeVore devoted more than 1200 hours to field observations and practically became an honorary member of several troops. He came to know some 80 baboons by sight and had names for all of them. He understood what they were saying to one another, a skill which helped considerably in interpreting their behavior—and, on at least one occasion, in interpreting his behavior to them. Baboons are reasonably tolerant of scientists, but one thing you must never do is frighten an infant. DeVore did just that by accident one day, the infant yelped, and immediately several large angry males dashed to the spot slapping the ground and lunging at him. Fortunately, he knew the appropriate signal. He smacked his lips loudly, which is a pacifying gesture among baboons and can be translated roughly as follows: "Sorry about that. It was a mistake. No harm intended."

DeVore followed troops all day for many days before he began to recognize some basic features of their way of life. Their comings and goings, which seem so haphazard at first, are actually quite predictable. Each troop confines its movements largely to a definite territory, a home range of about 10 to 15 square miles. The boundaries of the range are marked by an invisible fence, signs which we do not see but which are very real to troop members. Baboons become tense and watchful as they approach this line; they move away, and cannot be driven across it. They are not familiar with what lies on the other side. Novelty is always a reason for caution, and when the novelty is too great, it can be a powerful repellent.

The home range contains two or three core areas where the troop spends more than 90 percent of its time and does more than 90 percent

Irven DeVore
establishing contact
with baboons

of its traveling and feeding. Each core area is further specialized by the inclusion of at least one stretch of stream or river with trees growing along the banks, and trees are the only refuges on Kenya savannas. Escape is calculated by such things as the probability of predators being abroad, conditions of visibility, and distance from the nearest trees. Where lions are numerous, baboons move only within a safe distance from the trees. This is so even when they are hungry due to the scarcity of food in the area and abundant food exists outside the safety zone.

A collective wisdom exists in the baboon troop, as in every organized body of animals. As an organic repository of information, the troop knows more than any one of its members. The unique and unusual experiences of older individuals affect the behavior of the group. Once an investigator studying parasitic diseases shot two baboons from a car. More than eight months later, the troop was still giving cars a wide berth, although it had previously been quite approachable, and although the odds are that only a few of the troop's 80-odd members saw what happened. (A striking example of group learning is cited in Chapter 5.) About two years after Harding discovered meat eating among Kenya baboons, his colleague Strum found the practice considerably more widespread within the troop. Macaque monkeys have also developed traditions of a sort. Members of troops on Kyushu Island in Japan sometimes walk 30 yards or so from the forest to the beach to wash dirt off handfuls of sweet potatoes provided by scientists to entice the animals into open country where they can be observed. This baboon custom was learned about 20 years ago, and it spread rapidly and has been practiced ever since.

Such experiences may be remembered for years or generations and become part of the troop memory, a simple form of culture. In fact, the larger the troop, the greater is its store of accumulated information, its security from predators, and its general knowledge about the environment. If these were the only or the major factors operating, the forces of natural selection might well have produced larger and larger baboon troops and perhaps considerably more advanced social organizations. But other factors limit group size. When a troop has more than a hundred members, it tends to split. One of the reasons is a rise in tensions; when there are too many large dominant males they begin to form two rival groups. Also, when the population increases beyond the capacity of the land to provide food, part of the group must move away to less intensely exploited areas.

Every activity is the result of a balance among opposing tendencies, some of which you can see at work in a baboon when it feeds, which is most of the time. A baboon moves its head and shifts attention periodically. It feeds with head down, scanning the ground, and missing nothing as it passes, pulling up grasses and shoots, digging for juicy roots in the dry season, snatching eggs out of nests, occasionally

(a) Lone baboon on savanna, fair game for lions and other predators (b) Baboon troop near trees, where they can find refuge from predators (c) Baboons at water hole

turning over rocks to find insects underneath. But the baboon is not built to concentrate too steadily. Every five to ten seconds it stops, looks up, and glances about for a second or two before resuming feeding. (This pattern is also observed among people eating alone and may be a throwback to primate days.) At any given instant, about half a dozen individuals in an average-sized troop will be surveying the landscape.

Under certain conditions, particularly around densely overgrown places where predators may hide, baboons seem to live in a hair-trigger state. There are panic reactions—all of a sudden an entire troop, which has been sitting quietly, will scatter and make a break for the trees. Such behavior has obvious survival value, although many false alarms do occur. On one occasion, a dozen baboons dashed away from a resting place, turned to look back, and promptly relaxed when they saw two young impalas stepping out of the grass. A rustling of leaves may be enough to produce frantic scattering, and, in general, troops are ready for flight at an instant's notice.

Perhaps the most fascinating and subtlest thing about a troop is the fit between its natural behavior and the demands of the environment. Any predator attempting to get at baboons during a resting session would probably confront one or more of the vigorous young males distributed around the central group of females and infants and older males. An effective defense system exists, an outer ring of aggressive troop members. But the young males are there, not by choice or selection, but in large part because their close presence is not generally tolerated by the dominant males of the inner circle. In other words, the natural structure of the group determines their function as guards or sentinels.

A similar phenomenon may be observed as a widely dispersed troop passes from open terrain to clumps of bushes and tall grasses. Again the baboons organize for defense, moving to form a more compact group in a manner that tends to discourage crouching predators. But this cannot be considered a pure defense reaction. The mere fact that food is dispersed in the open areas and highly concentrated in the undergrowth would also tend to bring troop members together. A single natural maneuver serves a number of purposes at once.

This sort of behavior illustrates the workings of evolution, the fine adjustment of group to environment. It is the result of natural selection operating over periods of hundreds of thousands of generations, and the process is no less impressive because it seems to be largely automatic. Baboons make self-conscious plans far more rarely than people do, one reason why they rank lower on the evolutionary scale. But the closer one studies them, the more human they appear. Incidentally, the reasons for our own behavior are not always apparent. It also may often have an automatic quality.

A central difference between baboons and human beings con-

Yawn threat of adult male threatening competitors to hold place in hierarchy and maintain order

cerns levels of organization. A baboon troop is a close association of individuals feeding together and generally confining its movements to its home range. Now and then an individual, usually a male, shifts from one troop to another and becomes a loyal member of the new association, to the point of defending the new territory even against his former troop. In densely populated areas troops may feed side by side without fighting; but when there is plenty of space, they tend to avoid one another entirely. Superorganizations, alliances made up of two or more troops, have never been observed among baboons or any other nonhuman primate.

Seen from the outside in a broad context of social behavior, the troop operates a unit, a unified living system, moving about the savanna in search of food and avoiding danger. Seen from the inside, **239**

Glare threat of adult
male baboon
defending status

however, things become considerably more personal. The problem as usual is to bring individual members of the troop, each with their own temperament and needs, into a cohesive social structure. Peter Buirski of the City University of New York and his associates rated the personalities of the seven members of a troop of Nairobi National Park baboons and found that, like human beings, they varied in playfulness, aggression, sociability, and other traits, in general being somewhat more tolerant toward one another and possibly readier to explore than the average human being. These basic differences introduce stresses which must be given a measure of release and expression, and yet kept under control. The solution involves periods of excitement and relaxation, rising and receding tensions.

Every baboon receives a more or less continuous flow of information about the state of mind of other baboons and transmits information to them about its own feelings. The air is alive with signals. Lip-smacking and soft grunts are the most frequent signals and indicate peaceful intentions. Hard direct stares are the most powerful gestures of all. Threatening yawns revealing large canine teeth are typical of baboons who are standing stiff with shoulders hunched and neck hair raised. Every now and then there is a chase accompanied by loud grunting and screeches of fear. Little harm comes of the commotion. Most threats do not lead to a chase, for the threatened individual makes some sort of submissive gesture, such as moving away slowly or **241** screeching loudly with lips curled in a grin of appeasement. When chases do occur, they generally end with the fugitive pressing its body to the ground and the pursuer holding it there for a moment and then walking off. Bloodshed is rare, serious injury even rarer.

As a rule, quarrels last less than half a minute. They can be interpreted as letting off steam or maintaining a certain level of excitement and alertness among individuals that really have little else to do. The net effect is to achieve stability through a sort of regulated turbulence. All this activity goes on within the framework of a rigid social system, a hierarchy in which every adult member of the troop has a place. A few hours of observation are usually enough to figure out the status of various individuals in a general way. "The very bearing of a dominant baboon distinguishes it from the others," DeVore reports. "Besides having a confident gait, its fur is likely to be sleek and well-groomed. A subordinate animal will be less self-assured; it will have tousled fur and, frequently, many minor scars from old wounds."

More precise information can be obtained by noting which of two individuals gives way when both approach food or a shady resting place or a female in heat. Status also shows up during episodes of so-called redirected aggression. This is the baboon version of what happens when a man who has just been called down by his boss comes home and snaps at his wife—who then slaps her child, who, in turn, kicks the dog. The result is a flow of aggressive energy downhill through the troop's hierarchy. A dominant male usually starts things by chasing a subordinate male, who promptly expresses his feelings by chasing a still more subordinate individual. Low monkey on the totem pole during such activity is rarely an adult male, but often an adult female—the highest-ranking female still occupies a position below that of the lowest-ranking male. Sometimes baboons will even release their aggression on an inanimate object, bouncing against a tree or tugging at a large rock.

This sort of behavior may take place on a large scale when the troop has been frightened. The mere sight of a leopard, the most dangerous predator to baboons, was once followed by an extended burst of activity, dominant males chasing subordinate males, and subordinate males chasing females, to the accompaniment of much screeching and nipping. The episode lasted for more than five minutes before simmering down to a flurry of grunts, threatening yawns, and lip-smacking. It was something like waves and ripples dying out in a pond after gusts of wind. On another occasion a lion charged at a troop, and it took a full hour for the baboons to relax.

The hierarchy is not always a simple matter of A dominating B, B dominating C, and so on down the line. In one troop, for example, the strongest individual and the best fighter was Kula, an "aggressive, fearless, dominance-oriented" adult male in his prime. Kula could almost certainly have beaten any of the other adult males of the troop in single combat. But he never received privileges commensurate with his abilities because three older baboons, including a very old and formidable veteran, stayed close to one another most of the time and acted together in putting down the challenges of others. In other words, Kula was the victim of the establishment, or central hierarchy.

Adult males, particularly the establishment, bear the major responsibility for protecting the troop. The frequent quarrels and skirmishes among troop members serve constantly to reestablish and confirm status relationships. As with humans in fire drills or lifeboat drills, such rehearsals prepare all individuals for knowing their places and roles in times of crisis. Most encounters with predators come to a quick conclusion. When a pack of hungry wild dogs approached one troop, all individuals except the dominant male retreated, leaving him sitting between themselves and the pack; but he did not even bother to change his position; he merely turned his head and stared, and the dogs ran off.

Within the troop, adult males maintain order and stop fights. The number 1 male has a wide sphere of influence. If he walks toward trouble head up, leading with his chin, his presence may be felt at quite a distance. A long-range stare was once sufficient to break up a fight between two juveniles some 60 feet away and, on another occasion, to make a misbehaving infant scream as if it had been hit. On the other hand, the leader's power is not unlimited, and even females may intervene successfully by ganging up on him if he treats one of their number too roughly.

Patterns of mating behavior favor the inheritance of physical strength, fast reflexes, and other qualities contributing to the attainment of top positions in the hierarchy. Although dominance alone does not guarantee success in mating, a high-ranking male will probably have access to a female at the height of her estrus period, when she is most receptive and most fertile. Furthermore, the higher his rank, the better his chances of monopolizing her as a partner. Consequently, a large proportion of the offspring born into a troop may be sired by the most dominant male.

A hierarchy among females also exists, but its workings are more difficult to figure out during a limited period of observation. On a short-term basis, female relationships may change because of changes associated with the reproductive cycle. As a female in heat becomes increasingly aggressive, she arouses aggression within the troop, among females as well as males. She attacks other females more frequently and is more frequently attacked by them. Since she may be protected by adult males, her effective status in the hierarchy may rise a notch or two until the end of estrus (that is, for about ten days).

The Establishment: (top) adult male threatens two members of central hierarchy (bottom), who turn and chase him

The behavior of the adolescent female is particularly ambiguous.
She often joins forces with an adult female against another adult female,
and may come to dominate some individuals ranking low in the female
hierarchy. On the other hand, she generally makes it a practice to steer
clear of dominant females, and is thus half in and half out of the hierarchy. In general, since status is always shifting with changes in physiological condition, females apparently do not have a chance to establish
permanent coalitions. For the same reason, they quarrel much more
frequently among themselves than do males, although the consequences
are not as serious: "There is more or less continuous minor bickering
with very little real attacking and biting."

Females with young enjoy a very special status. In fact, in a sense
the troop exists for them. DeVore points out that by far the most important force in binding the troop together and creating a close-knit social
unit is the infant: "It is scarcely possible to overemphasize the significance of the newborn baboon. It becomes the center of interest, absorbing the attention of the entire troop. From the moment the birth is discovered, the mother is continuously surrounded by other baboons, who
walk beside her and sit as close as possible when she rests." An infant
is likely to come in a time of relative abundance. About four out of every five offspring are born between October and December, which is at
the onset of the rainy season in Kenya, when the food supply is about
to reach a peak.

One of the important features about the primate way of life is
that child rearing is essentially a group activity. Mothers aggregate at
the center of the troop, and other baboons, drawn by the enormous attraction of the infants, join the cluster. Juveniles and adult females come
near and smack their lips and try to touch one of the infants, although
the mother prevents any outside contact for the first week or two. Adolescent females also approach, and learn how to care for the infants they
will bear by carrying and fondling the infants of others. The central nucleus is ideally designed for the learning process, and infants born into
complex primate societies have a great deal to learn.

Dominant males are also powerfully attracted by infants. They
may carry an infant the way its mother does, by letting it cling to the
hair on their bellies. (Fortunately, it has a firm grasp.) In one troop, a
sickly female infant whose mother had died after nursing was adopted
not by a female but by a male member of the establishment. As a matter of fact, adult males will continue to protect a young baboon after its
mother no longer does. After about two years, when she is busy with
her next offspring, they will come to its rescue for another six months or
longer.

There is another interesting if somewhat perverse example of the
significance of infants for adult males. One day in the Amboseli Reserve, an adult male was running rampant through a troop, going after

Mother-infant bond: infant in mother's arms

females and juveniles and practically every individual in sight. He had just lost a fight to a higher-ranking member of the hierarchy. Another adult male, seeing the aggressor coming his way, snatched a nearby young infant and began to groom it frantically, knowing that with an infant in his arms he would probably be immune from attack. That is what happened. The aggressor passed him by for another victim, and he promptly released the infant. This sort of behavior, call it pretense or deceit, is peculiarly primate behavior; it is seen in no other species.

For the first month or so, mother and infant are practically a single organism. The infant is either in her arms nursing, being groomed, or clinging to her belly upside down as she moves with the troop. From then on it becomes increasingly independent. At first it may wobble only a few steps away during rest periods, but as its coor-

dination improves and it grows bolder, it spends more and more time
feeding at a distance and playing with other infants and juveniles. In
other words, at first the infant depends on its mother exclusively for
both companionship and protection, and later turns increasingly to its
peers for companionship and to adult males for protection.

By the age of 2 to 3, baboons are spending most of their time
playing, chasing and tumbling over one another, and dodging and
wrestling. Special signals distinguish playing from fighting. In fights
the pursuer may come on with a rush, loud grunts, and eyes fixed on the
pursued, who may dash away screeching with fright. Play is generally
silent, and the approach is made with a characteristic bouncing or hopping gait. It often seems to be a rehearsal, providing baboons with opportunities to maneuver body, face, and teeth into appropriate positions
for attack and defense.

There are sexual differences in play. Females chase one another
for relatively brief periods, the chase ending gently with the pursuer
simply touching the pursued. Furthermore, they devote increasing time
to infants and drop out of play groups entirely by the age of 3 or 4, that
is, toward the end of their adolescence. Males are adolescent longer, un-

til about the age of 7, and they play longer, harder, and rougher. Their chases generally end with romping and wrestling, and there is a greater tendency for excitement to build up until pain and serious encounters threaten, and such play may have to be broken up by adult males.

At about the age of 5 the male is larger than adult females, and his time has come to rise in the troop. So he starts fighting the females, who fight back for a time, although one has the impression that they expect him to assert himself and offer only token resistance. Some of his greatest problems develop later with the ending of adolescence, when he is at the top of the female hierarchy but at the bottom of the male hierarchy, and he begins to fight older males. He may be physically ready for leadership, but socially the time is not ripe. Although completely mature, he may have to wait another two or three years before finding his place in the upper levels of the male hierarchy.

The males, defenders and defenders-to-be, represent the chief locus of tension in the troop. Except for members of the central hierarchy, they do not actively seek one another out, and within the structure of the group younger males seem to prefer being by themselves. They tolerate one another politely but without warmth, which is less unfriendly than it sounds considering that males live at a high level of tension, particularly during periods when females are in estrus. Indeed, one test of any social group is whether it maintains its basic stability during such periods; by that test, the baboon troop is successful.

The locus of affection is definitely among the aggregated females and infants in the central group. Of all expressions of affection, grooming is by far the most frequent. Typically, one baboon sits or lies on its back as another baboon parts and searches through its fur, picking or licking off every speck of alien material. The picture is one of rapt concentration. The groomer scans the fur intently section by section, while individuals being groomed close their eyes or look to the side and wallow in contentment, always avoiding a direct look at the groomer, which is a sign of aggression.

Grooming almost certainly serves a hygienic function. Africa is a paradise for all forms of life, including a rich assortment of insects and parasites. After walks through grass I have frequently had myself inspected and inspected others for the presence of omnipresent ticks. Among the Kalahari Bushmen, boys delouse one another beginning early in the morning. Among baboons, mothers groom newborn infants every few minutes, and morning grooming groups of two to eight individuals form as soon as troops come down from their sleeping trees. The licking and picking of wounds may also have a cleansing effect and help account for the fact that healing often proceeds very quickly.

Above all, however, grooming brings individuals together. Sensual pleasure is involved, and the effect seems to be far more intensive when individuals are being groomed than when they groom themselves. The most common grooming cluster consists of two females and one infant. The next most common cluster is two females with additional infants and an adult male. Although females participate in the activity more often than males and devote more time to it, it has a special significance for the male. The grooming of one individual by another tends to be more frequent—and adult play less frequent—among baboons and other primates with rigid hierarchies, as if the very rigidity demanded a compensating increase of affection.

Like all social relations, grooming can be exploited, used with malice aforethought. Once a young female ran over to a dominant male for protection against a young male who wanted to attack her. The young male came over and began grooming the female, but gave her a nip as soon as her protector looked away. This can be cited as another case of deceit or, more broadly, of the evolving of complex tactics and strategies based on a knowledge of prevailing behavior forms. It is a characteristic developed to a fine point in people.

The baboon troop exists as a successful compromise, an equilibrium between individual aggression and cooperation. For all the tensions and chases, most of the day consists of peaceful feeding, resting, and grooming. Affection represents the pervading force, and the power of affection is indicated by its durability and continuity; fortunately, baboons do not have a great capacity for remorse. It is difficult to conceive

Male baboons wrestling, playing more roughly than females

Grooming group,
infant holding leg of
dominant male

of an organization better designed for the protection of infants than the baboon troop, with its inner cluster of mothers and dominant males; and yet probably less than half of all infants born survive beyond their second year, the rest becoming victims of injury, disease, and predators.

    An infant's death illustrates the persistence of affection, and also how abruptly it may cease. A mother may carry a dead infant for several days, clutching the corpse to her belly, letting it drop from time to time, and then going back and picking it up again. When the ultimate separation comes, it may be striking for its complete lack of apparent emotion. After clinging to her infant for four days, one mother simply let go of it without even breaking her stride or looking back, as if she were unaware of what had happened.

    Circumstances call for the shutting off of deep concern. The laws of necessity dictate that affection cannot be attached too strongly to any single individual. Death is too frequent. But affection itself must outlast all the endings and letdowns. In the case of the female, it must always be revived by the sight and touch of her next infant and the infants of others. The troop owes its existence to the fact that evolution and natural selection have made this enduring renewal possible.

249

CHAPTER 13   CHIMPANZEES: OUR CLOSEST RELATIVES

A high order of intelligence is generally associated with independence, individual initiative, and a capacity for novel and creative behavior. This implies that the more intelligent a primate is, the greater the difficulty of limiting its freedom in the context of rigid hierarchy. We see that tensions and frustrations have been observed even among baboons, and such behavior might well have caused more serious stresses among more intelligent prehuman apes. Severe conflict was probably a basic feature of the hominid line from the very beginning as a direct result of savanna life and the need for rules and discipline.

Baboon society provides a model of primate life in the grassy savannas of Africa, the sort of world our ancestors encountered when they moved out of open woodlands. They, like baboons, may once have lived sunrise-to-sunset lives, slept in trees for safety, and moved across open places in covered-wagon types of defense formations with infants and mothers protected at the center (see Chapter 4). Probably their sons also played rough-and-tumble games, while their daughters were attracted increasingly to infants and the care of infants. They also had hierarchies, an establishment, and the perennial problem of building individuals into stable social systems.

But the comparison can be carried just so far, and no further. Other species have adapted in other ways to exposed conditions. Ronald Hall found that the patas monkeys of Uganda, perhaps the most terrestrial of all nonhuman primates, survive by scattering rather than aggregating as baboons do. Individual troop members are often separated by distances of more than a hundred yards, on the principle of offering predators isolated rather than concentrated targets. Built like greyhounds, they are outstanding for their fantastic running and dodging abilities; they show little aggression. Much remains to be learned about survival in the savanna.

As for life in open woodlands, where the human family is be-   **250**

lieved to have originated, attention focuses on the chimpanzee. Of all **251**
living primates, the chimpanzee is most like people and, therefore, the
most difficult to observe objectively. In recent times, it has been described as a creature living in a state of primal innocence and as "a dia-
bolical caricature of ourselves . . . as common, as vulgar, as no other animal but a debased human being can be." In less gaudy terms, it ranks
high on the primate intelligence scale with a brain about twice the size
of the baboon brain. It spends much of its time on the ground and reveals an impressive capacity for complex and enduring social relationships. Moreover, observations suggest the sort of forces that might have
transformed the life-style of a forest-dwelling chimpanzee into a
hominid-savanna life style.

The wild chimpanzee prefers to keep its distance, at least in the
beginning; this usually presents far more problems in forests than in
savannas for investigators observing primates. In 1960 when Jane Goodall started her studies in Gombe Stream Reserve forests, she would arise
daily about half-past five in the morning and spend most of the day on
top of a rocky hill overlooking the forests and Lake Tanganyika, where
she could observe and be observed as a harmless and unassuming fellow primate.

Social acceptance was slow in coming. Some days she spent 12
hours in the field, climbing up and down slopes and forcing her way
through dense undergrowth without seeing a single chimpanzee. She
often heard calls in the distance, but the animals had moved off by the
time she managed to make her way to the area. "It wasn't just fear,"
she explains. "It was also resentment of your presence. Like people in
an English village, they don't care to be stared at." During the first few
months they would run away upon seeing her at distances of as much
as 500 yards.

The apes became tamer as they learned her ways, and as she
learned theirs. Part of her strategy, for example, was pretending not to
pay attention. Often a group that seemed nervous and about to take off
when being watched intently would calm down and stay if she started
doing something else, such as eating leaves or digging a hole. Gradually
she was able to come closer and closer—to within 50 yards by eight
months and within 50 feet by another half-year or so. In general, males
were bolder than females, "displaying" for five or ten minutes on occasion as they would to a fellow chimpanzee—that is, engaging in behavior such as screaming, hitting trees, and shaking branches. Then they
would ignore her and go about their business.

Chimpanzees enjoy a social life which is strikingly flexible compared to that of baboons. They are more human than baboons, or rather
they jibe better with the way we like to picture ourselves, as free-
wheeling individuals who tend to be unpredictable, do not take readily
to any form of regimentation, and are frequently charming. (Charm is

relatively rare among baboons.) Although baboon troops usually remain
together with all members clustered in a single area, this is rarely the
case for chimpanzees. According to Vernon Reynolds of Oxford University, who studied chimpanzees in the Budongo Forest of western
Uganda, they move about in four types of bands: adult males only;
mothers and offspring with occasionally a few other females; adults and
adolescents of both sexes without mothers or offspring; and representatives of all categories mixed together. The composition of a party may
change a number of times a day, as individuals wander off and groups
split or combine with other groups.

Chimpanzees live in such an easy-come, easy-go style that both
Goodall and Reynolds commented on their apparent lack of permanent
social organization. Japanese investigators were the first to note the
existence of loose but nevertheless definite troops. In 1967, Junichiro
Itani and Akira Suzuki of the University of Kyoto, working in Tanzania
some hundred miles south of the Gombe Stream Reserve, reported the
same invisible-fence phenomenon that was found among baboons (see
Chapter 12). Lines exist in the forest, boundaries which human eyes
cannot detect and which chimpanzees do not cross, turning back as if
obeying No Trespassing signs.

Recent research was done at Gombe by second-generation investigators—former graduate students including David Bygott, Patrick
McGinnis, Anne Pusey, Caroline Tutin, and Richard Wrangham of
Cambridge University; Geza Teleki of Pennsylvania State University;
and William McGrew of the University of Edinburgh. Their work has
done a great deal to extend our knowledge about chimpanzee behavior.
Three distinct communities have been observed in the region, two with
40 to 50 members and one with 20 to 30 members, and they occupy separate territories. The relationships among these groups are subtle. For
one thing, Wrangham has evidence that patrol groups visit boundary
ridges to keep tabs on one another's whereabouts: "The fact that parties
sometimes travelled to ridges without eating en route, and then returned after listening for 30 minutes or more, suggested that they were
monitoring the boundaries. Prime or dominant males were invariably
involved."

Judging by the typical behavior of dominant males, little love is
lost when parties from different communities cross paths. They avoid
one another or else threaten and attack, with the smaller party giving
way. On the other hand, there are also peaceful encounters, and there is
a potential for ties other than community ties. Females tend to be more
sociable than males, associating with males of different communities
from time to time and moving more readily from one community to another. Old males and even dominant males join alien parties on occasion without mayhem, although little is known about the circumstances

which make the joining possible. The individuals involved may once have been members of a single community, perhaps brothers, which split when the population increased.

Chimpanzees are nomads. They generally sleep in different trees every night and travel in individual core ranges or circuits depending on sex and the abundance of food. Wrangham's studies suggest that males tend to forage together in the same areas during times of abundance, and disperse when food is scarce. Females are dispersed at all times, except when sexually active. Chimpanzee paths are everywhere in the forests, miles and miles of them, including tunnels through the densest stretches of undergrowth, tubes just about big enough for an individual to scramble through on all fours. (Many animals have such tunnels, perhaps the most spectacular being the great elephant tunnels of northern Bengal, long corridors 10 feet high that wind through tangled places in jungles along the foothills of the Himalayas.)

There is nothing nonhuman for chimpanzees to fear in the forest. The most formidable predator, the leopard, tends to concentrate on other game. Chimpanzees hunt more often than they are hunted. Teleki, whose analysis of their predatory episodes is referred to in Chapter 6, has estimated that, on the average, a community of 50 chimpanzees may go after prey four or five times a month, and that the cooperation of 2 to 5 individuals is involved more than half the time. As among human bands, females rarely participate in hunting when adults males are around, but they may hunt in the absence of males.

Meat eating and sharing seem to go together. No primate is known to share plant food, but a successful hunt creates situations which definitely encourage giving or at least permissiveness. According to Shirley Strum, among baboons adult male-female and mother-infant pairs may eat the same piece of meat side by side: "Frequently, one individual moves to allow another access to the meat." This mild or passive form of sharing is also found among chimpanzees, together with rather more active and more elaborate forms. Out of 579 "exchange interactions" which Teleki observed during twelve kills, 395 were requests for meat. These included peering intently at or reaching out to touch the meat or the eater; emitting soft whimpers or "hoo" sounds; and extending an open hand, palm upwards, in the classical begging gesture. About a third of the requests produced results; most of the time they were firmly and not always gently ignored.

Three things that chimpanzees have never been observed doing indicate the nature of the gap between them and human beings. Chimpanzees never use weapons during the hunt; never gang up to kill or even to pursue animals bigger than themselves, confining themselves to prey weighing no more than about 20 pounds; and never teach hunting techniques, or anything else for that matter, to other troop members.

Learning proceeds without instruction, by imitation only, which means lengthy periods of trial and error and a tendency to limit the extent of cultural development.

Even so, hunting and sharing chimpanzee-style are highly significant. As James Chisholm of the Institute of Child Health in London emphasizes, although meat makes up only a small proportion of the apes' diet (probably less than 1 percent), it calls for the first steps toward a new and complex level of sociability—in effect, a kind of high-grade inhibition. When an adult male chimpanzee has a freshly killed animal in his grasp, he is temporarily king of the hill. He may occupy a low position in the established hierarchy, but his superiors waive rank and request food from him instead of grabbing it away and terrorizing him. They recognize that the possession of an extremely valuable resource somehow changes the rules, and that in the long run there is more to be gained by restrained, polite, and submissive behavior than by aggression. This quality developed to a high degree when our hominid ancestors relied increasingly on meat as part of their survival on the savanna.

Chimpanzees may become highly aroused at the mere sight of a killing, screaming loudly as they watch the action, and running about and throwing their arms around one another. In fact, a variety of conditions can throw them into a frenzy. As mentioned in Chapter 7, they perform rain dances to the accompaniment of thunder and lightning during tropical storms, and one of their most outlandish rituals is the carnival, when as many as 30 individuals come together in a period of fantastic noisemaking which may last several hours. The sound is difficult to believe even when you have heard it.

Reynolds has described what it is like to be caught in the middle of a carnival: "The noise is terrific, like a tornado or an audience-applause machine turned way up. It can be very frightening, because there is also a great deal of running back and forth, and the ground shakes, and you hear high shrieking and the thud of heavy feet coming toward you and violent drumming on the trees." No one knows what unusual events start such bursts of mass excitement. They may represent reactions to a killing of some sort, or perhaps elaborate greeting ceremonies between two communities which have not crossed paths for a long time.

Another sign of more complex social behavior is that the mother-offspring bond is more enduring among chimpanzees than among baboons. Chimpanzees mature far more slowly, requiring a prolonged period of infant dependency. The first separation between mother and infant, the first break in physical contact does not occur for 16 to 24 weeks, as compared to about 4 weeks among baboons. Although juveniles no longer need to be nursed after they are 4 or 5 years old or so, they may share their

Chimp mother
playing with son

mother's nest for another three years; they are dependent until about the age of 8.

Increasing independence, however, does not mean the severing of family ties. In fact, one of the most significant discoveries about chimpanzee behavior in the Gombe area, a discovery that would never have been made without long-term observations, is that family ties probably last throughout life. One mother estimated to be nearly 50 years old had two sons, both over 20, who often kept her company and groomed her. The two top-ranking males in a seven-male group support each other in times of trouble, look alike, and are probably brothers.

Other examples of close ties, including brother-sister bonds, indicate the complexity of social relations within the community.

The period of extended youth provides ample opportunity for many kinds of play. As among baboons, this consists in the main of silent chasing and wrestling. The chimpanzee is unique among primates, however, in the amount of time it spends playing with objects. It seems to have a special predisposition for manipulating certain kinds of objects, notably sticks and twigs, and manipulating them in a certain way, by poking and probing. Such a built-in bias helps to ensure that learning will not proceed at random but along broad, genetically guided lines.

One of the Gombe chimpanzees' outstanding accomplishments is inserting probes into termite-mound holes to extract the edible insects from underground nests (see Chapter 2). This is by no means a simple technique, as Teleki discovered during long periods of observation of

Chimpanzee family: sister nuzzling brother in mother's arms

an adult male (named Leakey after the Olduvai investigator). For one **257** thing, finding the covered holes demands considerable experience. Leakey would inspect a mound briefly, and then flick away a bit of dirt, almost invariably exposing an opening. Teleki never learned where to flick, nor could he detect any cracks, bumps, or depressions which might mark the location of a hole.

Leakey unhesitantly selected stalks or stems suitable for efficient probing, neither too stiff nor too flexible, while Teleki, who never mastered this trick of instant choosing, spent frustrating hours learning how to insert the probe into twisting channels and vibrate it gently so that termites would be aroused to attack the invading object by biting onto it firmly. Such difficulties are not surprising, considering that Teleki had only two to three months to learn, while Leakey had had a lifetime. The point is that nonhuman primates need and have an impressive ability to acquire elaborate new skills, to expand their repertoire of behavior patterns.

Another skill demonstrated by Gombe chimpanzees represents the anthropoid equivalent of drawing water from a well. The well is the crotch of a tree where rain water has collected, and the problem is to get a drink. Thirsty juveniles and young infants bend over and squeeze their faces into the hollow, but they get nothing because their faces are too big. An experienced chimpanzee knows precisely what to do. It strips some leaves from a convenient plant, chews them just enough to form a crumpled ball, dips the ball into the hollow, and then withdraws the soggy mass and sucks the water out of it. In other words, it makes a kind of artificial sponge.

The full range of tool use among wild apes is yet to be understood. Itani reports that chimpanzees in western Tanzania, occupying territories up to a hundred miles south of the Gombe Reserve, crack hard fruits with stone hammers, scoop honey out of honeycombs with twigs, and sometimes use sticks to attack one another (see Chapter 2). Different practices are observed in different areas. Presumably, the reason that Gombe chimpanzees employ the sponge method for getting at water in a tree crotch is because the trick was discovered at some time in the past and has been transmitted from generation to generation ever since. But Budongo chimpanzees have another method which happens to be less efficient, simply dipping their hands into the natural bowls and licking the water off their fingers.

Human beings go chimpanzees one better. They are also long-time eaters of insects, including termites, and one night Teleki had a chance to observe the methods of local Tanzanians. They took two short sticks, started drumming rhythmically on the top and sides of a termite mound, and then scraped off part of the mound with a machete, exposing swarms of termites which were promptly dumped into baskets. The purpose of the drumming? "We do that to imitate the rain." The regular beat sounds like raindrops to termites nesting deep underground, and they are fooled into climbing to the surface. Thus, baboons wait until relatively late in the rainy season and have about two weeks of termite eating; chimpanzees go to work early in the season and have two months or so; and human beings, by creating a fake rainy season, have at least four months.

Methods of catching termites are a measure of the intellectual capacities of baboons, chimpanzees, and human beings. Baboons have an avid appetite for termites and will watch intently as chimpanzees use probes to eat the insects by the thousands; sometimes baboons will pick up sticks, but that is where it ends. There is a world of brainpower between baboon and chimpanzee. The concept of a tool, the notion of using an object to make up for their own limitations, does not occur to baboons under these circumstances. They have never been observed trying to use probes, and they seem completely incapable of making a connection between the sticks they hold in their hands and the activities of the chimpanzees they are watching. Instead they wait until later in the season when termites are swarming and grab what they can on the ground or in mid-air, a far less efficient process.

Similarities between people and chimpanzees may be as striking as differences. Chimpanzees use familiar gestures to express their feelings. Upon meeting in the forest, old friends kiss and embrace, or one individual may reach out and pat the other on the head or shoulder. Another common form of greeting is to rest the hand on the thigh or genitals. This gesture may also signify reassurance, and men as well as chimpanzees have used it for that purpose. (In the Bible, for example, laying a hand on a person's thigh is a way of sealing a bargain, of swearing to do what he asks.)

There are other actions one would have no difficulty in interpreting; for example, chimpanzees scratch their head when trying to make up their mind. Before picking a piece of fruit off a tree, chimpanzees may squeeze it gently to test its ripeness, like a person selecting tomatoes at the local supermarket. Goodall saw a male fidgeting and absent-mindedly eating a flower while waiting for a companion, presumably female, and looking for all the world like an "impatient man glancing at his wristwatch." Chimpanzees are perhaps most human when they are at play. Infants may play tug-of-war with a stick; juveniles chase one another, and in the midst of a chase, the pursued may burst out laughing, presumably in anticipation of being tickled by his pursuer.

Presumably there were primates resembling chimpanzees 20 to 25 million years ago, before the coming of hominids, in forests that formed a broad band stretching from Africa to the Far East. They were prehuman apes (described in Chapter 2), and judging by recent studies, they were probably lively, easygoing, relatively independent creatures, with social systems sufficiently flexible to allow considerable freedom of **259** movement and individual action. Like present-day chimpanzees, most of these forest dwellers moved in and out of shadows and along old ancestral trails. Others, however, began to invade the strange new world where no ape had yet established a foothold, venturing away from the safe depths of forests and out into less dense woodlands toward the open savanna.

They were not alone in their migrations. Richard Estes of the Academy of Natural Sciences of Philadelphia points out that the ancestors of modern antelopes, wildebeests, buffaloes, and other hooved animals, creatures that had wandered solitary or in small groups in the forest, were also emerging into the savanna and adapting to new exposed conditions by coming together in large groups for mutual protection: "The herd was a passport to the grasslands. It substituted for cover, providing concealment for the individual." In other words, the individual increased its chances for survival by submerging itself in the group and becoming anonymous.

Our ancestors never went that far. They came well equipped for a life in the sun. They were large, agile, sharp-sighted, and had probably learned to use tools. Above all, they were intelligent and adaptable. Moving called for some radical changes. The invaders could not afford to travel through exposed places the way they had traveled among the trees, relaxed and with an almost careless lack of alertness. They had to contend with natives of the grassy plains, established species which were already admirably adapted for predation and had learned all the tricks of ambushing, harassing, and killing. A reasonable guess is that the new primates did what all pioneers, human as well as nonhuman, must do when they enter hostile territory. They became "baboonized," as it were, joining ranks and traveling together in disciplined troops.

Observations in the wild indicate that primates are capable of adjusting to different environments. Budongo chimpanzees, for example, change their behavior drastically upon approaching open terrain. They may amble unconcernedly through their forest, but they are tense and vigilant when it comes to crossing a road, looking left and right at the road's edge, running back into the undergrowth, and finally making a dash for the other side. Gombe chimpanzees become nervous on the slopes of hills where the forest thins out.

The effect can be considerably more extensive, as indicated by evidence from Itani and his associates. They have observed chimpanzees crossing wide stretches of open woodland country along mountain ridges lying between dense riverine forests, and report that these apes move in structured groups more like baboon troops on grassy savannas. The effect may also work the other way around. According to Rowell, baboons living in the comparative safety of Uganda forests do not have hierarchies and generally live more relaxed lives, more like chimpanzees with looser social structures. They are also freer to move from troop to troop, and adult males do not defend the troop during emergencies: "In fact, being larger they usually outdistanced the rest in a flight from danger, the last animals being females carrying the larger babies."

The environment is an important factor in determining such behavior, but it is not the only factor. James Paterson of the University of Calgary in Canada reports no apparent dominance hierarchy and hardly any fighting in a troop of baboons living on the edge of the Budongo forest, and a definite hierarchy and frequent fighting and chasing in a troop of savanna-dwelling baboons to the southwest. He attributes differences of this sort to the interplay between inherited behavior, different environments, and acquired protocultural patterns.

The primates that were our ancestors underwent a gradual evolutionary transformation. At first perhaps it was a matter of occasional crossings and the finding of new foods on the savanna, occasional excursions into savanna regions bordering forests, and back to the shelter of forests at night. Then there were moves farther and farther out into the open until the bond between apes and forest dissolved, and they left the forest for good and used tiny islands of forest, clumps of trees near waterways, for refuge and sleeping. This development, which may have required several million years or more, produced the first hominids. The new way of life was achieved at a price. Life in the open, exposed to predators in the wide grassy savannas, demanded tight troop organization and discipline, which, in turn, created new sources of tension clashes between the individual and the group, the one and the many, a result which has not yet been resolved.

Further insights are needed to help define more precisely what it means to be human. The German zoologist Karl von Frisch spent ten years studying some aspects of the behavior of bees and, incidentally, raising as many questions as he answered; it is safe to assume that considerably more time will be required for a primate species. To be sure, a great deal of information can be gathered in short-term research. One ten-month study alone produced 2,000 pages of handwritten notes and 50,000 feet of motion-picture film, as well as numerous maps, photographs, and tape recordings.

But for all the data, a year or a few years are not long enough. The period covers too narrow a slice of time, too short in comparison with the life spans of monkeys and apes, which may live up to 40 years in the wild. It may furnish a good idea of the structure of a hierarchy but tell us little about the dynamics of the hierarchy, how it changes and how individuals rise or fall in status. A troop must be observed over extended periods if insights are to be gained into such things as the development of personality, enduring bonds among individuals, and other rare but revealing events.

The most systematic long-term study yet conducted involves macaque monkeys living on the northeast coast of Japan's Kyushu Island, the "see no evil, hear no evil, speak no evil" monkeys of the Buddhist religion. One troop, which lives in a forest on a mountainside sloping down to the sea, has been observed on a continuous day-to-day basis ever since 1953. Studies of this sort can establish the existence of relationships at best only inferred from short-term studies and often missed entirely, as well as the existence of some major problems.

For example, a remarkably effective equivalent of the incest taboo prevails in the troop. In thousands of recorded copulations not a single one has involved a mother and her son, and brother-sister matings are surprisingly rare. Not all cases are as clear-cut as this one. According to Elizabeth Missakian of Rockefeller University, who studied rhesus monkeys on the island of Cayo Santiago off the coast of Puerto Rico, out of 26 mother-son pairs in which mating was possible, that is, in which the son was at least 3 years old, mating actually occurred among 8 pairs. But, in general, incest is much rarer than might be expected among nonhuman primates and among species other than primates as well. Norbert Bischof of the California Institute of Technology has completed an extensive study and concludes: "In the whole animal kingdom with very few exceptions no species is known in which under natural conditions inbreeding occurs to any considerable degree." He emphasizes that sex evolved as a most effective way of achieving genetic diversity, of producing offspring with mixed and varied hereditary traits; that this is a way of protecting and insuring species against extinction in environments that vary continually and unpredictably; and that widespread inbreeding would run counter to this basic principle. Incest taboos among human beings serve to reinforce what evolution and biology favor in the interests of survival.

Studies of Kyushu monkeys reveal another basic relationship, a marked tendency for the sons of dominant mothers to become dominant themselves. This seems to be a common mammalian pattern. Observed some 15 years ago among Japanese macaques and subsequently among baboons, it has also been reported in research on bison, wolves, and horses. It raises a number of questions. Perhaps the mother is dominant by association since she keeps company more frequently with dominant than with subordinate males, and so her sons tend to inherit genes for male dominance; in addition, they have the opportunity to emulate the ways of leaders. But the explanation may be more direct, namely, that the mother has her own genes for dominance which she passes on to her offspring.

But even with the best of backgrounds, males encounter many difficulties in trying to establish themselves among other males. In a special study, Hiroki Mizuhara of Kyoto University has found that there is not enough room at the top among Kyushu monkeys. At one point the troop contained about 200 members, and its male hierarchy was made up of 16 adult males (about 20 to 30 years old), 6 leaders and 10 subleaders. Several years later the troop had increased to 440 members, but without proportional representation. The hierarchy still consisted of 16 adult males. Although most of the younger males stayed on as second-class citizens, more than a dozen left to lead solitary lives outside the troop.

Even after making it to the top levels, a male must continue to assert his position, or else suffer the consequences. In the troop discussed above, an adult male, Pan, held position number 3 in the hierarchy for more than three years, and, together with the other five leaders, occupied the favored central area of the feeding ground, located at the forest's edge on the site of a Zen Buddhist temple. But then something very unusual happened. He began to lose status, without any decline in health or vigor and without any apparent pressure from other monkeys, as if he were relinquishing his position by choice.

The early part of the change took place gradually. Pan spent less and less time in the central area, and more time near its edges, where the subleaders generally sit or play when the leaders are around. But if he represented a weak spot at the top, no other troop member took advantage of the situation until nearly ten months had passed. The first sign of a challenge came one afternoon from Siro, a male ranking number 18 in the hierarchy. Siro lunged at Pan as if to chase him; Pan stood his ground.

The encounter ended there, except that Siro emitted a "gaa-gaa" cry, a threat frequently directed at solitary males who have left the troop. The cry proved to be prophetic. The next day, Pan had a vicious and inconclusive fight with a subleader. A few days after that, he permitted a young male to mount him three times, thus indicating quite clearly that he considered himself a subordinate and no longer part of the hierarchy. Within three weeks he had been chased from the feeding area. He was last seen alive sitting alone in a wheat field about 300 yards from the rest of the troop.

Mizuhara cites this case and others in emphasizing that, as far as enduring security within the troop is concerned, striking differences exist between the sexes. The female's role is relatively clear-cut and stable; no Kyushu female has ever become a loner. On the other hand, the male must always be ready to fight if necessary to keep or advance his position. The social structure of the macaque troop is put to an especially severe test when it comes to assimilating younger males into the hierarchy, a problem that is found in many human as well as nonhuman primate groups.

In general, as new observations accumulate, the importance of female members of the group becomes increasingly evident. Indeed, the increasing emphasis on the female's role is one of the chief developments of the past few years, reflected in continuing and extended **263** studies of particular troops. Short-term studies generally yield information heavily weighted on the male side, because male behavior tends to be more vigorous and dramatic. Long-term studies, on the other hand, indicate that actual changes in the male hierarchy may be frequent and drastic, while the female hierarchy changes relatively little.

Certainly, females have close relationships with more individuals, especially since fathers are not built into the family circle. In one Cayo Santiago troop, for example, 33 of its 89 members were related to a single female. Such ties become significant when major changes take place in social organization, a fact brought out in a study by Naoki Koyama of Osaka City University, who observed the splitting of a macaque troop of about 165 members into two roughly equal groups. He is convinced that a medium-ranking female named Mino was at the root of the trouble, which occurred as the result of a complex series of conflicts and status changes triggered off when she became dominant over her mother. This study and others, notably those of Donald Sade of Northwestern University, indicate that the social stability of a primate troop is related to the stable ranking of its older females.

Japanese investigators have also used feeding grounds in extended studies of the origin and spread of eating habits, for example, the habit of carrying sweet potatoes to the ocean's edge and washing the dirt off (see Chapter 12). This trick was invented some 16 years ago by Imo, a highly precocious female macaque only 18 months old at the time, apparently young enough so that she had not yet learned to share the traditional primate fear of water. Her playmates were soon washing their potatoes, but the rest of the troop continued to use the old and less efficient method of brushing the dirt off with their hands.

Five years later, the new method had spread from Imo and her playmates to their mothers and later to their own offspring. Today only a few of the adult males have not switched. In another test, the troop reacted in a similar fashion to a new food, caramels wrapped in paper. The candies were sampled first by young macaques, then by their more permissive mothers, and finally by adult males and mothers who had originally tried to discourage the practice. Acceptance required about three years. The pattern differed considerably, however, in another macaque troop, where the first to try a new food, wheat grains, was the dominant male; all troop members were eating the cereal within three days, a fine example of the power of the follow-the-leader principle. Troops differ in many other ways, in the intensity of aggression among leaders, the availability of females in heat to subordinate males, ways of seeking food, and so on.

Important new insights are expected to come from studies of kinship relationships in troops of nonhuman primates. In general, there is considerable evidence that troop members know their mothers, and

very little evidence that they know their fathers. In Robin Fox's words,
troops have "descent, but no alliance, kinship but no marriage." The
reasons for the emergence of marriage and the monogamous family
among hominids remain to be determined. Long-term studies, such as
those in Japan, Cayo Santiago, and the Gombe Stream Research Center,
are beginning to indicate the possible range of cultural or protocultural
behavior among nonhuman primates, and the implications for human
evolution.

Macaque monkeys raised as human infants; laboratory study of infant monkeys, mother surrogates, and development of abnormal behavior; Washoe and her security blanket; an orangutan that makes stone tools; studies of Ceylon elephants, wild dogs, and lions; human beings and social carnivores

CHAPTER 14 OBSERVATION AND EXPERIMENTATION WITH LIVING PRIMATES AND CARNIVORES

The colony of macaque monkeys of the Primate Laboratory of the University of Wisconsin was established more than 20 years ago, about the same time as Japanese investigators of wild macaques on Kyushu Island were beginning. The original purpose of the colony as described by Harry Harlow, the psychologist who founded the laboratory, was "to provide a steady supply of healthy newborn monkeys for the intensive study of learning and intellectual development from the day of birth until the attainment of full capacities."

Infants were raised in surroundings designed to promote vigorous physical growth. Taken from their mothers 6 to 12 hours after birth, they lived in clean and well-lit individual cages, where they could see and hear but not touch other infants. They were bottle-fed, transferred to solid foods at the proper time, and generally treated like human infants. As expected, the infants thrived on all the special attention. Their death rate was lower than that of infants reared by their mothers, and they gained about 25 percent more weight. After a year, they were moved to larger cages, to participate in a series of learning tests and eventually to provide offspring for continuing studies.

The monkeys never served as progenitors of a brave new laboratory breed, however. As they grew up, it became increasingly evident that they were physically fit but emotionally crippled. They sat motionless in their cages, staring into space or rocking, sometimes for hours at a time. Some individuals would start biting themselves as soon as they saw a human being approaching. Also, they were sexually incompetent. One male was aroused when put in a cage with an experienced estrus female which had grown up in the wild. He tried several times to mount her, but did not know how and finally gave up trying and began to attack her viciously. Females raised alone behaved similarly with experienced males.

Studies carried out in the wild direct attention to special areas of **265** behavior, such as relationships with predators, maternal care, communication, play, sleeping habits, and so on. They suggest interpretations and hypotheses which can be checked and modified by the results of experiments performed in laboratory environments. Experiments, in turn, may suggest things to look for when observing troops in their native surroundings. Sophisticated theories of primate behavior, theories capable of predicting new behavior patterns as well as explaining behavior already observed, are most likely to come from investigations which depend on an interchange of information between field and laboratory.

Expanding studies of our primate relatives in Africa and elsewhere are influencing work under way at scientific centers far from forests and savannas and predators. The effect may be traced in part to the long overdue reaction against drawing broad conclusions about natural behavior from the behavior of animals in cages. That does not in any way imply a downgrading of laboratory research, the need for which has never been at issue. It has become more important than ever now that we are acquiring more and more information about life in the wild.

In the future, investigators may be expected to devote more time to the natural behavior of primates, and less time to the study of animals in cages or the traditional and still prevalent kind of psychological experiment in which primates paint pictures, do arithmetic, or play tick-tack-toe. The effort, increasingly, is to discover how primates solve their own problems rather than problems we impose upon them. The trend reflects a change in our attitude toward all animals, a new respect for them as individuals adapted to their native environments.

Field work involves observed events, the specific activities of free-ranging primates. But observing itself is an extremely complicated form of behavior, many times more complicated than anything being observed. There is something to the notion that we tend to see things not as they are but as we are. Since investigators come to studies of primates, as to all studies, with various preconceived ideas, the problem is to bring these ideas into the open as fully as possible so that they may be modified by experience. The French biologist Claude Bernard used to tell his students that "observation shows and experiment teaches," a statement which applies with special force to primate research. Early experimental findings such as those involving macaque behavior have given rise to a great many studies of normal and abnormal behavior.

Harry Harlow and his associates investigated the response of infant monkeys to mother surrogates—that is, effigies, or dummies, built to serve some of the functions of real mothers. In one series of experiments infants were brought up in cages, each with two wooden-headed dummies, one made of bare wire and the other covered with terry cloth. There was no doubt which represented the preferred object to the infants. When bottles of milk were strapped to both dummies, infants in-

Love for mother
surrogate: macaque
infant clinging to
warm terry-cloth
surrogate (upper left);
reaching for milk on
bare-wire surrogate
(upper right); using
terry-cloth surrogate
for protection against
strange object
(bottom)

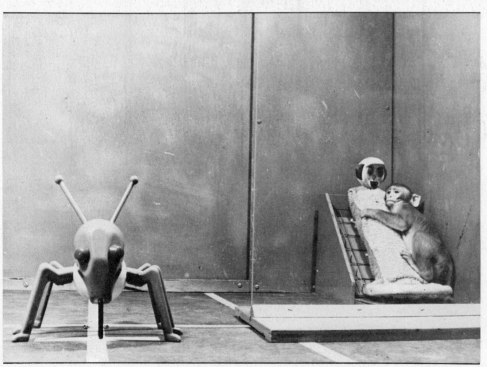

variably went to the terry-cloth dummy. Even when milk was available from the wire dummy only, they spent less than an hour a day there and 17 to 18 hours a day with the terry-cloth model. Softness and warmth were far more important than food in determining the strength of an infant's early attachment to its mother.

Further tests indicate that the mother is important for social rather than purely biological reasons. Infant monkeys raised with mother surrogates were put in a room where they had never been before, a traumatic experience in itself. More than that, the room contained a mechanical bear and a number of other playthings. For whatever it is worth, Harlow found that the toys of human children are among the most frightening objects to infant monkeys. In this test, if there was a terry-cloth dummy in the room, the infant would rush and cling to it. Then after a while it would start exploring, run back to the dummy, explore further, and so on, precisely as it would have behaved with a real mother. When put in the same room with a wire dummy instead of a terry-cloth dummy, however, infants found no solace or comfort or confidence. They were in effect utterly alone. They crouched and hid their faces and were generally too terror stricken to do any exploring.

Apes, but not monkeys, have been known to invent mother surrogates. Washoe, a young female chimpanzee who participated in a University of Nevada study of language (see Chapter 19), lived in a backyard trailer and did not usually venture out unless someone held

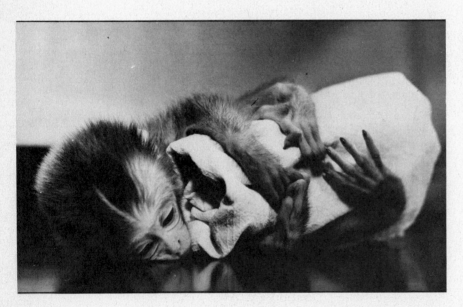

Macaque clinging reflex, prominent during first two or three weeks of life

her hand and accompanied her. But one day she came out on her own dragging a blanket, putting it on her head, lying on it, and leaving it for brief exploratory excursions around the yard, only to rush back to it whenever her courage ran out. The spontaneous use of a mother or security symbol has also been seen in a young gibbon. Perhaps this is an indication that investigators may yet discover surprising examples of advanced behavior among wild as well as among captive apes.

But Harlow makes it clear that dummies providing warmth and comfort are not substitutes for mothers: "The surrogate cannot cradle the baby or communicate monkey sounds and gestures. It cannot punish for misbehavior." Surrogates cannot provide active attention and emotional warmth, and for this reason, among others, strong attachments are sometimes formed with nonprimates. William Mason, formerly associated with Harlow and now at the University of California in Davis, reared rhesus infants for one to ten months, first with their mothers or other infants or cloth surrogates, and then separated

Surrogate mother: English sheep dog "adopts" deprived rhesus monkey

from these. The deprived infants quickly learned to accept gentle female dogs as substitute mothers.

Individuals brought up with terry-cloth dummies are practically as pathological as individuals brought up in complete isolation, without surrogates or real mothers. As adolescents and adults they are incapable of getting along with other monkeys. The few motherless females who became pregnant, because of the persistence of males rather than through their own initiative, showed no traces of affection toward their infants. They were indifferent and rejecting at best; at worst they attacked and killed their infants. In the absence of normal social relations, there is no such thing as a maternal instinct.

On the other hand, it is rather startling to note that some of these females gave birth to a second infant and that they performed far more adequately as mothers the second time. This represents a most revealing example of learning ability in primates, an ability that has somehow managed to survive the trauma of being reared without a mother and alone. That a female can experience such extreme deprivation in early life and still arrive at an appreciable capacity for learning indicates how strongly she is predisposed to develop into an effective mother.

Judging by the experiments of Stephen Suomi, one of Harlow's colleagues, infants can also make remarkable recoveries. He put normal 3-month-old females into the cages of 6-month-old male isolates, monkeys reared without mothers or social stimulation of any sort. The first response of the typical isolate was to huddle in a corner rigid with fear, and the first response of the infant female was to come over and cling to her cage mate for warmth and affection. In the beginning the isolate remained rigid and unresponsive, but within a week he was clinging too; within two weeks the monkeys were playing with one another. Improvement was steady, and today, after more than two years, the ex-isolates seem completely normal.

Anthony and Linda Pfeiffer of the Rutgers University–Lion Country Safari Chimpanzee Rehabilitation Project in West Palm Beach, Florida, have noted improvement among chimpanzees originally used in medical research and confined for long periods in telephone-booth cages. Like other animals, human and nonhuman, kept in cramped and unattractive quarters, the chimpanzees developed rocking behavior and other symptoms of mental sickness. After being released on a small island, however, they made incomplete but strikingly effective recoveries. Their development is still under close observation.

Such studies are of special medical interest; they suggest that the impact of even severe early deprivation can be appreciably reduced, a conclusion which runs counter to the views of some psychiatrists who feel that deprivation produces practically irreversible effects. From an evolutionary standpoint, Suomi's work highlights the role of the mother. She has always stood between the infant and terror, and it is

her function to help transform the infant into an individual ready for   **271**
outgoing social relationships.

Techniques developed at the Wisconsin laboratory are being used in long-range research on learning by Mason and Seymour Levine of the Stanford University Medical School. In general, they have found that infants with mother surrogates react to every variation of a standard test as if it were something entirely new, and react to novelty with screams of pain as if they were being tortured. One objective of current studies is to discover what biochemical changes accompany the emergence of pathological anxiety. A great deal of fruitful work is also going on in an effort to bridge the gap between nature and the laboratory. The laboratory provides opportunities for precise observation under conditions that may be varied at will, but does so at the price of oversimplification, especially in the case of isolated mothers and infants.

On the other hand, although the full range of primate activity is on display in the wild, it is difficult or impossible to vary conditions and obtain individual case histories. Therefore, studies are being conducted to deal with social behavior which is somewhat more complex than that typical of most laboratory experiments, while at the same time permitting observations somewhat more precise than those usually obtained in the field. Among investigators engaged in such work is Robert Hinde of the Subdepartment of Animal Behavior at Cambridge University, England. He has developed a most thorough procedure for recording the behavior of rhesus infants living in large outdoor cages connected with smaller indoor rooms.

The procedure makes use of checklists on which observers indicate details of the behavior of an infant—whether it is on its mother's nipple or off the nipple and on the mother or off the mother and more or less than 2 feet away (the distance within which the mother can pick up her infant quickly), whether mother is approaching infant or vice versa, various kinds of play activity, and so on. The system yields an enormous amount of data. In one group of monkeys these and other items were checked off at 30-second intervals for 234 hours as part of a study that lasted a year, making a grand total of more than 28,000 observing intervals for each mother-infant pair—and the group included nine pairs. Such data can reveal, and pin down in quantitative terms, important aspects of social behavior.

For example, Hinde found an unexpected set of relationships in a group consisting of an adult male, two adult females each with an infant, and an adolescent female. The adolescent female showed a normal desire to hold, groom, and play with the infants, and normally the mothers would have played a major and deciding role in granting or withholding the privilege. In this case, however, she was the male's favorite and he often intervened in her behalf when the mothers were trying to exercise their authority. They reacted by being especially re-

"Rehabilitated" chimpanzees: (a) huddling; (b) begging for food; (c) group at ease

strictive to their offspring. At the age of 18 weeks, the infants hardly ever stayed more than 2 feet away from their mothers for an interval as long as half a minute, while infants living in groups where their mothers could dominate other females stayed away in more than a third of the intervals.

This observation led to a year-long study planned especially to investigate under more usual circumstances the role of females other than the mothers in raising rhesus infants. The study involved four mother-infant pairs each living alone and, as controls, nine mother-infant pairs each living with a group of a male and three or four females and their young. Analysis of the results shows that, as compared with mothers in isolated pairs, mothers living in groups maintain physical contact with their infants a greater proportion of the time and,

when contact is broken, establish contact sooner. In other words, the fact that mothers restrict their infants more in the presence of other females is confirmed for conditions comparable to those prevailing outside the laboratory.

Notice that this effect would be difficult to demonstrate under natural conditions, although now that it is recognized it may be looked

273

for more carefully. The same thing goes for possible effects on the psychology of infants. In Hinde's test of infants' initiative and curiosity, the main cages had openings so small that only infants could enter, and the cages contained mirrors and other unfamiliar objects. As might be expected, compared with infants raised with their mothers only the two infants raised in a group which included the male-supported adolescent female were more upset by a strange environment and tended to cling to their mothers longer after being exposed to it, a cautiousness that would clearly increase their chances of survival in the wild.

As a rule, reactions to strangeness and novelty provide a very sensitive index to the existence and extent of emotional disturbance. Infants whose mothers had been removed from their cages for a brief period typically reacted to her return with a sharp increase in temper tantrums, distress calls, and other signs of anxiety. All of these tended to decrease rapidly as time passed, but responses to strangeness persisted. More than two years after their mothers had been absent for only six days, and after being with their mothers continuously ever since, young monkeys still showed aftereffects. They were especially wary of strange objects such as a big ball or Hinde himself dressed in mask and black robe.

Later the British investigator decided to separate infants from mothers instead of mothers from infants, removing infants for six days of isolation and then putting them back into their home cages. He expected that this sort of separation would prove more upsetting to the infants. Actually there was a great difference, but in the other direction. The isolated infants were far less disturbed, chiefly reflecting the fact that they had to deal with far less disturbed mothers.

Combined findings from field and laboratory indicate how relationships favoring mother-infant ties have become intricately intermeshed during the course of evolution. The tendency to exclude younger subdominant males from the center of the baboon troop creates an outer defense ring; the attractiveness of the infant brings clusters of individuals to the center; the resulting restrictiveness of the mothers produces properly cautious offspring; and if a mother should die, one of the females that have been hovering about is available to adopt the infant. (Such an adoption occurred in one of Hinde's experimental groups. Harlow has records of rhesus females which actually produced milk for their new charges.)

These investigations have clinical as well as evolutionary implications. Researchers cannot afford to overlook certain analogies between the behavior of monkeys and apes and the behavior of people. Psychiatrists have been struck with the fact that such symptoms as rocking and vacant staring and self-mutilation observed among monkeys deprived of their mothers during infancy are also seen in some mentally disturbed children and orphans. Some physicians believe that women without practice in caring for young brothers and sisters have a less strong urge than more experienced women to care for their own infants, a phenomenon which probably exists among lower primates.

The appearance in experimental primates of behavior resembling that of humans encourages investigators to feel that they are dealing with relevant situations, with principles that apply broadly. But it would be a mistake to deduce or expect too much from the parallels and to foster the notion that people are nothing but apes (what has been called nothing-buttery thinking). We study lower primates and the similarities between them and ourselves mainly so that in the long run we can arrive at a clearer and more precise understanding of the all-important differences.

Taking the full measure of our uniqueness demands further research along many lines. For one thing, we would like to know more about the bringing up of infants, and not only about the female's role. As far as the results of laboratory studies to date are concerned, the absence of subadult and adult males does not seem to make much of a difference in the development of young offspring. William Redican and G. Mitchell of the University of California in Davis, however, report continuing studies which are beginning to throw some light on the problem.

Their procedure was to place an adult male rhesus monkey about 10 years old in a large cage with a newborn infant and its mother, remove the mother after a month, give the infant a week behind a barrier to learn how to bottle-feed itself, and then allow adult male and infant to associate freely for seven months. They observed four such pairs, and in all cases grooming and playing started within two weeks. Although play fighting among young primates often turns into real aggression, this never happened among the experimental pairs. Furthermore, although the intensity of the attachment between mother and infant tends to decrease with the passing of time, the intensity actually increased between adult male and infant. The significance of these findings remains to be clarified. But it seems that, given a chance, the male of the species may have surprising and untapped possibilities as caretaker and companion when it comes to the rearing of infants.

Another important study is concerned with the development of self-recognition in chimpanzees. Gordon Gallup of the State University of New York in Albany put full-length mirrors just outside the cages of four chimpanzees, two males and two females born in the wild, and observed their reactions. At first the image in the mirror was an alien thing, an object inspiring curiosity and fear, something to be bobbed and lunged at. (This mixed response was reminiscent of that exhibited by wild Congo chimpanzees confronted with a photograph of a chimpanzee in color and slightly larger than life.) After two days, however, the four apes clearly began to realize that they were looking at themselves. They were soon making use of the mirrors for such activities as picking their teeth, and, most interesting, they promptly noticed red marks that had been dyed on their eyebrows and ears under anesthesia. In other words, they noticed changes in their image and responded by touching the marks repeatedly.

Such behavior contrasts dramatically with the behavior of monkeys, who were similarly confronted with full-length mirrors for three weeks and at no time indicated that they connected the image with themselves. Tests by Marc Bekoff of the University of Colorado indicate that coyotes are similarly unable to recognize themselves in mirrors. Gallup's research demonstrates that awareness of self is a sign of superior intelligence and advanced brain structure among higher primates. It has implications beyond that. Self-awareness must have developed further during the course of human evolution from *Ramapithecus* to early *Homo sapiens*, which raises the question of what new quality of self-awareness came with the appearance of modern humans within the past 50,000 years and with the first evidence of personal adornment and art. Perhaps it was a new kind of power, the realization that one can somehow change the order of things by changing one's image deliberately and by creating images and symbols outside oneself.

Apes may well have image-making capacities which are hardly

called on in their normal lives, but which might be more fully developed in appropriately designed experimental environments and social structures. The same thing goes for toolmaking. Chimpanzees could probably make tools far more sophisticated than termite probes if they had sufficient reason to do so, at least judging by the accomplishments of a 5-year-old orangutan named Abang currently resident at the Bristol Zoo in England. About a year ago Abang learned to make and use stone tools, his incentive being to have company and to please his teacher, Richard Wright of the University of Sydney, who was visiting England at the time.

In the first stage of the experiment Wright brought two items into the orang's cage, a smash-proof box of fruit, which could be opened only by cutting a tough nylon string, and a sharp flint flake, which was put on the floor next to the box. Abang put his heart into the game, trying everything from biting and tugging at the string to breaking the box and forcing the lid. At one point, he stopped and turned to Wright with an appealing what-do-I-do-now look on his face. Following several demonstrations of the flake being moved back and forth across the string, Abang got the idea—and had his first success after 69 minutes of training. From then on he had mastered the trick, performing it 15 to 20 times in a row.

The next stage involved the same setup, except that instead of a flake Wright put a large chunk of flint and a 3-pound hammerstone into the cage. It was up to Abang to make a cutting implement for himself by bashing the flint with the hammerstone and knocking off a suitable flake, a more difficult problem than learning to use a ready-made flake. After watching more demonstrations and tossing the hammerstone away at one point (his only sign of impatience), he took 134 minutes to learn the task; the total training period was about three and a third hours. Later for the benefit of British television he did it all over again in about 15 minutes.

Wright has plans for more ambitious experiments. For example, he would like to find out how a flake-making ape would go about passing its skill on to a novice, and whether it could work flakes into various shapes. Meanwhile Abang finds himself in a rather pathetic situation. At times during his training sessions, he seemed to have deliberately delayed opening the box, because he knew that once he succeeded Wright would probably leave him for the day—and the company was as important to him as the food. Now he sits in his cage with a rubber tire to play with, more bored perhaps than even his fellow apes who never had a chance to play really challenging games.

Some impressive tool-using feats have been accomplished without demonstrations or any sort of special training, merely by devising a favorable laboratory situation. Benjamin Beck of the Chicago Zoological Park put a male baboon, identified only as M-2, into a cage, in front of

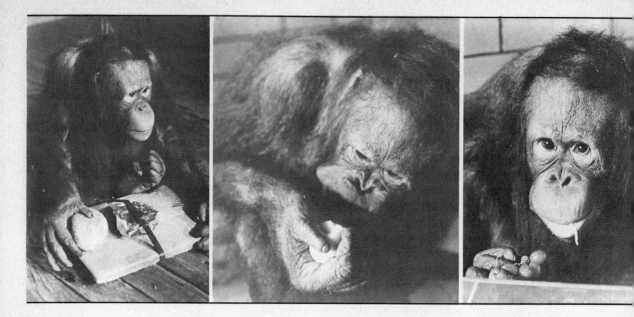

Abang the tool maker: before knocking off flake; examining flake; eating fruit from opened box

which was a pan full of fruits and vegetables—just out of reach through the bars. Normally, this situation would not have fazed M-2, because he had previously learned to get the pan using a steel rod with a hook at the end. Now, however, the tool was also out of reach. It was visible through an opening into another cage, but the opening was too small for M-2 to negotiate. He had only one recourse, to snatch the tool from one of a number of other baboons small enough to pass back and forth through the opening. He did this four times. The fifth time he and a female baboon were grooming one another when she saw the tool lying in the next cage, went in and picked it up, returned to M-2's cage, and sat holding the tool and looking at him for about six minutes. Then she put down the tool, and M-2 promptly took it and pulled in the pan. Subsequently the two animals developed this procedure into a routine, a case of spontaneous tool-using cooperation.

Such experiments are significant not only for their results, but also for the broad principle involved. The challenge is to create artificial setups, experimental environments, to which primates must adapt and which will encourage the development of specified behavior patterns, both among wild primates as well as among laboratory animals. As far as studies in the wild are concerned, the emphasis so far has been mainly on observing. For example, except for confronting chimpanzees with an occasional stuffed leopard or an awkwardly placed can of water or luring them to observing areas with bananas, the general policy has been not to tinker with natural conditions. But as accumulating evidence points up gaps in knowledge, some intervention may be useful.

The effect of regular savanna living might be investigated by actually moving a troop of chimpanzees into a sufficiently large tract of open country.

Another concern is the social impact of habitual meat eating. Suppose that some kind of small game, say hares, were fed to members of a chimpanzee troop until they became accustomed to the meat as a regular and necessary item in their diet. Then suppose that the troop was moved to an island or some other restricted area, where the only available source of meat consisted of wild hares. Would the chimpanzees rise to the occasion and invent hunting techniques? If so, would the techniques demand the development of sharing, appropriate new gestures and vocal signals, a more advanced communication system? (The problem of language is discussed in Chapter 19.)

The current overwhelming emphasis on monkeys and apes has sound reasons, the most obvious being that they are our kind, members of the same order. It is a problem to account for the fact that the research under way now was not started half a century ago. Full-scale studies of the behavior of primates in the wild have been so long in coming that every consideration dictates a major effort along these lines.

Furthermore, the emphasis on primates comes as a healthy reaction against certain other emphases of the not too distant past. As recently as three decades ago the social insects were almost certain to be cited in serious consideration of the nature of human beings. The Aesop's-fable approach, the tendency to present ants and bees as thrifty busy creatures and models of behavior, was on the way out, and the mood had become more somber. There were discussions about strict division of labor among ants and workers and slaves and armies; there were political warnings that postdepression big government men might evolve regimented anthill societies of their own.

Such discussions are taken less earnestly today. But to veer to the other extreme and study the primate order only would also be a mistake. We have much in common with mammals that live in herds, prides, packs, and troops, with all species from hooved browsers and grazers to lions and other social carnivores. Our ancestors, like many of the ancestors of other animals, had to cope with ice ages and wander across wildernesses and land bridges in search of living and feeding space.

Eisenberg is studying the Ceylon elephant as an example of a large animal with a life span comparable to ours and a record of having been able to coexist rather successfully with us, at least until recently. This elephant's basic social unit, or nuclear family, consists of a pregnant female with her offspring (aged about 8, 5, and 3), in close association with another female, often her mother or sister, with about the same number of offspring. Older bulls, in the age range of 20 to 30, go

about in less cohesive groups, occasionally accompanied by one to three
male "satellites" 11 to 14 years old. The oldest bulls, which may be 40
years old or more, are usually loners or else travel with a crony of about
the same age.

During dry periods, however, some 300 individuals may form
huge loosely organized herds, which provides Eisenberg with a chance
to check the idea that when an animal such as a person or an elephant "attains a certain body size and brain size, it is capable of unique
memory feats." Migration to isolated feeding grounds with sufficient
water in Ceylon may mean moving over any one of a number of complicated routes from lowlands into lusher highland country for distances
up to 40 miles, going over high passes and into the mountains, and
avoiding villages.

Since in addition to the annual dry season, there is a ten-year
drought cycle, details of certain special emergency routes must be remembered for periods of perhaps a decade or more by individuals who
cannot have participated in many migrations during their lifetimes and
who may have migrated only once. In other words, the elephant's bulk
not only helps protect it against predators but also pays off in terms of
proportionate brain size and memory capacity, permitting the shaping
of long-term survival strategies. Since the same point applies to people,
research on elephants may be expected to increase understanding of the
role of memory in human evolution.

The same thing goes for studies of predators and their prey. We can
learn a great deal about ourselves from the behavior of nonhuman hunters. As a matter of fact, Philip Johnson of the University of Arizona believes that in certain basic respects hunter-gatherers resemble social carnivores such as wild dogs, wolves, and lions far more closely than they do
primates. Hunter-gatherers regularly share and store food, and they engage in cannibalism, feed their young, kill more animals than they can eat,
and fight with competing predators—all characteristics of carnivores but
not of primates. Furthermore, in a study of the origins of social organizations, Glenn King of Monmouth College in West Long Branch, New Jersey,
finds the first traces of tribelike behavior among the social carnivores.

Of all predators, none comes closer to our ideals of cooperation
than the wild dog, which has been studied by many investigators
including George Schaller, Richard Estes, and Wolfdietrich Kühme of the
Max Planck Institute for the Physiology of Behavior near Munich, Germany, and John Goddard of the Ngorongoro Conservation Area in Tanzania. Kühme spent more than three months studying a pack of wild
dogs on the Serengeti Plain, the general area which includes the Olduvai Gorge. The pack consisted of 23 individuals, 6 adult males and 2
females, one with a litter of 4 and one with 11 newborn pups, all living
together in a borrowed den, one of the numerous vacant burrows dug

by aardvarks, wart hogs, and hyenas. The females nursed and cared for all 15 offspring on a first-come, first-served basis. They often competed for the privilege, even to the point of trying to steal one another's pups, a tactic which produced the only friction in the pack, mild bickering in the form of growls and snapping. Males were never seen fighting; there are no hierarchies among wild dogs.

Both sexes performed guard duty, usually the same individuals taking on the job of remaining with the young while the rest of the pack hunted. In other words, unlike nonhuman primates, the wild dogs had a home base where the very young and their guardians stayed while the rest of the pack hunted. When the hunters returned with pieces of unchewed meat in their stomachs, pups and guardians met them with a characteristic begging gesture, the beggar pushing its nose against the hunter's mouth or biting at the lips or jowls. The meat was then disgorged, and every pack member received its allotted portion. The stomachs of the mothers serve as secondary storage depots and processing plants. On a number of occasions, a female made a special point of chewing and swallowing disgorged meat intended for pups too young to handle the meat and provided them with small redisgorged titbits periodically during the next three to four hours.

Regular food sharing, a basic element in the pack's way of life, is unknown among nonhuman primates, as is regular communal hunting and division of labor in gathering food. However, as indicated in Chapter 13, a form of sharing has been observed among baboons, and chimpanzees share frequently. This is something which could be built upon and extended, given the proper set of circumstances. But human beings remain the only primates to go in for sharing and meat eating habitually and, whenever possible, on a relatively large scale.

Hunting in groups is another highly developed form of cooperation found among wild dogs and other carnivores. Estes and Goddard used Land Rovers to follow a pack in the crater of Ngorongoro, the volcano on the way to Olduvai which collapsed sometime during the past 3 million years. Some 25,000 herd animals and their predators live on the 104-square-mile crater floor, an open plain providing ideal observing conditions. The investigators obtained most of their information during the predators' two regular hunting periods, which last about an hour or two and begin early in the morning shortly before sunrise and in the late afternoon.

During the stalking phase of the hunt, wild dogs move with shoulders hunched, ears flattened, and hind legs in ready-to-spring position, like a runner at the starting block. The objective is to get within 300 yards or so of a grazing herd, usually gazelles, before breaking into a run and stampeding the prey. The leader of the pack selects a victim from the fleeing herd, perhaps one of the slower individuals; one or

two adult dogs follow at intervals of about a hundred yards, and the
other members of the pack run behind at distances of as much as a
mile.

Hunting strategies are simple and effective. Dogs running immediately behind the leader are ready to cut off the prey as it attempts to
dodge, but as a rule by the time it starts dodging it is too tired to get
away. At the end of the chase the victim is usually so exhausted and in
such a deep state of shock that it does not fight back. Estes and Goddard describe a large female antelope which "did little more than stand
with head high while the dogs cut it to ribbons, looking less the victim
than the witness of its own execution."

About 85 percent of all chases end successfully, that is, from the
pack's point of view—not surprising in view of the fact that a wild dog
can attain top speeds of more than 40 miles an hour, and run at an average speed of 30 miles an hour for several miles. Most chases last only
about three to five minutes and cover a mile or two. Schaller has found
that when game is plentiful, hunting packs on the Serengeti Plain kill
enough animals to provide about 20 pounds of meat per dog daily, at
least four times more than is needed.

Wild dogs have developed some amazing rituals. A typical prelude to the hunt might find them lolling about in the grass. One restless
dog will begin romping with a few of its pack mates. Soon others join
in, and gradually the play and the chasing build up into a wilder and
wilder climax, with the entire pack milling around in a circle and emitting, in unison, peculiar birdlike twittering calls signifying a high degree of excitement. The procedure, which has been compared to a pep
rally, brings the pack to a fever pitch for the hunt.

Sometimes a chain reaction occurs in the midst of the milling
about. It starts with two or three pack members engaging in particularly
hectic play. The play, in turn, apparently triggers a response among
other members, with up to half a dozen dogs taking part in a strange
melodrama. One dog seems to assume the role of victim and the others
gang up on it, pushing it over and rolling it about but never biting.
This so-called mobbing behavior is precisely what happens, more intensely, when the pack corners and starts ripping apart a large prey. Before the hunt, it may serve as a kind of dress rehearsal for the killing to
come, a procedure as potent as drugs or fire dances in arousing excitement.

Kuhme notes the existence of another ritual which has the opposite effect in that it serves to prevent violence within the pack. Adults
forestall aggression by habitually assuming postures of humility toward
one another when greeting or soliciting food. Again, it is a kind of acting. An adult male may pretend to be young and use the same begging
gesture infants and juveniles use, pushing its nose against the mouth of
another adult. At other times, adults behave like nursing pups, males

licking the udders of females and females creeping under males as if
seeking an udder. Such rituals achieve a "tolerance of competitors,
which human beings find so difficult."

Research on wolves, hyenas, jackals, and wild dogs is providing a
richer background of knowledge against which to view human behavior. The abandonment of stereotyped notions about other social carnivores may prepare humans to see themselves more clearly. For example,
although hyenas have been too readily dismissed as uncourageous scavengers, the fact of the matter is that they function as effective hunters
upon occasion. In early prehistoric times, hyenas probably preyed on
savanna apes and prehumans at least as much as on lions and other big
cats. As far as character is concerned, they display a rather subtle combination of shyness, persistence, and incredible gall.

A solitary hyena during the day is relatively harmless, and perhaps the animal's reputation as a skulking coward is based on the behavior of such loners. But there is nothing more lethal than a pack of 20
or so hyenas at night. A lion will move away from its kill at the attack
of a hyena pack, snarling but making no serious attempt to fight for its
meat. Schaller once saw a pack that had worked itself into a state of excited aggression and was mobbing a large male lion. Under these circumstances the lion was anything but a king of beasts. It was plainly
terrified.

The hyena is a superb waiter. According to Estes, "it will lie all
day near an ostrich nest, anticipating the time when the eggs may be
left momentarily unguarded . . . and cripples may be followed for days

283

until too weak to resist." He also observed hyenas waiting hours for a pack of wild dogs to begin hunting, often crawling to within a few yards of the pack and staring almost purposefully at the dogs "as though urging them to get started." Furthermore, like jackals, lions, the Gonds of India, and other tribes (and perhaps like early hominids; see Chapter 6), hyenas scan the skies for circling vultures and dash to the spot to share in the carcass.

Parallels exist between the evolution of canids, members of the dog family, and primates. As related species evolve increasingly complex social systems, they require increasingly complex signals to establish and maintain individual relationships within the group. In other words, there is selective pressure for more sophisticated communication and one result may be an increase in the mobility of the face and the number of possible expressions, a phenomenon being studied by Michael Fox of Washington University in St. Louis.

He points out that wolves, highly social animals with a system of cooperative hunting and sharing at least as elaborate as that of the wild dog, exhibit a far greater variety of facial expressions than canids such as the red fox, which does not live in packs and tends to be a loner when it comes to hunting. Similar tendencies have been observed among primates; as a matter of fact, social canids and social primates share a number of basic expressions signifying a playful mood (the so-called play face), threats, submissiveness, and so on.

Fox reports another difference between the wolf and red fox. Wolf cubs in a given litter seem to be born with widely varying temperaments, as judged by a series of tests designed to measure degrees of aggressiveness and fear of novelty, which is just what would be needed for pack formation and the establishment of stable hierarchies. The red fox, on the other hand, tends to have litters made up of cubs roughly on a par with one another as far as aggressiveness is concerned, but all of them are definitely individualists, a feature which may help ensure that they will ultimately disperse and lead more or less solitary lives. Primates do not have litters, of course, but it might be interesting to study differences among primate infants from an evolutionary standpoint.

Behavior, however, is a product of social as well as hereditary forces. The behavior of a wolf must be appropriate to its position in the pack, and its entire temperament may change when that position changes. The pack may have a secondary male, an individual ready to take over the number 1 spot when circumstances permit. The number 2 wolf of a captive pack studied by Erik Zimen of the Bavarian Forest National Park in southern Germany had been friendly to people and strange dogs until he beat the leader in a fight, when he became a snarling, aggressive animal. The previously vicious former leader promptly became friendly and affectionate, even to a keeper it once hated. A pack may include other role players, such as a scapegoat who may be attacked by any animal except a cub and a lone wolf who lives on the edge of the pack range and may associate briefly with other packs.

The behavior of the big cats is also of interest, and Schaller has spent a good deal of time among them, most recently during a three-year study of lions and other predators on the Serengeti Plain. His records show the advantage of hunting in groups. A lion alone, stalking its prey, lifting and placing each paw separately as it advances, and selecting a moment to rush from its hiding place, has a batting average of about 0.150 or a success rate of one kill in every six or seven attempts—considerably better than a one-in-twelve estimate for tigers, who always hunt alone.

On the average, a hunting group of from two to four or five lions is about twice as successful. As indicated in Chapter VI, lions use elaborate encircling tactics, but when a herd panics, they may simply move forward in an irregular line along a broad front and dash in for the kill. Sometimes, in the confusion, animals rush directly into the jaws of their predators. From the prey's point of view as well as from the predator's, there is an advantage in being a member of a group, provided the group is not too large. A zebra is far more vulnerable alone than in a herd, if the herd has no more than 75 individuals; but as herd size increases much beyond that level so does inertia. It may take longer to get moving, flight is inhibited, and the success of a killer rises correspondingly.

Lions, like most carnivores, conserve their energies and do not bother to kill if they can get meat in some other way. On the open savanna, they do more scavenging than hyenas; about half their food comes from moving in and taking the kills of cheetahs and other predators. When lions are not hunting or scavenging, they do nothing in particular, spending about 20 hours a day lying down, generally asleep. Incidentally, wild dogs spend even more of their time doing nothing, probably because their success rate in killing is so high; they lie down about 22 hours a day.

A pride of lions, like a troop of chimpanzees, tends to be very loosely organized; it has no rigid hierarchy and may be scattered over a wide area. It is essentially a female-centered group, averaging about 15 members. All males are ejected from the pride as soon as they reach sexual maturity, and become nomads wandering over the plains and joining prides for a time and then moving on again. Females, on the other hand, hardly ever change prides; they remain within a hunting territory of about a hundred square miles. In fact, Schaller suspects that generations of female lions have lived in their native ranges for centuries.

As a general rule, different species of predators tend not to get along with one another. Lions have been known to chase and kill leopards, cheetahs, and hyenas; leopards may kill cheetahs; hyenas may attack cheetahs and jackals; jackals may eat foxes. Furthermore, there may be within-the-species killing and cannibalism. Tigers may prey on tigers, lions on lions, and so on. Peace does not seem to prevail among carnivores. Such behavior contrasts with the behavior of antelopes, zebras, and other plant-eating herd animals, which normally live side by side without trouble; and the same thing is true within troops of non-human primates.

A rapidly growing body of firsthand knowledge about primates and other species, a wealth of new observations and experiences, now exists. At the same time, some investigators recognize that detailed accounts of how animals interact, and authentic anecdotes to replace the less reliable anecdotes of times past, represent an essential but only a first step. The facts cannot be expected to speak for themselves in the study of animal behavior any more than in the study of flint artifacts and other archeological remains. Hard science must follow soft science; a mathematical approach to relationships too complex to handle by intuition alone must follow the descriptive natural-history approach.

A beginning of systematic efforts along these lines may be seen in work such as that started by Stuart Altmann and his associates at the University of Chicago. His basic information is descriptive, but in a rather special way. Some of it comes from a two-year study on Cayo Santiago, the island off the coast of Puerto Rico which serves as a home for some 400 rhesus monkeys. The pioneer primate investigator Ray Carpenter brought the monkeys from India more than 30 years ago, and they have been studied constantly ever since 1956.

During his field observations, Altmann was not concerned solely with hierarchies, infant care, playing, and so on. He concentrated as much on the things a monkey does as on the setting or context of its doings, identifying and recording its concrete gestures and sounds and movements. In other words, he compiled a catalog of the elementary behavioral patterns of Cayo Santiago monkeys, listing actions such as "grooms," "gnashes teeth," "grimaces," "holds tail erect," and some 120-odd other items. This is a very restricted list in the sense that it includes only a fraction of all the things a monkey is physically capable of doing. But it does include all patterns which are known to serve in social communications and which thus make the survival of the species possible, a repertoire of behavioral units selected over millions of years of evolution.

The repertoire may be analyzed by using a mathematical theory—originally designed to deal with the behavior of human beings in telephone and radio communications. Claude Shannon of the Massachusetts Institute of Technology developed the theory more than 20 years ago, when he was at the Bell Telephone Laboratories investigating how to plan systems for handling large numbers of messages as efficiently as possible. Part of the problem involved ways of predicting messages. Of course, the full information content of a message generally cannot be predicted; if it could, there would be little reason to send it in the first place. On the other hand, a message is not entirely unpredictable. Certain rules for putting words together must be obeyed. The instant one is chosen, subsequent words are limited to an appreciable extent.

For example, if a sentence starts with *I*, the odds are that the next word will be a verb, such as *believe*, rather than a noun, such as *apple*; and the odds are that the next word after *I believe* will be *in* or *that* rather than *eat* or *elephant*. According to Shannon, the English language is about 50 percent redundant; when a person is writing in English, an average of about half the words are chosen freely and half are determined by the structure or rules of the language. This concept and others in communication theory are relevant to the analysis of animal societies, which are living communication networks.

Taking the rhesus monkey's repertoire of 120-odd behavior patterns as a vocabulary, as an analogy, certain "words" or patterns occur far more frequently than others. In fact, the six most frequent patterns — walks toward, walks away from, grooms, presents for grooming, grasps waist, and grips legs — account for more than half of all its observed activities. Furthermore, there is considerable redundancy in a monkey's life, a high probability that a certain pattern will be followed by a particular one of all the other patterns, and that those two will be followed by a third highly probable pattern, and so on, thus producing predictable sequences of stereotyped behavior.

Analyses of this sort are part of the effort to design increasingly refined models of primate interaction that will prove more and more helpful to us in understanding and predicting behavior. Perhaps the problem of how many behavioral patterns make up the human repertoire can also be investigated systematically. If so, the way will then be clear to compare in a precise manner our basic activities with those of our fellow primates. New intuitions may be expected to follow analysis and controlled experiments, new ideas about the workings of human and nonhuman societies.

CHAPTER 15 CONTEMPORARY HUNTER-GATHERERS: LAST REPRESENTATIVES OF THE STONE AGE

Many flashes or episodes of behavior reminiscent of human behavior occur in the daily lives of monkeys and apes. We see ourselves in the baboon, top-ranking member of the hierarchy—in the male as he scans the horizon for danger, hesitates, and finally leads his troop across a stretch of savanna; in the mother-infant pair surrounded by solicitous females; in the rough-and-tumble play of male juveniles. We see ourselves in the chimpanzee with a mischievous twinkle in his eyes, scratching his head in perplexity or laughing out loud at a bewildered playmate. Such similarities reflect the fact of continuity in human evolution, the existence of patterns which man and his ancestors share with lower primates. A great deal more could be learned from in-the-wild observations of the species even more closely related to human beings.

If ancestral hominids still roamed river valleys, savannas, and coastal plains, bands like those whose traces are found at the Olduvai Gorge or at Torralba and Ambrona, investigators could obtain firsthand records of early hunting methods and social organizations. In the absence of such bands, however, we ourselves can serve as subjects for research in living prehistory. We are all relics to some extent and, as such, provide a legitimate source of clues to the nature of prehistoric people. Much of what we do and think today is conditioned by what our ancestors did and thought long ago, when they were half wild and all of the world was a wilderness. Investigators expect to learn more about how human beings behaved in the past from studies of contemporary human behavior.

Much can be learned from contemporary hunter-gatherers, people who live on wild plants and animals. In March, 1966, at a native reserve on the southwest fringe of the Gibson Desert in western Australia, Richard Gould, an archeologist at the University of Hawaii, met an unusual two-family group of 13 aborigines (3 women, 2 men, and 8 chil-

288

dren ranging in age from about 4 to 15). They were among the very few **289** people in the world still making and using stone tools on a regular basis. A lost colony, one of the last remaining pockets of Stone Age existence in the twentieth century, entered the modern world from an isolation so complete that they had met their first white person only a few months before.

The aborigines soon had enough of the present and decided to step back into the past again, heading on foot for their homeland 155 miles away in the heart of the desert. Gould and his wife Elizabeth followed not long afterward in a Land Rover. They lived with this group and others for extended periods during the next 15 months, learning their language, sleeping at their campsites, and walking out with them in search of food among flat sand plains, long parallel sand ridges like ripples on a giant beach, and occasional cliffs and rocky outcrops jutting out of the sands.

This investigation is the first of its kind ever undertaken. The writings about the world's primitive tribes which have accumulated during the past century or two include page after page, volume after volume, describing myths, kinship, inheritance, systems, birth, puberty, marriage, and death rituals. They are complete with details about rattles, masks, and other associated paraphernalia. Embedded in it all is a strikingly sparse amount of useful information for the framing of hypotheses. The focus has often been on the bizarre, on practically everything that makes people appear alien and exotic, a tendency which reveals as much about the authors as about their subjects. Going through such material is an ordeal, part of the initiation ceremony which students must endure on their way to degrees.

More and more investigators seriously concerned with understanding human evolution are going into the field in an effort to learn for themselves before it is too late. Such studies are important because contemporary hunter-gatherers are disappearing rapidly. According to an estimate made in 1966, the world included only 30,000 hunter-gatherers in a total population of some 3.3 billion, about enough to fill a medium-sized football stadium. Their ranks have thinned appreciably since then, as they continue to die out or give up their ways and join farming and industrial communities.

Gould is the first professional archeologist to use his training in a systematic and intensive study of a group of hunters and gatherers. He has watched them living off the land with the specific objective of collecting information that bears on the interpretation of prehistoric sites and the reconstruction of prehistoric social behavior. The information includes details about toolmaking, hunting, camping, living floors, and the elaborate system of beliefs which the aborigines have created to endow their world with meaning and purpose.

The past treatment of hunter-gatherers, and others living in primitive societies whose behavior patterns resemble those that prevailed for more than 99 percent of human's time on earth, marks a low point in colonial history. As mentioned earlier, a common notion was that such people belonged to subhuman breeds, occupying "at best a middling position among the species," somewhere between apes and men but rather closer to apes as far as mentality and morals are concerned. In the name of this belief, they were widely dispossessed, enslaved, hunted, raped, slaughtered, fed poisoned food, and otherwise exploited.

The classic case of this viewpoint in action involved the wiping out during the last century of 3000 to 5000 aborigines living on the Australian island of Tasmania. Rhys Jones of the Australian National University in Canberra comments on the process: "The fate of the Tasmanians constitutes one of the few examples in written history where an entire people has become totally extinct. . . . It is the example *par excellence* of genocide. . . . Savage and barbarian met face to face, and the savage died."

A later and somewhat more enlightened attitude, but one based on the same belief, was that they should be preserved together with other forms of wildlife as "living fossils" or lower species that never attained the evolutionary status of modern people. The report of a scientific expedition to central Australia in 1894 indicated the prevailing bias of the times toward members of all primitive societies, a bias found not only among laymen but also among specialists.

In appearance [the Australian aborigine] is a naked, hirsute savage, with a type of features occasionally pronounced Jewish. He is by nature lighthearted, merry and prone to laughter, a splendid mimic, supple-jointed, with an unerring hand that works in perfect unison with his eye, which is as keen as that of an eagle. He has never been known to wash. He has no private ownership of land, except as regards that which is not overcarefully concealed about his person. . . .

Religious belief he has none, but is excessively superstitious. . . . He has no gratitude except that of the anticipatory order, and is as treacherous as Judas. He has no traditions, and yet continues to practice with scrupulous exactness a number of hideous customs and ceremonies which have been handed down from his fathers, and of the origin or reason of which he knows nothing. . . .

After an experience of many years I say without hesitation that he is absolutely untamable. . . . Verily his moods are as eccentric as the flight of his own boomerang. Thanks to the untiring efforts of the missionary and the stockman, he is being rapidly "civilized" off the face of the earth, and in another hundred years the sole remaining evidence of his existence will be the fragments of flint which he has fashioned so rudely.

Today's attitudes are generally more in keeping with times that have seen the undermining of white supremacy and the passing of an empire upon which the sun never set. Anthropologists make a special point of recognizing all extant hunter-gatherers as members of the club

World Distribution of Hunter-Gatherers: 10,000 B.C.

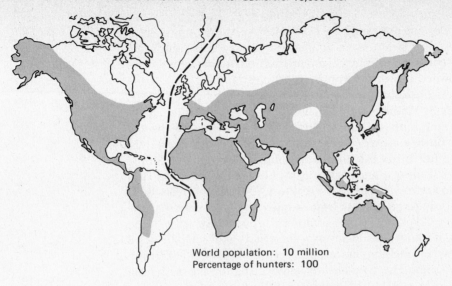

World population: 10 million
Percentage of hunters: 100

Known Living Sites of Contemporary Hunter-Gatherers

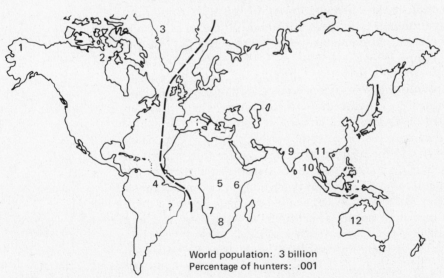

World population: 3 billion
Percentage of hunters: .001

1. Eskimos; Alaska	8. Kalahari Bushmen; South Africa, Botswana
2. Eskimos; Northwest Territory	9. Birhar; Central India
3. Eskimos; Greenland	10. Andaman Islanders; Andaman Island
4. Akuri; Surinam	11. Mrabri; Thailand
5. Pygmies; Congo	12. Australian Aborigines; Australia
6. Ariangulo; Tanzania	13. Tasadays; Philippines
Boni; Tanzania	14. Sevnany; Malaya
Sanye; Tanzania	15. Kubu; Sumatra
7. Koroka; Angola	16. Panan; Borneo
Bantu; Angola	

Known Living Sites of
Contemporary
Hunter-Gatherers

of *Homo sapiens.* They are people living exactly as we would be living if
we had regarded nature in the same way and had adapted to the same
conditions. Their societies are much simpler than ours, but nonetheless
sufficiently complicated to warrant continuing investigation.

In the lives of the aborigine families who were the Goulds' hosts,
a typical December or January day, the height of the Australian summer, begins in darkness about half an hour before dawn. The people
are awakened by nature's alarm clock, the sound of parrots, cockatoos,
and half a dozen other birds bursting into song. They join the chorus
with yawns, throat-clearings, and exchanges of morning greetings and
banter. There is no formal, communal breakfast. During the next hour
or so each member of the group eats from a supply of food prepared the
night before, usually cakes and loaves of ground-up seeds or fruit.

Work starts at about six or seven, when it is still cool by local
standards, that is, when the temperature is below 95 degrees. The group
divides into two parties. The women are responsible for the gathering
of plant foods and may walk 4 or 5 miles — with long wooden bowls of
water balanced on their heads and nursing children carried on their
hips or slung over their backs — perhaps to one of the areas containing
bushes of ngaru, an abundant pale green fruit about the size of a small
tomato. Dogs and children old enough to walk come along too; no one
stays behind at the camp.

Meanwhile the two men from the family group go off together to
attend to their job of hunting, a less dependable way of obtaining food
under desert conditions. In general, they go to a place where they can
ambush game instead of tracking and chasing it, especially in the summer heat. Perhaps they make use of a water hole as a kind of trap. They
may travel a mile or two to the nearest creek bed, where they scoop out
a pit or soak hole exposing a small pool, and then select a spot on the
bank overlooking the pit about 15 feet away to build a circular blind or
hiding place of bushes (preferably in the shade of a tree). They lie there
and wait, ready to hurl their spears at a thirsty emu or, very rarely, a
kangaroo or a wallaby.

Everyone is back at camp by ten-thirty or eleven. By that time
the temperature may have risen to 120 degrees, and not even the aborigines go out in that noonday sun. The women return the wooden
bowls empty of water and filled with ngaru fruit. The men are usually
not as successful. Sometimes they manage to kill a large animal, but on
most days they have little to show for their patience, perhaps only a
single goanna lizard. Most of the aborigines' diet is made up of plant
foods, gathered mainly by women; the meat consists chiefly of lizards,
rabbits, snakes, birds and other small game, also frequently provided
by women. According to Gould, "about 90 percent of the time women
furnish at least 80 percent of the food."

The midday resting period is devoted to sitting in the shade, tak-

Yuwi, the hunter

ing naps, making tools, gossiping. At three-thirty or thereabouts the women go to another area for a fruit related to ngaru. At this time of year, the fruit is parched and looks something like large raisins. The two fruits provide more than half the aborigines' food during dry summer months. One man decides to try his luck at the blind again; the other considers that to be a waste of time and goes lizard hunting. The people reassemble at camp before dark, in two hours or so, and the women prepare food for the evening and the next morning. Fires are built even in the hottest summer nights to keep *mamu*, or night cannibal spirits away. There is much talking, and everyone is asleep by eight-thirty or nine.

The desert dictates rules governing the course and rhythm of **293**

Nyapurula, elderly
aborigine woman,
and child

daily activities. Some of the rules are harsh. In the absence of cultivated
cereals and milk-yielding domestic animals, suitable children's foods
are limited, and breast feeding generally goes on for three years or
more. Since women can neither carry nor nurse two infants at once,
there is no choice but to establish some form of birth control, and the
most common type has been infanticide. Joseph Birdsell of the University of California at Los Angeles, who has gathered quantitative data
relevant to the custom, estimates that in the not too distant past the aborigines killed at least 15 percent of their infants and perhaps up to 50
percent.

Killing the infant was the mother's decision and her job. She disciplined herself to do it quickly, usually within an hour after birth. Her
only consolation, and the only consolation for the group, was the belief
that the soul of the infant would enter the body of another infant some
time in the future. As indicated in Chapter 10, this practice probably
played a part in limited prehistoric populations; the population boom
believed to have occurred in Magdalenian times may have resulted in
part from more settled living conditions and the decline of infanticide.

Nothing is denied to the children that are reared. Whenever they
want food, either from the breast or from stored supplies, they get it.
Aborigine mothers rarely spank or otherwise punish their offspring,
even under the most provoking circumstances. In all 15 months of observing, Gould noted only one exception, when a mother reached out
and smacked her son who was behaving in a particularly annoying
fashion. As children grow up they learn to resent being told what to do,
so perhaps the most insulting remark one aborigine can make to another is to call him *wati tjukumunu*, a bossy man.

Whenever people live together, even in small groups, tensions
build up and there is always a chance of violence. The aborigines do

everything in their power to avoid conflict. They discourage arrogance or high-handedness or bragging of any sort, anything that could lead to heated arguments; but trouble always comes, and when it does, they have special rituals to control aggression which stop just short of all-out fighting to the death. Nicolas Peterson of the Australian National University, who has lived with aborigines for extended periods, recently witnessed a confrontation between two men who had been enemies for several years. Man A threw a boomerang with just the right speed so that man B (who had stolen A's wife) could dodge by moving fast. Then they ran at one another, knives in hand, dropped to their knees, and man A proceeded to make a short slash across man B's chest, just deep enough to draw blood and exact blood vengeance. That was the end of the feud.

There are bloodier and less bloody rituals, all calculated to let off steam with as little mayhem as possible. Sometimes adversaries call each other names, throw a few boomerangs, and then rush together, hugging and weeping and swearing to be friends forever. On occasion, controls may break down completely. Murders do occur, along with raids and rare pitched battles involving entire bands. In general, the easiest way of avoiding conflict is to pack up and move away. Band membership is a flexible thing, with fairly frequent comings and goings.

The aborigines of the western desert have survived under the severest of conditions, including less than ten inches of rain a year on the average, which means that rainfall is often less than that. They may travel as much as 250 to 350 miles in search of food, particularly during droughts, and Gould met one band which had to move nine times in three months over an area of nearly a thousand square miles.

The remarkable adaptation of these people to desert conditions includes a technology that would have been familiar to a toolmaker living 30,000 or more years ago. A distinctive and common tool, the so-called adz flake with a thick and fairly steep edge, looks much like the sort of scrapers archeologists find at prehistoric sites the world over. The edge may be made by removing tiny chips with a hammerstone or a wooden stick or, most unusual of all, with the teeth—a technique first reported by the Spanish explorer Coronado in 1541 among the Great Plains Indians of North America. Evidence for the practice in more remote times exists in the form of tiny chips of quartz found in human coproliths, preserved feces excavated at a prehistoric cave in Utah.

The dental method involves placing the flake in a nutcracker position and nibbling with the side or premolar teeth. It requires teeth worn flat at the crowns to form an even working platform and exceedingly strong jaw muscles, both of which the aborigines have developed during years of using their teeth to chew tough meat, soften sinews, and rip the bark off branches. (They have no trouble in remov-

ing the top of a tin can by making successive bites along the rim.)
There are reasons to believe that Magdalenian and Azilian toolmakers
may have used this same method (among others) in the delicate job of
fashioning microliths, very small scrapers and blades.

The need to travel light in the desert puts a premium on multi-
purpose or combination tools rather than elaborate tool kits. Of these
the most impressive is the spear thrower, a flat wooden tool which may
be used as a firemaker upon occasion. When an aborigine wants to start
a fire, he splits a piece of wood, puts bits of dried kangaroo dung in the
slot, and then rubs the edge of his spear thrower back and forth in the
slot like a saw blade, hard and fast, until friction ignites the dung, a
procedure that generally takes less than 20 seconds. This versatile tool
serves other functions, such as shaper and cutter, with the aid of an adz
flake hafted to one end; mixing board for preparing pigments and a
special blend of premasticated wild tobacco and ashes; and noisemaker
for beating out rhythms at dances and other ceremonies.

Spear throwers also provide a crude kind of archives, the closest
thing to written records among people who do not write. Decorations
carved in the wood have practical and religious as well as aesthetic purposes. The aborigines believe in a remote "dreamtime" before the coming of mortals, when their ancestors, supernatural beings in the guise of
humans and animals, rose from eternal sleeping places undergound and
roamed the earth's surface and created the world. In their wanderings
they changed themselves into boulders, water holes, cliffs, trees, lakes,
sand ridges, and other natural features which now mark their tracks

Yutungka, drinking at
clay pan

through the desert. The features are represented on spear throwers by wavy and zigzag lines and a variety of irregular and geometric forms.

These symbols do not make up a language. They are not universal in the sense that only a fixed number of standard patterns exist and that each of them means the same thing to many men. They operate as personal symbols, different for different hunters and interpreted strictly on an individual basis. On the other hand, they can be regarded as private pictographs or hieroglyphics which help the hunter to establish firmly in his mind a map of his land, the locations of sacred places and water holes upon which his life may depend, and to pass the knowledge on to youths entering manhood. It is noteworthy that the Magdalenians also had spear throwers and also decorated them, often with abstract designs, suggesting that they may have used symbols for similar purposes.

Gould provides an example of what it means to be at home in your part of the world, to know your land. He estimates that aborigines remember the locations of more than 400 places with water—rock clefts and hollows in trees where rain may collect as well as temporary and

Close-up of aborigine branch shelter

permanent water holes. They know about 300 places firsthand, from visits in person, and 100 more from other aborigines. The living-prehistory approach offers the enormous advantage of having people who make spear throwers and other tools right on the spot, people who are ready to explain everything.

Watching and helping aborigines build and use blinds made of bushes or rocks are also ways of bringing the past a bit closer and making it more vivid. Some of the blinds are natural rather than man-made, large boulders or rock shelters close to water holes or in narrow gorges, and while a hunter waits he may take a piece of red ocher and draw animals or designs representing animal tracks on rock walls. A drawing of a line and side markings that looks something like a feathered arrow or a branch with twigs might well be interpreted as such, or even more likely, as another mysterious abstract sign if there were not firsthand information to the contrary. Actually it depicts the footmarks of a kangaroo as it hops slowly along dragging its tail behind through the sand. Such drawings are generally done as a loose form of magic, in the belief that they will attract animals to the blind, although now and then they seem to be mainly a matter of doodling to pass the time.

Stalking is done more rarely than waiting in blinds, but if an aborigine sees a possible kill he loses no time in going after it. "That happened late one evening about twenty minutes before sunset," Gould recalls. "There was not much wind, the landscape was very red from the setting sun, and a kangaroo was browsing about a thousand feet away. A hunter started walking directly at it, moving over the sand with the graceful and smooth motion which is second nature to the aborigines as

Spearthrower as "map": Gibson Desert landmarks and water sources along a 150-mile track of a totemic snake in the dreamtime

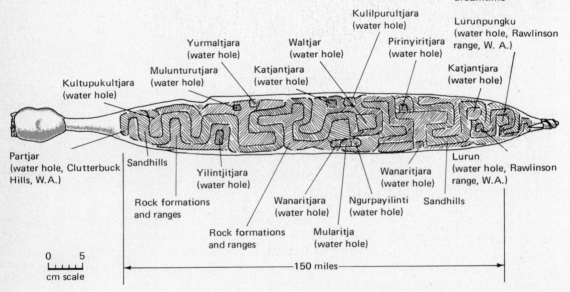

Kulilpurultjara (water hole)

Lurunpungku (water hole, Rawlinson range, W. A.)

Yurmaltjara (water hole)

Waltjar (water hole)

Pirinyiritjara (water hole)

Mulunturutjara (water hole)

Katjantjara (water hole)

Katjantjara (water hole)

Kultupukultjara (water hole)

Partjar (water hole, Clutterbuck Hills, W.A.)

Sandhills

Yilintjitjara (water hole)

Wanaritjara (water hole)

Lurun (water hole, Rawlinson range, W.A.)

Rock formations and ranges

Wanaritjara (water hole)

Ngurpayilinti (water hole)

Sandhills

Rock formations and ranges

Mularitja (water hole)

0   5
cm scale

150 miles

sea legs are to sailors. "He kept his eyes fastened to the animal's head and ears, and the instant it started to look up he froze in his tracks, sometimes for two or three minutes until it looked down again and continued feeding. Then he moved forward again. After about half an hour of stalking he came to within seventy-five feet of the kangaroo— but missed his prey! He used a rifle, and many Gibson Desert aborigines are still very bad with rifles. He would never have missed with a spear."

Gould has devoted much time to a study of contemporary living floors, occupation patterns representing the activities of aborigines he knew well or the activities of their friends and recent ancestors. Such evidence can be used in interpreting prehistoric living floors not only in the Australian desert but elsewhere. For example he gathered considerable information during visits to Tika-Tika, a major open-air site covering several acres. The site includes ample supplies of fruit and berries in midwinter and late summer, small game and occasional kangaroos, and five water holes on a limestone flat, one of which can be counted on to furnish some water even during severe droughts.

One important feature of the layout here, and at other sites in the desert, is that the people never locate their occupation areas close to water holes. The general practice is to build camps at least 200 to 300

Yutungka, in permanent water hole

Tjakamara, making a
spear thrower

feet from the nearest source of water; if they were much closer, camp
noises would frighten game away. Another reason for having the water
hole farther away is to reduce social tensions and preserve peaceful
coexistence among neighboring groups. Under the system of rules that
governs the behavior of relatives toward one another, for example, a
man is strictly forbidden to talk with his mother-in-law, and if a family
lived near a water hole it might be difficult to avoid awkward encounters.

In all, Gould and his wife spent the better part of a summer
month living at Tika-Tika with the family group they originally followed into the desert. Shade is the primary concern during the summer
season, when daily temperatures may average more than 100 degrees
for four or five months in a row, and a typical shelter includes a basic
structure of eight branches set into postholes about a foot deep and arranged in a rough semicircle. Thick clumps of grass piled on top of the
branches provide protection from the sun, while the interior of the
semicircle is scooped out to a depth of 2 to 3 inches to permit sleeping
snug to the ground. The aborigines camped in two such shelters, making small fires just outside the entrances.

A winter visit to the same area called for different kinds of
scooped-out shelters, for nights when the temperature may fall to freezing or below. One campsite consisted of a cleared oval area about 14

Aborigine hunting blind

feet long with a windbreak of dense brush constructed along the windward side. A large hearth was located at one end of the clearing between the windbreak and bushes growing nearby; two small hearths burned at the other end. The aborigines make no clothing for cold-weather living, and their custom has been to curl up naked near hearths and behind windbreaks. Dogs may furnish additional warmth when wrapped around the chest or legs like furs or blankets, a procedure which the animals seem to appreciate as much as the people.

A deserted campsite located nearby also had a windbreak and three hearths. What distinguished it was that the hearths were arranged in a row like those found at the Abri Pataud in France and at Kostenki in the Soviet Union. The aborigines explained the pattern. It was the sort of camp constructed by all-male groups, probably two men in this case, since one man usually lies in each of the spaces between hearths. This modern site included such signs of a hunting ceremony as those found at Terra Amata on the French Riviera and other sites, some of them more than 250,000 years old. A stone slab weighing about 25 pounds was covered with red ocher, indicating that the men had ground the pigment on the slab and painted their bodies, probably with designs representing water holes and the tracks of their dreamtime ancestors.

Artifacts collected from deserted sites at Tika-Tika included digging sticks, pieces of wooden bowls and spear throwers, and an unusual pad made of emu feathers and designed to be worn on the foot during revenge expeditions (organized when a group of aborigines believes one of its members has been bewitched by another group's sorcerer). Of course, such items are perishable and may disintegrate within a couple of years under desert conditions, usually devoured by white ants. Among the durable items were grinding stones and slabs, several

301

Aborigine food, a
day's catch of lizards
by two women

dozen adz flakes, and hundreds of waste chips, all of them made of various forms of quartz obtained from quarries 40 or more miles away.
Such material may accumulate for many years, because campsites tend
to be used over and over again.

Gould visited nearly a hundred sites, including sites occupied by
only a few persons, complexes with clusters of as many as 20 camps and
more than 80 persons, ceremonial sites, butchering sites, and ambushing sites. In all, his maps represent several hundred living floors and
some new features of special archeological interest. At the dead end of a
steep gully, he came across a ring of rocks which, on the side facing a
nearby water hole, were piled neatly to form a wall. A similar ring in
another gully a quarter of a mile away and near another water hole had
an even more carefully built wall almost 3 feet high.

Such structures had never been reported before, so Gould turned
to the experts for an explanation. The aborigines identified them as
blinds used by hunters at night. The gullies are natural traps for kangaroos and emus, and some hunters hide in crevices along the gullies and
at the entrances, ready to intercept animals trying to escape. Large animals killed far from camp are roasted whole on the spot in earth-oven
trenches (another archeological feature that may endure for many years).
The animals are butchered and divided among the hunters, who may

Nyampitjin, summer camp in the Gibson Desert

subsequently subdivide their shares among as many as 50 or 60 individuals back at camp.

There are also features of religious significance. Certain sites are transformation places, dreamtime tracks where special events occurred which caused supernatural ancestors to change themselves into various landmarks, often into rocks and rock formations. At one such site, the bed of a dried-out creek winds down from the Clutterbuck Hills about 40 miles northwest of Tika-Tika through a low canyon. On a terrace at the upper part of the canyon is a structure built centuries or perhaps millennia ago, a line of 436 rocks, 39 of them being upright slabs a foot or two high.

There is a tale behind these rocks, in Gould's words "a storyline that proceeds up-canyon from north to south." The story, as recounted by the two elderly aborigines who were his guides, concerns the legendary circumcision of a novice Kawan-kawan in the dreamtime. Signs of the ceremony are found all along the way to the terrace—depressions in the bedrock of the creek, where the novice sat and knelt while waiting **303**

Aborigine women
winnowing wangunu
seeds

to proceed to the circumcision site; two slabs of rock marking the spot where he was picked up to be carried to the site; and, at the end of a billabong, or long pool of water, a tall eucalyptus tree believed to be Kawan-kawan himself. One of the 436 rocks on the terrace, the one with red stripes on it, is his freshly circumcised and bleeding penis; the other 435 rocks are dreamtime beings who assumed the shapes of marsupial cats and attended the ceremony.

The canyon is a sacred place to these aborigines, who belong to the marsupial-cat totem, or cult lodge. They identify themselves with the marsupial-cat people and believe themselves to be descended from these people in a direct male line going back to father and grandfather and so on to the beginning of the dreamtime. It should be emphasized that circumcision, occurring at the age of 14 to 16, is only the first of a series of initiations in which the male aborigine participates. Other initiations take place during the next 10 or 15 years, all designed primarily to impart knowledge of one of the most elaborate religions known. Songs and legends are memorized note for note and word for word, together with a vast store of details about numerous rituals, and everything is passed along from generation to generation.

Increase ceremonies ensuring the reproduction of plants and animals are involved as well as initiations. One increase site lies on a track where dreamtime water-snake ancestors became sick after eating the yellow flowers of a local shrub; they vomited up the flowers, which promptly turned to stones now represented by a cluster of eight piles of yellow rock. As one of the rare sources of sugar in the desert, the flowers represent a much-sought food, and members of the water-snake totem come to the site regularly to sprinkle their blood on the rock piles. The aborigines describe the act as "just like rain," indicating that they consider their blood as important as rain in bringing about growth of the shrubs. There could be no more vivid expression of the fact that they are laying their lives on the line in the business of survival.

Their art is intimately connected with religious themes, with pre- **305**
serving a unity with the world and the desert. They still paint on rock
surfaces, and Gould has watched them applying pigments of charcoal
and red and white ocher mixed in emu fat. He has also listened to explanations of various works from the artists themselves. Their rock
paintings consist mainly of abstract designs, representing events that
occurred along dreamtime tracks. In one rock shelter, an artist of the
water-snake totem drew a long wavy line in red ocher for the snake's
track, elongated red dots for its eggs, and black dots for the hearths at
its campsites.

The designs are basically different from those used on spear
throwers. In fashioning the tools, individuals use a variety of symbols
which may be meaningless even to members of their own totem group.
But rock-art patterns come from a set of recognized symbols which are
also used in painting the body for ceremonial dances. These symbols
resemble the abstract designs found painted in the art caves of France
and Spain and suggest that prehistoric people may also have had a "vocabulary" of symbols to express myths and beliefs. If so, investigators
face a major job of deciphering.

The aborigines consider their paintings sacred but, being man-
made, of a second order of sacredness. Thus it is no crime to paint over
them, and superimpositions occur commonly, as in the prehistoric caves
of western Europe. Rock engravings, rock alignments, and rock piles, on
the other hand, belong to an entirely different category. They are not
representations, but the real thing. To the aborigines the eucalyptus tree
in the Clutterbuck Hills *is* the novice Kawan-kawan, and the aligned rocks
are the dreamtime marsupial-cat people who attended his circumcision.
Furthermore, Kawan-kawan and the people are alive, merely sleeping,
and capable of moving and acting at any time.

Gould reports that the old guides who brought him to the canyon
in the hills "spent about twenty minutes clearing away weeds and
rubble which had accumulated around the rocks of the alignment since
their last visit." And every time one of them set upright an aligned rock
that had fallen over, he addressed it as "my father." The world of the
aborigine has been described by Theodor Strehlow of the University of
Adelaide, who has spent his life studying their religion:

> Mountains and creeks and springs and waterholes are, to him, not
> merely interesting or beautiful scenic features in which his eyes may take a
> passing delight; they are the handiwork of ancestors from whom he himself was
> descended. He sees recorded in the surrounding landscape the ancient story of
> the lives and deeds of the immortal beings whom he reveres; beings who for a
> brief space may take on human shape once more; beings many of whom he has
> known in his own experience as his fathers and grandfathers and brothers, and
> as his mothers and sisters.
>
> The whole countryside is his living, age-old family tree. The story of his

own totemic ancestor is to the native the account of his own doings at the beginning of time, at the dim dawn of life, when the world as he knows it now was being shaped and moulded by all-powerful hands. He himself has played a part in the first glorious adventure, a part smaller or greater according to the original rank of the ancestor of whom he is the present reincarnated form. . . . Today, tears will come into his eyes when he mentions an ancestral home site which has been, sometimes unwittingly, desecrated by the white usurpers of his group territory.

In the last analysis the similarities of aborigines, modern people, and prehistoric representatives of *Homo sapiens* are much greater than the differences. On the other hand, this emphasis can be carried too far. Differences must be recognized, otherwise even logical and convincing hypotheses will never match the facts. Perhaps the most obvious difference between the aborigines and prehistoric people living in western Europe 35,000 to 10,000 years ago is their different environments. The technologies and philosophies that evolved in glacial climates with abundant big game naturally differed from those evolved under desert or semidesert conditions.

Among the aborigines themselves, there were differences in prehistoric times between those who lived in the desert and those who lived along coasts and rivers, where food was considerably more plentiful. Changes occurred even more among the desert people. The original settlers of Australia probably did not have dogs, spear throwers, stones for grinding food, and spears as well designed as those of modern times. Over the course of millennia, they borrowed techniques from others and developed techniques of their own. In fact, Gould has discovered a procedure that seems to have come in quite recent times, a way of using rock slabs as foundations for shade-providing structures in summer camps. There are more than enough differences to keep investigators occupied for decades.

Meanwhile, the search for similarities goes on. The aborigines and the Magdalenians may or may not have had radically different religions, but what they have in common with one another and with us is more significant, a capacity for seeing beneath the surface of things and expressing their ideas in art and ritual, and a need to see the world as an orderly and meaningful place. More specifically, the similarities known to exist between some of the stone tools and living floors of prehistoric and recent times hint that further similarities remain to be discovered. Recognizing such things as rock blinds, rock alignments, earth ovens, and so on in the occupation area of the aborigines helps to free the mind when it comes to interpreting possibly related features of other living floors in Australia and elsewhere. According to Gould, "it suggests new possibilities and analogies to us, and helps us get unstuck from a limited range of ideas."

By the time he conducted his most extensive excavation, Gould

Aborigine art on
rocks of a hunting
blind: kangaroo
tracks (left) and
unidentified object

had learned a great deal about aboriginal life styles in the region. He
and a group of students dug for 11 summer weeks in a rock shelter at
the foot of a steep cliff, under hot and dry conditions very much like
those that prevailed in prehistoric times. Less than half an inch of rain
had fallen there in two years, and all of it fell in a single day during the
third week of the dig.

The shelter was first used about 10,000 years ago, and is still
being used for brief visits today. In fact, within two years or so before
excavating started, aborigines had left a number of stone tools at the
site, tools like those made and used throughout the history of the site.

The original settlers, perhaps two families, found an ample shelter 40 feet long and 15 feet deep. One day, after they had been living there for a long but undetermined period, and fortunately when no one was in the shelter, part of the roof collapsed, covering most of the living space with tons of quartzite debris. The people returned, however, and cleared two oval-shaped areas, presumably one for each family.

Gould drew on his knowledge about the behavior of living aborigines to help understand the behavior of their remote ancestors. The two oval-shaped areas are exactly the same size and shape and contain many of the same kinds of artifacts as 41 current-style camps which he mapped over a period of a few years, suggesting that then as now such areas were probably occupied by three to four persons. Some of the stone tools recovered from the site are identical to tools from other Australian sites dating back about 30,000 years, and to tools still being used today. Furthermore, microscopic studies reveal that the wear patterns of modern woodworking tools are identical to those of similar prehistoric tools.

Experience gained from living with aborigines also helped explain one of the most unusual features of the site. Next to the main rock shelter is a smaller one, too small to live in, but containing a pit 5½ feet deep, with many thin tilted layers of differently colored soil, some **309** containing ash or charcoal. Excavators were surprised to find moist soil within the pit, suggesting that it had served as a water source, a trap for moisture percolating down through cracks in the cliff.

Gould believes the pit is a "fossil" well, and he has seen similar structures actually being used by modern aborigines. They are dug down to the water table, sometimes 15 feet deep or more, and provide virtually permanent supplies of water. But it may be months or years between visits to a native well, and during that period the openings may be clogged with dense growth of grass and thorny bushes, which are cleared away by burning. The same procedure was probably practiced in times past, which would account for the thin layers of burned material found in the prehistoric rock shelter.

At times the shelter must have served as a place for magical and sacred activities, as indicated by rock paintings, quartz crystals, tektites, or glassy objects which may be the remains of shattered meteors, and other unusual stones brought in from surrounding areas and presumably used for charms and talismans. Also, some time between 7,000 and 10,000 years ago, grinding stones and the charred remains of seeds and other plant parts appeared in excavated layers, perhaps a sign of more intense exploitation of local food resources.

For all the information that has come from the aborigines during past investigations, considerably more can be expected in the years ahead, as interest in living prehistory continues to grow. Findings in Australia already bear on problems encountered in the digging of European and Near Eastern sites. For example, Nicolas Peterson and Carmel Schrire of Rutgers University have spent time in Arnhem Land along the north-central coast of Australia, the home territory of some 5000 aborigines. They present reasons for believing that the differences between tool kits found at coastal and inland sites and once attributed to different cultures actually reflect local adaptations to seasonal rains and flooding. In other words, the same people were doing different things at different times of the year, and comparable situations may have existed among prehistoric hunter-gatherers living at sites like Combe Grenal in southern France (see Chapter 9).

At the broadest level, research on the ways of aborigines, past and present, furnishes an example of our genius for adapting. Wherever we live, we do what must be done in order to survive—and that includes finding a reason to survive in the first place, a harmony between necessity and belief. Necessity dictates that the land be used as effectively as possible, especially in inhospitable desert regions; as Peterson emphasizes in a recent study, belief ensures that this does indeed happen.

Where food is limited, people cannot live together in large groups. If they did, they would soon eat themselves into extinction,

consuming food like a swarm of locusts and ruining the land in the
process. Survival depends on living in small groups over a wide area,
and on remaining dispersed. Aborigine men, not women, are brought
up to be powerfully attached to their homeland. When a young man
marries he may have to move a hundred or more miles to live with his
wife's family. But as he grows older and accumulates daughters, perhaps another wife or so, and status, he generally returns to the region
of his dreamtime ancestors.

This attraction, a kind of cultural homing instinct, is created by
aborigine rituals, which include a whole series of painful procedures,
such as knocking out a front tooth, circumcision, scarring the chest, and
bloodletting. One function of the ordeals is to engrave as deeply as possible in memory an identification with place, to make knowledge about
the features of the landscape and their meanings unforgettable, to ensure that the native son does indeed return.

Sometimes this is difficult, for instance, when the homeland is
not particularly attractive. Annette Hamilton of the University of Sydney points out that in the central Australian desert, the tendency is to
force young men to go through all the ordeals and mutilations, while in
Arnhem Land, where rain and food are more abundant, the atmosphere
is more permissive, and such severe ordeals may not be compulsory.

Yet, there is less tension in the desert, and life is more equitable.
Young men are hostile toward the older men who initiate them, but
they also feel admiration and respect, perhaps because women tend to
be fairly distributed. As a rule, the practice is one man, one wife. But in
Arnhem Land, for some reason older men may have two or three wives;
the young must wait until they are 25 or 30 to marry, and their hostility
is mixed with less respect and more hatred. Women have a higher
status in the desert. They are excluded from initiations and other male
rituals but may have rituals of their own, and generally they seem more
sure of themselves and less anxious than Arnhem Land women.

Although there are differences among the aborigines, the similarities are even more outstanding and enduring. In everything from
artifacts to religious beliefs and practices they tend to be extremely conservative, and their past demonstrates the strengths and weaknesses of
extreme conservatism as a way of life. For them everything had a completed quality; everything was accounted for, once and for all. The
dreamtime was a kind of cultural high-water mark against which subsequent events could be measured, a lost golden age of heroes and he-
roic deeds and abundance and easy hunting. Every change since then
was a change for the worse, a step backward. The duty of the living
was a rear-guard action to hold the line and prevent changes that would
result in a further falling away from dreamtime days.

The memorizing of songs, myths, and dance sequences was a
way of preserving the *status quo*. So were the mutilations which served

to dramatize the desperate seriousness of remembering and doing **311** things as they have always been done. Everything was spelled out detail by detail so that there would be no questioning. No one thought of modifying ideas about dreamtime tracks and sacred places, much less of inventing new ideas, because every feature of the desert had long since become part of a time-honored and firmly established legend. The landscape was effectively used up.

This system stands as one more example of the fact, amply documented in civilized as well as primitive societies, that people can be programmed or indoctrinated with practically any set of beliefs, and that change itself can be put off if those beliefs are implanted deeply enough. The complexity of the aborigines' religion contrasts sharply with the simplicity of their technology, and suggests that they may have poured most of their creative energies into the dreamtime world. Their struggle to preserve things succeeded for a long time; it failed, not because of any change in themselves or in their land, but because of the coming of people who had been programmed to regard change as both possible and desirable.

The old problem of observing and registering what goes on as objectively as possible is intensified as we study our nearest ancestors. The difficulty, serious enough in the case of simpler creatures such as baboons and chimpanzees, is multiplied many many times in the case of human beings. Preconceptions are more massive and die harder the closer we come to our own species. There is a deeper commitment to belief and assumed knowledge, more to be justified and defended. But recent developments in every branch of the behavioral sciences indicate that a beginning has been made in breaking loose from notions no longer relevant to the times.

CHAPTER 16   THE BEHAVIOR OF PRIMITIVE PEOPLES

There are basic relationships among people living together, laws or hints of laws yet to be discovered. This is a major reason for studying living prehistory, which includes the search among contemporary societies for clues to the nature of prehistoric societies. Although certain behavioral patterns of elementary responses and reactions apparently apply to all people, whether they live in highly industrialized communities or in remote backcountry areas, chances of finding such patterns may well be greater among primitive groups, where they may be seen "pure" and detected more readily.

One pattern has to do with so-called magic numbers. Two of the numbers are 25 and 500; the first refers to the size of hunter-gatherer bands, and the second to the size of their tribes. Some 20 years ago Joseph Birdsell was studying rates of population growth among the Australian aborigines and noted that their band sizes ranged from about 20 to 50; he selected 25 as a representative figure. His choice has turned out to have a wider significance than he may have realized at the time.

An unpublished census of ten bands of aborigines indicates an average size of precisely 25, and this number has also been reported in a survey of Kalahari Bushmen. The average for the Birhar, a hunting-gathering tribe of northern India, comes to 26. Other analyses involve similar figures. For example, evidence indicates that adult males tend to form working groups of six to eight individuals, which is the number generally included in a 25-member band. Incidentally, certain living-floor studies suggest about the same size for prehistoric bands.

There is nothing absolute about the number 25. Birdsell and others emphasize that it represents an "equilibrium" value, and that while actual counts may come to more or less than 25, they tend to cluster around that value. It is somewhat higher than the range for gorilla troops (about 12 to 17), fairly close to that for Indian langur monkeys (18 to 30), and lower than the averages for baboons (about 40), forest-

312

dwelling rhesus monkeys of north India (about 50), and African chimpanzees (40 to 50). We do not know the reason for the human average, although, as indicated above, it may have something to do with the most efficient working groups of adult males. But it is not radically out of line with the general range for the order of primates as a whole.

The magic number 500, on the other hand, represents something really new. As a common average for a dialectical tribe of hunter-gatherers—that is, a group of bands all speaking the same dialect—it is a purely human number in the sense that organizations of such interrelated bands have not been found among other primates. Birdsell directed attention to the number during the course of his population studies of the aborigines: "The Australian data show an amazing constancy of numbers for the dialectical tribe, statistically approximating 500 persons. This tendency is independent of regional density. Since the data cover mean annual rainfall variations from 4 inches to more than 160 inches, the size of the dialectical tribal unit is insensitive to regional variations in climatic . . . factors."

This is also an equilibrium value and not an absolute figure. Birdsell himself has noted that the sizes of individual tribes may range from extremes of about 200 to more than 800 persons. The phenomenon becomes clear and meaningful only after taking census figures for a large number of tribes. Such studies reveal a central tendency to cluster at the 500 level, and this tendency is widespread. It holds for the Shoshoni Indians of the Great Plains and the Andaman Islanders in the Bay of Bengal, as well as the Australian aborigines and other peoples.

This number apparently reflects certain fundamental features of human communication systems. The unity of a hunting-gathering tribe depends on face-to-face meetings, a degree of intimacy among members of its component bands which creates the feeling of belonging to the same extended community even though they may live many miles apart. The intimacy involves not only the same language and dialect but the same familiar intonations, expressions, and gestures, and a common store of idioms, jokes, myths, and allusions. All this signaling or communicating activity is implied in the notion of sharing a common cultural background.

Apparently there are laws governing the extent of such sharing. There seems to be a basic limit to the number of persons (1) who can know one another well enough to maintain a tribal identity at the hunter-gatherer level; (2) who communicate by direct confrontation; and (3) who live under a diffuse and informal influence, perhaps a council of elders rather than an active centralized political authority. Knowing one another well enough is a qualification that is difficult to define and measure. George Murdock of the University of Pittsburgh, who has looked into the problem, provides some unpublished results. To obtain a rough index of familiarity he asked students, colleagues and friends to estimate the number of people they associated with on a first-name basis. His main finding was that for most of us, the number ranges from about 800 to 1200, the unofficial champion being James Farley, an influential member of the Democratic party during the Roosevelt administration, who estimated that he knew between 6000 and 7000 persons by their first names.

The range of 800 to 1200 of course applies to citizens of a highly mobile and densely populated nation. Contacts are less frequent in the hunter-gatherer's world, however, where visits require long walks. The 500 figure for tribal sizes may be related to this limitation. As an interesting sidelight, there is an architect's rule of thumb to the effect that the capacity of an elementary school should not exceed 500 pupils if the principal expects to know all of them by name—and it has been stated that when a group exceeds 500 persons, it requires some form of policing.

The underlying phenomena which account for magic numbers have yet to be discovered, but some clues come from recent studies by Martin Wobst. It would be ideal to have detailed records indicating the success of hunter-gatherer bands over many generations, bands of different sizes and different social systems. Since this sort of information has never been collected, however, the second-best course is to play a kind of let's-suppose game and simulate what might have happened with the aid of a computer.

The first step involves feeding into computer memory some assumptions, probabilities, and instructions: the original size of the group, the number and ages of all its members, certain social rules such as incest taboos and exogamy, and the odds that each individual will get married, have offspring, leave the group, die by accident, disease, or old age, and other information. Then the computer can go to work and run through the probable history of the group over a specified period. Using a modern high-speed computer, a single run simulating the events of 500 years can be completed within six minutes.

Wobst has obtained a variety of theoretical prehistoric case histories. For example, he assumed for the sake of simplicity that the smallest possible bands, lone adult male hunters on their own, have a half-life of about a year—which means that half of them will die within a year, half on the surviving half will die during the second year, and so on. Put 5 persons together, a family of father, mother, and 3 children, and the half-life increases to a generation, while for a 5-family band of 25 members the figure increases to from 250 to 500 years. Cultural factors probably limited band sizes much more than that, since the more members the greater the chances of conflict and splitting up.

Other computer runs suggest that what has been referred to as the magic number 500 concerns the size of the group from which mates may be obtained. The stricter the mating rules, the less chance a band member has to find a mate nearby and the greater the number of other bands needed to provide an adequate pool of possible mates. For a band with incest taboos and a rule that a man can choose a woman of any marriageable age, the number of other 25-member bands would be 7 for a tribal total of 175 persons.

This number increases to 19 bands or 475 persons if the age rule is stricter, if it specifies that a man must marry a woman younger than himself. Interestingly enough, removing the ban against incest has little effect on tribal size because, among other things, it increases the number of possible mates only slightly. The undesirable thing about incest in a prehistoric hunter-gatherer context is that it increases competition for mates within the band and requires more males to travel farther in search of mates, so taboos are of definite survival value. As indicated in Chapter 13, incest is also undesirable in a wider biological context, since it works against the principle that genetic variety effectively helps insure the survival of a species.

There is certainly more to the 500 figure. The memory capacity of the human brain probably plays a fundamental role of some sort, since that influences the number of persons one can know by sight. Incidentally, Wobst's work suggests that the need for wider kinship-mating networks may have arisen some 35,000 to 40,000 years ago in Cro-Magnon times, when increasing population favored the large-scale hunting of herd animals. This period also saw the appearance of personal adornment, art, and probably rituals designed to promote group solidarity (see Chapter 11). Other problems are sure to arise as research uncovers other regularities and tendencies in the behavior of people adapting in complex ways to one another and to their environments. Evolution builds on these regularities and tendencies.

Funds may not be available soon enough for large-scale research into living prehistory and the behavior of living primitive peoples. It is already too late for further studies of the Hadza, for example, a group of some 400 Africans who occupied a remote area of bush country not far from the Olduvai Gorge and Ngorongoro Crater in Tanzania. About eight years ago they were living in beehive-shaped grass huts and, during the rainy season, in rock shelters. Although visitors from affluent lands described their land as an inhospitable wilderness and their life as a bitter struggle against starvation, they had a generous food supply, no enemies, and a surfeit of leisure.

The people considered themselves to be hunters, and game was abundant. But more than 80 percent of their diet consisted of wild honey and various plant foods collected by the women; about half the men did practically no hunting at all. From early morning until dark they spent a major part of their time gambling, betting arrows on whether wooden disks tossed against a tree would land barkside up or barkside down. (Gambling probably arose as an antimonotony device, a way of creating unpredictable events under all too predictable living conditions. Australian aborigines living on government reservations where there is little to do have taken to a weird form of poker with rules that seem to change from hand to hand.)

The Hadza had adapted successfully to their native territory. In 1960, visiting pediatricians from the Makerere University Medical School in Uganda reported that their children were among the healthiest in East Africa. Recently, however, most of the people were forced to change their way of existence. Government officials relocated them to a reservation 50 miles away, where they lived in much closer contact with one another. Within a year, about a quarter of their children had succumbed to an epidemic, a turn of events that has occurred many times before during similar forced moves.

Another vanished society is that of the Ainu people, who are concentrated on Hokkaido, an island north of the mainland of Japan. Although some were still engaged in hunting and gathering no more than a generation ago, their world began changing rapidly in the early 1880s, when the Japanese government adopted the policy of encouraging them to become farmers. Fortunately, according to a study based on extensive field work and interviews conducted by Hitoshi Watanabe and his associates at the University of Tokyo, their former way of life has been reconstructed.

The Ainu lived basically as our ancestors did in western Europe some 15,000 years ago, settling into river valleys and gearing their existence to natural cycles, the seasons, and the predictable comings and goings of migratory animals. Their major source of food was the salmon, the "divine" fish which was sent to the people by spirits living in the sea and which returned year after year to the same spawning grounds. And every spring and fall, deer came down from hills and mountains in the central part of the island, going along the same fixed trails through dense forests, and swimming across rivers at the same points, the traditional places for ambushes.

Hunting and fishing served future as well as current needs. Provision had to be made for subsistence during a period of two or three months in the dead of winter, when snows were deepest and deer retreated to the hills and salmon to the sea. Everything depended on the salmon. When they ran in large shoals, as they generally did, the people were assured of ample stores of sun-dried fish for cold-weather eating supplemented by sun-dried venison—and winter became a season of leisure, celebration, and visits from friends and relatives. Less abundant runs meant going after deer in their forest retreats and a greater dependence on nuts and other plant foods. One year, in one valley, salmon were extremely scarce; during the winter, some 200 persons died of starvation.

These studies put the past in perspective. In prehistoric Europe, longer and colder winters may have prevailed during glacial periods in the valleys of the Les Eyzies region, for example, confronting the Neanderthals and Magdalenians with the same essential problems that the Ainu recently faced. Survival for them, as for the Ainu, demanded ways of preserving and storing food and getting about in the snow when food was scarce.

Evidence has been obtained which bears on the storage problem. The Neanderthals almost certainly used natural permafrost and ice refrigeration and stockpiled meat in some of their caves; possibly, they used sawtooth flint tools to shred reindeer and horse meat into strips for drying in the sun or over slow-burning fires. The question is how they managed to cope with snow. Watanabe points out that they probably were able to follow game across open tundra country, where winds freeze and harden the snow cover. But snowshoes are needed to move through forest areas where the snow is soft and deep, and that invention may not have come until Magdalenian times or later.

Current efforts to learn more about life in arctic and sub-arctic climates include the research of Binford and his associates in the Brooks Range of Alaska. Some of their archeological work has been mentioned in Chapter 9. They have also been observing hunting and other activities among some 135 Eskimos living near the main pass through the mountains, a pass used for millennia by people and caribou.

Some years ago Binford had a firsthand, unplanned adventure in the region. He came specifically to see the caribou, the people's major source of food, moving through the pass. But the herds did not appear. More than 7 feet of snow fell during a six-day blizzard; the animals stayed in forests to the south, and the community faced its most severe food shortage in decades. Snows covered everything, changing the landscape of familiar contours and paths and willow stands into a vast, blank, white expanse—with all the landmarks gone except for the tallest trees, the highest bluffs, and the mountains themselves.

In this transformed world, the people turned to strategies and tactics originally learned in prehistoric times. One group of hunters saw tracks in fresh snow, set 150 snares and caught 65 arctic squirrels, although as far as a square meal is concerned, a squirrel compares to a caribou as a hummingbird compares to a Thanksgiving turkey. The hunters also decided to try ice fishing in a nearby lake, but gave it up after hacking a hole more than 4 feet deep into the ice without any signs that water was near. They had better luck, but not much better, finding meat put away in special places around the countryside for just such emergencies, locating two out of ten caches. Meanwhile the women were beginning to tap another source of food, marrow bones and the frozen carcasses of wolves and foxes kept on the roofs of houses where the dogs could not get at them.

At about this stage, the situation started improving, and there

was no need to use last-resort emergency foods such as fern roots and
the inner bark of willow trees. A herd of moose headed south, where
there was food in the forests; hunters saw their tracks and came back
with 3700 pounds of meat. Not long afterward, as temperatures soared
from 30 degrees or more below zero Fahrenheit to a "warm" 5 or 6 degrees above, the caribou showed up. But for nearly a month, Binford
had a glimpse of what things must have been like during prehistoric
emergencies, when weather often did not improve and hunters were
wiped out. Even today and given the favorable change of weather, the
community would have suffered far more severely if he had not
brought an ample supply of antibiotics with him, because all but half a
dozen of the people caught influenza.

Binford and his associates have hunted with Eskimos, observed
their butchering methods, and obtained detailed records of the remains
at some 280 kill sites at different seasons—all of which will help in reconstructing prehistoric activities. For example, skulls, necks, and vertebrae are generally left behind at the kill site, while thigh bones and
other long bones may be saved for their marrow and brought back to
the main camp. The same sort of distribution exists among fossil reindeer bones excavated at a Neanderthal site in England, suggesting that
it was a kill site and not, as had previously been concluded, a home
base. Similar analyses are scheduled for material found at Olduvai, Torralba, Combe Grenal, and many other sites.

Such research has implications far beyond its use in interpreting
findings at individual sites. In a new study, Binford has calculated
many of the values which Brooks Range Eskimos place on caribou parts,
analyzing their hunting, butchering, and caching strategies at different
seasons and under different conditions of weather, abundances, scar-
cities, and so on. He indicates the extent to which Eskimo behavior is
shaped by the behavior and ultimately by the anatomy of their prey.
This is hard evidence for the existence of a kind of built-in calculus of
subsistence among hunter-gatherers, a strict and precise relationship
between the food quest and social organization.

Time is running out for such hunters as the Eskimos, and for the
scientists who would learn from them, even in the few remaining areas
where civilization has not yet produced radical changes. Such territories
still offer sufficient supplies of food, but human resources continue to
dwindle. In Australia an estimated 3000 to 4000 aborigines are still living the old hunting-gathering life, and they can no longer stay away
from the missions, reserves, and farming communities where most of
their people have settled. They must find mates for their sons and
daughters, which means visiting civilized centers and often never returning to the desert.

So the emphasis in living-prehistory research has been increasingly on immediate large-scale projects conducted in depth. One such

project involves a region thousands of miles from the aborigines' home country, a region in southern Africa where more than a third of all existing hunter-gatherers (some 9000 persons) are concentrated. Specifically, it has focused intensively on a very small area of unusual interest, a speck in the 350,000-square-mile Kalahari Desert of Botswana. The area has a radius of less than 20 miles, is surrounded by vast stretches of waterless terrain, and includes 11 permanent water holes and wells, between 400 and 500 plant and animal species, and about 450 Bushmen.

For about ten years these people and their neighbors have been the focus of a continuing study, one of the most comprehensive of its kind ever undertaken. Irven De Vore played a leading part in organizing the study, which involves investigators from Harvard University, the University of Michigan, the University of New Mexico, and a number of other institutions. Research on the health of Bushmen and their nutrition, subsistence techniques, child rearing, sex roles, rituals, and so on has yielded some basic results. For one thing, it has amply confirmed the effectiveness of the hunter-gatherer way of life.

Richard Lee of the University of Toronto has concentrated on the economics of that life style, on the amount of effort individuals put into the business of obtaining food. Local Bushmen are fortunate in having an abundant and dependable food staple, a staff of life, in the form of the high-energy, high-protein nut of the mongongo tree. Although some 85 desert plants are considered edible and may be used for variety or as second-best fare, this single species provides from half to two thirds of the total vegetable diet. The selection of campsites is determined by the locations of mongongo forests found on the crests of long sand dunes or, more precisely, by the distances between the nearest water sources and the forests.

According to Lee, "the Bushmen typically occupy a camp for weeks or months and literally eat their way out of it." During January or February, when most of the rain falls, they may camp at a temporary pool within a mile or so of the nearest trees, and exhaust that supply of nuts in a week. Then on successive weeks they may have to walk 2, 3 and 4 miles to progressively more distant forests, all the time camping at the same pool. They will never walk more than 6 miles, however, since women, the main food providers, are not willing to undertake longer trips in a single day at temperatures averaging 100 degrees and carrying 20 to 40 pounds of nuts on their backs, plus infants or tired children.

This is the departure point, and the group will then move to another water source near other forests, that is, in relatively wet weather. But in the driest season, in October and November, there is no choice because all temporary pools have vanished and the people must stay near one of the permanent water holes. Most of them forgo mongongo nuts and other preferred foods, living on poorer fare which can be gath-

Kalahari mongongo forest

ered within a few miles of their homes. Some hardier groups, however, travel up to 20 miles to mongongo trees in waterless places where they may camp for a week or two.

Life becomes exceedingly difficult under such conditions. Indeed, it would be impossible without a certain type of shrub that has bulbous root organs which are about the size of a football and store water in the form of milky juice. Even with these natural reservoirs, the campers barely make a go of it in dry seasons; so much of the water they get from the roots is needed simply to replace the water lost in the process of digging for the roots, which lie a foot or two underground in the hard compacted soil of basins between sand dunes. Incidentally, on one occasion Lee asked a group of Bushmen to go through this ordeal, even though he could easily have driven them to a mongongo forest and back again in his Land Rover, which is something like asking city dwellers to walk to work in a heat wave without using available buses and subways. But they promptly agreed after he explained that they were the only people in the world who could cope with the Kalahari at its worst, and that he and others wanted to know how they did it.

Food gathering requires only a bare minimum of equipment. The basic tools are a pair of unworked stone hammers to crack nuts with and a sturdy digging stick about 3 feet long and ¾ inch in diameter, **320**

Kalahari dietary
staple: roasting
mongongo nuts

Kalahari woman
gathering food with
child on back

sharpened to a blade at the business end. The most important item of **322**
equipment is the kaross, a combination garment and receptacle made of
antelope hide which women wear draped over the shoulder. It forms a
pouch for carrying nuts, berries, edible roots and bulbs, ostrich-shell
water containers, firewood, and babies. These three simple items, the
two tools and the kaross, are all that is needed to obtain vegetable
foods.

Going after animals demands more ingenuity and a correspondingly more elaborate set of tools—including bows and arrows, arrow
poisons made from crushed beetle pupae, rope snares, nets, firemaking
kits, knives, and a dozen other items. John Yellen of George Washington University has gone with Bushmen on hunting trips and studied
their tracking techniques. Judging by a variety of scuff marks and in-
dentations in the sand, they can tell the kind of animal as well as its
size and sex and which way it is going. They can also tell how old the
track is. Some tracks are so recent that sand is still falling into the hollow, while old tracks may be blurred and faded. Such abilities are relatively routine, roughly the equivalent of reading and writing.

The finer points of the art come into play in deciding what the
animal is doing and whether or not to go after it, decisions based on an
intimate knowledge of the land and animal behavior. Yellen emphasizes
that an eland's tracks may be only half an hour old, but if hunters feel it
is "going somewhere far" and moving at a steady pace, they will not
bother to pursue it. On the other hand, tracks several hours old may
represent a call to action if they indicate that the animal is moving irregularly within a limited area, which may mean that it is stopping
frequently to rest or keeping watch on a young offspring hidden in
some bushes.

One of the most impressive things about these and many far
subtler deductions is what they imply about the quality of the brain required for advanced forms of hunting. During the following of game
trails one discusses the nature and meaning of tracks, assesses the probable merits of different theories about what is happening, decides on a
course of action, and frequently checks and rechecks one's theories in
the light of fresh evidence. One distinguishes clearly between fact and
hypothesis. The hunter's brain is also the scientist's. Whether they are
deciding where to gather the day's food or predicting the movements of
game in a wilderness or of satellites in space, people everywhere use
the same basic thought processes.

Big game is not as plentiful in the Kalahari as it once was, so
considerable effort is devoted to smaller animals. The most commonly
caught game, the springhare, is taken in its burrow with the aid of a
flexible pole 13 feet long. The hunter pushes the pole into the burrow
slowly as it bends to follow underground turns; he proceeds by "feel"
and is ready to detect vibrations or sounds that indicate the location of

the cornered prey. Then at the proper moment the pole is moved backward and then forward in a swift thrust, impaling the hare on a hook attached to the probing end. A digging stick is used to get at the animal and kill it.

Trapping requires expert skill and involves far more than merely finding tracks where snares may be placed. The trick is to influence patterns of animal movement, deliberately creating places suitable for snares. For example, when hunters notice antelope tracks on a sandy area of bush country, they sometimes toss some branches across them. When they come back to the area a day or two later, they note changes in the tracks and put down more branches. After a number of days there is a seemingly haphazard brush fence with gaps 2 or 3 feet wide. The next step is to add just enough branches to narrow the gaps still further, and then set nooses in them. By this time, and it requires considerable patience, the animals have been conditioned to walk right into the traps.

There is also a clever way of catching guinea fowl. If a hen sees that one of her eggs has rolled out of the nest, she tries to roll it back with her head and beak. This is an automatic reaction, triggered by the sight of the misplaced egg, and the way to take advantage of it is to remove an egg from the nest, place it about 8 inches away and lay a buried noose around it. As soon as the hen returns to her nest and notices what has happened, she is doomed because she cannot help nudging the egg toward the nest and springing the trap.

Kalahari hunter-gatherers have an enormous repertoire of techniques which they can modify to fit special circumstances. They spend their lives learning these highly developed techniques of their ancestors, so despite the hard times of hot dry seasons, they are remarkably successful at extracting a living from desert lands. Lee has measured the success in a detailed study of one group of about 30 persons camping near a water hole. The study continued for 28 consecutive days in July and August, a time when food was neither exceptionally abundant nor exceptionally scarce.

It yielded a precise and revealing subsistence balance sheet. During this period, the diet was made up of 37 percent meat, mostly small game, 33 percent mongongo nuts, and 30 percent other vegetables. Sufficient supplies were obtained daily to provide each member of the group with 1.4 pounds of food—about 2140 calories, 165 more than the basic daily requirement. Furthermore, obtaining food is by no means a full-time job. Only from one to three days a week was devoted to hunting and gathering and the rest of the week was free for resting, playing games, and visiting friends at nearby camps.

As a matter of fact, earning a living is even more efficient than these figures indicate. During their few days of working time, the providers manage to obtain sufficient food not only for themselves but for dependent individuals under 15 and over 60 years old, who make up about a third of the group and contribute nothing or very little to food supplies. It is worth noting that about 8 percent of all 248 hunter-gatherers in the Kalahari area were persons 60 to more than 80 years old. The study was conducted during a year of drought which had less than 7 inches of rain, and foraging achievements would have been even more impressive in better times.

There are many reasons to carry out such analyses. They tend to pin down, and sometimes to show up, anecdotal information and general impressions. In this instance, they contribute to an entirely new picture of the hunting-gathering way of life, contemporary and pre-historic. The old picture was less a solid theory than a fine example of the tendency to judge all human beings by the standards of middle-class life in a modern city. Many investigators assumed that people who have few and simple possessions are impoverished, long-suffering, and pitiable.

Certainly that assumption does not hold for the people of the Kalahari. Their way of adapting stands as a living reminder of earlier adaptations, details of which can only be inferred from patterns of fossils and artifacts found in excavated occupation layers. Their success illuminates earlier successes that set the stage for the coming of modern people. Evolution that was uniquely human arose with the rise of subsistence strategies on the savanna, prolonged infant and child dependency, a home base, and elaborate social customs hitherto unknown in the order of primates. The result was a degree of leisure unattainable in a troop of primates where there are no home bases or stored foods and all troop members except nursing infants spend time seeking food every day of their lives. A hunting-gathering society probably provides more free time for its members than any other type of society yet evolved. For most people, leisure vanished with agriculture, cities, and the Industrial Revolution; it may yet return with computers and automation.

On the other hand, that does not mean that life was idyllic. Hunter-gatherers were never noble, nor, on the other hand, were they evil. They were and are merely human, which is rather more complicated. There has never been anything natural about living together, if by natural we meany easy or effortless. Every individual must devote an appreciable proportion of time and energy to maintaining a reasonably peaceful place in the scheme of things, to keep from rubbing other individuals the wrong way or being rubbed the wrong way. The continual boiling and spilling over of tensions is as characteristic of human groups as of baboon groups.

The people of the Kalahari, like the Australian aborigines (see Chapter 15), have a life style designed to keep conflict at a minimum. They discourage bosses and bossiness of all sorts, and any tendency to play the role of big man. George Silberbauer of Monash University in

Australia, who has lived among them longer than any other investigator (about 14 years), speaks of the ephemeral quality of leadership, where an individual may lead today and follow tomorrow, and of dispersed leadership, where several persons take the initiative in suggesting, amending, compromising, and creating a consensus. Naturally, there are prominent specialists. The best hunters plan hunts, the best witch doctors heal, the best story tellers entertain the group around fires at night. But full-time leaders do not exist, and one reason is that Kalahari people fear violence. It is this fear that above all dictates their ethics and humility.

Any boasting or pompousness, even the faintest hint of arrogance or an attitude that might eventually lead to arrogance, becomes sufficient reason for a firm put-down. A hunter may come into camp with a fine antelope kill at a time when game is scarce and the people are craving meat, but if he merely utters a noncommittal "I have killed an animal," the response is likely to be "only one?" or some such mild disparagement which is only half joking. Lee himself was the victim of this treatment when he bought an ox for a Christmas feast, and was told repeatedly in a dozen different ways by a dozen different people that the animal was scrawny, that he had been cheated, and that there would not be enough meat to go around. Actually, it was a fine animal, and everyone had more than enough to eat. But the people were acting to avoid any show of pride: "When a young man kills much meat he comes to think of the rest of us as his servants or inferiors. . . . Some day his pride will make him kill somebody."

Accumulating things, another source of pride and potential domination, is also discouraged. A particularly beautiful or useful object arouses mixed emotions. It may be desired and cherished, but not for long. It is also dangerous, a threat to the security of the individual and the group, something that may stir up envy and resentment. So the tendency is to keep it for a while, perhaps a few days or weeks, and then pass it on to someone else who will eventually feel the same way and get rid of it. The passing-on has positive as well as negative aspects. The Bushmen are continually giving things away, skins decorated with beads, knives, arrows, cattle, sandals, safety pins. Goods of all sorts pass from relative to relative, from band to band, along gift or exchange networks that involve dozens of persons and may extend for as much as 300 miles. Polly Wiessner of the University of Michigan has studied these networks in detail and points out that they serve, above all, to establish good will over wide areas so that people in search of food, a new home, or simply of companionship will find a welcome in many places.

The shaping of behavior can be seen in the way Bushmen raise their children, a process based on customs and instincts which have evolved over many generations. Training in generosity starts a few months after birth; strings of beads are put around an infant's arms, neck, and waist, and not long afterwards, generally between the ages of 6 months and 1 year, the infant is provided with new beads and encouraged to give the old ones to a relative.

The process of growing up in the Kalahari was investigated by Patricia Draper of the University of New Mexico. She kept records of the activities of some 35 children up to 14 years old, each of whom was observed in a series of spot checks for a total of three to four hours each over a period of 12 months. Analyses based on this evidence provide a quantitative and vivid picture of the intimacy of life in the wilderness. Taking the entire age range, from birth through 14 years old, children were in physical contact, actually touching another individual, about a third of the time. For the age range from birth through 5 years, the proportion of contact time was more than 50 percent, and in only four observed cases was the child unaccompanied, that is, without another person less than 3 feet or so away.

From the young child's viewpoint, the Kalahari camp is a self-contained world, an island in the bush which extends pathless in all directions without obvious landmarks. The camp is a cluster of eight to ten family groups living in as many little beehive-shaped huts, made of saplings, palm fronds, and grass, which are arranged in a circle or semi-circle. The child grows up in a close-knit group. Families sitting at night in front of their huts and around their fires do not have to raise their voices to speak with one another across the camping area. A disturbance of any sort moves swiftly like a ripple through the group. In such an atmosphere, there is little aggression and no sustained fighting among children. Potentially disruptive encounters are halted at the very start by an adult, usually but not necessarily one of the children's mothers, who is within arm's reach and, more often than not, separates the would-be antagonists casually, without interrupting work or conversation. "Aggression is never allowed to build up," Draper comments, "and children do not get a chance to learn the satisfaction of making someone cry or humiliating a person."

Nevertheless, for all the training and traditions of humility and generosity, aggression exists in the Kalahari as it does elsewhere. Individuals get on one another's nerves, tensions mount, and there are arguments and fights and occasional murders. Bushmen, like the rest of us, have difficulty maintaining the peace, which is one reason for staying small, for living in bands of only a few families, since conflict tends to increase in larger groups. Another reason is that food resources are too widely dispersed to support concentrated populations.

Many aspects of Kalahari living remain unexplained. For example, what is the significance of the tendency to prolong further the already prolonged period of dependency? Among Bushmen, as among Australian aborigines, breast feeding may continue until the child is 3 or 4 years old. Furthermore, until the age of 5, children are carried most of the way during hikes from camp to camp, and responsibility is delayed for a long period after that. Although 7-year-olds regularly take care of their younger brothers and sisters in many primitive societies, in Bushman societies, young children have nothing to do but play, and they are still playing at the age of 12 or more when boys of the same age among neighboring Bantu peoples are herding cattle. As a matter of fact, Bushman girls do not begin regular food gathering until they are about 14, while boys generally do not begin hunting seriously until at least two years later.

Such practices are part of a pattern that was once universal, the pattern of raising children for a life of hunting and gathering. The first stages of the process are of special interest to Melvin Konner of Harvard, who is focusing on development and behavior during infancy and early childhood. Among other things, he has been studying the reflexes which Bushman infants are born with, the same repertoire of reflexes observed among infants born in urban societies—except that more of them seem to be important in a hunter-gatherer context.

Some reflexes, such as sucking, blinking, and crying, are useful to infants in all societies, but others seem to be useful only in primitive societies. For example, an infant placed on its stomach a few days after birth is very likely to try to raise and turn its head from side to side and to drag itself along by using its legs in a crawling action; if held upright with its feet touching a flat surface, it will probably exhibit stepping and walking movements. These reactions serve little purpose for a baby who spends most of its time lying on its back in a crib. But they may be important to a Bushman infant who is held upright in a sling on its mother's side or hip, particularly when it is sleeping with its face pressed against her. Under such circumstances automatic moving of the head and body can be expected to reduce its discomfort and the risk of smothering.

Konner points out that other reflexes considered "vestigial" may also play an important role in primitive societies where infants spend practically all their time in a vertical position rather than in the horizontal position typical of urban-society infants. Further research will be required to learn what effect, if any, the difference in positions has on subsequent development and behavior. Perhaps the most striking difference between Bushman and urban infants, although in most respects they are very much alike, is how they react to strangers. Infants of all societies generally begin to fear strangers at about 7 to 9 months old, but the response tends to be relatively mild among American and European babies, who may frown, turn away, and cry in protest if a stranger does not leave. But the response of the Bushman infant is spectacularly more intense.

One day Konner and a British colleague stopped their Land Rover to pick up a family of Bushmen, including a mother with a sleeping infant. During the ride the infant woke up, lifted its head, saw the Britisher in the back seat, and unleashed an ear-splitting scream—the same sort of scream which babies emit when they are in severe physical pain. This was a typical response. Furthermore, tests show that practically identical responses occur whether the stranger is a white visitor or a Bushman, native to the Kalahari. The reaction probably has a sound basis in experiences of the prehistoric past. At least until recent times, the appearance of a stranger was presumably a rare event, and an event that meant trouble more often than not.

Another phase of research in the Kalahari concerns the relationships between behavior and beliefs. At the core of the Bushman's religion is the healing dance, and at the core of the dance is the trance of the healer. The Bushmen believe that medicine lies cold in the pit of the healer's stomach, and that it can be released and transferred to sick persons by a laying on of hands. But first the medicine must be brought to a boil, which is the purpose of the dance.

Proceedings usually start in the evening as women, and often children, make a fire and sit about it clapping and singing. Soon some of the men move into the area to dance for brief periods in circles around the fire, shoulders hunched, feet stamping, and arms pressed against their sides in a casual sort of warm-up period that may last for two hours or so. Then the frenzy comes. A vacant stare appears in the eyes of the dancer and he trembles, sweats heavily, and stamps so hard that, in Lee's words, "shock waves can be seen rippling through the body."

The trance state is marked by moaning, shrieking, and intense physical exertion. Sometimes a dancer, a novice as a rule, loses control and runs wild into the bush or burns himself by dancing through the central fire. One man described the experience as follows: "I see all the people like very small birds; the whole place will be spinning around and that is why we run around. The trees will be circling also. You feel your blood become very hot just like blood boiling on a fire and then you start healing. . . . When I lay my hands on sick people, the medicine in me will go into them and cure them." As a rule, healing hits a peak between midnight and two in the morning, simmers down for a while, hits a second peak at sunrise, and comes to a close around ten or eleven. During this period a large proportion of the group participates in the sessions. A few women, especially very old women, also go into trances, and some of the younger men simply use the occasion to demonstrate their dancing skills.

Healers are not members of an elite class of exalted beings who are regarded by the rest of the people with fear and trembling. The ambition of all boys is to become "doctors" and, after many trials and several years of apprenticeship for promising candidates, about half of

Beginning of Kalahari trance dance: preparing for laying on of hands and healing

them make it. These rituals serve a number of purposes besides healing. The people also organize dances out of sheer exuberance, to celebrate the killing of a large antelope or to greet old friends coming for a visit. Drawing attention to the resolution of conflict, Lee emphasizes that in the course of their dancing activities the Bushmen experience hallucinations, distorted body images, and related effects, things that members of other societies, primitive and otherwise, experience with the use of drugs, and that certain features of the dance, such as violent exertion and shrieking, help provide harmless relief for resentments, fears, and insecurities.

Psychological testing, extensive interviews, and a number of **329** other techniques have been used to gain a deeper understanding of what the trance ceremony expresses. Ritual has always been difficult to get at. Like poetry, it has meanings at many levels and demands complex types of analysis. But if fruitful studies of poetry are any indication, such work may yet yield important insights. Meanwhile, it is evident that the ceremony can no longer be viewed as a sort of circus display put on by quaint savages, that they are by no means as exotic or remote from us as was once believed. Their rituals and ours express common needs and frustrations and have common roots in human prehistory.

All phases of survival in the Kalahari are interrelated in the sense that they represent an adaptation, one of many possible adaptations, to a particular type of environment. The Bushmen live in a diverse and scattered world. Food is available in different areas at different times of the year; and since rainfall is not always predictable, they must be able to take advantage of every local opportunity as it arises. Henry Harpending of the University of New Mexico stresses that this flexibility shows up in a number of genetic and breeding patterns.

For example, he has studied nine areas containing a total of about 2300 Bushmen, and finds that only about 60 percent of the parents in a particular area were born in that area, as compared to a figure of 95 percent or more for some settled agricultural villages of similar population size. This situation reflects the basic nature of the band. The band does not exist as a fixed group of individuals living and moving together as one big family. It is a dynamic unit where people, singly and in groups, arrive and depart according to such things as the availability of food and how well they happen to be getting along with one another.

These and many other observations raise the basic question of continuity. How completely have Bushman ways of doing things been preserved over the ages? How do the people's lives compare with the lives of their remote prehistoric ancestors? Intensive studies still being conducted under the direction of Yellen and Alison Brooks, also of George Washington University, suggest that traditions do indeed endure for long periods. For one thing, the Bushmen seem to have lived in the region far longer than was previously believed. The old notion that they had been forced out of more abundant lands into desert refuge areas during relatively recent colonial times is contradicted by the discovery of typical Bushman sites dating back at least 20,000 years and probably a good deal longer.

The George Washington investigators are comparing archeological remains found at these sites with remains found at sites abandoned within the past generation or so, and find no signs of radically different life styles. Furthermore, the Bushmen who excavated with them are helping interpret various findings, just as the aborigines of the Western Australian Desert helped Gould in his studies (see Chapter 15). The search is always for new insights, for patterns that may provide a more complete picture of behavior in times long past. There is a newly discovered pattern in recently abandoned Bushman camps. The camps include a central or nuclear zone where remains tend to be heavily concentrated, where people sat around communal hearths and performed the day's chores, everything from making arrowheads to cracking nuts and cooking. A definite mathematical relationship exists between the zone's area and the size of the camping band. For example, if the zone measures 1800 to 1900 square feet, it was probably occupied by about half a dozen families, 25 to 30 individuals.

As long as the band's population does not change, this zone stays the same size. But it is generally surrounded by another zone which is used for special, often messy, activities requiring extra space, such as cleaning and drying skins or roasting heads in pits—and which tends to grow larger the longer people occupy their camp. Thus, if the half-dozen families settled for about a month, the total area of their camp, nuclear zone plus special-activities zone, would gradually increase to nearly 5300 square feet. The question now is whether similar relationships also hold for prehistoric sites, and this is one of the problems currently confronting Brooks and Yellen.

All the evidence indicates that the Bushmen have adapted effectively to Kalahari environments. Reports by Nancy Howell of the University of Toronto, who has gathered and is analyzing records of about 850 Bushmen, indicate that their population has been increasing slowly over the years and that their death rates have been moderately low in the recent past and probably for a long time before Europeans came. Their maximum life span seems to be the same as it is for human beings everywhere, with perhaps one person in a million living to the age of 110. (The oldest known Bushman is almost 90.)

There is an increasing interest in living among and studying today's hunter-gatherers and conducting local excavations which they can help interpret. A number of people have never been observed by modern methods, although their existence has been known for some time, for example, people in the forests of the Amazon Basin, Borneo, Thailand, Malaya, and South America. More such groups are still being found. For decades explorers, anthropologists, and other strangers have moved through forests without coming across people camped unobtrusively off ancient trails.

Now, new kinds of strangers, commercial pioneers such as road builders, mining engineers, and land prospectors, are going increasingly into places where there are no paths. The first contact with natives may be a glimpse of forms retreating into the shadows. Face-to-face encounters come later, and there are headlines about the discovery of lost tribes such as the Tasaday, a group of some two dozen persons living in a limestone cave on the Philippine island of Mindanao.

The problem of introducing these newly found people constructively into the modern world is taken more seriously than was once the case. So is the closely related problem of how to learn most effectively from them. In the days when all primitive people were regarded as bizarre inferiors, it was customary to come in with beads and other gewgaws and come out with the traditional sort of information which features anecdotes, general descriptions, and impressions, generally romantic. The tendency is still with us, as indicated by Anthony Pfeiffer in an analysis of research on Congo pygmies. It draws attention to some "neglect in collecting quantitative data on pygmy economics" and presents a tentative economic interpretation of one of their major ceremonies.

The current swing toward using quantitative data and statements precise enough for checking has been stimulated to an appreciable extent by the presence on university campuses of high-speed computers, which can be extremely powerful tools but are no good at all without numerical information and a set of unambiguous instructions. Although the machines have yet to play their full role in the study of prehistory, indications of a change are already evident.

One sign of the change is the interest in magic numbers. Another sign is renewed thinking about what June Helm of the University of Iowa calls "a life style transcending grossly different environments." As examples she cites three features which seem to be widely found in hunter-gatherer societies: the basic right of a man to live and work with any group where a relative of his or his wife serves as "sponsor"; bride service, involving a man's duty to live with and help support his wife's parents for a period of months or years, a custom which reinforces alliances between local groups and expands hunters' knowledge of terrain and resources; and an ethics of sharing, the readiness to give generously of one's time and goods. These and other practices are "continually reweaving a set of localized camps into a greater society," an effort which concerns us still.

Participant observers' reenactment of a prehistoric way of life; relearning extinct skills in use of tools and survival techniques; necessary revision of old hunting and farming theories; construction of artificial prehistoric sites for experiment and teaching

CHAPTER 17 EXPERIMENTAL ARCHEOLOGY

There are ways of entering more actively into the life of prehistoric people that take us out of the laboratory, into the open wilderness, and a small step closer to their world. Sometimes opportunities for experiments arise unexpectedly. One July evening in 1966, a group of excavators was camping in an isolated part of the Fort Apache Indian Reservation of eastern Arizona. Among them were William Longacre, an archeologist at the University of Arizona, and a group of students. They were engaged in digging an 800-room pueblo community dating back to the fourteenth century, a continuing long-term project.

The camp routine was upset an hour before midnight when a student stringing up a hammock heard a rustling in the leaves and turned his flashlight on a big black bear who had been attracted by the smell of baking banana bread. The animal was fair game. The bear population in the area had increased rapidly, and the Apaches were losing cattle regularly. Several nights earlier, bears had killed a couple of calves at a nearby dam. The cattle manager for the Indians was called to the scene and killed the animal with a single 30-30 carbine shot.

The problem of what to do with the carcass became a valuable lesson. It happened that Don Crabtree of Kimberly, Idaho, a specialist in stoneworking, was visiting the camp to demonstrate toolmaking techniques to the students. The bear represented an unprecedented chance to see his tools actually in use by an expert hunter and skinner, the man who had killed the bear. The expert, Gene Seely, gracious if not highly enthusiastic, obviously preferred rather more conventional methods, but agreed to give it a try.

Everything was ready early next morning. Crabtree had prepared a little kit of eight tools, all made of obsidian, a hard volcanic glass. The students had gathered around to watch, and there in the center of the circle were the dead bear and Seely, who was chewing tobacco and shaking his head skeptically. He took a backed blade and started the first cut from below the jaws down the chest, but he was shocked to find himself off balance in a peculiar way. On the basis of his experience with steel knives, his muscles were set to overcome a certain amount of resistance in cutting through the tough skin. The obsidian blade had gone through the skin as if it were butter.

From there on it was smooth sailing and a clear-cut victory for the stone tools. Seely, muttering to himself in surprise, completed in less than two hours a task that would have taken up to three and a half hours using his favorite Swedish steel knife. Of course, the one advantage of steel is its superior durability, although the volcanic glass can be resharpened in a few seconds by removing tiny chips along working edges. After the demonstration, Seely requested and received a kit of obsidian tools to commemorate the occasion.

As indicated in Chapter 5, Louis Leakey also conducted a number of similar experiments. He skinned and butchered wild game with stone tools of his own making, for example, the antelope dismembered one Christmas Eve at Olduvai before wondering Masai tribesmen. Moreover, his experiments also involved activities which come earlier in the chain of food-getting events. They included efforts to duplicate methods which prehistoric people may have used to capture animals in the first place, such as the technique of running down hares by anticipating which way they will dodge.

One of his most successful performances occurred a number of years ago in open country near a lake outside Nairobi. Leakey saw a herd of nine fleet-footed Thomson's gazelles, or Tommies, about 250 yards away, and decided to stalk one of the group that was grazing apart from the others. First he fastened leafy branches to his belt as part of a crude camouflage, not to hide himself, but to break up the telltale silhouette of the human body. Then he started closing in: "The essence of stalking is to appear not to move."

The trick is to move directly forward and to move very slowly, because that way the shape of your silhouette does not change and the size increases imperceptibly. But any sideways movement, particularly of the hands, which are a sure sign of a person, changes body shape and may cause animals to flee in panic. So Leakey kept his hands against his sides, moved his legs straight forward, and kept his eyes on the gazelle he was stalking as well as on the rest of the herd.

As long as the animals were feeding, as long as their heads were down, he advanced steadily. But the instant they looked up in his general direction, he had to freeze to the spot, and he knew how to anticipate that instant: "There's a subtle movement just before a Tommy lifts its head. One shoulder seems to rise just a bit higher than the other." Leakey advanced in a series of stops and starts and changes of direction as his prey moved about. Several times he had to wait motionless for birds, which emit sharp alarm calls when startled, to fly away. Finally, after two solid hours of stalking, he reduced the distance between him and the gazelle from 250 yards to about 6 feet, and brought it down with a perfectly timed flying tackle.

During the entire period Leakey played two roles alternately. Part of the time he identified himself with the gazelle he was stalking, drawing air through his nostrils for the scent of predators, listening for a snapping twig or the rustle of branches, and anticipating, not only by overt signs but with a sixth sense for its rhythm of alertness, the moment to stop grazing and look up. When the animal pricked up its ears and turned suddenly, Leakey felt an uncertainty, a tension, that was not relieved until it resumed feeding. And a split second before the final tackle he felt the burst of fear and confusion of his prey.

At other times he was a prehistoric hunter, applying what he had learned as a child from Kikuyu hunters who lived near his home in Kenya. He observed a thousand details while frozen in position, noting things nearby as well as at a distance, particularly things that meant food—a large snail, an anthill, tracks and trails where snares might be set, and weaverbirds' nests lined with grass on the inside so that there are few openings and little light gets through, a sign that rats or mice have moved into the abandoned nests. "You try not to take risks, not to strike until you're quite certain," Leakey explained. "But I've failed many times and Stone Age man did, too, so he always noticed second-best foods as he stalked, in case his quarry escaped."

Such attempts to learn as much as possible about life in prehistoric times go one step beyond observation. No matter how hard most observers work at recording and reconstructing the past, their approach is necessarily passive. They are always on the outside looking in. Investigators like Crabtree and Leakey chafed at being perpetual spectators. They found a way to enter, however briefly and superficially, the world of prehistoric people. An analogous process takes place in acting. When an actor learns to move as he believes a character would have moved, when he assumes the gestures and intonations and garments and bodily rhythm of the character, he is beginning to feel another's feelings and to live another's life. We say he lives his role.

No investigator has gone to the extreme of immersing himself so deeply into the role of a prehistoric person. On a more restricted scale, experimental, do-it-yourself archeology has made efforts to recreate a small part of the past so as to obtain by direct action a measure of insight into what it might have been like to work in, say, Magdalenian times or earlier. It is primarily an active approach, a matter of trying out a technique to see how it works, modifying it if necessary, seeking fresh archeological and behavioral evidence, and trying again. Anything that helps translate hypothesis into action helps to make prehistory come alive, and thus serves teaching as well as research purposes.

Many experiments concern the making of stone tools, by far the most numerous traces of prehistoric people. Tools can be found in isolated places everywhere, on all continents, often in fantastic abundance. I have seen stretches of semidesert peppered with artifacts lying exposed on the sand, sites where you can still collect several dozen hand axes and cleavers and other tools within half an hour or so, even though amateur archeologists, professional archeologists, and tourists in search of souvenirs have been collecting from the area for 20 years or more. One part of South Africa alone, the Springbok Flats just outside Johannesburg, contains an estimated 17 billion artifacts.

No material is familiar to us in the way stone was familiar to our ancestors. Toolmaking was second nature to them, part of their daily lives, something like driving a car is today, only learned much younger. They acquired a feel for the qualities of stone, for the way it had to be held and struck and the way it broke; and every step of the shaping proceeded according to traditions thousands of years old. They accumulated a kind of muscular knowledge, only a fraction of which could be conveyed by words.

Prehistoric children probably learned mainly by watching and imitating rather than by verbal instruction, at least as far as most early tools are concerned. A number of experiments suggest that such instruction is not necessary to make reasonably good hand axes or, according to Gould's observations, to make the sort of tools produced by the Australian aborigines. On the other hand, when it comes to the most refined techniques and the shaping of such items as Solutrean blades and some of the projectile points to be discussed in the following paragraphs, experts almost certainly had to tell novices what to do.

Much of what we infer about prehistoric stoneworking techniques comes from the experiments of modern stoneworkers. One of the acknowledged masters is Don Crabtree, whose tools skinned the Arizona bear. For more than 40 years, Crabtree has devoted a major part of his time to this highly specialized work, first as an expert on American Indian artifacts at the Ohio State Museum in Columbus and later at the Idaho State University Museum. He has made more than 50,000 blades, scrapers, projectile points, and other stone tools, and probably broken three or four times that many in the course of his research.

In flintworking, technique is everything, and during recent years Crabtree has become far more interested in techniques and the behavior of materials than in making artifacts. As part of an effort to understand more fully the muscular habits of prehistoric hunters, he may spend hours trying out a single style of removing flakes. When he finds a good source of flint, he may make several hundred pounds of blanks and preformed pieces for future practice sessions. He will take pieces worked on both sides and make them thinner and thinner until they break or practically melt away, just to develop a mastery of the thinning process. One of his major projects is a continuing effort to duplicate the work and learn the "extinct" skills of certain virtuosos among the American Indians.

Outstanding examples of stone toolmaking include the laurel-leaf points of the Solutreans (described in Chapter 10), Danish daggers, and Egyptian bracelets, and beautiful flint knives made in Europe and the Near East when stone was already on the way out, a lost-cause attempt to imitate and compete with new metal blades, even to the point of reproducing in the stone the seam lines made during the casting process. Incidentally, to the expert toolmaker, many rough and ungainly items represent the work of craftsmen who were fully as skilled as the makers of museum pieces, but who had to cope with inferior material.

The project which has occupied Crabtree's attention on and off ever since the start of his career involves a New World tool as remarkable as any produced in the Old World, a projectile point discovered in 1926 at a buffalo-kill site near the town of Folsom in New Mexico. Folsom points come in a variety of forms. But Crabtree has concentrated on a type which, in his opinion, "reflects the very ultimate in working skill and control . . . being as thin and perfectly shaped as the technique would allow." It is an artifact generally about 2 inches long, shaped something like a rowboat, and featuring a full-length groove or fluting along each side.

Crabtree has taken the measure of the vanished craftsmen whose work he is trying to reproduce. He has examined many of these points, as well as the waste chips produced during their manufacture, with all the care of an art student examining the brush strokes of a fine painting. For example, he notes the delicate retouching, the removal of 152 tiny flakes along the edge, all of them practically identical in shape, their widths varying by no more than a few hundredths of an inch. Crabtree emphasizes that such uniformity indicates a high order of skill: "For each flake removal requires the same platform preparation, the same spacing, the same downward and outward pressure, and the force must be applied each time at exactly the same angle."

He has tried 11 different methods of making this type of Folsom point, each calling for the control of up to 35 variables, from the selection of suitable flint to final retouching. One of his current methods is based on a procedure observed half a century ago in Mexico. It includes use of a chest crutch, a wooden tool which may have an antler tip at one end and a crosspiece at the other. The crosspiece rests against the chest of the stoneworker, and by leaning forward he can apply forces of as much as 300 pounds to the working end of the tool and remove flakes from a flint piece held firmly in a special clamp.

The technique is extremely difficult. Although Crabtree can turn out almost perfectly notched arrowheads at a rate of one every five or ten minutes, it takes him three hours or more to make a single Folsom

Don Crabtree
demonstrating chest-
crutch to make
Folsom point

Contemporary
flintworkers: Don
Crabtree and
Francois Bordes in
Crabtree's Idaho
workshop

point. The final product may look very much like the real thing to less accomplished stoneworkers, which includes the great majority of arch-eologists. But the Idaho stoneworker knows that he still cannot dupli-cate the craftsmanship of people for whom properly made tools meant survival. He feels that his most important contribution to date has been to demonstrate that certain previously suggested methods will not work. For example, he has ruled out a number of notions about the making of Folsom points and believes they could have been produced either by the chest-crutch or other pressure-flaking methods or by in-direct percussion, that is, by using a punch to strike off flakes. Indirect percussion appears to be more convenient and less demanding.

Crabtree has conducted many other experiments. He has used rounded stone hammers as large as basketballs to obtain pieces of raw material from quarries; tried flaking tools made of ivory, horn, wood, and a dozen other materials; compared the qualities of hundreds of varieties of flint by feel, appearance, and sound (a piece that rings sharply, for example, will probably be of good working quality); and used the tools he made to produce other tools. In every case the objec-tive of such studies is to learn by doing, to come closer and closer to a working knowledge of stone and of the stoneworkers' original pur-poses.

There are no final answers, but we know a great deal more than

Four Crabtree-made
Folsom points

we did about the significance of our finds, including the Folsom point. For one thing, it appears that the striking beauty and symmetry of the tool is purely a coincidence from an aesthetic point of view, a by-product of practical considerations. Crabtree does not believe in the art-for-art's-sake theory which suggests that Indian craftsmen took extra pains to embellish their work, going beyond strictly functional requirements. He is convinced that every feature of the Folsom design is necessary to produce a point that can be hafted securely to a spear shaft, plunged into an animal, and easily withdrawn for subsequent thrusts in a repeated stabbing action.

His work on Folsom points and other tools has resulted in a discovery that provides further evidence of the ingenuity of prehistoric stoneworkers. Some time ago, he observed a difference between flint as it came from the mine and flint used in artifacts. For example, finished arrowheads usually have a characteristic greasy or glasslike luster, while the same material is a relatively dull green in its freshly quarried state. He also found that the shinier material is less brittle and easier to work and, after many trial-and-error experiments, learned how to convert the native material to glassy form by heating it for at least 24 hours at more than 400 and less than 900 degrees Fahrenheit under carefully controlled conditions.

The procedure is a form of annealing or tempering like that used to toughen steel. In flint as in steel, tempering reduces crystal size, transforming a coarse-grained into a fine-grained material which is more elastic and more readily shaped. All the evidence indicates that the American Indians preheated most of their flints and other coarse minerals; and what may have been a flint-heating pit has been reported

339

from one western site. Furthermore, similar pits may be identified in the Old World, because there is reason to believe that various forms of heat treatment were used widely during prehistoric times by the Solutreans and perhaps earlier peoples.

So museum and home-workshop experiments have had widespread repercussions, suggesting new features to look for in artifacts and at prehistoric sites. The National Science Foundation has provided funds for the publication of Crabtree's research as well as for high-speed motion pictures of his toolmaking techniques. (The filming of certain phenomena, such as detachment of a blade from a flint core, requires speeds of more than 10,000 frames per second.) It also supported the first special conference on lithic technology, or stoneworking, which, fittingly enough, was held at Les Eyzies, the unofficial capital of French prehistory.

Such activities represent a new trend in archeology. Not that working with flints and other materials is anything new; it is as old as archeology itself. But it has not always attracted funds or the active attention of most professional investigators, and only a decade ago it was generally tolerated as an absorbing if rather unfruitful hobby. The increasing interest in experimental toolmaking is significant as one further example of the current focus on behavior in all areas of evolutionary research. It expresses the idea that exploring possible ways of doing things may help in arriving at theories of what people did in times past.

Often the result is to eliminate or at least to cast considerable doubt on theories which have little evidence to support them, and yet are commonly cited in research papers and textbooks. Another experienced present-day stoneworker, John Witthoft of the University of Pennsylvania, has commented on the hammerstone as "the basic implement used by Stone Age man in tool manufacture." He emphasizes that in many cases it is mistaken for something else, mainly because, if it has a roughly spherical shape to begin with, it tends to become increasingly spherical with use since irregularities and projections wear away faster than other surfaces.

Investigators insufficiently acquainted with stoneworking procedures have offered a variety of interpretations of objects which experienced toolmakers immediately recognize as hammers. Spherical stones found at Neanderthal and earlier sites have been interpreted as evidence for the use of a weapon called a bola, two or more stone balls attached to leather thongs and whirled around and flung at the legs of escaping animals to trip and entangle them. Witthoft mentions another case of mistaken identity: "The stones of the Pyramids were shaped by pecking with spherical hammers, but most of the Egyptologists have identified these hammers as ball bearings used to roll the masonry blocks into place."

Perhaps the most important contribution of experimental stone-working to our understanding of prehistoric behavior was made by François Bordes (see Chapter 9). His theory that there were four different Neanderthal cultures or tribes, a theory which has opened the way for a new approach to the study of tool assemblages, arose directly out of his firsthand experience with the use and making of stone tools. It depends on the careful identification of more than 60 types of scrapers and other implements which make up the four basic Neanderthal tool kits—an analysis which could have been carried out only by someone with a worker's knowledge and feel for the shaping of flint tools. Incidentally, not long ago Bordes visited aborigines in northern Australia and had a number of toolmaking sessions with them: "I chipped stones with them and taught them a lot of techniques they did not know. Of course, this comes a little late to change things. I also learned a lot from them."

Other investigators have conducted experimental studies designed to provide insights into the evolution of the human hand. Tool use involves two types of grip. In the precision grip, used in delicate work such as inserting and turning a small screw in a socket, the tool handle is held between thumb and fingertips. When the screw is in place, however, you tighten it by shifting to a power grip, so that for the last turns, fingers are flexed around the handle of the screwdriver and the thumb is acting as a kind of clamp. This is the standard grip for applying full force.

According to the English anatomist John Napier, whose studies of the hand are mentioned in Chapter 4, the precision grip has evolved to its highest form in humans. He believes that certain primitive tools could have been made without a fully developed precision grip, which requires a long and mobile thumb capable of being placed readily opposite the tips of the other fingers, or without any precision grip at all. To prove the point he has performed some stoneworking feats with his thumbs glued firmly to the sides of his hands, thus in effect permitting him to use a power grip only. He found he could use a hammerstone to strike flakes off a large pebble and produce the sort of ancient chopper found at the Olduvai Gorge and elsewhere. He even managed to turn out a crude hand ax. He believes that making more advanced tools, however, required not only a larger brain and new purposes and plans, but also a more advanced hand with a fully opposable thumb. The human hand may have evolved to its present form a million years ago, or a million years or so after the earliest known tools.

The fact remains that we still can only guess at the functions of many tools, and here again experiments can help us obtain a better picture of prehistoric workers in action. Making a good replica of a specialized tool and then successfully cutting or scraping with it demonstrate only how it *could* have been used. Further research may indicate how it was actually used. One effective approach takes advantage of a kind of built-in evidence, obtained from the original implements themselves as they are found in excavated sites. For more than 30 years, Sergei Semenov and his associates at the USSR Institute of Archeology in Leningrad have been studying microwear, tool marks which cannot be detected by the naked eye. Certain gross features, such as gloss, or polish, and nicks and scratches, provide general clues to the way a particular implement was used.

But a far more detailed record can be obtained by treating tool surfaces with metal powders and other chemicals, and then examining them magnified as much as several hundred times under the microscope. This procedure reveals an entirely new landscape of wear, a topography of lines, pits, scars, facets, cracks, dull patches, and so on. It is something like the difference between viewing the moon from an earthbound telescope and from a telescope mounted on an artificial satellite flying only a few hundred miles above the lunar surface.

For example, on the basis of naked-eye inspection, archeologists had tentatively identified one flint tool from Neanderthal times as a knife, since the working edge was polished on both sides as if it had been used repeatedly to cut down through some material. Microscopic examination, however, revealed a system of many fine grooves and indicated a different function. The grooves were not parallel to the edge as they would be if it had been used in a regular back-and-forth cutting action. They ran at various angles, often crisscrossing one another, which is precisely the sort of pattern produced with experimental tools serving as scrapers.

The rounded edge that appears under the microscope and the presence of grooves on both sides of the tool show that it had been used with a two-way motion, left to right and right to left. Furthermore, the material involved could only have been animal skins since previous skin-scraping tests created identical microwear patterns and since different patterns result from the scraping of wood, bone, stone, and other materials. A final deduction: the skins were probably fresh and damp, because skins dried in the open generally contain tiny wind-blown sand grains, which produce grooves considerably deeper than those actually observed.

Another study concerned a more recent flint tool, perhaps about 15,000 to 20,000 years old, found at Kostenki on the Don River. It is about 5 inches long and almond-shaped, with a point at one end and a rounded butt at the other; the working edge on the butt contains nicks and scars produced by heavy blows. For a number of years, investigators had debated about the nature of this tool, a debate settled by microwear analysis. The microscope shows very slightly curved grooves on both sides of the working edge, most of them parallel to one another at an angle of about 25 degrees to the line running longitudinally from

Working edge of scraper used by Australian aborigines, magnified 25 times, showing typical fractures. Same kinds of fractures found on the Quina-type scraper of the Neaderthals

butt to tip. This pattern is a fingerprint of a sort, a positive identification for ax blades whether made of flint, bronze, or high-grade steel.

Engravers, saws, perforators, and other stone tools also have characteristic patterns, although not all mysteries are solved as completely as those cited above. So do many tools made of bone and antler, which are often only slightly worked or not worked at all, so that shape may not be a clue to use, and identification may depend entirely on microwear studies. Similar research at laboratories outside as well as inside the Soviet Union confirms Semenov's basic finding that tools may bear permanent records of their motion through and across various materials, records of the movements and rhythms of workers who vanished tens of thousands of years ago.

Getting the most out of the microwear approach may call for combining it with observations of today's hunter-gatherers, as shown in one of Richard Gould's experiments. First, he took two dozen scrapers obtained from Australian aborigines, who had been using them to make spear throwers and other objects of extremely hard mulga (acacia) wood, and examined them under the microscope. In every case he detected characteristic markings produced by the breaking off of tiny **343** chips, fractures that terminated in an abrupt, steplike fashion along the working edge. Then he made a replica of an aboriginal scraper out of native stone, hafted it to a wooden handle with resin made from a special kind of native grass, and used the tool to shape a mulga wood shaft the way the aborigines do in preparing a spear. After exactly 1000 strokes, he examined the tool under the microscope and found fractures identical to those on the aborigines' own scrapers.

Of course, activities other than scraping might have produced the same wear pattern, a possibility explored in recent and continuing studies. Gould and his associates at the University of Hawaii have performed similar experiments holding all variables but one constant—in some cases changing the type of stone used, in other cases changing the angle of the working edge, and so on. To assess the effects of accidental forces they walked over freshly made stone flakes buried in sand, and shook freshly made flakes together in a bag for varying periods. Indications to date are that typical fractures with steplike terminations occur mainly on flakes with steep edge angles and almost never on acute-edged flakes, and rarely except after use in scraping hard wood. Similar microscopic fractures can be seen on the Neanderthal Quina-type scrapers with steep angled edges that were used by people living at La Quina rock shelter in southern France 50,000 and more years ago. This suggests that their tools also served to scrape bone or some other resistant material similar to hard Australian mulga wood.

Prehistoric gathering has also been investigated experimentally. Some years ago Jack Harlan of the University of Illinois, a specialist in early plant domestication, joined an archeological expedition to southeastern Turkey, one of the Near Eastern regions where farming was first practiced. The region is still rich in plant foods. Harlan saw "vast seas of primitive wild wheats" still growing on mountain slopes, the same varieties of wheat used by early farmers some 10,000 to 12,000 years ago. One day, he went out into the fields to see how much grain he could harvest.

During his first tests, he used the simplest of tools, his bare "urbanized" hands, which soon became red and raw. But even so he had no trouble gathering an average of about 4.5 pounds of grain per hour. Then he made himself a crude sickle by gouging a slot in a sturdy branch and inserting a flint sickle blade obtained from a 9000-year-old early agriculture site in Iraq. The blade cut wheat about as well as a steel sickle blade, yielded nearly an extra pound of grain per hour, and spared his hands. His conclusion: "A family group . . . working slowly upslope as the season progressed, could easily harvest wild cereals over a three-week span or more and, without even working very hard, could gather more grain than the family could possibly consume in a year."

Harlan also tried various ways of preparing wild wheat. He removed hulls by using an Osage Indian mortar and pestle, a process made somewhat easier by pretoasting in an oven for 15 to 30 minutes at 350 degrees. The pounded material could be cleaned by passing it through a sieve of woven grass, or simply by winnowing it in the wind, and then made into a soup or boiled like rice. Harlan reports that wild wheat is nutritious as well as tasty, chemical analysis showing that it contains nearly 60 percent more protein than modern cultivated varieties.

Of course, those who have actually lived with primitive people on a day-to-day basis gain a kind of firsthand knowledge that can be obtained in no other way. In his studies of the Bushmen, for example, Lee had to learn their difficult language, which includes four different clicks and five tones. He has gathered mongongo nuts with them, and lived for three weeks on a diet consisting mainly of this staple. On one occasion he managed to keep up with hunters walking through the Kalahari at a speed of 5 to 6 miles per hour, although doing that as a regular practice was something else again. His most arduous experience was an effort to live as Bushmen live at the height of a drought, accompanying a group on an overnight hike to a mongongo forest where the only local source of water were the juices in deep underground roots.

This was too much for Lee. After spending hours looking for game and digging for roots and walking some 9 miles under the sun in temperatures of well over a hundred degrees, he realized that he would be a burden to the others. He felt feverish and dry, could not swallow, and decided to go back to the base camp near a permanent water hole. Upon his return early the next morning, Lee made a dramatic beeline for the nearest water bag and emptied it with evident relief, a sight that set the Bushmen laughing for an hour.

There is an advantage in trying to share a way of life and a language, an advantage beyond coming closer to people and earning their confidence and good will. Although one can never learn to think as prehistoric people thought or learn exactly how they did things, every increase of knowledge adds a bit to reconstructions of times past. The problem of improving the reconstructions, of understanding human origins better, is sufficiently important to merit the exploration of every possible lead. Perhaps the ultimate step, the ultimate experiment in living archeology, is to "go prehistoric" for a time and live entirely on what you can get from the wilderness.

As far as I know, no one has yet undertaken such a project in an organized fashion, although there have been occasional efforts. One archeologist in his undergraduate days spent several months hunting and trapping alone in the wilderness, and provided very well for himself. But his motive was personal rather than scientific; he simply wanted to get away from people. And more than a decade ago ten French investigators spent three weeks in a cave living off the land in what they considered to be the style of Neanderthal man.

Leakey evolved a more ambitious plan covering several million years of human evolution in six weeks, each week representing a different stage of development. According to this plan, Leakey would live during the first week the way hominids presumably lived before the regular making of tools, say, some 3 million years ago. Equipped with clubs, rocks for bashing, digging sticks, and cord for snares and traps (made from the inner bark of trees), he would subsist chiefly on plant foods and small game which could be ripped apart with bare hands.

During the second week, the second evolutionary stage of perhaps 2 million years ago, he would make simple choppers and flake tools. That would permit systematic scavenging for the first time, because such tools make it possible to cut through tough antelope skin and separate joints and do general butchering, all of which cannot be accomplished with hands and fingernails and teeth (Leakey has tried). The third week would involve increasing independence of other killers; the decline of scavenging and the rise of big-game hunting; the development of hand axes, cleavers, and other heavy-duty butchering tools; and the invention of wooden spears with whittled and perhaps fire-hardened tips, or antelope-horn tips.

The plan calls for reliance on more and more advanced techniques during the last three weeks, which cover the period from 10,000 or 15,000 to about 100,000 years ago. Leakey would begin by making stone points and hafting them to spears with natural resins, gums, and sinews, and later turn to backed blades and spear throwers and harpoons. Up to this point all his weapons would be designed primarily to cripple animals and slow them down, but the final week would see the first case of shooting to kill with finely balanced spears and, above all, an efficient bow and arrow. Throughout the six-week period he would live in increasingly advanced quarters: rock shelters; caves; crude tents, half-sunken pit houses, or artificial caves, and huts with solid walls and roofs.

Leakey had an explanation for not undertaking such vigorous living off African savanna lands: "I'd have done it long ago, but Mary wouldn't let me. She thought it was too dangerous." But a review of what has already been done and of what has not yet been done indicates that the time may be ripe for some such plan. Making tools, and using them to make other tools for butchering animals and gathering plant foods, trying out primitive hunting techniques, and many studies have all contributed blocks of information to our understanding of hunter-gatherers. But each study has been a piecemeal effort, isolated from the others and representing the skills, enthusiasm, and interests of the individual investigator acting pretty much on his own. The next step might well be a coordinated series of field expeditions where the objective would be to duplicate the complete range of actual Stone Age living as closely as possible by organizing volunteers into prehistoric-type bands and having them camp out in the wilderness for extended periods.

Another type of experimental archeology which has many unexploited possibilities is the construction of artificial prehistoric sites, full-scale living floors prepared mainly for research purposes. A number of such sites exist, for example, there is one on the Santa Barbara campus of the University of California. In one series of studies, John Chilcott and James Deetz used a machine to dig square pits 7 feet on a side and some 5 feet deep. They put artifacts and other materials in predetermined positions, filled the pits up again, and planted grass on the surface. Six months later, after the elements had aged the area, they returned to excavate.

One of the pits was designed to test the effectiveness of various digging techniques in recovering small objects, in this case glass beads about the size of BB shot. Among other things, the study indicated just how important the type of soil may be in this connection. Ninety-six percent of the beads placed beforehand in the natural silty soil of the region were recovered by simply scooping up the soil in a trowel and sifting through it. But the recovery rate dropped to less than 60 percent in damp earth formed by decayed organic matter, which is oily and tends to cling to the beads, a fact underlining the need for special measures when working in such soils.

A second site served as a proving ground for students. It had three made-to-order occupation layers, the deepest containing a hearth, scrapers, projectile points, and other carefully placed items that might be found in Indian deposits 6000 years old or more. Above this layer, the California archeologists arranged a more recent type of living floor, including coyote and human bones and pottery; and above that a modern or "historic" layer, with a beer bottle, pieces of glass, a metal bank, and other human remains. Five crews of students representing different age groups and different degrees of experience worked at five parts of the site. As expected, the more experienced students did a more careful job of excavating than novices (breaking fewer items and leaving more items in their original positions). In other words, this sort of setup provides a good way of training and testing students.

Even with the best of excavating techniques, however, there is always the problem of how to interpret the evidence. For example, it is often taken for granted that if bones are relatively scarce at a living site, the people probably did not eat much meat and that a predominance of bones of small animals means a diet heavy on small game. Actual tests show that these assumptions are not necessarily valid.

Glynn Isaac once dumped 55 large bones and bone fragments and more than 60 bone splinters on a 1-square-yard plot in the Rift Valley. He came back four months later to see what was left, and found that more than 70 percent of the material was gone, destroyed and scattered mainly by hyenas and other scavengers. In the Kalahari, Yellen observed that large bones are often splintered for their marrow and that the splinters tend to disintegrate swiftly, while small bones tend to become buried and remain intact. Such factors must be taken into account before drawing conclusions about early hunting practices.

British investigators are conducting more elaborate tests. Peter Jewell of Royal Holloway College near London and his associates have built an experimental earthwork, or barrow, with a ditch and bank such as prehistoric people built to house their distinguished dead. Jewell et al. placed inside it cremated human bone, numbered pieces of pottery, burned and unburned wood, leather, dyed and undyed cloth, and other items. The exact position of each item has been recorded. The project is designed to determine how, and how fast, materials decompose, how their positions change as a result of the heaving of freezing and thawing soils, and the action of earthworms and other burrowing animals. Some notable changes have already taken place. For example, pieces of unburned wood and undyed cloth have disintegrated, but not the burned and dyed specimens. The experiment will last at least a hundred years. The earthwork was built in 1960 and has been opened up half a dozen times since then, most recently in 1976. The next excavation is scheduled for 1992 and the last for the year 2088.

Unfortunately, professional archeologists have not used the experimental approach as widely as they might in their own research work. But their greatest failure lies in education, where the gap between what has been accomplished and what could be accomplished is enormous. Indeed, there is no better example of missed opportunities than the lack of significant and exciting activities in the classroom. Although much effort has gone into the preparation of more stimulating and challenging courses, the shortage of really imaginative ideas continues.

A promising exception is the work of Errett Callahan of Virginia Commonwealth University in Richmond. For a number of years he has been developing programs in subsistence living, or living archeology. They are increasingly sophisticated efforts to learn more about prehistoric peoples by firsthand experience and by "resurrecting 'dead' information, information supposedly locked in time." High points of his studies occurred in the summers of 1974 and 1975 during experiments in living on a wild 1500-acre tract on the Pamunkey River 25 miles from Richmond, not far from the Pamunkey Indian Reservation.

Before moving into the area, Callahan and his students trained for the project by getting used to meals made up of wild foods and by weight lifting and daily jogging (a mile in less than eight minutes). They lived on the land in the style of Woodland Indians more than a millennium ago; they used tools they made themselves to construct shelters, traps, fish weirs, and a raft; and they contended with a drought in 1974 and almost ceaseless rain in 1975. It was an adventure, but no lark. Callahan is still analyzing the results of this project, which he intends to continue in future seasons.

At other schools, some interesting work is being done in the lower grades. Teachers at Solebury in New Hope, Pennsylvania, have used artificial sites in a new way that goes beyond the University of California project as far as creative pedagogy is concerned. Part of one experiment involved a game between eighth and ninth graders. In the fall, eighth-grade students dug a large square hole about a yard deep, and at the bottom arranged a hearth with ashes, flint chips, a broken scraper, and some fossilized bones—representing remains as they might be found in an actual Indian site 10,000 or more years old. The students made a map indicating the position of each object, and then filled in the hole with earth.

Next spring ninth-grade students excavated the site, the aim being to plot the positions of the uncovered objects precisely enough to duplicate the map drawn by the eighth-grade students. Although the soil was clayey and difficult to dig, they managed to reconstruct appreciable portions of the original patterns. The experiment gave students a chance to think up their own living-floor patterns, and in the process to gain a firsthand feeling for the basic notion of living floors and the importance of slow and careful excavating. Similar games have been devised by William Turnbaugh of the University of Rhode Island, who is developing a variety of new ways of teaching archeology.

Such studies are beginning to interest a few educators. Experi-

Solebury School students at experimental site

mental archeology can do much—for students who are not planning to **350**
enter the field as well as for professional archeologists and arch-
eologists-to-be. Making the past come alive in a truly meaningful way
and introducing into humanities courses the notion of evidence and experiment can help students gain, among other things, a better understanding of human origins and also of the cultural process itself.

The pace of early learning; what the frog's eye tells the frog's brain; the human infant as explorer, observer, imitator; the developing smile, a way of reaching out and communicating; the evolution and prehistory of smiling; crying, maternal responsiveness, and feeding schedules; mother-infant bonds and rigidities

CHAPTER 18   THE HUMAN INFANT: A STUDY IN LIVING PREHISTORY

The human infant is born primed for action, ready from the very beginning to reach out and make sense of the world and the people moving around in it. Infants start exploring almost immediately, not long after they leave the womb, just about as soon as there is anything worth exploring. Changes come throughout the course of life. But the swiftest and most spectacular changes of all come during the first few years, nature having arranged things so that we do most of our growing up when we are most helpless, most immobile.

Research on early development has a number of evolutionary implications. For one thing, by providing clues to the nature and pace of learning, it suggests ways of improving education, improving the species, and thereby guiding and accelerating future evolution. It also provides clues to the remote past. The human infant was to a large extent shaped in a world that no longer exists, adapted primarily for survival in vanished wildernesses among small bands of hunter-gatherers—which raises the possibility of deducing from its behavior something about the course of events in prehistoric times.

Learning takes place rapidly during infancy, so rapidly that it is difficult to observe and analyze. In this respect, the human condition contrasts sharply with that of most other animals. Generally speaking, the lower a species ranks in the hierarchy of evolution, the more likely its young are to be born ready-made and prepared to participate in life with a minimum of learning. The leopard frog, for example, comes fully equipped for keeping itself alive. Its brain and sense organs are built to perceive only those elements in the environment strictly necessary for survival, and to exclude everything else. It sees only what it is designed to see. Its world is a mere fragment of the real world.

Experiments conducted by Jerome Lettvin and his associates at the Massachusetts Institute of Technology show that a frog is blind to stationary insects. It actually sees nothing in its field of vision until the thing moves toward it. Insects moving away are invisible, and do not exist in the frog's world. Furthermore, the things it sees are not insects as we know them, creatures with six legs and wings and iridescent colors. As far as the frog is concerned, all that information is utterly useless. It sees abstracted insects stripped of everything but a few essential details, standardized symbols like the black dots used on maps to represent cities, small objects with curved front edges.

The frog operates largely as an automaton, and automata are notoriously vulnerable to experimental tricks. If a frog is put in a cage with freshly killed flies, it will starve to death unless it is rescued and provided with a supply of live flies. It cannot see motionless food. But in the context of evolution and adaptation, such behavior is a strength rather than a weakness. Frogs are admirably designed for their real world, where small objects that are curved in front, and move are almost always insects. The probability of being confined in a place where the only insects are dead insects is exceedingly low, so low that the frog has endured for some 200 million years.

Whether or not humanity manages to survive that long, and there are powerful arguments on both sides, we are committed to survival by different means. Our forte is flexibility of behavior, which depends as heavily on inheritance as rigid behavior does. In fact, our behavior is being studied with the aid of techniques developed by Niko Tinbergen and other investigators during research on less flexible species, techniques being applied increasingly to human as well as to nonhuman primates (see Chapter 12). This is the field known as ethology, roughly speaking, the biology of behavior.

The marks of the past are deeply embedded in us. The past has given us a selective advantage that enables us to survive and multiply. Although the range of observed human patterns is vast, it is still only a fraction of the even vaster range of possible patterns. We do not move along narrow and strictly determined paths like robots on monorails; but neither are we completely at liberty. Like all species, we represent a compromise between freedom and constraint.

The infant is born with enormous potentialities. Its brain will develop a system for storing and rapidly retrieving a vast number of memory traces, enough information, according to a recent estimate, to fill a thousand 24-volume sets of the *Encyclopaedia Britannica*. In nerve centers, the traces can be put together into new combinations representing possible actions, and a kind of switching circuitry permits choices among many alternatives.

The special structures develop automatically. They take shape according to the same genetic schedules which shape the rest of the body. They dictate the human way of life. In the last analysis we have no choice but to be true to our genes. It is as impossible for us to stand pat as a species, to resist the forces for change embodied in the brain, as it is for animals of lower species, such as frogs, to unlearn their built-in habits. We are born free in comparison with other animals. Our world is wider and richer in events because of inherited behavior patterns, products of an evolutionary process involving a hominid line that goes back some 15 million years.

Some of the patterns that appear earliest in life seem to have no use; other patterns may be more important in a hunter-gatherer than in an urban context (see Chapter 16). Infants have an amazingly tenacious grip as early as the first or second week after birth, in some cases hanging from a stick and supporting their weight up to 15 seconds or so, an ability that might have saved lives when our ancestors lived in trees. A more complex pattern which also involves grasping and has been called the embrace reflex may be a vestige of the infant monkey's efforts to obtain a firmer hold on the belly hair of its mother as she rises to walk. These reflexes disappear within a few months.

Other early patterns come to stay. Infants are born with a bias to explore actively, to seek out the extraordinary. They proceed promptly to divide the world into parts, making out the differences and boundaries that distinguish objects from one another. Experiments show that on the very day of their birth some infants track triangles displayed in their field of vision, following the outlines with their eyes. Also, when a newborn baby is confronted with a plain black background, it may keep looking away, looking from side to side and up and down as if in search of something more interesting. It is designed to focus on edges and discontinuities, marked differences of light, shade, and color, any and all unusual features.

It also possesses remarkable and, until recently, unsuspected powers of observation. Experiments conducted at Oxford University indicate that it is not only capable of watching intensely, but it can also imitate what it sees, puckering its lips, opening and closing its mouth, and sticking out its tongue in response to the changing expressions of investigators. The surprising thing is that this ability may appear as early as two to four weeks after birth.

Such tendencies are innate in the same sense as the frog's tendency to go after small moving objects with curved front ends. We enter the world with a whole battery of built-in biases, and a number of them involve getting along with people. In a study of 25 mother-infant pairs Mary Ainsworth of the University of Virginia observed a definite "disposition to obey," which she suggests may have evolved in prehistoric hunter-gatherer times when obeying was a matter of life and death.

There also seems to be a general tendency to move toward rather than away from people, at least in the beginning. The baby loses no time in learning to communicate with the world. All newcomers face the need to establish relationships with others; of all human undertakings there is none more important than the infant's first efforts to find its place in society. The infant starts out as well equipped for entering into and maintaining relationships as it is for breaking them off if they turn out to be irritating or damaging. Whatever happens later on, it has a tendency to reach out and approach and bring things closer. Of all ways of reaching out, the smile is one of the most effective.

The fact that smiling is universal and appears in all human societies suggests that it has deep roots and that it arose in response to strong prehistoric needs and demands. Its development is a process of unusual interest to investigators as well as parents. The act itself, the mechanics of drawing back the corners of the mouth and associated facial movements, appears very early in life. In fact, the first smile of the infant appears so early that it is usually never seen. Judging by observations of premature babies, it may occur in rudimentary form two or more months before birth. The role of subsequent learning is to attach that reflex to appropriate things in the environment and that involves other biases.

The first public smile comes several months later. It appears as early as the third week after birth, as late as the twelfth week, and in most cases between the fourth and sixth weeks. In the beginning the infant smiles not at its mother, but at a visual symbol of its mother, an abstraction related to her the way pictographs are related to actual objects. The symbol may involve sounds and physical content and other sensations. But the central factor is the sight of the face—and at first the sight of only a part of the face, that part which the infant, with its primitive capacity for seeing, finds most compelling, namely, the eyes, especially when the face is moved about a bit.

Studies indicate that an image of the eyes is a minimum requirement to arouse a smile in a young infant. Investigators used masks to eliminate lips, nostrils, hair, and every feature other than eyes, and the infant still smiles. Both eyes are necessary; smiling stops when one eye is masked or when the investigator shifts from a full-face to a profile position so that the infant can see only a single eye. Two glass balls or any other pair of shiny objects will also produce smiling, as long as they have roughly the same size, shape, and spacing. Human eyes are most compelling, however, because they stand out against the more uniform background of the forehead and cheeks. They have color and movement, and reflect a high proportion of the light falling on them.

This reaction involves the decided preference for variety and contrast which babies seem to be born with. The reason an infant looks away from a black background is partly because of the monotony of a scene without features, and it naturally glances toward places where the action is, where there are edges and areas of dark and light. All shiny objects are of unusual interest, and the infant's world is full of them:

keys, dishes, chrome-plated handles, and all highly reflecting surfaces of **355** polished wood, glass, and metal.

But the infant goes beyond the mere taking of a general inventory. Out of the entire collection of attractive items it begins to learn to know the one that is and will continue to be most meaningful, the pair of bright objects which at first represents all it can notice of its mother. It picks out one image from all the rest, the one usually associated with soothing sounds and other pleasant sensations and answers that particular brightness with a brightness of its own, the brightening of its eyes when it smiles. The infant learns to smile at a selected image in its new world because of a built-in ability that will serve it throughout its life, an ability to sort things out and distinguish those of special importance.

A great deal is going on along with the subsequent development of a smile. After two months or so, an image consisting of two bright spots no longer causes the infant to smile. It requires something more before it will respond, the outline of a nose in addition to two eyes and later, a mouth and lips and hair and so on. In other words, the infant's impression or picture of the face is filled out in finer and finer detail until it becomes complete and is identified with a specific person, generally the mother.

This process has been investigated in some detail by the British psychologist Anthony Ambrose, director of the Behavior Development Research Unit of St. Mary's Hospital in London. His technique was to stand before a baby and simply look at it for 30 seconds without moving and without expression. Then he would step away, record observations of the infant's smiling responses and other behavior for 30 seconds, return to watch for another 30 seconds, and so on until he had completed a run of 12 consecutive observing periods. In one of the many experiments he conducted 30 runs, one a week, on four infants starting when they were 6 weeks old.

Among other things, he found that the total smiling time per run, a measure of response strength, changes in a characteristic way. For example, one infant did not smile at all during the first three runs, smiled only a few seconds during the fourth run, and not at all again during the fifth run. Practically nothing happened between the ages of 6 and 11 weeks, a situation which contrasted with the infant's response to the face of its mother, to which it smiled increasingly over this period—because the sight of her face was usually accompanied by movement and by her voice, touch, and warmth. So the first part of the experiment showed that during the early weeks, the image of a face alone, without movement or other accompanying sensations, produced hardly any response.

Then a striking change appeared in the record. The infant rapidly became more and more responsive until at the age of 14 weeks it was smiling more than 40 percent of the observing time, about two and a half out of six minutes, indicating that it had learned to react with feelings of pleasure to the image of a face by itself, isolated from voice, touch, and other sensations. At this stage, the infant was responding to a general, broad-gauge symbol rather than to a particular human being. Any appropriate image or properly designed mask besides that of its mother or Ambrose would have produced a smile.

The next change came even more rapidly; one week later there was a sharp decline of smiling. The infant smiled only fleetingly at Ambrose, and for no more than 20 seconds in all. The rest of the time it stared without expression, turned away, sucked its thumb, or whimpered. But during the same week its smiles had become even more frequent and brighter for its mother. The infant had passed the peak of indiscriminate and impersonal responding. Mother had suddenly become a unique individual. The image of her face had filled out in sufficient detail so that it could be compared with and distinguished from other faces. Later the infant's response to Ambrose reached a second peak, considerably lower than the first peak, that represented a level of habitual smiling reserved for all people not members of the family.

Infants differed widely as far as the timing and intensity of their changes were concerned, but they showed the same general changes in the same order. The sequence of little or no response, sharp increase in smiling, sudden decline, and so on turns out to be a basic pattern which involves not only certain built-in biases but also a bias to learn in a certain way. Ambrose used his observations and the observations of others to develop a theory of the origin of smiling. As a matter of fact, his theory goes further than that; in effect, it includes a partial analysis of the evolution of facial expressions in primates. (It also elaborates on some of the ideas of Michael Fox, which were presented in Chapter 14.)

The process started more than 65 million years ago among practically dead-pan prosimians or premonkeys, the first primates to take up life in the trees. The most primitive surviving prosimians, such as the lemurs of Madagascar, simply do not have the proper equipment for a fine play of emotions. Their facial muscles consist mainly of broad bands of fibers, which tend to contract all together and produce gross movements. It happens that lemurs are capable of only a single clear-cut facial gesture, the original primate expression. It consists of a drawing back of the lips to bare the teeth for biting, a sign of fear or anger.

Refinements of this fighting posture came with the reshaping of the face. The earliest prosimians had long snouts, like terriers, and they lived mainly by the sense of smell as their ground-dwelling ancestors had lived. But chases and escapes and games played high in the trees favored the rapid development of vision at the expense of the sense of

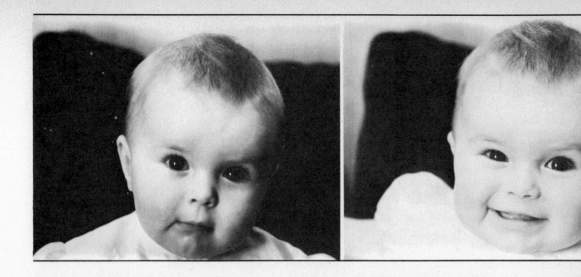

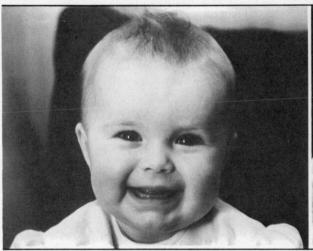

smell. The snout retreated, the face shortened and flattened somewhat, and the eyes shifted from the sides of the head to an up-front position. Evolution in effect created a kind of natural screen, or surface, for visual displays.

The muscles of the face became more specialized among higher primates and primates living in more complex social groups, forming small bundles of fibers which branched off from the broad bands like secondary roads and side lanes from superhighways. A particularly elaborate system of muscles developed around the eyes and lips, and nerves running to and from the brain permitted finer control and greater variety of expression. For example, laughter seems to have emerged in apes as a composite form of behavior. When a chimpanzee

357

laughs it draws back its lips and bares its teeth as if confronted with a dangerous situation, but at the same time its muscles are relaxed and its eyes brighten as if it is playing.

These and other mechanical characteristics of laughter may be regarded as signs of ancient emotional conflict between opposing tendencies. The dominant tendencies were enjoyment and an attraction toward the object or situation being enjoyed; the subordinate tendencies were fear or anger and running away. This interpretation fits in with what we know about the arousal of human laughter, which generally occurs in response to a surprise of some sort, that is, to sudden or startling stimulation such as takes place in tickling or in mock attacks and chases during games. Of course, a delicate balance is involved. The lightness and good humor can vanish swiftly as a result of overstimulation, that is, from too much tickling or playful fighting that becomes too rough.

Ambrose believes that smiling evolved from laughter, and that the social smile, which is unique to humans, evolved as a special adaptation designed to strengthen bonds among people. The first such bond is with the mother. In prehistoric times, however, there were forces tending to weaken that bond. Imagine that you are observing a troop of hominids on an African savanna perhaps 15 million years ago, not long after the start of the hominid line. A troop of small slender near apes or prehumans, the earliest representatives of the human family, is taking its midday rest; at its center is a cluster of mothers with offspring, young females, and dominant males.

The cluster exists as an island of stability and safety in the wilderness. The main social task of every adult member is to look after and protect the infants. One mother sits near a tree and is being groomed by another female, while its infant, which is only a week old, clings to her hair, as it will continue to cling for another three or four months. Another mother moves off to a spot where fruits are growing and ignores her infant, which is old enough to follow her. When the entire troop moves, it moves as a single unit. No one stays behind. There is a certain amount of evidence to support this picture. It is based to a large extent on observations of wild baboons which have been living reasonably well-adjusted savanna lives for more than 25 million years. Their early prehuman ancestors probably lived according to the same fundamental patterns.

This situation began changing in *Australopithecus* times. The earliest human infants had to contend with conditions different from those confronting the earliest hominid infants. Their parents were practicing a new kind of division of labor, with hunting chiefly performed by men and gathering chiefly performed by women. As a result, in one sense at least, the human band was and is less of an organic unit than the prehuman troop was. Its members no longer went everywhere together. There was a home base, where women, the young, and the old remained waiting while most of the men went away to hunt and often stayed away for long periods.

The infant was still a major center of attraction. It was still carried practically 100 percent of the time during the first year of life, or somehow in contact with its mother, judging by Draper's observations of the Kalahari Bushmen. But it no longer enjoyed quite as much undivided attention as infants had enjoyed in earlier times. Society had become a great deal more complicated, and parents had more things to do—making tools, preparing meals, talking, collecting wood and plant foods, taking care of fires. Furthermore, the infant found itself in a frustrating position largely because of the increasing complexity of social organization, which favored an increased learning ability, larger brains, and a longer period of development and dependency after birth.

Not only was the infant born helpless, and not only did it remain helpless longer than the offspring of monkeys and apes, but it was physically ill equipped to do anything about it. Presumably, its mother had to put it down on occasion and walk off to perform a chore, if only for a few minutes. When that happened, it could neither cling to her nor follow effectively. It could only watch as she moved out of sight, a predicament guaranteed to produce emotional disturbances in the young of any primate. The tendency to explore was also frustrated since the prehistoric infant depended completely on its mother for transport. Unless she carried it, it could not go where it wanted to go, nor could it establish contacts with new people and objects.

The smile may have evolved as a signal or communication to help make up for the handicap of infant immobility. Of course, crying could always be used to bring the mother to the spot. But crying alone was not enough. Infants of other primate species have vocal signals of some sort which indicate at a distance the nature and intensity of their distress; and something extra was called for to deal with the human predicament, something to hold the mother's attention longer and after the nursing and the burping were done. The infant represented only one of several alternative social contacts available to the mother. It had a high priority, to be sure. But it still had to compete for her time against other individuals and groups of individuals with demands of their own. Smiling became an essential way of meeting this competition.

The forces of natural selection come into play under such circumstances. Ambrose's research indicates that the smile is simply mild and low-intensity laughter minus chuckling and other sounds, and more relaxed. When it first appeared after nursing, mothers no doubt responded with cooing sounds, or the prehistoric equivalent thereof, and other forms of affection. Infants capable of making a ready connection between such pleasant responses and their mothers, who at this stage were seen merely as pairs of shining dots, learned to smile more and more and received more care and attention than other infants and prospered accordingly.

In other words, it was extremely important for the infant to form a deep attachment to its mother and to form it swiftly. Conditions existing in prehistoric times favored rapid learning at an early age. Judging by the records of contemporary infants, the process may have started during the third month of life with a sudden decrease in smiling at any human face and an increase in smiling at the mother's face. The odds are that if an infant had not formed a firm attachment by the age of 6 or 7 months, it never would. So the evidence suggests the evolution of a sensitive or critical period, when the infant is particularly ripe for learning the smiling response and associated behavior.

Critical periods exist in other species, notably birds. For example, a newly hatched gosling separated from its mother and all other adult geese will accept a substitute mother. It will attach itself to any one of a wide variety of moving objects, a blue balloon, a cardboard box, an investigator studying mother-infant bonds. The gosling responds to the object as to a real mother, follows it closely, and cries when it disappears. Studies indicate that in many cases this phenomenon, known as imprinting, must take place within 24 hours of hatching or else it may not take place at all.

For obvious reasons no comparable research has been conducted on human infants, and if it were, the situation would certainly turn out to be far more complicated. But evidence exists for a critical period in monkeys, and many aspects of the behavior of the human infant indicate that similar reactions are involved. For example, consider one of the ways a 4-month-old baby may behave when its mother comes into the room. It has just learned to distinguish her face from other faces, and as soon as she enters it turns its eyes on her smiles and tracks her while she moves about, looking and smiling intently all the time.

This is an impressively powerful response, a silent response. The infant seems to be compensating with all its might for its immobility. It is doing with its eyes and its smile what other primates can do more directly by clinging or following—keeping in close touch with its mother. The tracking could hardly be more efficient if its eyes were actually connected with the target. Such observations indicate strongly that tracking can be regarded as a substitute for following; that imprinting or something like it played a major part in the evolution of the human smile and continues to play a major part in the development of the smile during infancy.

The infant had much to gain by its positive reactions. The longer its mother remained close, the greater the chances that its immediate physical and emotional needs would be satisfied. So it would presumably be healthier, and even a small raising of the odds in that direction could have had an appreciable selective impact among populations in

which more than half of all infants died before they were 12 months **361**
old. But helping to meet the demands of the moment was probably not
the only or most important function of the smile.

Everything points toward its predominant role in a long-range
social context, in promoting the capacity to get along with other individuals. The increase in complexity of social systems during hominid
evolution, everything from toolmaking and meat eating to the shift from
small-game to big-game hunting, put increasing pressure on the infant.
Indeed, evolution seemed to be painting itself into a corner. It was
shaping an infant which had to learn more and sooner, and which at
the same time remained helpless longer. In such circumstances its first
close associations with an adult inevitably assumed an overriding importance.

Judging by activities in primate societies simpler than ours, the
trend seems to have begun much earlier. For example, in troops of macaque monkeys, the infant may obtain many things from its mother
over and above the satisfaction of immediate needs. Perhaps the most
telling point in this connection is the finding, originally reported by Japanese investigators (see Chapter 13), that the offspring of dominant
mothers tend to grow into dominant adults, another indication of the
fact that it pays to start at the top. In general, the infant's relationship
with its mother also serves as a model for future relationships in gorilla
and chimpanzee troops.

The uses of the smile reveal a great deal about the position of the
mother in human societies and about her special meaning to the infant.
One interesting response may occur after an infant tracks her movements around a room. Notice that such behavior implies that it is not
hungry or cold or uncomfortable in any way. For such things, crying
serves and has long served as a highly effective protest and summons.
In this case, the infant wants something else, and what it wants is indicated the instant its mother comes over and picks it up and holds it
in her arms.

At that point smiling usually ceases abruptly, almost as if shut off
by a switch, in a gesture that says, more plainly than words, "mission
accomplished." Then, secure in physical contact with its mother, it proceeds to look around the room. This is the exploring tendency in action.
It is the beginning of an adventure, a brief adventure to be sure, but a
prototype for all subsequent adventures. Later, when the infant crawls,
it continues to use its mother as a base of operations from which to explore the mysterious world. It leaves her to play with things it cannot
touch by reaching, and then comes back to her and leaves again. Still
later there will be other departures and returnings.

The mother also has problems, although they are more complicated and more difficult to investigate than the infant's. Evolution
has confronted her with dilemmas and conflicts. The same forces that

increased the dependency of the infant increased her dependency as well. The longer it remained helpless, the longer she had to stay nearby and be ready to come at its call. At the same time, her own security was threatened by the departures of hunters. She often had to watch people whom she needed passing out of sight, and often felt a fear of being abandoned analogous to that experienced by her infant when she left it to carry out other duties.

Mother love, like infant love, had to be learned and learned quickly. The mother's natural bias, like the infant's, was toward the positive, toward all the feelings and actions that would foster a close and deep coming together. Her smiling and associated behavior became part of a self-enhancing communication that worked both ways. But there were negative as well as positive aspects of infant care. Upon occasion, especially after prolonged crying, the mother came to her infant with resentment and anger, and one of the main functions of its smile was probably to help soften her feelings.

Incidentally, a related function can be traced back long before the coming of humans. Some time quite early in primate evolution, a modified form of the baring of the teeth developed as a sign of submission displayed by a low-ranking member of the hierarchy to a dominant member, a so-called appeasement grin, and the human smile may serve a similar purpose in adult life as well as in infancy. Under such conditions smiling loses its warmth, and it and the gesture that evokes it may be an extremely ugly thing.

I remember how one man responded to a hard look from his superior. It was toward the end of a conference in the vice-president's office of a large corporation, and he flushed and his smile was a cringing and a humiliation. All of us in the room, all human relations, seemed to shrink as he turned and left the room. It was a perversion of the smile, and we were all back in earlier times, behaving like members of a troop of prehuman primates.

The smile is only one aspect of infant behavior which has been studied for what it may suggest about possible courses of early social change. Crying also has evolutionary implications, although it seems to be more complicated than smiling, at least during infancy. For one thing, it is more difficult to classify. There are degrees of intensity and tone which make all the difference between hunger cries, pain cries, and so on. In addition, crying may come in regularly or irregularly spaced bouts, and distinctive patterns may exist within individual bouts. Preliminary studies suggest that it may be necessary to consider eight or more types of infant crying.

In most cases, however, the general message is clear and basic. Crying is designed to elicit a fast maternal reaction, and the faster the better. But the infant requires time to learn how effective its crying is, and to adjust its behavior accordingly. Ainsworth and her associate Sil-

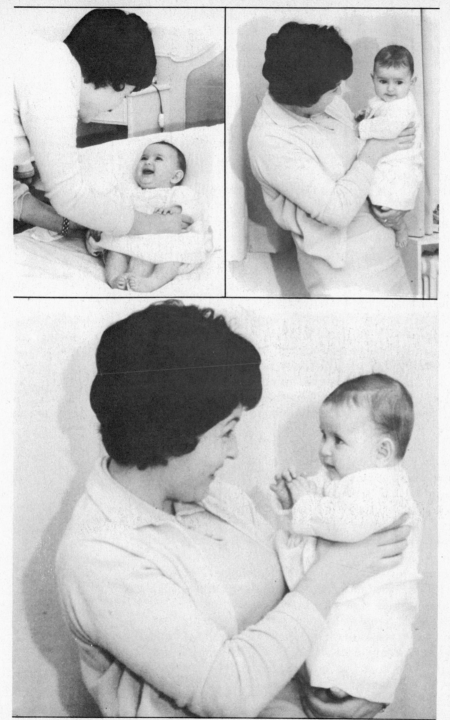

The smile in action: infant attracts mother (upper right); smile ceases after infant is picked up (above); secure in mother's arms, infant, unsmilingly, explores its world (lower right)

via Bell report that although the amount of crying varies widely during the first three months of life, from more than 20 minutes per hour to practically no crying at all, it has little to do with maternal responsiveness. At that stage, babies tend to cry at their own individual levels no matter what their mothers do.

Differences begin showing up during succeeding months. By the end of the first year there is appreciably less crying among babies whose mothers are quick to respond than among babies whose mothers delay responding or do not respond at all. If myths were not so enduring, such findings would be enough to discredit once and for all the notion that a crying infant is trying to get away with something and, for the good of its character, must not be spoiled by getting too much attention.

The primal urgency of most crying, its deep-rooted nature, is revealed by the observation that what counts most is the promptness of the response. Some mothers know better than others why their babies cry and precisely what to do—whether to feed the baby, change its diapers, pick it up, or simply to utter soothing words. But as long as she appears promptly, its crying will tend to decrease.

The real point of appearing promptly is what it does for the baby's expanding world view. Equipped with its appetites and desires and biases, it must identify objects and events, learn their regularities, and to some extent control their movements. When crying brings a dependable response, its world makes that much more sense—and making sense of things can be extremely difficult, perhaps even more difficult during infancy than later on. What happens outside and around the infant must often seem erratic and unpredictable.

The work of Ainsworth and other investigators indicates that a rather high proportion of mothers, perhaps one out of every three or four, frequently misinterpret infant signals or even overlook the signals entirely. Part of the problem is a tendency to underrate infants, to treat them as if they were too small and too underdeveloped to have anything to communicate. A baby may feel hungry and cry, but its mother, who may or may not be going by some sort of schedule, figures that the last feeding was too recent for another one just now. So she comes over with a toy. A while later the baby, having been distracted for a while, is busy playing with the toy and suddenly finds it must stop, its mother having decided that the time has come for a feeding.

It is on the basis of many many such strange incidents that the infant must learn to modify its wants in appropriate ways and build its model of reality. Feeding seems to be a perennial problem. The notion of feeding every four hours that was originally recommended without benefit of evidence by a discipline-minded German physician about a century ago is no longer as popular as it once was. On the other hand, modern living conditions do not permit the baby to obey its natural inclinations.

Evidence relating to feeding during prehistoric times has recently been considered by Nicholas Blurton Jones of the Institute of Child Health in London, who, in addition to studying English children, observed Kalahari children during a visit to the Kalahari. (He is the British stranger mentioned in Chapter 16, the sight of whom caused a Kalahari baby to scream.) Comparative studies of a hundred mammal species show that the chemical composition of mother's milk provides clues to the frequency of infant feeding. Mother's milk containing high proportions of protein and a fat is characteristic of rabbits, who feed their offspring about once every 24 hours, and tree shrews who feed their offspring about once every 48 hours. At the other extreme, among some rats, some marsupials and most monkeys, the young are fed every half-hour or so; rat mothers have low-protein, low-fat milk.

Human mothers and chimpanzee and gorilla mothers have milk very low in these essential compounds, indicating that frequent, almost continuous feeding was the rule in the remote past. The same conclusions follow from the observation that frequent feeders tend to suck slowly, and human infants are very slow suckers. Judging by Konner's estimate for the Kalahari Bushmen, infants who are carried most of the time and have ready access to the breast probably feed at least twice an hour, each time for 30 seconds to 10 minutes.

Such behavior represents the result of intensive selection and suggests some of the fundamental characteristics which humans share with other mammals. It may serve the special purpose of developing a close bond between mother and infant. Blurton Jones asks the question: Why carry babies? His provisional answer, based on admittedly incomplete evidence: "The association in the mammals between frequent feeding and a following or carrying system of child care is not nutritionally necessary, but rapid onset of hunger and satiation in the baby would be a simple mechanism for ensuring that it stays with the mother."

The fact that the infant can adapt to a rich variety of feeding practices and schedules, most of which are hardly geared to its basic biases, is as significant an example of the unique flexibility of humans as is the capacity for surviving and multiplying in widely different environments. Studies of smiling, crying, and other forms of infant behavior reinforce the notion of the infant as an active participant in its own development. It is not waiting, unformed and undirected, for us to make impressions upon it. It takes the initiative in responding, approaching, and establishing relationships, and makes up for its physical helplessness by a surprisingly advanced ability to communicate.

Ainsworth emphasizes an interesting point in this connection, namely, that you can often tell a great deal about the quality of an infant's communications with its mother by watching its face. A highly mobile face, a face that shows a varied and vivid interplay of emotion, is usually a sign that the infant has established satisfactory and sensitive communications. On the other hand, less fortunate infants tend to be "pudding-faced," a bit on the deadpan side. It may be that prolonged infant dependency and the importance of a close mother-infant bond have a close evolutionary relationship with the increasing capacity for facial expression.

Facial expression and the expression of emotion may also have a racial basis according to a report by Daniel Freedman and his Chinese wife Nina Chinn Freedman of the University of Chicago, who studied 24 Chinese-American and 24 European-American infants. The infants were only 7 to 75 hours old, yet even at that early age sharp differences in temperament occurred between the two groups. In one test, a cloth was placed over a baby's face for a few seconds, a procedure which proved highly upsetting to most European-American newborns, who struggled to remove the cloth by trying to brush it off with their hands and turning their heads. Chinese-American babies did far less thrashing around, most of them simply lying still until the cloth was lifted off.

This test and several others yielded similar results. Chinese-American babies are not only born more imperturbable than their European-American counterparts, but they also tend to calm down sooner when they do become upset. Such findings, which Chisholm has partly confirmed in studies of Navajo babies, raise many questions. If they are confirmed by other investigators, it should be possible to learn more about the origin of modern races during the past 10,000 to 30,000 years and about how long it takes to establish genetically based behavior changes in people. (A number of investigators believe that in some cases it may take less than 500 years.)

Research in living prehistory includes living infants and all representatives of *Homo sapiens*, not just members of the last remaining bands of aborigines in desert places. It was only a few hundred generations ago that we, the citizens of technologically advanced nations, were also hunter-gatherers. Contemporary people are close enough to those days to behave "prehistorically" upon occasion. Their behavior provides clues to the behavior of prehistoric people.

The differences between the most civilized and the least civilized among us are striking, but hardly basic. They are cultural differences chiefly, learned programs of behavior expressed and conveyed to us in traditional codes, and such programs are completely interchangeable. Any child from an American or Japanese family, for example, could be brought up to believe as firmly as the Australian aborigines in dream-time beings and a world that can only change for the worse. What we want to understand better are things relatively independent of upbringing, the sort of biases all humans share, the built-in tendencies for **367** all individuals to feel and think and react alike under comparable conditions.

The tendencies must first be identified and then accounted for in evolutionary terms. In the process of reconstructing the past through studies of contemporary behavior, we can also work things the other way around, using what we learn about prehistory to see ourselves more clearly here and now. It is a matter of obtaining new perspectives on life in our times. The present and the future are also part of human evolution, the part that must concern us most directly in times of accelerating transition. So it may help to turn in a serious and systematic manner to prehistory as part of our current efforts at self-understanding.

For example, evolutionary studies indicate that the mother-infant bond may not be as adaptive as it once was. In fact, any other conclusion would be amazing, considering how much the world has changed. Society was much simpler in prehistoric times. There were fewer people and fewer kinds of people. Not only that, but customs and traditions endured to an extent that we can hardly conceive. Individuals lived their entire lives in societies that had not changed appreciably for thousands of years, and would not change for thousands of years to come. They faced exactly the same dangers that their ancestors had faced, chiefly swift and sudden attacks by predators.

Survival in this kind of world favored rapid learning and, even more to the point, once-and-for-all learning, the formation of relatively fixed actions and attitudes. It was a steady-state, predictable world, the sort we yearn for in our weaker and more nostalgic moments. Time and life had a monolithic quality. Expectations were high that everything would endure in its present form forever, that the future would continue to be very like the past. In other words, what the infant learned fast and early would in all probability serve it admirably for the rest of its life.

Ours is a different world, with the wilderness gone. Even danger is not what it used to be, and instead of predators we face diseases that tend to develop slowly and strike late in life, a kind of violence which is as uniquely human as mercy or tolerance, and the enduring insecurity of change itself. The emphasis must be increasingly on flexibility. The mark of the new evolution which sweeps us along is that unlearning and learning anew have already become as important to survival as learning used to be. What people know is far less important than their capacity for modifying or discarding what they think they know.

So self-examination includes a harder look at the mother-infant bond and the speed, depth, and intensity of early learning. Much of what the infant learns during its first years may block its ability to learn later in life and create rigidities, an outcome somewhat more appropriate for prehistoric than for modern societies. The question for the future is whether built-in flexibility, one of the most distinctive marks of being human, is great enough to permit the erasing if necessary of information learned early—whether in a sense we can be taught to forget as effectively as we remember.

Infants' discovery of language; their inherent sense of grammar; nonverbal conversation of trained captive animals; tool using and children's play as steps toward prehistoric language, call systems, and development of abstractions; invention of a vocal alphabet; the anatomy of learning

CHAPTER 19 THE EVOLUTION OF LANGUAGE

More than half the people in the world can neither read nor write, but practically all individuals everywhere speak their native tongue. And, at the deepest levels, all languages are built according to the same fundamental blueprint. They all involve a very small number of basic voice or speech characteristics, about 15 or so ways of producing vowel and consonant sounds. These sounds are building blocks which in various combinations make up a very large number of words (several million words in the English language, which is increasing at an estimated rate of tens of thousands of words a year). The number of sentences, the hierarchies and patterns of words used, is infinite.

The origin of language is one of the great problems of science. If we understood how speech emerged from a system of calls—from the assorted grunts, barks, screams, hoots, and whimpers of nonhuman primates—many of the mysteries of human evolution would be solved. Such insights are yet to come. They demand nothing less than a step-by-step reconstruction of the evolutionary process, and for that the evidence is still lacking. There are no fossil clues to the nature of the earliest human languages and no living representatives of early stages on the way to present-day languages.

But there have been a variety of theories. The theologians of 300 or 400 years ago had no doubts and rather less evidence. They assumed that human beings were created fully articulate and that Adam and Eve spoke Hebrew in the Garden of Eden. A Scandinavian, dissenting from prevailing opinion, suggested that God addressed Adam in Swedish, Adam answered in Danish, and the snake tempted Eve in French. These are among the less plausible theories about the coming of language. Although a complete list of all theories, variations of theories, and related studies has yet to be made, Gordon Hewes of the University of Colorado has taken on the formidable task. His bibliography, still not complete, includes more than 6000 references.

Papers speculating about these matters but offering little by way of scientific evidence were so numerous that the Linguistic Society of Paris banned all such writings in 1866 and in 1911. Clearly, the ban was not highly effective. But it may have discouraged investigators from tackling the problem on a full-time serious basis. The situation has changed radically since then, as indicated dramatically in 1975 by a four-day New York conference on the origins and evolution of language. Hundreds of scientists and students packed a large hotel ballroom to hear some 50 reports on work in progress.

The past few years have seen an increasing interest in the problem, and a number of promising new approaches. For one thing, investigators are probing deeper than ever into events that occur during infancy and early childhood, the only chance we have to observe language taking shape. It is an exciting process, especially when viewed in the perspective of recent and rapidly accumulating evidence about the remarkable ability of apes to acquire language. The fact that the use of words, like the use and making of tools, is not an exclusive feature of the human species is stimulating new speculations about the evolutionary forces that brought human language into existence, and about accompanying changes in the structure and workings of the brain.

Life begins in chaos or near chaos. As a newcomer, a recent arrival from the womb, the infant faces a problem it will never solve completely. It is born into a turbulence of noises and odors, smooth places that suddenly become rough, cold places that suddenly become warm, lights and shadows that rise, fall, appear, and disappear. Plunged into this commotion, the infant must start to find a way and a place for itself. Its job is to create out of all the random strangeness a system of familiar objects, landmarks, rhythms, and laws.

So the infant investigates because it must, because that is what it is designed to do. It seeks and sorts out the elements of its world, including the sounds. It distinguishes meaningful from meaningless sounds, which sounds to heed and which to ignore, and, among the heeded sounds, which have the precisely patterned qualities of words. And it eventually makes what is probably the greatest discovery it will ever make, a discovery which is no less great because it is made over and over again by every infant. It proceeds to discover language.

This is a true discovery in the sense that the child learns but is not taught. Most of us have little or no knowledge about the intricacies of syntax and semantics, and even if we did, we would not be able to impart such abstruse information to our offspring in the nursery. We play a vital but more passive role, supplying language to them as we supply food and shelter. We provide them with a flow of sounds, words, and intonations which they may imitate, and that is the full extent of their imitating. Given this raw material, this sample of developed speech—an estimated total of 50 million words overheard during the first thousand days of life in the utterances of older children and adults, including speakers on radio and television—they go to work and create language anew on their own.

Out of that massive flow of words and sentences, the infant somehow deduces for itself the elements of speech and of effective communication with other individuals. In little more than two years it progresses from baby talk to an excellent command of its native tongue. The process, at least that part of it which we can observe, probably starts at about the age of 6 months with babbling, a kind of practice for producing basic sounds deliberately and for discovering and refining syllables. The infant utters its first words at 10 to 14 months, its first sentences of two or more words at 18 to 26 months. By the age of 3½ to 4 years it has a speaking vocabulary of up to 1500 words and, since the ability to comprehend language outruns the ability to use it, probably understands another 3000 to 4500 words which do not appear in its sentences. This situation continues throughout life, and the reading vocabulary of the average adult may be some 100,000 words, ten times larger than one's speaking vocabulary.

The full-scale investigation of language development among young human primates is a demanding task, which may be one reason that until recent times it has been generally avoided. Roger Brown and his associates at Harvard University have summarized their problems, tape-recording the utterances of children between the ages of 2 and 3: "There were those who warned that the child would be shy and speechless in our presence; this was not the case. Mothers told their children that visitors were coming and, in general we were eagerly welcomed, shown a parade of toys and games, and talked to rather steadily.

"It became clear that the child expected a guest to put in some time as a playmate, and so the recording was a two-man job with one of us taking data and the other prepared to play cowboy, horsie, coloring, trains, and the mule in 'kick the mule.' . . . We found that by about noon we needed a rest and so we went away for lunch, returning about two; the child took his nap in the interval."

The patience and endurance required to cope with such conditions have proved rewarding in a number of ways. For one thing, the evidence shows quite clearly that the child takes the initiative in learning language. Its first sentences, mostly strings of two or three words, are not formed at random. They indicate an inherent feeling for subject-predicate and verb-object relationships. Furthermore, they are often completely original. The child continues to surprise us with a rather high proportion of phrases—such as *that doed, more up, allgone shoe* and *hi, milk*—which cannot be the result of any parroting process since it does not hear any such remarks from its elders.

Learning proceeds at an impressive rate. Brown's studies indicate that starting at the age of 26 to 34 months or so infants learn special ways of modulating simple sentences, expressing meanings. English-speaking infants, for example, begin to use the present progressive tense correctly in sentences involving activities under way here and now, as in *me going* and *me eating*. Next they master the use of *in* and *on*; then sounds of the plural forms *iz*, as in *roses*; *z*, as in *dogs*; and *s*, as in *cats*; then the past irregular *went* instead of *goed*; and so on.

The process seems to obey its own laws and develop according to a predetermined timetable, no matter what anyone does about it. According to Charles Hockett of Cornell University, language acquisition "is practically impossible to prevent, save through environmental insults so drastic that the child has little chance to survive at all. . . . The earliest steps, moreover, are remarkably alike for children in all different speech communities, suggesting that all the languages of the world are, and for a long time have been, erected on a single groundplan." On the other hand, the coming of language cannot be rushed. Children make progress when they are ready to make progress, and not before.

For example, at about the age of 3, when they are still learning the rules of negation, they tend to produce double negatives and, as the following exchange indicates, until they grow out of this stage nothing can be done about it:

> *Child:* Nobody don't like me.
> *Mother:* No, say "nobody likes me."
> *Child:* Nobody don't like me.

This mother put up a game but losing fight. After the above dialogue was repeated word for word eight times in a row, she tried one last time:

> *Mother:* No, now listen carefully; say "nobody likes me."
> *Child:* Oh! Nobody don't likes me.

The double negative was ingrained in the child's mind. It could not change, because no matter how often its mother repeated the correct sentence starting with *nobody*, the child heard something else. It listened with its inner ear and heard not one but two words, *nobody don't*. Of course, within a month or two it had learned to hear differently and was producing perfect negatives. So let the teacher, parent or otherwise, beware. Individuals younger than we are may not always be ready to profit by our greater experience and wisdom.

By the time the child is 4 or 5 years old it has learned the great majority of more than a thousand basic rules of grammar. But many fine points remain to be mastered. For example, consider the difference between *John told Mary to go to Boston* and *John promised Mary to go to Boston*. The first sentence obeys the rules; it is Mary who is to go to Boston. The agent, Mary, and the verb *to go* are next to one another, in accordance with the so-called minimum distance principle.

In the second sentence, however, the principle does not hold.

John is the agent of the verb *to go,* but the two words are not next to **373** one another, and a child may be confused and unable to use the verb promise properly until it is 9 or 10 years old. Another difference which may confuse children even more is the distinction between *Tell Mary what to put in the box* and *Ask Mary what to put in the box.* There are several thousand more rules and exceptions to rules, most of which are learned unconsciously by the age of 10 or so, although there are rules some people never learn.

The way children acquire language hints at what might have happened in the remote past. "The two fundamental developments were naming and grammar," Ben Blount of the University of Texas points out, "and . . . these emerged out of increasing complexity in social behavior and cultural information. The same is true for children learning the words of their language and for the highly efficient organization of grammar. Just as our protohominid and hominid ancestors did, children create and discover finer and more precise ways of relating information about the environment and themselves to other individuals."

Another important parallel is that infants manage to communicate a great deal before they begin using words. Smiling and crying convey a wide range of feelings, some subtle and some not so subtle—hunger, pain, discomfort, anger, pleasure, the need for affection, the desire to explore. Emotion or expression without words preceded the coming of language in evolution. Blount suggests that conveying information dispassionately, the first steps toward "the freeing of utterances from affect," represents a later and continuing development. As a matter of fact, our capacity even today to engage in emotion-free communication is probably more limited that we imagine.

Language develops with the pace and sweep of a biological force. We can see that force taking shape, the beginnings of the human kind of communication, in the striking and hitherto unsuspected capacity for language among the most advanced nonhuman primates, notably chimpanzees. Current studies and studies planned for the near future all stem from the pioneer successes of Allen and Beatrice Gardner, a husband and wife team at the University of Nevada. They worked with the young female chimpanzee named Washoe who used a blanket as a mother or security symbol (see Chapter 14.) For five years, starting in June 1966, when Washoe was 1 year old, she lived in a trailer with free access to a yard containing trees and a jungle gym. All her waking hours were spent in the company of one human being or more, usually the Gardners and their graduate students; but she never heard human speech. Observers never uttered words in her presence, only hoots and other chimpanzee calls. In addition, people made gestures based on those of the standard American sign language for the deaf.

There is a logic behind this unusual experimental arrangement. Chimpanzees cannot learn to talk, a point proved once and for all nearly

20 years ago when another husband and wife team brought up another female chimpanzee named Viki. Viki learned to brush her teeth, dust furniture, open cans and bottles, and eat at the table with manners at least as respectable as those of the human children who were her only playmates. But she could utter only three words *mama,* and *papa,* and *cup,* and only with extreme difficulty. In fact, she often rocked back and forth and exhibited other symptoms of severe emotional distress when called on to say her words.

The Gardners designed their experiment partly as a consequence of seeing motion pictures of Viki's behavior. They did not conclude that the chimpanzee is inherently incapable of language, but simply that it is incapable of imitating human speech sounds and acquiring spoken language. On the other hand, gestures come quite readily to it, and it often imitates human gestures when playing. So it seemed reasonable to take advantage of this natural ability and explore the chimpanzee's linguistic potentialities by using sign language.

Washoe responded enthusiastically. She learned her first word at about the age of 15 months, an insistent *come gimme* represented by a beckoning gesture with fingers or wrist. Her second word, *more,* which involves bringing the fingertips of both hands together, came within another week or two—and by the time she was about 3½ to 4 years old she used more than 50 signs, including those representing *hear listen* (index finger touches ear), *toothbrush* (index finger rubs front teeth), *flower* (index finger touches one or both nostrils), *dog* (slaps thigh), *cover blanket* (one hand moved over the back of the other and toward the signaler's body), and *please* (draw open hand across chest).

When Washoe was about 2 years old she spontaneously made the *come gimme* sign and then wagged her tongue and touched it with her index finger, the sign for *sweet.* It was her first sentence. But even more significant, it was a creative sentence. Although she had learned the individual signs by imitating, the combination was not imitated and could not have been because Washoe had never seen that particular combination of gestures. The Gardners had never used sign language to ask her or one another for candy. Many of her subsequent sentences were also original combinations, such as *come gimme tickle, please up,* and *hurry open.* She has used five gestures in a single sentence (*more more more sweet drink*) and as many as four different gestures (*drink sweet please hurry* and *out open please hurry*).

Washoe recognizes herself in the mirror, an ability she shares with other chimpanzees such as those studied by Gallup (discussed in Chapter 14). The big difference is that in their case, the ability had to be inferred indirectly because they did not know how to communicate with people. In Washoe's case, the evidence is direct. While looking into a mirror one day, she was asked, "Who is that?" and promptly responded, "Me, Washoe" in sign language.

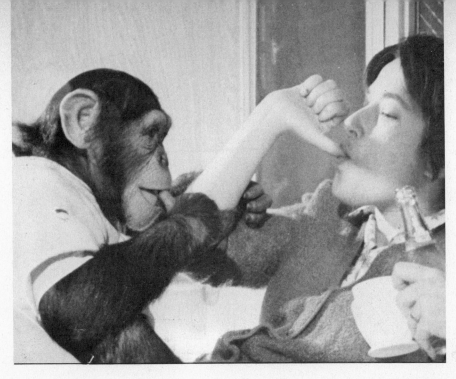

Nonhuman primate learns to "talk": Washoe says "drink" to Beatrice Gardner

SIGNS WASHOE USES

(Listed in approximate order of appearance from June, 1966, to December, 1967)

Sign	Description	Context
(ASL indicates correct American Sign Language form)		
Come gimme	Beckoning, with wrist or knuckles as pivot.	To signal persons, dogs, etc., and to indicate food, toys, and other objects out of reach. Often combined with another sign, e.g., *come tickle, gimme sweet.*
More	Fingertips brought together, usually overhead. ASL form: tips of tapered hands touch repeatedly.	Asking for continuation or repetition of some activity— spinning, tickling, second helpings of food. Also used to ask for second demonstration of some performance, e.g., a somersault.
Up	Pointing up with index finger or thumb.	Wants a lift to reach object, e.g., grapes on vine, leaves, or wants to be placed on some-one's shoulders.

Sweet	Index or index and second fingers touch tip of wagging tongue. ASL form: use index and second fingers extended side by side.	Asking for dessert; occurs spontaneously at end of meal, also when sweets are offered. (A common interchange: W: "Gimme, gimme." P: "What do you want?" W: **"Sweet."**)
Go	Opposite of *come gimme*.	While walking hand-in-hand or riding on shoulders of companion, usually indicates direction desired.
Hear listen	Index finger touches ear.	For loud or strange sounds— bells, car horns, sonic booms, footsteps, etc. Also, solicits someone to hold a watch to her ear.
Tickle	Draws index finger of one hand across back of other hand. Related to ASL *touch*.	For tickling or for chasing games.
Open	Places flat hands side by side, palms down. Draws them apart while rotating to palms up.	At house, room, car doors, refrigerator, cupboards; and for jars and other containers.
Toothbrush	Using index finger as brush to rub front teeth.	At end of meals. Used when W noticed toothbrush in strange bathroom.
Hurry	Shaking the open hand at the wrist. ASL form: use index and second fingers extended side by side.	Frequently follows signs such as *come gimme, out, open, go,* particularly when there is a delay before she is obeyed. Also used when watching her meal being prepared.
Funny	Tip of index finger presses nose, and W snorts. ASL form: use index and second fingers, no snort.	Soliciting interaction play and used during games, occasionally, when being pursued.
Hurt	Extended index fingers are jabbed toward each other. Can be used to indicate location of pain.	To indicate cuts and bruises on herself or others. Can be elicited by red stains on a person.
Drink	Fist with thumb extended, thumb placed in mouth.	For water, formula, soda pop, etc.

Sorry	Rub bent hand on chest. ASL form: rub fist in circular motion.	After biting someone or when someone has been hurt in some other way (not necessarily by W). When told to apologize for mischief.
Please	Draw open hand across chest. ASL form: use fingertips and circular motion.	Asking for objects and activities. Frequently combined: *please go, out please, please drink,* etc.
Food eat	Several fingers of one hand are placed in mouth. ASL form: fingertips of tapered hand touch mouth repeatedly.	During meals and meal preparation.
Flower	Tip of index finger touches one or both nostrils. ASL form: tips of tapered hand touch first one nostril, then the other.	When seeing or wanting flower. Elicited by actual flowers and pictures of flowers.

Washoe's subtle grasp of language often shows up unexpectedly. One day when she went riding in a car with the Gardners, they used the sign for a dog in conversing with one another. She "overheard" the sign and looked out the window in search of a dog, indicating that she had acquired a kind of built-in cerebral dictionary which matches gestures and images. Washoe often "talked" to herself privately and made signs in her bedroom before going to sleep (an activity observed among human children) as she thumbed through a magazine or picture book or sneaked toward a forbidden part of the yard (using the sign for *quiet*) or ran for the toilet (using the sign meaning *hurry*).

The Gardners emphasize that their work with Washoe represents only a beginning. After all, she received no language training until she was about a year old, and that presumably retarded her development as an analogous delay would have retarded the development of a human child. This point is being put to the test. Among the Gardners' current projects are studies of two new chimpanzees, Moja and Pili, whose language training started a day or two after birth and who, judging by observations to date, may well exceed the accomplishments of Washoe.

Meanwhile Washoe continues to learn in a new setting, the University of Oklahoma's Institute for Primate Studies, under the watchful eye of Roger Fouts, a former student of the Gardners. The move called for some readjustments. Washoe had seen another chimpanzee only once before, and now, living among half a dozen chimpanzees, she did not regard them as fellow apes. She apparently considered herself superior to them, calling them "bugs." This attitude was somewhat reminiscent of when Viki, more than a generation ago, sorted photographs of human beings and apes into two piles. Viki accomplished the task with 100 percent accuracy, until she came to a picture of herself; without hesitating, she placed it in the "human" pile, along with Eisenhower, Roosevelt, and Joe DiMaggio.

Eventually, Washoe came to recognize the facts of life, and she began using her vocabulary, made up of more than 175 words, in an effort to communicate with other chimpanzees on more equal terms with the signs for *tickle, come hug, go drink* (when she wanted to have some fruit to herself), and so on. At first she received no answers, which was hardly surprising considering that none of her companions knew sign language. That situation has since been remedied; there are other users of signs around. In one study, Fouts trained two male chimpanzees, Bruno and Booee, separately, then brought them together; soon they were signaling to one another, generally to be tickled or hugged, and not always with success. Once Booee gestured, "Tickle Booee," and Bruno, who was being fed some raisins at the time, replied, "Booee me food"—which may be freely translated as, "Not now, Booee. I'm eating."

Now that communications have been established at an elementary level, the Oklahoma investigator is extending the scope of his studies. Ally, a young male chimpanzee, lives with a psychiatric social worker who is serving as his human mother. He is scheduled to learn all about ownership and possessions and eventually to convey the notions of *mine* and *yours* to another chimpanzee, probably Booee. What might develop is unpredictable, but there could be arguments and perhaps even fair-trade exchanges of books, toys, fruit, and other objects. Washoe herself, now sexually active, is expected to be involved soon in a study of the transmission of language from mother to infant.

Another African-born female chimpanzee, named Sarah, is also assured of a prominent place in the annals of man-animal communication. She is the 15-year-old protege of David Premack of the University of Pennsylvania, who started her education back in 1968 with a simple procedure. In the first step, designed mainly to achieve a good working relationship between ape and teacher, he put a ripe banana on a table and watched benevolently as she ate it. Having established that routine, he put a banana just out of her reach, and within reach, a small pink plastic square with a steel backing. Sarah quickly learned that to get the banana she had to pick up the piece and place it on a magnetic language board. In similar fashion, she learned that a purple triangle meant *apple* and so on for a total of half a dozen different fruits and their corresponding plastic pieces. Confronted with two pieces and one

Give

Chocolate

Sarah

Sarah and trainer:
learning to "talk"

fruit, two fruits and one piece, and various combinations, she showed that she knew which pieces and fruits went together, and had chances upon occasion to indicate her preferences.

The next stage was teaching Sarah a new class of words, the names of her different teachers. She found that to get a banana from Mary Morgan, a research assistant working with Premack, she had to place a plastic M on the language board and under it, since Sarah writes vertically Chinese style, the square banana symbol. After learning the names of several teachers, she learned that fruit would not be forthcoming unless she constructed a three-word sentence—for example, M for *Mary*, the purple triangle for *apple*, and, between the two, a third piece shaped something like a vertical bow tie and representing *give*.

Slowly, step by step, Premack built up Sarah's linguistic skills until she learned about 130 words, that is, plastic shapes that she can manipulate to produce sentences on the language board. She has learned to use proper word order—for example, *Mary give apple* will bring results while *apple give Mary* will not. She can indicate whether two objects are the same or different, answer *yes* or *no* to questions, ask questions, deal with *if then* sentences, and so on.

Premack feels that up to this point Sarah actually learned very little which was new to her: "Mostly our procedures had been merely teaching her the names for concepts she already knew." Subsequent

379

training sessions have shown definitely that she can advance to new and more sophisticated concepts. She dealt with the equivalent of the question, What is the relationship between an apple and the plastic word for apple? by indicating that the purple triangle was the name of the fruit. She also learned to answer questions involving abstract ideas of color, shape, and size.

Future plans involve new members of the University of Pennsylvania's chimpanzee colony, and a special project for Sarah. She is being prepared to learn a new language in a new way. Instead of plastic pieces and a language board, she is working with an electric typewriter with special keys which are small images of word symbols and which appear on a color television screen in sharp outline. Details of the symbols remain to be worked out, but they will all appear in a standard-sized rectangular box and be made up of abstract elements. Premack plans to teach Sarah individual words by using entirely arbitrary symbols. For example, *eagle* might be

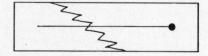

and *sparrow* might be

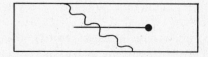

After acquiring a vocabulary and skill in using the typewriter keyboard, Sarah will be trained to see that many of her newly learned words are composed of basic elements, syllables of a sort. For example, the two symbols above are made up of the following words and their symbols:

large: ——————————
small: —————
flying object: ●
fierce: 〰〰〰
peaceful: ∿∿∿

The payoff in this study will come when Sarah learns to put these and many other elements together to form new words and new concepts.

The impressive linguistic capacities of chimpanzees as revealed in these and other laboratory experiments contrast sharply with what apparently happens, or does not happen, in the wild. Everything we know leads us to expect something special from the most human of nonhuman primates that are at large in wilderness forests, something as impressive as their toolmaking. For example, we might expect the use of combinations of calls to form crude sentences. But for all their intelligence, observations have been disappointing. According to Jane Goodall, chimpanzees have about two dozen calls which, like the calls of many other primates, express such things as threats, rage, greetings, and satisfaction; but the calls exhibit no prelanguage features.

Among those interested in confronting the problem and gaining a deeper understanding of primate communications under natural conditions is Emil Menzel of the State University of New York, Stony Brook. In a typical experiment, he hid a bunch of bananas in a bush in a 1-acre field, about 75 yards from a cage containing a colony of half a dozen "compatible" chimpanzees who had lived together for several years; they could not observe his actions. Then he took a young female named Belle out of the cage, carried her to the bush so that she could see the hidden fruit, and put her back in the cage. Ten minutes later he released her and the rest of the colony and watched what happened from an observing tower.

Belle led the way to the fruit, but not without some trouble. Her fellow apes wanted to climb trees and wrestle with one another, and she had to stop repeatedly. She would take a few steps, glance back, grimace, beckon by waving her hand in a come-along gesture, tap laggards on the shoulder. In other words, she used body language to convey information. Many variations and elaborations of this kind of test have revealed a great deal about cognitive, or mental, maps; the ability of chimpanzees to remember the locations of as many as 18 different objects and to act accordingly. Menzel is now working with Premack to find out, among other things, whether symbols can be used instead of actual showing to tell chimpanzees where objects are hidden and, if so, whether chimpanzees can learn to use symbols in directing other chimpanzees to the hiding places.

Another approach to investigating the language-learning capacities of chimpanzees is under way at the Yerkes Regional Primate Research Center in Atlanta. Lana, the star of the project, lives in a room with rows of push buttons on one wall, each marked with a symbol representing a word. By pressing appropriate buttons in the appropriate order she can ask for a variety of things—candy, apples, bananas, milk, music, movies, slides, companionship (human, not simian). Similar buttons outside the room permit experimenters to communicate with Lana.

According to latest reports, Lana now knows about 90 pushbutton words, or lexigrams, and is in the process of learning 30 or 40 more. Duane Rumbaugh of Georgia State University, director of the project, points out that the study, like all such studies, is a continuing adventure in the sense that no one knows when experimental apes will make some unexpected linguistic breakthrough on their own. One morning, for example, Lana saw a new object and spontaneously asked for its name, indicating not only a grasp of the abstract notion of naming, but also the possible potential for building up a much larger vocabulary. Interestingly enough, although such tests were designed primarily to explore the implications, evolutionary and otherwise, of chimpanzees' linguistic powers, they promise to pay off in terms of direct benefits to human beings. Some retarded and pathologically withdrawn or autistic children are learning to use push-button and keyboard techniques to communicate increasingly with the outside world, a process which at the same time may encourage them to talk and increase their vocabularies.

The gap between human and nonhuman is enormous as far as language is concerned and the odds are that, even with the most ingenious training procedures, no ape will ever learn more than a fraction of what the young child learns mainly on its own. Nevertheless, the gap is not as large as once thought. Clearly, as Blount points out, "the prerequisites for labelling or naming have been present in the primate line of descent for a long time, perhaps ten to fifteen million years." Continuing studies of primates in the laboratory and in the wild will lead to a new appreciation of their powers and limitations. Apparently chimpanzees are capable of far more sophisticated communicating than they are actually called on to demonstrate in their native forests. They certainly seem to outdo themselves linguistically under the pressure of associating with psychologists.

The great evolutionary question is what pressures were at work on our remote ancestors, and part of the answer seems to be the steady increase in the complexity of things. Even before the appearance of hominids, the world was richer and more diverse for primates than for most other species. Equipped with an outstanding visual apparatus, they saw more objects more vividly and in finer detail. Items viewed in three dimensions and in color stood out with a new prominence and demanded a new degree of attention. As a matter of fact, from one standpoint, objects did not exist in the fullest sense of the word before the coming of advanced stereoscopic color vision.

The quality of objects was further enriched by the evolution of hands with mobile fingers. In contrast to most of the earliest prosimians, monkeys and apes could reach out and pick up things for inspection — feeling, sniffing, and mouthing. Things were moved more readily from their natural positions, and regarded more closely and from more angles. The brain, particularly the most recently evolved cortex or outer bark, took over the task of synthesizing new information from a number of sensory channels and of creating more detailed models of objects. The result was a partial taking apart or fragmenting of the environment. It became less of a continuum, less an uninterrupted expanse of blurred and merging forms, and more a system of distinct and more numerous items.

This development was characteristic of primates in general. Something more must have put a premium on the origin of language among those primates that were members of the human family, something that appreciably increased the complexity of life and that involved the quest for food and related activities. As omnivores, our remote ancestors exploited to the limit every possible source of food. They learned about hundreds of other wild species and, among that extensive inventory of potential and possible dietary items, concentrated on a relative few, depending on circumstances and the seasons. They were also doing things which further multiplied the number of meaningful objects in their world and the number of possible relationships among the objects, for example, using tools. Sticks for digging opened up new sources of nourishment—underground roots and tubers and small game hiding in burrows. Stones with sharp edges helped cut through skins and sinews; rocks for bashing served to mash tough fibers and break bones.

Above all, the first hominids were social creatures in the process of becoming even more socialized. The nature of their vocabularies on the open savanna may be hinted at in certain aspects of the linguistic behavior of Washoe and other experimental apes. "What chimpanzees communicate about primarily," according to Blount, "are social relations among individual members. Signals concern dominance, submission, threats, mating, play, in sum, how individuals work out how they relate to one another, what the activity of the relating is." He emphasizes that most of Washoe's first signs, such as *come gimme* and *go,* referred to activities rather than objects: *more* often meant she wanted more tickling or playing of some sort; *funny* referred to playing games and being chased.

Perhaps many of the earliest words of our earliest ancestors were also more like verbs than nouns. There may have been a long period of prelanguage signaling, a time before the course of evolution demanded revolutionary changes in communication and before speech became more and more a serious life-and-death business. Perhaps in the beginning children were the chief innovators, specifically children at play. The very nature of play makes for invention in language as in other forms of behavior; novelty flourishes wherever there is freedom and a certain lack of responsibility for taking care of the world's immediate problems. At one time our ancestors presumably had a call system not too different from that of contemporary chimpanzees, which means that as far as vocal communications were concerned, they lived almost exclusively in the present. Their calls were generally immediate responses triggered by the emotional impact of immediate events. The bonds between calls and intense emotion were loosened somewhat during play only, with its elements of make-believe and incomplete involvement.

Radical changes came later, in all likelihood among the children

of tool-using hominids, who were preparing to participate in a more
elaborate world and were playing more elaborate games. Of course,
their repertoire must have included such perennial primate favorites as
chases, mock fights, and various versions of hide-and-seek. But probably some games were being played that had never been played before.
Pursuers may have carried rocks in their hands and may have thrown
the rocks, the chases sometimes ending with something more serious
than a playful nip or an appeasement gesture.

Mock danger may often have turned into real danger, mock pain
and terror into real pain and terror. Perhaps such pursuits were gradually modified or abstracted, stripped of the fear and much of the excitement and the risk of pain and injury, stripped of everything except the
elements needed to improve throwing accuracy and coordination. The
result may have been something like the game of catch, which can be
regarded as a watered-down or domesticated pursuit, a disguised target
practice in which the participants take turns at throwing and being
thrown at, at being predator and prey.

New symbolic activities which developed during play were probably accompanied by new symbolic vocalizations. Action and utterance
were part of the same behavioral process, with natural selection always
favoring detachment, the ability to free objects from their positions in
the environment and to free utterances from their connections with intense emotion and the present. A ball game required some delay, some
anticipation, as compared with the old standard primate games. It called
for organization, perhaps a choosing up of sides, and an object—often a
prepared object at that, something worked into a roughly spherical
shape to remove sharp edges and projections.

A rich system of calls could have evolved in such a setting. Before the start of a play-chase many primates approach with a kind of
hopping gait, a signal which indicates that what is about to happen is
all in fun, and perhaps an analogous point was expressed vocally as a
prelude to games with objects. Perhaps a hominid who wanted to play
catch went through the pantomime of throwing, and at the same time
uttered a standard call indicating excitement modified by a sound signifying a game. If the game became popular, the combined gesture and
modified call could have spread rapidly to other children in a group,
and later the call by itself could have meant Where is the ball? or Let's
play catch.

At some later stage, a child acting on the spur of the moment, or
as the outcome of an accidental turn of events during play, may have
invented a more complicated game, say, a game involving throwing and
then running, and uttered the calls for *throw* and *run* together, in that
order. Perhaps the two-part call came first and inspired the idea of the
two-part action, or it might have happened the other way around. But

in either case the result would have been a dual creation, a new game **385** and a sentence or protosentence.

What would adults have been doing all this time? For one thing, they may have wondered then as they sometimes do now at the offbeat utterances of their children. Part of their influence would have been negative in the sense that mothers warning players to be more careful probably helped to transform violent chases and the hurling of missiles into something as innocuous as the game of catch. Also, on occasion adults may have adopted some of the new calls and the new games that went with the calls, although it can be assumed that as far as acceptance in general was concerned, they always lagged a bit behind their offspring then as they do now.

The most receptive adults, however, were those who had participated most actively in innovation during their youth. The longer the period of infant and childhood dependency, the longer the delay in assuming responsibility, the greater the opportunity for playing together and forming close associations. Games and utterances learned during childhood provided the sort of experience in cooperating found among team members who have competed so long together that they can anticipate one another's intentions and actions. Linguistic habits carried over into adult life served well in hunting and fighting, thus setting a prehistoric precedent for the notion that Britain's wars were won on the playing fields of Eton.

This is only one of many possible processes. But it seems reasonable to suppose that some sort of transition stage existed between call systems and language and that it took place not within the confines of a single band but in many bands over very long periods. There was certainly time and energy enough, millions of years, and billions of individuals interacting with one another. As noted, evolution put a premium on the survival of bands including members who could reconstruct the past in their minds and express their images and conceive new sequences of actions to serve as the basis for future plans.

Certain elements of this faculty can be seen among nonhuman primates. Only primates seem to be capable of the sort of behavior where a male baboon, threatened by an angry and higher-ranking male, will snatch up an infant and begin grooming it, because he knows that he is safer from attack with an infant in his arms (see Chapter 12). This form of pretense is deliberate plotting, and uses symbols. It requires not only a second-nature familiarity with complex hierarchal relationships, but also a certain ability to disengage oneself, to stand apart and observe the relationships and exploit them for new ends. It amounts to a kind of tool use in which a behavioral pattern is displaced from its natural setting and put to work in the service of a special purpose. Using the grooming of an infant as a device for turning away wrath demands a certain detachment not unlike that involved in the early evolution of language.

Detachment implies certain things about the structure and workings of the brain. It implies the development of an ability to respond negatively. For example, in connection with the increasing need for self-control and for biding one's time in an increasingly complicated world (see Chapters 1 and 7), one would need the ability to inhibit flight and the display of anger and other actions. If language evolved from call systems, it demanded reacting to sounds not as emotion-laden, here-and-now signals, but as abstractions referring to something that had happened or was yet to happen. Incidentally, the same basic ability to postpone impulses, perhaps indefinitely, is heavily involved in two other uniquely human characteristics—incest taboos and the use of tools to make tools. When a stone is used to sharpen a digging stick, as George Miller of Rockefeller University emphasizes, the stone acquires a value not only as something immediate but as something to help in fulfilling a delayed purpose.

The rudiments of language may have developed in the easygoing context of play and other leisure activities, and later been incorporated into more elaborate systems under the rising tensions of evolutionary necessity. Tool use, the novelties and hazards of savanna life, and cooperating and sharing in the food quest helped spread the coming of language. So did the family, as it evolved into an increasingly complex institution with the change from closed inbred groups to open groups in which matings outside the band became a policy supported by ritual. This change marked the creation or invention of the uniquely human sort of group made up of a number of bands held together by kinship ties. Such systems, of course, could not have appeared until our ancestors had brains and languages sophisticated enough to conceive and identify a variety of near and remote kin.

All this involved new pressures. It added up to a mounting and enormous flood of activities and relationships and objects to be named, a pileup of signals. At some stage, the strain on memory may have approached the breaking point for many individuals. Furthermore, they may have been hard pressed to invent new signals that could be readily distinguished from one another. The problem can be illustrated by a hypothetical case of picture writing in which each symbol is a simplified sketch or caricature of a house, a man running, a wounded animal, and so on. If an evolving tribe kept adding new pictures for every new object and relationship generation after generation, it could sooner or later run out of symbols which were simple and compact, and at the same time sufficiently different so that the eye could tell them apart. This situation, or something very close to it, arose about four centuries ago in Chinese writing, which had accumulated an overwhelming total of more than 45,000 pictographic characters. Comparable difficulties **387** may have arisen in the development of language.

Recent thinking takes account of such difficulties. For instance, Hewes has a theory which was inspired partly by the achievements of Washoe and Sarah that is a refined version of ideas first presented 200 or more years ago—namely, that man's original language was a silent gesture language. He suggests that at first groups probably got along with a small number of gestures, perhaps 50 or so, for landmarks, common plant and animals foods, water sources, and directions—such as *up, down, near, far, here, there.* Later developments required more and more gestures until, at about the 1000-gesture level, the number approached the limit of readily distinguishable signs, at which point selective forces brought about a greater emphasis on modified calls and the beginnings of speech.

The first or primordial spoken language is the subject of a bold theory offered by Mary Foster of California State University. She was led to the theory by "the accidental discovery that resemblances between presumably unrelated American Indian languages were too widespread to be due to chance or borrowing" and by the subsequent finding of further resemblances in the Indo-European, Turkish, Hittite, and other languages. She believes that people originally spoke a language consisting of 18 sounds, each of which had a distinctive cluster of related meanings.

The units were gestures of a sort, hidden gestures based on the mechanics of pronunciation, the way the tongue, lips, and other parts of the apparatus produce the sounds. For example, sounds such as *p, t,* and *k* (stopped sounds), produced at the front of the mouth and requiring complete closure of the expelled-air channel for a fraction of a second, represented the general notion of movements away from or outward. Resonant sounds such as *m, l,* and *r,* produced further back in the mouth together with vocal-cord vibrations, represented a class of internalized or subjective meanings involving mental activity, beginnings, desire, and so on. Foster has reconstructed a theoretical basic vocabulary made up of more than a hundred primordial words built from various combinations of the 18 sound-meaning units, or oral signals.

Perhaps such units or something like them arose and were refined in the process of trying to name more and more objects and activities. If some of the differences between sounds became so subtle that they could no longer be recognized readily or uttered as distinct patterns, one result would have been a high level of ambiguity. Hunting-gathering bands with such overloaded communication systems may have tended to cross their signals rather frequently. Presumably there were misunderstandings and ineffective or confused responses, a situation which might have been particularly unfortunate in matters involving complex plans and social relationships. In other words, pressures of living favored the ability to reduce ambiguity, to make further refinements in the classification and interpretation of sounds.

Specifically, they were able to dissect calls into their components and discover categories or common elements. Hockett suggests that the change required a heightening of awareness or sensitivity, a shift of attention from whole sounds to parts of sounds. It was something like the difference between writing with pictorial symbols, representations of familiar objects and activities, and writing with the individual letters of an alphabet, which are not intended to be images of anything in particular, but which make possible the invention of an indefinite number of readily distinguished words. What happened, in fact, was the invention of a kind of vocal alphabet, a small set of acoustic units, the vowel and consonant sounds which we use to form words.

The accumulation of names, the ceaseless adding of new words to human vocabularies, called for increasing efficiency. As Blount puts it, "grammar is a very powerful device for organizing meaning." He points out that grammatical rules increase the possible number of unambiguous messages which can be composed and conveyed. For example, a hypothetical language of ten words allowing only one-word and two-word sentences has 55 possible messages. If word order made a difference, if word A plus word B meant something different from word B plus word A, the number of possible messages increases to 110. Three-word sentences, with each combination of words having a different meaning, yield a total of 1110 messages. For today's actual languages, with many thousand of words and many special rules, the number of available messages is practically infinite.

There is no generally accepted time scale for the evolution of language. But the first small steps toward language may have been under way at least 10 million years ago with the appearance of a few special gestures among creatures like *Ramapithecus,* or a few changes in the quality and structure of ancestral primate calls. Perhaps *Australopithecus* attained a vocabulary of 50 or more gestures by about 3 million years ago, and the next 2 million years or so brought an accelerating increase in naming, during the transition from *Australopithecus* to *Homo erectus,* and a near doubling in the size of the brain, partly in response to the need for a larger memory to store the new words of an expanding cerebral dictionary.

François Bordes sees a significant connection between the evolution of toolmaking and the evolution of a capacity for abstract thought. An early stage involved the concept of a cutting edge, as something which is absent but imminent and possible to create in a suitable unworked pebble. We can credit this insight to *Australopithecus,* and the trend ever since has been toward more and more abstract concepts. The concept of shape in addition to cutting edge developed perhaps 350,000 years ago with the making of hand axes like those found at Torralba, while in the Levallois technique, as established some 150,000 years ago (see Chapter 9), humans not only pictured the desired shape in their mind but actually predetermined it, by trimming the stone beforehand in such a way that the shape would come into being all at once with the final striking off of the flake.

Investigators disagree on many points in the above timetable, some believing that language came much later and never had a gesture stage. But they all agree that something very special was happening about 50,000 years ago, when social forces not yet clearly specified started shaping modern-type human beings. One important fore-shadowing of things to come appears in the archeological record, the graves which the Neanderthals dug for their dead, and the memorial objects they placed in the graves. Chunks of meat, presumably left for nourishment during the trip to another world, ibex horns, and bear skulls arranged in patterns at some gravesides were symbols of imag-ined worlds, worlds conceived but invisible.

The burials represent the first hints of a revolution on the way, the explosion of symbols that gathered rapidly increasing momentum with the emergence of full-fledged modern Cro-Magnon people 40,000 years ago. The following millennia saw an enormous increase in the variety of tools, marks of new and more complex purposes, including tools such as the Solutrean laurel-leaf blades which were nonusable symbols (see Chapter 10). The number and size of sites also increased, and, above all, the world's earliest known art appeared in the form of paintings and engravings on the walls of caves.

The evidence is intriguing in itself, and the implications are even more so. We can only guess at the linguistic significance of these devel-opments. Bordes speaks of "an ability to separate the shape from the object shaped . . . reproduction of a real shape, taken from the outside world and transferred into two dimensions to a flat surface." The art-ist's depiction of shapes may signify a new ability to make images and to picture or imagine things, fictitious as well as real; language would be richer in symbols, theories, similes, and metaphors. It is interesting to note that the fossil record suggests that the brains of Cro-Magnon people were somewhat smaller than the brains of their Neanderthal an-cestors. If so, perhaps new grammatical rules evolved which put less of a premium on sheer number of nerve cells and sheer memory capacity, and more of a premium on imagination and association—a possibility indicated by an apparent increase in the size of the front parts of Cro-Magnon brains, the regions involved in abstract thought.

In any case there seems to be a good argument for the general point that our sort of language represents a refinement of the Neander-thal sort. It arose during the period which saw population increases, larger settlements and confederations, mass cooperation for mass killing

in the hunt, burials, cave paintings, advanced ceremonies, and kinship
systems. The continuing rise in social complexity and the continuing pileup of words almost certainly favored the further development of grammatical rules.

According to a theory proposed by David McNeill of the University of Michigan, there may simply have been too much to remember. For example, every form of every verb may once have been a distinct word; at one time people may have had completely different words for *he is running, he was running, he will be running,* and so on. Learning such a language might take at least twice as long as learning a modern language with its rules for the use of auxiliary verbs and special endings. McNeill believes that modern children learn so rapidly because prehistoric children invented rules which their own children acquired by the usual process of inference. So perhaps, like the new artificial languages man is devising to communicate with electronic computers, natural languages began as rather complicated and unwieldy systems and became increasingly easy to learn and use.

Present knowledge, taking account of some recent findings about the behavior of chimpanzees and human children, can carry the story no further. New findings will certainly alter current ideas. What seems central to all arguments is the notion of increasing complexity, of a world becoming steadily richer and wider with the successive phases of hominid evolution, and the rise of increasingly complicated mechanisms to deal with it. To put it in the most direct terms, if objects of significance to ancestral primates in the trees could be numbered in the dozens, hundreds of thousands of natural and man-made objects had special importance for prehistoric *Homo sapiens.* Taking command of the world means classifying the objects and imposing regularities upon them, and language is our most effective way of doing precisely that.

In the last analysis, understanding these and other basic processes depends on understanding the relationships between brain and behavior, the biological basis for language acquisition. Something in the brain, some structure or set of structures, is designed to scan the environment from infancy on and to seek and discover, out of all the hubbub, certain very special kinds of order. Just enough is known about phenomena at the cerebral level and about the organization of cell-to-cell nerve connections to hint at some of the problems that lie ahead.

One of the elementary requirements of learning a language is the ability to associate things seen and things heard, to learn that certain sound patterns or words are the names of objects and persons. Laboratory experience shows that it is very difficult to produce such associations in most lower primates. According to one investigator, "you have to hit them in the guts to accomplish anything," which means that if you want a macaque monkey to associate the word *circle* with the image of a circle, you must subject it to considerable emotional stress. You must punish it for making mistakes by applying an electric shock or some other painful stimulus, or keep it hungry and then reward it with food. And even under such conditions the experiment may not succeed.

Anatomy suggests one of the most important reasons for the difficulty. A certain visual area on the surface of the monkey's brain, on the sheet of nerve cells forming the cortex, is concerned with the shaping of images; another auditory area is concerned with patterns of sounds. Learning to associate an image and a sound is primarily a matter of establishing communications between the two areas. But it happens that there are very few direct connections from one to the other.

The main pathways in the macaque brain take an indirect course. They include nerve fibers running down beneath the auditory area on the cortical surface to nerve structures which appeared relatively early in evolution and are involved in emotional and biological needs. The fibers then make connections with other fibers ascending from these structures to the visual area at the surface. Many problems encountered in the laboratory arise because such roundabout routes are involved in efforts to train monkeys to associate complex sounds and images.

The situation in people is entirely different. The human brain includes a rich system of direct routes, fibers within the cortex itself which by-pass the depths and connect not only visual and auditory areas to one another but also both these areas to a similar area concerned with the feel and texture of things. In fact, the fibers are so numerous that a special switching station, a superassociation structure, has appeared during the course of hominid evolution. It is somewhat bigger than a half-dollar piece and occupies a strategic position on the side of the cortex, just behind the temple, at the junction of the three areas.

Medical research indicates that this structure may be involved in the development of language. According to Norman Geschwind of the Harvard Medical School, it plays a major role in the formation of connections which enable children to associate the image and the feel of a teddy bear with the sound pattern for the words *teddy bear*. Injury to the center later in life may produce strange disorders of language, the result of difficulties in establishing connections between things heard and things seen. For example, a patient may have only minor difficulties in speaking, but he or she may lose the ability to read or write. Recently Geschwind and Marjorie LeMay, also of the Harvard Medical School, reported that among right-handed persons, nerve centers in the left-hand side of the brain, regions long known as major language centers, generally tend to be larger than corresponding regions in the right-hand side of the brain—a difference which may be related to an increase in the size of the superassociation structure.

The anatomy of this structure helps account for something we know from observations of behavior. The calls of lower primates are bound to emotion, occurring almost invariably in response to immediate satisfactions and dissatisfactions, a fact which makes sense considering the strong links that connect their visual and auditory areas to underlying nerve centers concerned with emotion. On the other hand, since such links are much weaker in the human brain, we are capable of a certain detachment and can even upon occasion communicate dispassionately. By the way, although the superassociation structure is absent or exists in only very rudimentary form in monkeys, it may be somewhat better developed in the chimpanzee, which helps explain the talents of Washoe and Sarah.

Here is an example, however hypothetical it may be at the current stage of human ignorance, of what it means to know. The point is not that we have an answer or a partial answer to our problems. Geschwind's ideas will surely have to be revised or they may well be discarded within a few years; but the approach, the fundamental nature of the search, is meaningful and appropriate. Sooner or later things must be confronted at the biological level; we must seek explanations in the behavior and organization of nerve cells.

We do not really *know* unless we *know* anatomically and physiologically, and in most cases even conceiving plausible models is enough of a problem. How would one design a brain so that it automatically classifies things? The information received through sense organs passes into some kind of sorting structure, some system of precisely interconnected nerve cells or molecules within cells. It must be categorized, arranged in hierarchies of classes, subclasses, subdivisions of subclasses, and so on. The information is stored in retrievable form so that answers can be given, usually in short order, to questions like Have you ever eaten at the Golden Horn? and Do you know an elderly carpenter named Jim? The anatomy of grammar will be better under-

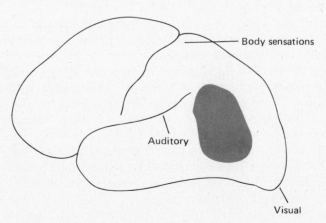

The "superassociation" center, a brain area believed to be involved in language acquisition

Body sensations

Auditory

Visual

stood when we learn how the brain cross-indexes its remembrances of **393** things past.

In general, it seems that the mechanisms involved are not primarily a matter of brain size. Size is important if only to provide sufficient storage space, and the elephant's famous long memory is related to the massiveness of its cerebral hemispheres. But language may be acquired with surprisingly little nervous tissue. There are dwarfs with perfectly proportioned bodies scaled down to a height of 2½ feet or so, and their brains weigh only some 14 ounces, the weight of the chimpanzee brain and about a third of the weight of the average human brain. They are mentally retarded, but they speak fluently. Their undersized brains still retain intact the uniquely human mechanisms which embody the capacity for language and probably arose early in hominid evolution.

These mechanisms have certain built-in biases, as indicated by the observation that all children acquire certain habits of using words. For example, Joseph Greenberg of Stanford University points out that in all languages studied to date the word for *good* appears more often than the word for bad. (In English, *good* appears five times more often than its opposite.) The phenomenon may reflect at the linguistic level our tendencies to expect the best and to start by approaching things rather than turning away. But what are we to make of the fact that *long* occurs far more frequently than *short?* and similarly that *many*, *deep*, and *wide* occur far more frequently than *few, shallow,* and *narrow?*

Also, it may be significant that some rules of grammar are learned later than others. The fact that proper use of the verb *promise* does not generally come until the age of 9 or so may imply a later appearance in the language itself of the complete notion of promising— and that, in turn, may imply something about the nature and sequence of evolutionary events. The order in which individuals learn rules of grammar may reflect the order in which the species encountered and dealt with various social problems.

Perhaps language is full of such relics, clues to prehistoric experiences and ways of thinking. Perhaps language, like the brain itself, is a thing of many coexisting structures which are inherited from times past and can provide insights into our remote heritage. The past has not vanished or been discarded in the continuing process of becoming human.

Behavior patterns in rhesus monkeys and children; first-grade hierarchies and children at play; the evolution of play as practice for real-life situations; play as discovery and research; play and the origins of art; war, the most human form of hunting; evolution and mental disease; Freud's concern with primate behavior; the male-male bond; the new study of humans

CHAPTER 20   STUDY OF HUMANS: POWER OF THE PAST AND POTENTIAL FOR CHANGE

Everything that is being learned about human evolution points to the power of the past. Patterns of behavior developed in prehistoric times and in the process of adapting to conditions that prevailed hundreds of thousands of years ago continue to influence current behavior. We may respond prehistorically to present-day situations, thinking and acting in flashbacks, as it were, living upon occasion in a world that has vanished long since. We may at times turn back to a dreamtime of a sort, attempting to understand and handle contemporary problems as if we were still small-band members of a wild species at large in a wilderness.

The modern scene, in other words, provides abundant examples of premodern behavior and of basic and revealing insights into prehistory. There is a great deal to be learned not only from chimpanzees, the most human of nonhuman primates, and from hunter-gatherers in the Kalahari and Australia, but also from those living far from wildernesses in the spreading urban centers of industrial societies, in highrise apartments, squatters' settlements, and suburban homes. Primitive behavior that has ancient roots and may, therefore, suggest how human beings coped with ancient environments is widespread among all present-day peoples.

New information about the past is coming from studies in human ethology, the application to human beings of techniques developed by Niko Tinbergen and other zoologists for the observation and interpretation of behavior patterns among birds, fish, and other species. More and more investigators are watching children and adults go about their daily business at work and play in schools, offices, and churches. Perhaps stimulated by the presence of rising populations, by a future that is no longer quite as limitless as it once appeared to be, they are taking an especially hard look at the human species.

In studying children, for example, they are using the same kind   **394** of approach that Stuart Altmann used in his research on rhesus monkeys (see Chapter 14). Altmann compiled a list of more than 120 behavior elements for the monkeys, such as "gnashes teeth" and "holds tail erect"; similar lists for children generally involve 125 to 150 separate items, although many more could probably be identified. William McGrew of the University of Edinburgh has observed striking similarities between play groups of human and nonhuman primates. He reports practically identical "flashing" or eyebrow raising and other common elements such as "play face," "play crouch," "gaze fixate," "kiss," "stamp," "beat," "hug," and so on: "I would estimate that at least 80 percent of the behavior patterns we have defined for nursery-school children have counterparts in nonhuman primates."

Similarities are also found in more elaborate activities. In many ways children's rough-and-tumble play is identical to the play of other primates. There are chases, flights, and wrestling, all typically preceded by a kind of I-dare-you posture and expression. A child about to be chased often stands side-on to the prospective chaser, slightly crouched and with a mischievous play face resembling the play face of the macaque monkey or chimpanzee under comparable circumstances; they display an open-mouthed smile with the teeth hidden. Another characteristic pattern, jumping up and down on both feet, is reminiscent of the baboon's hopping gait in mock fights. There is also an open-hand beating movement, without actually hitting, an overhand movement very much like that used in throwing a ball or spear. Incidentally, boys tend to play harder and rougher than girls, a difference noted among baboons and other primates (see Chapter 12).

The patterns for fighting, including frowning, a cold stare, and real blows, are entirely different. In fact, the differences are greater and more clear-cut for children than for the offspring of any other primate. Play fighting has been distinguished in a very special way, isolated and set apart from real hostility, identified by a system of signs so that the chances of misunderstanding are reduced to a minimum, which has a double implication for what apparently happened in the remote past. Hostility became especially dangerous and lethal in a species that wielded rocks and clubs and hurled missiles. At the same time play acquired an extra importance not only as practice for real-life fights and escapes, but also in developing social competence and perhaps a mastery of language.

Spontaneous social organization starts relatively young. In a study of more than 400 school children, Donald Omark and Murray Edelman of the University of Chicago found the first signs of hierarchies emerging in the first grade, around the age of 7, "with boys being placed near the top, girls near the bottom, and considerable overlap in the middle." There were other interesting sexual differences. Boys formed larger groups, generally at some distance from their teach-

Play-fighting face,
open mouth and
sparkling eyes

Real hostility: human
primate

ers and other adults, and were more competitive and aggressive; girls "talked quietly in groups of twos and threes," generally closer to their teachers. Furthermore, when discussing their positions in hierarchies, boys tended to overrate themselves, exaggerating their true rank more than girls.

Real hostility: non-human primate

Most of these and other classroom observations are consistent
with observations in the wild among nonhuman primates, as well as
among hunter-gatherer bands in the Kalahari. Hierarchies and certain
male-female differences apparently have ancient roots, evolving in times
when survival depended on a sharp division of labor between defense
against predators and caring for the young. Whether the differences, or
the hierarchies, make as much sense today is another question. New information bearing on this problem may be expected from research still
under way, including research by Blurton Jones. Trained by Tinbergen,
Jones pioneered in child studies about a decade ago after observing
fleeing reactions, threat and attack displays, and meeting ceremonies
among chickadees and geese in England and seagulls off the Bering Sea
coast in western Alaska.

His early work included more than a hundred hours spent among
children 3 to 5 years old at a London nursery school. He simply sat on a
chair in a corner, notebook in hand, and began watching: "On your
first visit the children make an enormous fuss about you. They either
stand and stare or run up and give you things, and then go away if **397**

your response is polite but uninvolved. They make a fuss again at the beginning of the second visit, but it does not last as long. It takes about three visits to be completely ignored practically from the start."

Jones and his associates recently completed a project that started in 1972 and involved intensive observations of 60 middle-class first-born children from the age of 15 months on. The information has not yet been analyzed, but everything points toward the importance of the mother in the development of the child's language and relationships with others. For example, Jones points out that when a child presents an object to its mother, the act may have "some social significance over and above the object given, and possibly even independent of the response to the object." Older children commonly do the same thing upon meeting a stranger, and the feeling is that in some ways giving of this kind is a deeply symbolic act of fear and appeasement.

Such work inevitably draws attention to current problems in child-raising, and hints at conditions that may have prevailed in times past. Current practices, as a matter of fact, may clash with prehistory in the sense that they run counter to tendencies evolved long ago. Strains arise from middle-class customs which may work against the child's apparent capacity and perhaps need for wide intimacies, and may tie the mother-child bond too tightly. The child is ready for associations with other individuals, particularly its peers and older brothers and sisters, earlier than most people realize, early in its second year or some two years before nursery school usually starts.

In other words, the child may be prepared for the sort of environment or home setting which existed throughout the main course of human evolution, during the 10 to 15 million years from early hominids and *Australopithecus* to recent times. Children once lived continuously in a world of people close at hand, as individuals in intimate contact with many other individuals, suggesting that, at least in certain basic respects, life in the remotest of human and prehuman times closely resembled life among today's hunter-gatherers and other nonindustrialized peoples. As far as present-day behavior is concerned, some of the pressure of child-mother relationships might be relieved if society were organized to provide more opportunity for the child, and the mother, to form wider associations. Increased freedom of this sort might increase rather than decrease the closeness between mother and child and the stability of the family as a whole.

Sooner or later investigators studying childhood must deal with play, the child's most characteristic, most common, and least understood activity. There are many theories about this highly complex form of behavior, about its role in evolution, particularly in the evolution of mammals, and about its present functions. It has long implied something frivolous and evoked an admonition to grow up and put your toys away. This is the voice of puritanism, which Darwin heard and was influenced by. It still speaks out strongly today. It speaks in the tendency to concentrate, in evolutionary studies of humans and other animals, almost exclusively on feeding, reproduction, and fighting; and to underrate the significance of casual leisure-time activities, all varieties of behavior without immediate relevance to the "important" things of life.

The notion of play can be overextended. Corinne Hutt of the University of Keele in England has observed nursery-school behavior in a test situation. A familiar playroom included both familiar toys, such as a truck and a panda doll, and a brand-new object, a red metal box with four brass legs and a kind of four-position gearshift lever on the top. Under the conditions of one series of experiments, moving the lever operated a bell, a buzzer, and four clicking counters.

Children were set free in the room for six ten-minute sessions, usually two days apart, and their actions at first were decidedly not playful. At first they were afraid. When an adult was in the room with them, the fear did not last long and they approached the red box within 30 seconds or so, generally after asking what it was. But when they were alone they delayed longer and approached more hesitantly, and never approached without bringing a familiar toy along. Boys brought the truck, girls the panda doll. And even then the children did not play.

As might have been predicted, they paid special attention to the new object, spending up to half their time with it, holding the lever in one position, listening to the noise, watching the counters, shifting positions rapidly, and trying to twist it and pull the lever off. Such activity might have passed for play in this study, as has been the case in many other studies, except for the key observation that the children did not seem to be having fun. There was a certain amount of tenseness in the air as they concentrated on the object with intent, earnest attention. The entire pattern of behavior, from the first hesitation on, was clearly serious business.

Novelty is a threat to children as well as to their elders. The fear comes from the remote past, when the sight of a stranger or an unfamiliar object had the impact of a criminal loose on the street or a house on fire. Children and adults may be reacting appropriately for that early world if not for their own. Working against the fear of novelty, however, is the tendency to approach and inspect and above all to remove the mystery and the insecurity. Novelty is also a necessity. It cannot be wished away. It can be assimilated and transformed into the familiar and made part of the environment. It can be built into the scheme of things as a landmark, as something dependable and therefore something that can usually be ignored. All this represents a special need for the human child who is dependent for so long.

Hutt's nursery-school children first hesitated and then investigated, an activity that tapered off rapidly after the third or fourth experimental session, after the red box had lost its mysteries. Now at last they were ready to enjoy themselves. Starting at the second session and reaching a peak at the fifth, their posture and facial expression relaxed, and they spent more and more time treating the box as a familiar thing. In effect, it became a toy for the first time. One boy ran around the room pulling the truck, and every time he passed the lever he shifted it to produce bell-buzzer sounds. He had finished exploring and had turned to play.

Hutt stresses the significance of the shift: "The emphasis changes from the question of 'what does this object do?' to 'what can I do with this object?'" Play is thus active in a creative rather than a purely exploratory way. It is a fragile thing, as fragile as joy itself, which vanishes with the first hint of fear or uncertainty. Play flourishes among familiar objects in a familiar setting, as at savanna feeding grounds where dominant males are nearby and at home bases. Among hominids it has become increasingly associated with pretending and acting and the invention of games, and perhaps of language. Regarding pretending, the boys in Hutt's studies did more of it more elaborately than the girls. She observed 20 out-of-the-ordinary cases of playing with the red box, such as using the gearshift knob as a microphone and crooning into it, and in 16 cases the player was a boy.

We can deduce certain things about the conditions under which play arose in times past. The odds are that little if any play existed on

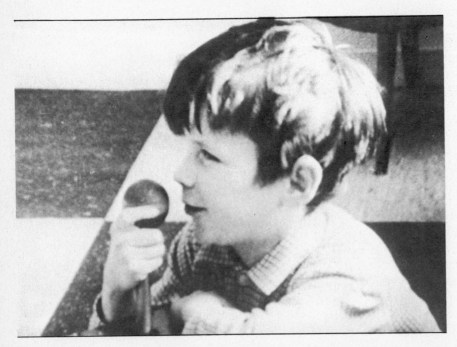

Make believe crooning

earth before the appearance of warm-blooded animals 200 million years ago or more. If dinosaurs were indeed warm-blooded and swift-moving rather than sluggish as commonly believed (see Chapter 1), their young may have wallowed and frolicked on the shores of shallow seas and marshlands. Among today's species, play has never been reported as an important activity in reptiles, fish, insects, or lower species; it seems to be confined to birds and mammals.

There is no easy explanation for this state of affairs. But one factor may be that, generally speaking, warm-blooded animals tend to spend more time and energy feeding and exploiting a wider variety of foods than cold-blooded animals—a difference which, according to Robert Fagen of the University of Illinois, might well favor play as a form of stamina-building scrimmages which prepare for active foraging in the future. Also, play may have prepared individuals to predict one another's behavior and to cooperate. Certainly powerful selective forces must have put a premium on the emergence of play, which had a number of serious disadvantages in the wild and would never have become prominent without important compensating advantages.

Fagen emphasizes that play tends "to put an animal in double jeopardy: First, the animal is penalized for not using its play energy for growth and maintenance, and then it is penalized over and above this effect due to specific risks associated with play." In other words, play uses up energy which might be better spent in satisfying immediate needs, and also creates new dangers. Animals at play lower their guard and may not be on the alert. Absorbed in their make-believe fights and pursuits, they are notoriously vulnerable to the sneak attacks of predators.

To investigate factors favoring the rise of play, Fagen used a computer to help evaluate comparative costs and benefits, simulating the life histories of hypothetical animals devoting various proportions of their time and energy to reproduction, play, feeding, and other activities. Certain results of the computer experiment check with well-known observations. Among simulated as among real-life animals, the young tend to play more than their elders. Furthermore, play appears more frequently among relatively secure species established in stable, predictable environments than among species under stress in the process of trying to adapt to short-lived environments. The cost-benefit analysis also indicated that the amount of time spent playing could vary enormously, not only among different species, but within different populations of the same species, a phenomenon noted in squirrel monkeys, for example, some troops of which play frequently and others not at all.

Other model studies suggest that although play may provide training for real-life situations, such as hunting, fleeing, and establishing social relationships with other individuals, its basic payoff is discovery. Most of what happens most of the time in the relaxed world of make-believe involves activities which are new to the individual but **402** old to the species, tactics, maneuvers, and ideas which have been part of the species' heritage for many many generations.

But now and then something new arises, a new dodging strategem or a new mock alarm call or a new variation in an old game, and some of the things discovered at leisure (perhaps a very small proportion) turn out to have survival value later when the pressure is on, for example, when hominid life demanded more effective communications and the beginning of language (see Chapter 19). In Fagen's words, "play behavior might even be described as extraordinary scientific research performed by animals."

The implication is that the human variety of such basic research, a luxury activity supported most liberally in boom times, has roots in the urges to play, to solve problems, and, upon occasion, to invent problems. There may be an analogous relationship between play and the arts. The element of pretending, of something standing for or symbolizing something else, is prominent in both play and art. So are the elements of surprise, adventure, pleasure, experimentation in the sense of trying out new patterns and contrasts, and uselessness in the sense of not fulfilling any immediate biological function.

In a recent study, Ellen Dissanayake, an art historian from Kandy, Sri Lanka (formerly Ceylon), emphasizes these similarities; she suggests that art arose from play and later went its separate way, acquiring formal and ritualistic qualities in the course of serving social needs. The precursors of art may have been a variety of representations used originally in games—pieces of wood resembling animals and infants, circles and other shapes drawn in the dirt with sticks and fingers, colored clay smeared on faces, on pebbles, and on cave walls.

Art may have been associated with religion from the very beginning. The archeological evidence indicates that religion became an established institution at least 75,000 years ago, some 30,000 years before the first signs of painting, suggesting that the earliest art, like the art of medieval times, may have been sponsored by individuals in charge of memorial ceremonies, burials, and other rituals. Art was probably also involved in teaching, in designing ornaments and marks of social status, and in arousing people to a pitch of excitement for fighting, hunting, and worshiping.

As far as the role of most modern art is concerned, at least the avant-garde variety, Dissanayake has strong reservations. She has reached the unpalatable conclusion ("a conclusion I did not expect to find") that art is no longer a positive force in human evolution, that it may no longer be adaptive and indeed may run counter to social development in existing solely "for the private delectation of the individual." There is a sharp controversy here. Other scholars point out that the same sort of criticism was being leveled a century or so ago at Cezanne and other painters, yet they turned out to have a great deal to say to **403** wide audiences. Art probably continues to serve evolutionary ends. It continues to be a medium of assertion, rebellion, and communication at the social as well as the individual level, as well as a form of exploration and a way to provide continual surprise and novelty.

The search for novelty, in science as well as art, may be a sign that in the human species evolution has taken a new tack. It seems to have produced a new kind of deliberate, long-term instability. It is no longer a matter of adjusting to change and to the variety which the world offers. Apparently an important part of being human is to discover and invent more and more variety. Some day perhaps, when investigators study adults as intensively as they are beginning to study children, they may learn a great deal more about these things. Until then we will have to go mainly by impressions and a minimum of solid data in approaching such basic problems as the source and control of our chronic restlessness. There is no peace for us. Even as we strive to attain stability we upset things anew; our way of striving increasingly involves changing our environments, our social and physical milieus— then we must adapt all over again to new conditions by changing our environments again, and so on, and on.

Life is further complicated by the fact that we have never yet been able to foresee many of the important consequences of the changes we bring about. Thus, we continually try to adapt, and, in the process, we make new adaptations necessary. Changes occur continually as a result of our own activities and of increases in population, knowledge, and the acceleration of the pace and complexity of life. The irony is that in the beginning we were innocent—anything but revolutionaries. We once were, and may still be, basically conservative. But in our relationship to the planet earth, events seem to thwart our conservatism at every turn, as if we and evolution are chronically at odds, even as we move creatively to adapt ourselves.

There is no better example of this tension, this strange quality of the human condition, than the story of fire (see Chapter 7). It all began in a rather straightforward fashion. The first fire users were probably hunters who curled up near red-hot embers on cold nights to keep warm. They wanted no new worlds. They simply wanted to make the world as they knew it more comfortable, and they had no idea of what they were getting themselves and their descendants into. They could not begin to know the consequences of their invention.

They could not know that fire would bring light as well as heat, creating a new and longer day whereby people could gather in bright glowing places after sunset and talk to one another, looking back at yesterday and forward to tomorrow. Nor could they know that fire would bring pain and fear; would be used more and more over the millennia to drive other animals out of their lairs and caves and into a variety of deathtraps; would bring wonder at the flickering of shadows, visions among the shadows, and intimations of spirits, demons, and other worlds. In short, the first fire users could not know that the simple act of bringing warmth into their camps would play a leading role in transforming their lives radically and irrevocably.

The same forces continue to operate in our times, only far more swiftly. We move to forestall death, to save the lives of a greater and greater proportion of our young, to confront in all its stark ramifications the prospect of exploding populations and a hungry and overcrowded world. The effort to decrease suffering increases the threat of suffering on a wider scale than ever before; the rise of larger and larger communities, in part the result of saving lives, creates new tensions, as it did in the past among hunter-gatherers and sometimes among nonhuman primates.

Charles Southwick at Johns Hopkins University reports that the chief problem among rhesus monkeys of northern India is crowding. Encounters among the monkeys are particularly vicious in and near Hindu temples, where they occupy the same sort of position as pigeons do around churches and other buildings in American cities. (A similar phenomenon is observed among human beings.) The monkeys are fed by local people and treated somewhat as pets; they multiply freely and produce larger and much more aggressive troops than those found in the forests. Fighting breaks out more often, not only within the ranks but among entire troops. There are dominant and subordinate troops, hierarchies of hierarchies, whose positions are usually determined by the number of members. Subordinate troops always retreat when they see a higher-ranking troop approaching.

But not infrequently, perhaps once every three or four days, sudden encounters take place. A subordinate troop may be so absorbed in its feeding that it fails to notice the approach of a dominant troop, and then violence flares up. Adult males generally begin the fighting, but females and juveniles also join in. According to the Johns Hopkins investigator, temple monkeys are particularly vicious aggressors: "These fights were ferocious and dangerous . . . often resulting in severe wounds, and most adult males bore wound scars around the face, shoulders, or rump. Wounded individuals were fewer among the rhesus monkeys in rural habitats and forest areas."

Most fights end after only a few minutes with the retreat of the subordinate and smaller troop. Now and then, however, the sides happen to be evenly matched and a pitched battle results, lasting as long as 15 to 20 minutes. On one occasion, part of the top-ranking troop suddenly came upon the entire membership of the number 2 troop. The subordinates seemed to be enjoying a distinct advantage until the rest of the dominant troop, like reinforcements of Federal cavalry in a Western movie, arrived to save the day.

Even though war, like language, is uniquely human, it has roots at the subhuman level. Indeed, the case of the temple monkeys suggests how war may have arisen as an established institution among humans. As long as people lived in the wilderness, the excitement and glamour of the hunt had meaning in the context of survival by promoting aggression against prey and predators. But agriculture and the domestication of animals gradually reduced the importance of hunting; once truly vital work, it became a sport for people with time on their hands. Agriculture also accelerated the growth of populations and cities, bringing more people, and more different kinds of people, closer together than ever before.

Deprived of hunting as a major source of prestige and of wild species as a major focus of aggression, people began playing the most dangerous game of all and began to go after each other, as if their peers were the only creatures clever enough to make hunting really interesting. So war, the cruelest, most elaborate, and most human form of hunting, became one of the most appealing ways of expressing aggression. (War has always been more exciting than peace, robbers more so than cops, hell more so than heaven, Lucifer more so than God.)

Counteracting tendencies are nevertheless at work in the efforts of people to reduce the tensions they create for themselves. When asked why they live in small groups, the Bushmen of the Kalahari reply that they fear fights. Living in small groups is not a possible solution for people who are no longer hunter-gatherers. But something related to it may be observed in urban and suburban communities. An instinctive cutting down of social contacts occurs; in its pathological form this may become a total shutting off and withdrawal from the world, but it normally amounts to behaving continuously as if one is living in a small group. It also recreates the possibility of privacy.

The traditional readiness of people to form and join organizations has become if anything more intense in urban settings. People tend to associate themselves with certain fellow workers at the office and, outside the office, with a widening variety of community and business associations—political groups, hobby clubs, historical societies, and so on. Individuals have roles in many organizations; on their way from one to another, they may pay little attention to their other fellow creatures—one reason for the impersonal atmosphere newcomers feel in cities and for the reluctance of many passersby to come to the aid of strangers in trouble.

The tendency to form social islands in population oceans can be regarded as a kind of provincialism, a throwback to the small-band living and psychology of prehistoric times. It can also be seen as another example of mass pathology. A countertendency exists, however, to form larger and more inclusive organizations at national and international levels. There is no reason to believe that the two tendencies are incompatible.

Local organizations, furthermore, serve to relieve tensions as well as to get things done and to provide some of the trappings of rank and status associated with presidents, vice-presidents, treasurers, and executive committees. They are hierarchies, but hierarchies without the tensions and intensities of the past. Swearing blood brotherhood in secret by the light of the full moon is inappropriate for stamp clubs and groups dedicated to keeping the countryside beautiful. The more archaic qualities of rituals, such things as vigils, ordeals, and fighting for positions in hierarchies, somehow become obvious when people meet to enjoy themselves or to cooperate rather than to compete.

Much human behavior has a strong hereditary bias and tends to be automatic and stereotyped. The power of the past is indicated by what comes easy to us and what comes hard. It is hard to think things through before acting, to develop long-range master plans and abide by them. It is easy to act quickly for quick results on a day-to-day basis.

In many ways we still behave like members of a small-band species with a small-band mentality; we are still creatures wandering in close-knit groups through wildernesses. It is easy to love family and a few friends, hard to love more widely, to care about anyone outside one's immediate circle, and to trust people who look different. To be aroused to quick anger and a fight, even when the arousal works against one's interests, is easy; to become aroused about community projects is hard. We respond too readily to the call of the wild.

People interacting with one another show many of the characteristics found in troops of nonhuman primates. Direct stares, frowns, forward movements of the lips, and other expressions indicate aggression; hunching the shoulders, drawing the chin in toward the chest, closing the eyes, and moving away are among our natural flight reactions. People living together in groups in hospitals, homes, offices, and military units use such signs to establish hierarchies much like those observed among wild baboons, or to form a coalition of two or three individuals which becomes a dominant core or establishment (see Chapter 12).

The fact that we are partly geared to the past is reflected in physiological processes over which we normally have no control. Body temperature falls about 3 degrees Fahrenheit during the course of a night's sleep, reaching a low point at about four in the morning, and begins to climb sharply from then on. Blood pressure follows the same general pattern and so does the concentration in the blood stream of certain adrenal-gland hormones which mobilize natural body fuels. During the last hour or two before awakening, dreaming tends to increase and heart and breathing rates become more irregular.

This entire complex of changes which exists in certain lower primates has been interpreted as an alerting mechanism. Although humans no longer live in open country, sleeping on the ground or in trees or on rocky ledges, the brain, at least those parts of the brain responsible for such reactions, does not know about these changes. Morning after morning we are prepared for events that no longer occur, for responding to emergencies that confronted our ancestors, for the hours before sunrise on the savanna, which represent a period of special danger as far as stalking predators is concerned.

The past is with us also when we wake up and go about the day's business. Unpleasant encounters, frictions, a bitter argument at home, an accident barely avoided while driving, a belittling remark from a superior at the office all produce changes which prepare the body for violent and sudden exertion on the spot—for bursts of anger or fear and for attacks and flight. Many predawn reactions are accentuated; for example, a sharp rise in the output of adrenal hormones produces a corresponding rise in the blood level of fatty substances that can be burned or metabolized rapidly to provide energy for the muscles.

Usually people do not act impulsively because they have learned not to act; certain parts of the brain play an inhibiting role on other parts. But self-control may take a toll in the long run. If excessive fatty substances in the blood are ready for burning and do not burn, in the opinion of David Hamburg of the Stanford University Medical Center, people may suffer as a consequence because while most of the substances are excreted unused, very tiny amounts may accumulate and form deposits on the inner walls of arteries, including the arteries that bring blood to the heart itself. Consequently, as the deposits thicken, the arteries become narrower and narrower, until blood supplies are seriously reduced or cut off entirely, and a heart attack results.

Such attacks are far more common among men since women burn fatty fuels more completely. Possibly, this is because women are brought up to be less ashamed of emoting and hence tend to release tensions more openly and directly. In a sense they live more in harmony with their metabolism and their inherited physiology. Probably, men emote less readily and are called on more often to disguise their feelings. They often encounter situations demanding inhibition, so they seethe inside, smile, and delay the settling of accounts. Vital statistics suggest that the woman's way may be healthier than the man's; she lives seven to eight years longer than he does.

Evolutionary factors may also be partly responsible for a number of other diseases that come increasingly after middle age. The body's immunity system reflects the notion that in the remote past people too old for hunting, fighting, and reproducing played minor roles at best in society. Active participation after the age of 40 or 50 is a relatively new phenomenon, and the body has not caught up with the times. It is precisely during this period that the immunity system, which not only combats bacteria and viruses but may also destroy abnormal cells, begins to go into a decline.

This amounts to a lowering of the guard. One result may be increasing vulnerability to a variety of infections which were held in check during earlier years, to cancer and other conditions involving uncontrolled cell growth. Robert Good of the Sloan-Kettering Institute in New York comments: "After all, nature is not basically interested in individuals who have passed the age of maximum reproductive efficiency. The coming of language and brains capable of intricate learning and long memories, factors that helped make old people important as bearers of tradition, is a very recent development in evolution."

Mental illness may also involve evolutionary throwbacks, behavior patterns more appropriate to prehistoric times than to the contemporary scene. Primate studies indicate that the shift from forests to savannas, the same move that presumably brought about an increase in meat eating and hunting, was accompanied by a shift from the relaxed and loosely organized hierarchies characteristic of chimpanzees to a more rigid hierarchy like that of baboons. The change was a matter of survival. Individuals can go about alone or in twos or threes in the forests, but not in open country, the hunting grounds of lions, wild dogs, and other predators.

Evolution favored bands made up of individuals who knew their places and behaved accordingly. John Price of the Maudsley Hospital Institute of Psychiatry in London believes that mental disease originally appeared in early human hierarchies, and that many present-day patients behave as if they were still living in such a context. For instance, certain disorders may have been associated with low-ranking members of the hierarchy who fitted into the scheme of things because they were predisposed to be sensitive to and expect trouble, and who adjusted by responding with apprehension, appeasement gestures, and withdrawal.

Price suggests that the first cases of anxiety neurosis and schizophrenia were diseases of humility, arising among subordinate individuals subjected to unusually severe stress, perhaps during periods of food shortage or overcrowding. Dominant individuals, on the other hand, would have been vulnerable to other conditions; endowed not only with physical strength and fighting ability but also with a suitable temperament, in readiness to fight and a capacity for impatience and anger, they suffered from diseases of arrogance—megalomania, delusions of grandeur, and abnormally aggressive behavior. Depressive states could have arisen among individuals losing caste and on the way down in hierarchies, manic states among individuals on the way up. Our current disorders may be reversions to such behavior under stress, reenactments of conflicts in prehistoric hierarchies.

There are two important things about this theory. In the first place, it is a theory thoroughly in line with and in spirit with recent research findings. It has an evolutionary perspective, takes account of what has been learned about primates, and is based as far as possible on direct observation in the wild and in the clinic. In the second place, it can be tested. If the theory is sound, patients should benefit from any measure which works against the formation of hierarchies, thus reducing rivalries among them.

According to Price, one measure might be a no-nonsense approach involving clearly specified and strictly enforced rules and regulations in mental wards: "The allocation of beds, places at meals, and ward chores . . . should be seen to be rigid, immutable and insusceptible to influence by any behavior on the part of the patients or their relatives. All social activities would be controlled by the staff, and no opportunity allowed for jockeying for position." He and his associates are planning to investigate the beneficial effects, if any, of this approach and others calculated to discourage competition and dominant or submissive behavior.

Another interesting development in research on mental illness comes from Christopher Brannigan of the Department of Psychiatry at the University of Birmingham in England and David Humphries of the University of Aston in Birmingham. They report an episode that occurred during a group therapy session in which one patient's homosexuality was being discussed. At the uttering of the word *homosexual*, another patient, Mr. X, responded with an involuntary gesture, a characteristic movement in which he placed his hand on the back of his neck. The gesture was a message, and the British investigators were prepared to read it because they had conducted studies of child behavior which, like those described earlier in this chapter, were based on detailed observations of gestures and expressions.

They had observed 136 separate elements including 42 hand-arm gestures, 17 eyebrow patterns, and 7 types of smile. The hand-to-neck gesture of Mr. X made sense in the context of this silent language and its special vocabulary. It is related to gestures of preschool children who are preparing for fights and who raise their hands to a ready-to-strike position, assuming a so-called beating posture. As children grow older, usually starting at about the age of 5, they begin to modify this reaction; they are learning other ways of settling disputes, mainly exchanging well-chosen words instead of blows. But often they are unable to prevent early patterns entirely. At the start of trouble, the hand goes up by instinct; then, as controls take over, instead of moving forward for a blow, the hand retreats and hides as it were, ending up concealed at the back of the neck.

The gesture in childhood is a sign in disguise, something like a message written in code. It can express hostility, feelings of being threatened, and a readiness to fight if necessary, and it is carried over into adult life. For Mr. X the word *homosexual* uttered in an open group discussion represented the threat of being discovered, and it came out later that he had strong homosexual tendencies. So the child appears in the adult, and the species appears in the child. The case of Mr. X is not **410** only part of the history of an individual; it is also part of human history, since the hand-to-neck gesture is a pattern developed in remote times when words were just becoming a serious alternative to violence.

There are many other basic gestures of this kind, most of them yet to be interpreted with any degree of precision, and all of them making up the elements of an evolutionary sign language. The ability to read this language will advance our understanding, not only of emotionally disturbed persons, but also of the forces that shaped prehistoric people and made them vulnerable to new varieties of mental disease. Other behavior patterns generally thought to be solely abnormal states with no particular evolutionary significance may also reflect prehistoric ways of life. One recent study suggests that epilepsy or something very much like it may once have served a useful purpose in human survival—if one can judge by the results of animal research.

Michael Chance, head of the University of Birmingham's Subdepartment of Ethology, who has conducted a special investigation of epilepsy in humans and other species, points out that in many cases it can be better understood in terms of the prehistoric past. For example, laboratory tests show that certain strains of deer mice inherit a tendency to have violent epileptic seizures upon hearing sudden loud noises. The reaction is clear-cut, swift, and dramatic. Typically, an individual runs and crouches alternately, then lapses into a running fit, during which it runs blind and collides with anything lying in its path; then it attacks cage mates and inanimate objects, sinking its teeth in and holding on; finally it collapses, stopping dead in its tracks and going rigid all over. The entire reaction generally lasts only a minute or so.

This behavior appears to have nothing to do with survival mechanisms when observed among caged animals; investigators have usually dismissed it as the result of an undesirable mutation. But it makes more sense when one considers the behavior of deer mice in the wild. They do not make burrows. They live on the surface in sparsely wooded country where at any moment they may encounter a predator out in the open. Under such circumstances, chances for survival would be increased by a pattern of automatic flight, vicious fighting if flight fails, and, if fighting fails, freezing or playing dead. So epilepsy among hypersensitive deer mice, as well as among other animals, seems to be a hereditary and pathological form of normal defensive behavior.

The same principle may apply to human epilepsy. Early people also lived in open country with few places to hide and had to develop a variety of flight tactics. There seems to be a connection between this behavior and an observation of sexual behavior. According to the Kinsey report, about one out of every six preadolescent boys and a small proportion of men occasionally have violent convulsions during or after orgasms, which may reflect the well-known and very ancient association of sexual activities with flight and aggression.

Certain forms of seizure may have acquired special importance by helping to control the flow of fuel to various parts of the body. Brain cells demand liberal supplies of oxygen, and suffer irreparable damage when supplies fall too low. The threat of such emergencies must have arisen frequently 1 to 2 million years ago when the brain was expanding rapidly with the coming of *Homo erectus.* If so, epileptic attacks may have served a protective function by prostrating the body and increasing the flow of oxygen-rich blood to the brain.

In general, the more that is learned about human behavior, the more patterns seem to be rooted in prehistory. A growing concern with such problems is one of the reasons for the relatively generous if somewhat belated support of long-term primate research. In fact, some of the most prevalent notions about the underlying causes of human behavior, human drives and impulses, might have been considerably different if such research had been carried out half a century or so ago. Robin Fox of Rutgers University points out that Freud recognized what most biologists and few psychoanalysts recognize today, namely, the importance of basing any theory about the origins of human behavior on the behavior of other primates.

Unfortunately, the best sources available to Freud were highly colored and unreliable. The only evidence he had during the early 1900s consisted of second- or third-hand tales about gorillas. Their basic social unit was supposed to include a single dominant male, a number of females, whom the male monopolized, and younger males continually trying to gain access to the females and continually being outfought. Using such material, Freud conceived of a "primal horde," the original human family made up of an all-powerful, jealous, and aggressive Jehovah-like father who maintained a harem and drove his sons out of the household when they became sexual rivals, thus providing the basis for Oedipus and Electra complexes.

Freud, like Darwin, was influenced by the puritanism of his times. His picture of the folks at home, as well as the stories upon which it was based, reflected the attitude that sexual passions, the root of all evil, were animalistic and inherited from devilish subhuman savages. The observations of Schaller and others do not support these notions. Gorilla bands usually contain more than one adult male; the head of the hierarchy may be completely unconcerned when other males copulate with receptive females, even when they are males who have only recently joined the troop; and younger males are not driven off. Aggression of any sort is rare.

Human violence and conflicts cannot be foisted on less-advanced primates. On the other hand, tendencies that exist within primate troops bear on the nature of human problems, and Freud was on the right track in directing attention to the adult male animal. The beginnings of a more intensive study along these lines are evident in the recent work of Lionel Tiger. As indicated in Chapter 7, his is an evolutionary and biological approach, and a very tough-minded approach, to the nature of all-male associations.

Many familiar observations acquire new significance when one begins to regard groups of men in a strictly behavioral context, in the same spirit which guides recent studies of children and wild primates. The basic fact which emerges is that men seek each other out and find pleasure in being together. They engage in a wide variety of activities (all essentially male monopolies) from which women have long been excluded—war, the top councils of organized religion, finance, politics—in addition to their tendency at parties to converse in groups away from the womenfolk.

According to Tiger, men are attracted to one another, and the attraction is as powerful and deep-rooted as that between men and women or between mothers and infants. He suggests that the very pleasure involved in all-male associations, particularly in sports and fighting, is an index to the intensity of the attraction: "An emotional current or perhaps an esthetic excitement adheres to manly militant strength which seems biologically equivalent to the sexual excitement between men and women." In this connection, many ceremonies may play a role in male-male relationships analogous to the role of courtship in male-female relationships—for example, the circumcision rites of the Australian aborigines, initiations into fraternities and secret societies, and, at a somewhat less ritualized and communal level, businessmen's luncheons.

Men are predisposed to associate with men, another way of saying that the tendency has a genetic basis and a long prehistory. It may have arisen very early in hominid evolution, at least judging by certain observations of wild chimpanzees. One of the most remarkable features of chimpanzees' remarkably relaxed and informal life in the trees is the spirit of camaraderie which prevails among top-ranking adult males. Even investigators trained to avoid easy comparisons between apes and humans describe what they observe as friendship.

The biggest and most powerful chimpanzees in a given territory seem to enjoy one another's company, and often travel about together in groups of half a dozen or more individuals. Such behavior probably arose out of necessity; group action had an important selective value when it came to defending the troop in times of emergency. But eventually it may have come to serve some other function as well, perhaps helping to promote and maintain amicable social relations. In any case, the attraction of males for males continues in contemporary forests, even though dangers are few and chimpanzees have little to fear from predators.

As forest dwellers, the earliest hominids in the male line may have been very much like chimpanzees in their readiness to form close associations. Furthermore, developments during the subsequent course of evolution almost certainly worked in a positive way to reinforce the tendency. The existence of a home base where individuals met at the end of the day, a specific site to be protected and defended against all comers, certainly fostered feelings of solidarity among the defenders. Long hunting trips must have had a similar effect, particularly hunting trips that called for camping out overnight away from the home base in unfamiliar and uncertain territories.

Male-male bonds had to be strong, because opposing forces came into play. If the tensions of the human condition emerged in the shift from forests to savannas, as suggested in Chapter 13, the shift affected males in particular. Irven DeVore and others have observed that things may be anything but relaxed among highly organized primates of the savanna. Dominant male baboons, like male chimpanzees, associate with one another upon occasion. When trouble appears, they come together to form a formidable wall between would-be predators and the rest of the troop; in peaceful times, they are close at hand as part of the core group that includes females with infants.

Adult male baboons may act together, but they do not become friends. Most encounters involve mild but firm assertions, tensions, and latent threats in which the dominant male expects and receives standard gestures of appeasement, almost as if he were deliberately reminding lower-ranking males of the way things are. There is little real warmth or affection, even among members of the central hierarchy or establishment who may join forces to keep stronger individuals in subordinate roles. At best, adult males tolerate one another with a cool and restrained politeness. They do not seek one another out.

Life in the open may have produced a similar tendency among forest-dwelling hominid males. When they moved into savannas on a full-time basis, their natural warmth must have been somewhat tempered by a guarded tension which, like that found among male baboons, involved elements of fear and aggression. The savanna subjected them to a special strain, bringing threats from new predators and demanding a higher degree of alertness. One result may have been a divisive tendency: if trouble is sought and prepared for long enough, it may be found—if not from the outside, then within the ranks.

In all areas a realistic picture of human behavior is only beginning to emerge, and, as indicated in Chapter 12, nothing discovered to date is more remarkable than our long resistance to such studies. The resistance has been so intense and so effective that it must have been of special value to the species, serving some vital adaptive need. Perhaps it was a matter of survival for early people to feel supremely confident and all-powerful, especially when the wilderness seemed most alien and daily routines most futile. Feelings of superiority are not easy to maintain in the face of too much self-knowledge.

In any case, if insight once threatened our security, today ignorance is an even greater threat. More than 90 percent of current knowledge about primate behavior has come during the past decade, and a great deal remains to be discovered. Considering our biases and our deep-rooted tensions and instabilities, one can no longer be quite so confident about the future of humanity as was the fashion before our most recent world war. The new study of humans starts off with a new realism. It avoids the unwholesome spirit that causes us to speak of black Americans as one-third middle class instead of two-thirds impoverished and that impels us to put rouge on the faces of corpses and to suggest that the effects of atomic radiation be measured in "sunshine units."

People are beginning to be watched as they have never been watched before; the elements of their behavior are being noted and the repeated patterns are being analyzed from an evolutionary standpoint. Among those conducting such investigations is Woodrow Denham, who has shifted his attention to human primates after watching the nonhuman variety (see Chapter 12). He observed some 260 aborigines as they went about their business in the desert of central Australia, sitting on top of his Land Rover and recording what he saw in a special shorthand code. The code for an event, for example, 28 34 189 321 631 617 1137 284, would be translated as follows: Event 28 takes place in residence number 34 where individual number 189 makes (321) a fire (631) out of small branches (617) at 11:37 A.M. (1137) on 11 March 1972 (day 284 of the project). This event was one of 50 noted during one 16-minute recording session, and Denham's project involved about 200 hours of watching. All that information has been transferred to the magnetic-tape memory of a computer, a grand total of 41,800 events plus birth, death, and marriage statistics, genealogies, kinship data, weather records, and other details.

So far Denham has asked only a few questions of the computer, but there are already indications of what might be expected from more extensive studies yet to come. Already preliminary analyses have yielded such interesting information as the following: male infants are carried about more than female infants, more than seven times as frequently among 3-year-olds, while females do practically all the carrying; aboriginal infants tend to be carried in front to start with, and as they grow older in other positions, generally on the back, a shift also observed among monkeys, apes, and also among human beings observed in public places in Washington, D.C. Also common to human and many nonhuman primates is a distinctive class of young unmarried males, sexually mature and socially immature, highly mobile, and trying to find places for themselves in the group.

Along these lines, there will be further studies of human beings **415** in schools, offices, homes, and churches as well as in deserts; and also studies of nonhuman primates and other animals. An enormous amount of raw data remains to be gathered. Accumulating masses of detail demands intense concentration and attention falters after half an hour or so of observing and recording without a break. Like all research designed to get at fundamentals, such work is tedious most of the time; the real work of sophisticated analysis starts only after information has been painstakingly coded and entered into computer memory. The results, however, should be exciting and revealing. The search is for nothing less than basic patterns of human behavior seen in broad evolutionary perspective—fresh insights into our origins and guidelines for the future.

The probability that species outside the solar system confront problems like those of humans; the symbiosis between people and computers; computers as devices that speed the pace of evolution; the interaction of people and environment, an experiment in violence; an urban environment to meet the need for close human contact; the limited value of hierarchies in the modern world; conditions promoting aggression in young people; the future of home and family

EPILOGUE OUR FUTURE AS FORMER HUNTERS IN A WORLD WITH NO PLACE FOR HUNTERS

The problem of the future is whether there will be a future fit for human beings to live in. The question arises now after some 15 million years of evolution in the hominid line, after the transformation of a clever ape into a creature with unprecedented and increasing powers to create and to destroy. The crisis humans face is the first of its kind on earth, the first involving the entire species. As the only remaining members of the human family, we may or may not survive. The issue will almost certainly be decided within the next hundred years.

There will be a future if people can avoid nuclear warfare for that long. If they are sufficiently impressed by the sheer horror and impracticality of the "ultimate solution" they will probably survive to create and surmount other crises, and human evolution will probably continue for millions of years on earth and other planets. If they do not avoid nuclear warfare, they can expect extinction and not the swift and sudden "big bang" sort. Such an ending would amount to mercy killing, and we dare not count on that. It would probably be a slow process, the fading of a species that had lost will and purpose and the capacity for caring.

In the last analysis, one's notions about what will actually take place must rest on a personal and essentially aesthetic basis. No precedent exists for the human situation, that is, no known precedent. Looking at the problem from a wider point of view, however, there is good reason to suspect that ours is not the first species to find itself facing such a crisis. The Milky Way is one of many islands or galaxies in the universe, a concentration of some hundred billion stars, and practically every one of them is a solar system complete with central sun and set of planets. It would be a miracle if life had arisen only on the planet earth, if evolution were not taking place in billions of solar systems.

There is good reason to believe that the universe contains planets in various stages of development—planets forever barren because con-   **416** ditions are not right for life of any sort, planets so young (say, half a billion to a billion years old) that life has not yet appeared, planets with species just starting to make nuclear weapons and nuclear power plants. On slightly more advanced planets, species may have recently formed stable world governments and be well on the way toward tapping unlimited sources of thermonuclear energy, establishing permanent settlements on other planets, communicating with creatures in other solar systems, and accomplishing other feats that we may yet accomplish. Planets may also exist which have had their all-out nuclear wars and have passed out of the community of civilized worlds.

There are a great many possible universes, and a universe of evolution everywhere, of survival of the fittest on a cosmic scale, may not be the real one. But it is a probable universe, sufficiently probable so that those convinced of the complete uniqueness of what is going on here must bear the burden of the argument. The notion that the human species will be among the survivors may turn out to be unduly optimistic, since there may be a tendency for new civilizations to destroy themselves. In that case, our consolation will have to be that others probably survived before us and will survive after us.

Assuming that human beings do not succeed in bringing about their own destruction, they will certainly be involved in changes more radical than any which have occurred in times past. And of all inventions, the one that hints most strongly at the spirit of things to come is the large-scale electronic computer. This machine has the feel of the future about it, marking an area where evolutionary forces are active and change seems to be particularly intense. It represents a taking-off point, a new direction in the human journey, and its effects promise to be as far-reaching and unpredictable as those of fire.

As a matter of fact, it is the fire story all over again, the sort of story that opens uneventfully, almost in a humdrum manner, and then, slowly at first and later at an accelerating pace, takes on the aspect of a major evolutionary adventure. The first electronic computer was not intended to blaze any trails, and was not regarded as a bold experiment. A development of World War II, it was known as ENIAC (Electronic Numerical Integrator and Computer), and it was designed primarily to do something that had been done ever since the invention of guns—to prepare ballistics tables indicating the trajectories of shells for different elevations, wind directions, and so on. Under peacetime conditions such tables had generally been produced by groups of mathematicians working at hand-operated desk calculators, but the war brought a serious shortage of mathematicians and the only alternative was to turn to automatic methods.

Today's computers are far more than devices for handling routine problems. A new relationship is being formed between people and machines, a relationship amounting to a kind of organic-inorganic union, a system which may turn out to be rather different from either people or machines. Computers are strong where we are weak, and weak where we are strong. Compared with the human brain, they are puny indeed when it comes to thinking creatively, dealing with novelty, recognizing patterns, discovering and exploring new problems.

On the other hand, they are enormously more efficient at calculating and following elaborate, detailed instructions. The hunting-gathering life did not foster an outstanding ability to do arithmetic. People are sloppy and inaccurate in working with large numbers. They cannot carry out even a moderately difficult series of calculations without making errors. For example, a person using pencil and paper might take about five minutes to multiply 3,696,437,692 times 9,731,991,327 and arrive at the correct answer, 35,973,699,559,339,897,284. The fastest electronic computers can do about 50 million such calculations in a single second, running for weeks on an error-free basis.

With such speeds at their disposal, as well as electronic memories storing tens of millions of words worth of information, investigators can deal with problems which could not have been considered or conceived of in precomputer times, because they would have taken centuries to solve. The computer permits the doing of things that could never have been done before. It promotes basic changes in the nature of research and planning, serving as an accessory of the brain, a thinking aid built specifically to carry out arithmetic and logical operations which the brain cannot carry out by itself.

People are inclined to view the world in terms of chains of events, to see things as simple cause-and-effect sequences, a phenomenon reflected in written sentences. Sentences, as formal items each starting with a capital letter and ending with a period, are symbols or models of a linear approach. This tendency is another example of living partly in the past. Many aspects of the world of prehistoric people were linear. Tasks were generally one-person, one-material tasks. Making scrapers, for example, involved four broad activities in a fixed order: finding a flattish flint nodule, trimming the edges, striking off flakes, and retouching the flakes. Present-day tasks require hundreds of materials, thousands of workers and activities, the putting together of hundreds of thousands of parts. Producing a new-model automobile or airplane, a space vehicle, or a housing development may require tens of thousands of interdependent activities, all of which must be coordinated in flowcharts and master plans.

Problems featuring the interaction of a great many variables are a sign of the times. They may be found everywhere, not only in factories and on production lines but also in projects involving urban renewal, medical care, crime control, and the administration of justice, economic opportunity, and education. The brain alone cannot handle these problems. But the combination of brain and computer can. The computer, instructed to apply special mathematical techniques to the analysis of complex systems, enables things to be seen whole. It happens that so far these techniques have been used widely to deal with business and military projects, and not so widely to deal with matters of public welfare. More attention seems to have been devoted to the mathematics of competition and warfare than to the mathematics of cooperative endeavors.

Computers have been developed to serve human purposes, and their duties have been abundantly publicized. The most impressive are general-purpose machines which do anything they are told to do—anything from calculating payrolls, insurance premiums or the orbits of man-made satellites, to predicting election returns or playing tournament-level chess—depending on the software, or the sets of instructions or programs investigators prepare for it. Computers also make it possible to explore possibilities more thoroughly and more precisely than ever before. How will a river behave if dams of specified dimensions are located at specific points along its course and along the courses of its tributaries? What will be the flight characteristics of a supersonic plane or rocket-powered spaceship built according to certain design principles? What would be the effect of a new housing development on the social and economic life of a community?

Such questions can be investigated by writing out appropriate programs, simulating simplified versions of actual processes on computers—in short by creating mental models of a sort, which amounts to expanding human imagination and amplifying intelligence. A person at a computer terminal, communicating with the machine, is in effect many times more intelligent than a person without a computer at his service. Freshmen sitting at terminals located in classrooms, laboratories, and dormitories are easily solving problems that were far too difficult for seniors to solve in the days before computers, and the same increase in brain power will continue throughout life. The computer, one of the latest and most remarkable products of human evolution, permits individuals and groups to cope with new complexities of their own making. It is thus actively speeding the process of evolution.

Engineers concerned with solid-state problems continue to pack more and more computing and memory capacity into less and less space. In the present state of the art they can incorporate between 5,000 and 10,000 transistors and associated elements into a chip of crystal no bigger than the letter M and about as thick as this page. Using such circuitry it would be possible to put ENIAC, the original electronic computer which occupied about the size of a tennis court, into a shoe box. Hand-held pocket calculators are only a hint of what is to come, signs of a technology still in its infancy. Joel Moses of the Massachusetts Institute of Technology estimates that in 10 to 15 years high-power computers which now cost half a million dollars will cost $500 or less, take

about as much space as a suitcase, come equipped with printers and
television-type screens, and find a place in millions of homes. These
compact information consoles of the future will give people on-the-spot,
living-room access to libraries, games, motion pictures, and a variety of
educational experiences.

The impact of such developments is unfolding everywhere
among us, part of the shape of things to come. As people continue to
multiply, they form larger and larger clusters. All the cities of the
United States, urban places which include more than 140 million
people, or 60 percent of the nation's population, have a combined area
of about 40,000 square miles, less than 2 percent of the total land area.
Meanwhile elaborate networks are growing up within and among population centers. Not long ago, most large-scale computers were islands
where information was processed, each confined chiefly to serving the
needs of a single institution, company, university laboratory, or government bureau. Now the machines are being interconnected with one another by telephone and broadcasting channels, across institutional, city,
state, and national borders.

Their memories, computing capacities, and programs are now in
the process of becoming, in effect, one vast communication system, accessible to people throughout the world. This supernetwork is nothing
less than a social nervous system which, one may hope, will be part of
a one-world trend. In other words, social evolution is taking place out
in the open, before our eyes—except, of course, that we are participants
as well as observers.

So all things, even our most ingenious thinking machines, seem
to be pushing us along, emphasizing the pace and the prevalence of
change, the need to reorganize ourselves in transit as it were, on the
run. We have yet to develop artificial environments as appropriate for
contemporary populations as natural wilderness environments were for
prehistoric hunters and gatherers. But that is our job, and a renewed
search for such environments is under way. It is characterized by increasing efforts to understand people in groups, grownups as well as
children, and to base the design of living and working places on observations of what people do and prefer.

A number of studies indicate the existence of biases that seem to
hold for people in many cultures. For example, Dutch investigators find
that visitors to parks and other public recreation areas tend to concentrate in transition zones where two different kinds of terrain merge—
along seacoasts, the banks of rivers, and the edges of forests. At the
same time they naturally seek out locations providing some cover at
their backs, a cliffside, sand dune, or dense growth of trees, with expanses of open space in front of them.

This tendency is made up of many things—a feeling for freedom
and privacy, a preference for shady spots, and a strong attraction to

panoramas and unobstructed views of distant horizons. One thinks of forest-dwelling hominids or prehominids venturing into the plains and ready to dash back into the trees or of later bands of early hunters living in shelters and caves high on rocky ledges, relatively safe from predators and with a wide view of valleys and grazing animals. Such places offered beauty and security in a world where people were few and bands rarely came across one another.

Today, beauty and security must be sought in artificial settings, practically all developed with other things than beauty and security in mind. People move in environments which often promote tension, anxiety, and conflict as effectively as if they had been designed for that very purpose. Not long ago a special conference was held in Washington, D.C., to consider "the office building as a current-day artifact in our society . . . not only what an office building is but what it could be—what it should be."

One discussion concerned the headquarters of the Central Intelligence Agency, about as unattractively and unimaginatively designed as most government buildings, only a bit more so, being dominated by gray, narrow tunnel-like corridors 400 feet long and generally dismal decor to match. In such a wasteland environment people tended to dress drably and be suspicious of one another, and on at least one occasion fighting broke out in a corridor. The simple expedient of painting walls and doors with brighter colors produced a notable effect. Employees, female employees in particular, soon began wearing more cheerful and colorful clothing, and there was a marked improvement in morale.

Another case cited at the conference concerned an unplanned experiment in violence, a situation involving two school buildings built at the same site for the same group of high-school students. One building was designed according to the notion that young people naturally tend to rip things apart. It incorporated so-called maintenance-free construction consisting of "hard" spaces enclosed in massive bare walls which are easy to keep clean and difficult to destroy. Vandalism was common in this building; extensive repairs were required. The setting, like most institutional settings, was alien to the student and represented an invitation to trouble.

The other building was based on an entirely different notion of human behavior, the notion that people respond positively to places which they feel belong to them and which incorporate some of the elements of a home setting. The building was designed from the beginning with the needs of the students in mind. There were carpets on the floor, as much for warmth as for appearance, large windows, informal comfortable spaces, and there was plenty of light. Students have done very little damage here.

These examples come as no surprise to architects, who have long been sensitive to the impact of environment on behavior and of behavior on environment. They know how often people have painted walls brighter colors, put in large picture windows, and added extra wings in an effort to undo what has already been done, to humanize the inhumanity built into structures. They also know how much a creatively designed setting, house, housing development, or city can help reduce tensions and contribute to a fulfilling life.

In fact, one of the most original preliminary designs for an urban environment grew directly out of a consideration of human needs and the causes of human anxiety. Christopher Alexander of the University of California at Berkeley started from scratch with the notions that cities are meeting places and that the most elementary human need of all is the need for intimate contacts with other individuals. He defines an intimate contact as a situation in which people see one another very often, almost every day, not in offices or public places, but under informal and private conditions.

Contacts of this sort were commoner in prehistoric times and in times not long past. Small farms and villages were commoner, as were homesteads with large families made up of representatives of three or more generations. Contacts were closer then, although we should guard against becoming overly nostalgic since in many cases the contacts were too close and people tended to be ingrown and conservative and to regard all outsiders and outside ideas as alien. But the modern city, for all the opportunities and variety it may offer, produces another form of alienation. Although people may accept or tolerate one another more readily, it is often distant and impersonal.

Alexander approaches the problem directly with a plan for a new kind of made-to-order city, including, within densely populated areas, zones designed to encourage certain living features once provided by village-farm settings. He cites psychiatric studies suggesting that mental illness is especially likely to develop among persons with few intimate contacts or none at all, and that an individual needs at least three or four such contacts. The environment must be organized so that close friends can drop in on one another on the spur of the moment, which means that they should live no more than ten minutes apart. In today's cities, friends or, rather, potential friends usually live half an hour to an hour apart, enough to prevent casual dropping in.

This general requirement leads to certain design requirements. Each house must be located on a through street for automobile traffic, the street being a thousand feet long at the most and connected with a major traffic artery at both ends. Each house must lie within a hundred yards of 27 other houses, and have private bed-living rooms as well as a transparent communal room which opens onto a private garden and can be looked into from the street. Also, the entire residential area must consist of uncluttered countryside and rolling hills.

In all, there are 12 requirements or "geometric considerations"; a residential area that meets them all will include an artificial landscape where hills are constructed so that the highest and steepest may be nearest the theater-shopping-commercial center of the city, and the lowest and flattest are furthest from the center. All roads and houses in the area are underground, providing unbroken expanses of countryside. Each house is located so that while its street-side entrance is buried, its garden-side entrance lies on a hill slope and is wide enough to let in daylight for communal and other rooms.

According to Alexander, planners who start with his objective, namely, to create an urban environment fulfilling our need for one another, will arrive at a design that may differ from this one in details but not in any fundamental way. He is also stressing something even more important, a principle that holds independently of this or that particular plan. Design is no cure-all; it cannot by itself solve problems of mental illness and violence. But it is not arbitrary either. It depends on and is determined to a large extent by human needs.

The fundamental concepts of urban design are bound up with what is known about those needs, and it will change as more is learned. For example, there are no carefully controlled studies to support the notion that every individual needs three or four intimate contacts or, as a matter of fact, to support most notions about the negative and positive aspects of living in large groups. Most knowledge about the effects of living and working spaces consists of impressions and anecdotes like those discussed at the Washington conference on office buildings.

Solid evidence can be obtained from research on behavior. Cities and communities designed today must take account of tendencies and biases shaped during the course of prehistory, a period representing more than 99 percent of humans' time on earth. Until recently this approach has received little more than lip service, partly because architects were preoccupied with other matters and partly because computers and other tools for the analysis of complexity were not widely available. The work of Alexander and others, however, indicates that such an approach will play a larger role in planning and building in the future.

The problem is whether thinking and feeling can evolve accordingly, whether people can design institutions and philosophies as imaginatively as they design machines and structures. There is certainly a need for new designs. Living in a hierarchy is often about as appropriate for modern times as living in a cave. In small savanna-dwelling bands including only a few adult males, the hierarchy was a most effective way of controlling aggression and maintaining order. Dominant individuals were always close at hand to curb fighting and, when necessary, to inflict punishment with a minimum of mayhem. Furthermore, during most of prehistory, each band lived alone and isolated from

other bands most of the time, so that conflicts among competing hierarchies were rare events.

Under certain circumstances the hierarchy is still an effective way of doing business. In fact, studies indicate that the hierarchy is still by far the best way of organizing individuals to deal with situations involving firmly established rules and regulations, where procedures have already been spelled out to the letter and must simply be applied. Hierarchies flourish, along with rituals and rote learning, in settings dedicated to preserving traditions. But a hierarchy is completely ineffective when, as frequently happens in a modern context, there are no precedents and the task is to discover new rules and patterns.

Current demands for dominant and submissive behavior often clash sharply with our purposes. In a troop of baboons, keeping the peace is a matter of establishing subhierarchies within a hierarchy. Males are ranked in order, from the most to the least dominant; but as a rule the lowest-ranking male dominates the highest-ranking female, and naturally the subhierarchy of infants and juveniles is the lowest of all. Human beings are biased to organize things along similar lines, only with a few variations. For example, they tend to keep older and older individuals in the lowest-ranking subhierarchy, prolonging too long the already prolonged period of juvenile dependency.

It is difficult to conceive of a situation better calculated to promote aggression. Schooling tends to work along the same lines, serving to separate students as completely as possible from essential community activities. For many children the word *school* has acquired the same connotations that the word *home* has acquired for many women as a place away from the action, where one is put to be kept busy and out of trouble.

Meanwhile, at home as well as at school, young people learn to want to rise in hierarchies, although most of them will never make it, because there is not much room there. So to some extent we are educating them for frustration and a measure of defeat. Another source of aggravation is the fact that sexual maturity has been coming at an earlier and earlier age. Records from many countries show that young people are reaching puberty three to five years sooner today than they did a century ago, largely the result of improved nutrition. Their unrest is a product of biological as well as social forces.

As regards adapting to such new conditions, we are moving slowly and reluctantly into the future. Changes are under way almost involuntarily, certainly without large-scale, sensitive planning. The human family is evolving into something less and less like the family of any other primate. Its ties are based more on the evolving needs of independent individuals than on strict rules of dominance and submission. The child is obtaining more of what it needs from the outside world, and obtaining it earlier. In line with preschool training programs, for example, educationally underprivileged children 4 and 5 years old are attending classes, and with such promising results that the practice is sure to be extended to all children.

The parent's role will also involve the outside world to a greater extent. The bond between mother and offspring may be as intense as it ever was but, at least after the period of infancy, it demands less and less of her time. This is the latest phase of a development that started perhaps a million or more years ago when the woman assumed major responsibility for gathering plant food, cooking, and keeping the home fires burning, while the able-bodied men were out hunting. Her most important concern was still the infant, but it was not her only major concern as it is for the mother in a chimpanzee or baboon troop.

Today, for the first time, prolonged juvenile dependency need not mean prolonged maternal dependency. The increasing availability of outside services such as preschool training and day nurseries means that mothers can share on a larger scale the responsibility for the care and education of their children. Furthermore, the attitude toward having children is changing and will have to continue to change. Over-crowding once existed somewhere else, in slums and across oceans. Now it is here among us, and its effects can be seen in the dwindling of the wildernesses and villages, in traffic jams on Main Street, in streams clogged with garbage, in the paper cups and beer cans left on river banks.

Under such conditions, and they can be expected to become much worse, birth control ranks with the control of aggression, nuclear weapons, and pollution, as a prerequisite for survival. Unlimited motherhood and unlimited fatherhood cannot be supported quite so whole-heartedly and without serious qualifications. We will be as proud of our children as ever, but considerably less proud of large families. So, for many reasons, women will have more time available earlier in their lives for activities outside the home, associating more with other adults and other people's children.

How will men, the former hunters among us, behave in such a setting? Even today, even during times of violence, there are still signs that all is not well with a number of the more violent manifestations of male-male bonding tendencies. In this connection men seem to be obtaining assistance from an unexpected quarter, from television's engineers, technicians, directors, writers, and performers. We can forgive television most of its offerings, and that is a lot to forgive, if it continues to show and show up some of the most archaic all-male activities.

Seeing is believing, and the eye of the television camera has a way of putting behavior into perspective. Prizefighting, as a regular form of home entertainment, was an early victim of the cold hard camera look; it showed many people things that a few people had been viewing all along—men being battered past the point where they could offer any defense and the passions of the fans themselves. Political conventions have also felt the pressure of television cameras looking on, and there are signs that the delegates' less essential parading and posturing may abate somewhat. Although we cannot yet evaluate the long-range effects of television coverage on war, we can hope.

It is not only research in the social sciences, in prehistory and primate behavior, which puts up a mirror to us. Other developments heighten self-consciousness and self-understanding and indicate more clearly the forces that tend to divide people or bring people together. Most of prehistory has been a record of small bands on the loose, the efforts of a minority species to survive in an alien and mysterious world. Most of history has been a record of a painful but steadily increasing inclusiveness, of letting more and more people into the club of first-class citizens, commoners as well as kings, nonwhites as well as whites, women and children, all minorities, and pseudominorities; human liberation, if you will.

Human evolution proceeds as it has during times past, in an atmosphere of uncertainty and adventure. People are just beginning to explore outer space, the final wilderness, and to see themselves as creatures moving always in response to basic biological forces, as one among many social species. Nothing in the record proves that our kind will become extinct, or that we will endure. Whatever our viewpoint, it is and will continue to be a matter of belief, an act of faith. We shall continue to behave as we are designed to behave, proceeding positively on the assumption that we represent not an ending but a beginning.

The following is a personal bibliography in the sense that it includes only publications of most direct use to me in developing the main ideas of this book. The publications themselves include bibliographies which the reader may consult for a fuller listing.

BIBLIOGRAPHY

PROLOGUE: TECHNIQUES AND PROSPECTS IN THE SEARCH FOR MAN

BATES, MARSTON, AND HUMPHREY, PHILIP S. *The Darwin Reader.* New York: Scribner, 1956.

BEER, GAVIN DE. *Charles Darwin.* Garden City, N.Y.: Doubleday, 1965.

BORDES, FRANÇOIS. *The Old Stone Age.* New York: McGraw-Hill, 1968.

BRAIDWOOD, ROBERT J. *Prehistoric Men.* 8th ed. Glenview, Ill.: Scott, Foresman, 1975.

BUTZER, KARL W. *Environment and Archeology.* 2nd ed. Chicago: Aldine, 1971.

CLARK, J. DESMOND. *The Prehistory of Africa.* New York: Praeger, 1970.

COUTTS, PETER, AND HIGHAM, CHARLES. "The Seasonal Factor in Prehistoric New Zealand." *World Archaeology,* February 1971.

DOBZHANSKY, THEODOSIUS. *Mankind Evolving.* New Haven: Yale University Press, 1962.

GOLDING, WILLIAM. *The Inheritors.* New York: Harcourt Brace Jovanovich, 1962.

GUMERMAN, GEORGE J., AND LYONS, THOMAS R. "Archeological Methodology and Remote Sensing." *Science,* 9 April 1971.

HOWELL, F. CLARK. *Early Man.* 2nd ed. New York: Time-Life Books, 1971.

MAYR, ERNST. *Populations, Species and Evolution.* Cambridge, Mass.: Harvard University Press, 1970.

OAKLEY, KENNETH P. *Man the Tool-Maker.* 6th ed. University of Chicago Press, 1976.

———— *Frameworks for Dating Fossil Man.* Chicago: Aldine, 1964.

OSBORN, HENRY FAIRFIELD. *Men of the Old Stone Age.* 3rd ed. New York: Scribner, 1925.

PFEIFFER, JOHN E. *The Search for Early Man.* New York: American Heritage, 1963.

———— "Man Through Time's Mists." *Saturday Evening Post,* 3 December 1966.

PILBEAM, DAVID. *The Ascent of Man.* New York: Macmillan, 1972.

427

BAKKER, ROBERT T. "Dinosaur Renaissance." *Scientific American,* April 1975.

CALDER, NIGEL. *The Restless Earth.* New York: Viking Press, 1972.

CARTMILL, MATT. "Rethinking Primate Origins." *Science,* 26 April 1974.

CLEMENS, WILLIAM A. "*Purgatorius,* an Early Paromomyid Primate." *Science,* 24 May 1974.

EIMERL, SAREL, AND DEVORE, IRVEN. *The Primates.* New York: Time-Life Books, 1965.

KING, JAMES E., AND FOBES, JAMES L. "Evolutionary Changes in Primate Sensory Capacities." *Journal of Human Evolution.* 3: 435–443 (1974).

KURTEN, BJØRN. "Continental Drift and Evolution." *Scientific American,* March 1969.

MARTIN, R. D. "Towards a New Definition of Primates." *Man,* September 1968.

———. "Ascent of the Primates." *Natural History* 84: 52–61 (1975).

SIMONS, ELWYN L. "The Earliest Apes." *Scientific American,* December 1967.

——— *Primate Evolution—an Introduction to Man's Place in Nature.* New York: Macmillan, 1972.

TUTTLE, RUSSELL H., ed. *Paleoanthropology: Morphology and Paleoecology.* Chicago: Aldine, 1976.

VAN VALEN, LEIGH, AND SLOAN, ROBERT E. "The Earliest Primates." *Science,* 5 November 1965.

2. FIRST MEMBERS OF THE HUMAN FAMILY

BARTHOLOMEW, GEORGE A., AND BIRDSELL, JOSEPH B. "Ecology and the Protohominids." *American Anthropologist,* October 1953.

CONROY, GLENN C., AND PILBEAM, DAVID. "*Ramapithecus:* A Review of Its Hominid Status," in *Paleoanthropology,* Chicago: Aldine, 1976.

FRAYER, DAVID W. "Is *Ramapithecus* a Hominid Ancestor?" in press.

——— "A Reappraisal of *Ramapithecus.*" *Yearbook of Physical Anthropology* 18 (1974).

GOODMAN, MORRIS, TASHIAN, RICHARD E., AND TASHIAN, JEANNE H. "Progress in Molecular Anthropology." *Current Anthropology,* September 1976.

HEWES, GORDON W. "Hominid Bipedalism: Independent Evidence for the Food-Carrying Theory." *Science,* 16 October 1964.

HOCKETT, CHARLES F., AND ASCHER, ROBERT. "The Human Revolution." *Current Anthropology,* June 1964.

JOLLY, CLIFFORD J. "The Seed-Eaters: A New Model of Hominid Differentiation Based on a Baboon Analogy." *Man,* March 1970.

KING, MARY CLAIRE, AND WILSON, A. C. "Evolution at Two Levels in Humans and Chimpanzees." *Science,* 11 April 1975.

KORTLANDT, ADRIAAN. "New Perspectives on Ape and Human Evolution." *Current Anthropology,* December 1974.

LAWICK-GOODALL, JANE VAN. *In the Shadow of Man.* Boston: Houghton Mifflin, 1971.

LEAKEY, L. S. B. "Adventures in the Search for Man." *National Geographic,* January 1963.

———— "An Early Miocene Member of Hominidae." *Nature,* 14 January 1967.

MANN, ALAN. "Hominid and Cultural Origins." *Man,* September 1972.

PFEIFFER, JOHN E. "When Man First Stood Up." *New York Times Magazine,* 11 April 1965.

PILBEAM, DAVID. *The Ascent of Man.* New York: Macmillan, 1972.

———— The Evolution of Man. New York: Funk and Wagnalls, 1970.

SARICH, V. M. "A Molecular Approach to the Question of Human Origins," in *Background for Man.* Boston: Little, Brown, 1971.

SIMONS, ELYWN L. "Some Fallacies in the Study of Hominid Phylogeny." *Science,* 6 September 1963.

———— "On the Mandible of *Ramapithecus.*" *Proceedings of the National Academy of Sciences,* March 1964.

———— "The Early Relatives of Man." *Scientific American,* July 1964.

———— AND ETTEL, PETER C. "Gigantopithecus." *Scientific American,* January 1970.

———— AND PILBEAM, DAVID R. "Hominoid Paleoprimatology," in *The Functional and Evolutionary Biology of Primates.* Chicago: Aldine, 1972.

SIMPSON, GEORGE GAYLORD. "The Biological Nature of Man." *Science,* 22 April 1966.

SZALAY, FREDERICK S. "Hunting-Scavenging Protohominids: A Model for Hominid Origins." *Man,* September 1975.

VERCORS. *You Shall Know Them.* Boston: Little, Brown, 1953.

WASHBURN, SHERWOOD L. *The Study of Human Evolution.* University of Oregon Press, 1968.

———— AND AVIS, VIRGINIA. "Evolution of Human Behavior," in *Behavior and Education.* New Haven: Yale University Press, 1958.

3. THE UNFOLDING STORY OF HUMAN EVOLUTION

BRAIN, C. K. "A Hominid Skull's Revealing Holes." *Natural History* 83 (10):44–45 (1974).

———— "New Finds at the Swartkrans Australopithecine Site," *Nature,* 28 March 1970.

BUTZER, KARL W., et al. "Recent Thinking on Human Evolution." *Current Anthropology,* December 1974.

DART, RAYMOND A. "*Australopithecus africanus:* The Man-Ape of South Africa." *Nature,* 7 February 1925.

———— Adventures with the Missing Link. New York: Viking, 1961.

DAY, M. H., AND LEAKEY, R. "New Evidence of the Genus *Homo* from East Rudolf, Kenya." *American Journal of Physical Anthropology* 41:367–380 (1974).

HAYS, J. D., IMBRIE, JOHN, AND SHACKLETON, N. J. "Variations in the Earth's Orbit: Pacemaker of the Ice Ages." *Science,* 10 December 1976.

HEEZEN, BRUCE C. "The Rift in the Ocean Floor." *Scientific American,* October 1960.

HOWELL, F. CLARK. "Omo Research Expedition." *Nature,* 10 August 1968.

HOWELLS, WILLIAM. "Piltdown Man: His Rise and Fall," in *Mankind in the Making.* New York: Doubleday, 1959, chap. 17.

ISAAC, GLYNN L., LEAKEY, RICHARD E. F., AND BEHRENSMEYER, ANNA K. "Archaeological Traces of Early Hominid Activities East of Lake Rudolf, Kenya." *Science,* 17 September 1971.

JOHANSON, D. J., AND TAIEB, M. "Plio-Pleistocene Hominid Discoveries in Hadar, Ethiopia." *Nature,* 25 March 1976.

KING, GLENN E. "Society and Territory in Human Evolution." *Journal of Human Evolution,* 5:325–332 (1976).

LAWICK-GOODALL, JANE VAN. *In the Shadow of Man.* Boston: Houghton Mifflin, 1971.

LEAKEY, RICHARD. "Man and Sub-Men on Lake Rudolf." *New Scientist,* 56:385–87 (1972).

——— et al. "New Hominid Remains and Early Artefacts from Northern Kenya." *Nature,* 18 April 1970.

PATTERSON, BRYAN, BEHRENSMEYER, ANNA K., AND SILL, WILLIAM D. "Geology and Fauna of a New Pliocene Locality in Northeastern Kenya." *Nature,* 6 June 1970.

——— AND HOWELLS, W. D. "Hominid Humeral Fragment from Early Pleistocene of Northwestern Kenya." *Science,* 7 April 1967.

PILBEAM, DAVID, AND GOULD, STEPHEN JAY. "Size and Scaling in Human Evolution." *Science,* 6 December 1974.

SWEDLUND, ALAN C. "The Use of Ecological Hypotheses in Australopithecine Taxonomy." *American Anthropologist,* September 1974.

TAZIEFF, HAROUN. "The Afar Triangle." *Scientific American,* February 1970.

TOBIAS, P. V. "The Taung Skull Revisited." *Natural History* 83 (10): 38–43 (1974).

WOLPOFF, MILFORD H. "Some Aspects of the Evolution of Early Hominid Sexual Dimorphism." *Current Anthropology,* December 1976.

4. FOSSILS AND TOOLS AS CLUES TO HUMAN BEGINNINGS*

CONNOLLY, KEVIN, AND ELLIOTT, JOHN. "The Evolution and Ontogeny of Hand Function," in *Ethological Studies of Child Behavior.* New York: Cambridge University Press, 1972.

*A special 87-page section in the October 1965 issue of *Current Anthropology* includes articles on the dating of finds at the Olduvai Gorge as well as on the finds themselves, together with comments from investigators throughout the world.

HALL, K. R. L. "Variations in the Ecology of the Chacma Baboon, *Papio Ursinus.*" *Symposia of the Zoological Society of London*, no. 10 (1963).

431

LEAKEY, L. S. B. "Olduvai Gorge." *Scientific American*, January 1954.

———— "Finding the World's Earliest Man." *National Geographic*, September 1960.

———— "Exploring 1,750,000 Years into Man's Past." *National Geographic*, October 1961.

LEAKEY, MARY D. "A Review of the Oldowan Culture from Olduvai Gorge, Tanzania." *Nature*, 30 April 1966.

LOVEJOY, C. OWEN. "A Biomechanical Review of the Locomotor Diversity of Early Hominids," in *African Hominidae of the Plio-Pleistocene*. London: Duckworth, 1976.

NAPIER, JOHN. "Studies of the Hands of Living Primates." *Proceedings of the Zoological Society of London*, September 1960.

———— "The Evolution of the Hand." *Scientific American*, December 1962.

———— "The Antiquity of Human Walking." *Scientific American*, April 1967.

OAKLEY, KENNETH P. "The Piltdown Problem Reconsidered." *Antiquity*, March 1976.

PAYNE, MELVIN M. "Family in Search of Prehistoric Man." *National Geographic*, February 1965.

PEACOCK. D. P. S. "Forged Brick-Stamps from Pevensey." *Antiquity*, June 1973.

PFEIFFER, JOHN E. "Dr. Leakey and His Olduvai Digs." *Think Magazine*, September 1963.

SPETH, JOHN D., AND DAVIS, DAVE. "Seasonal Variability in Early Hominid Predation." *Science*, 30 April 1976.

STILES, D. N., HAY, R. L., AND O'NEIL, J. R. "The MNK Chert Factory Site, Olduvai Gorge, Tanzania." *World Archaeology*, February 1974.

WASHBURN, S. L., AND DEVORE, IRVEN. "The Social Life of Baboons." *Scientific American*, June 1961.

ZIHLMAN, ADRIENNE L. "Interpretations of Early Hominid Locomotion," in *African Hominidae of the Plio-Pleistocene*. London: Duckworth, 1976.

5. EARLY MIGRATIONS OF HUMAN ANCESTORS

BUTZER, KARL W. *Environment and Archeology*, 2nd ed. Chicago: Aldine, 1971, chap. 2.

———— AND ISAAC, GLYNN LL., eds. *After the Australopithecines: Stratigraphy, Ecology and Cultural Change in the Middle Pleistocene*. Chicago: Aldine, 1975.

CHARD, CHESTER S. "Implications of Early Human Migrations from Africa to Europe." *Man*, August 1963.

CLARK, J. DESMOND. "Africa in Prehistory: Peripheral or Paramount?"
Man, June 1975.

GAULIN, STEVEN J. C., KURLAND, JEFFREY A., AND STRUM, S. C. "Primate
Predation and Bioenergetics." Science, 23 January 1976.

HARDING, ROBERT S. O. "The Predatory Baboon." *Expedition*, Winter 1974.

HOWELL, F. CLARK. "Observations on the Earlier Phases of the European
Lower Paleolithic," in *Recent Studies in Paleoanthropology*,
American Anthropologist Special Publication, April 1966.

HOWELLS, WILLIAM W. *"Homo Erectus." Scientific American*, November
1966.

JU-KANG, WOO. "The Skull of Lantian Man." *Current Anthropology*,
February 1966.

PERPER, TIMOTHY, AND SCHRIRE, CARMEL. "The Origin of Flesh-Eating,"
in *Second Conference of the Monell Center for the Chemical Senses
and Nutrition*. New York: Academic Press, 1977.

SHAPIRO, HARRY. "The Strange Unfinished Saga of Peking Man."
Natural History, November 1971.

STRUM, SHIRLEY C. "Life with the 'Pumphouse Gang'." *National
Geographic*, May 1975.

WASHBURN, S. L., AND DEVORE, IRVEN. "Social Behavior of Baboons and
Early Man," in *Social Life of Early Man*. Chicago: Aldine, 1961.

WATANABE, HITOSHI. "Running, Creeping and Climbing: a New
Ecological and Evolutionary Perspective on Human Locomotion."
Mankind, June 1971.

6. FOOD QUEST AND BIG-GAME HUNTING

BORDES, FRANÇOIS. *The Old Stone Age*. New York: McGraw-Hill, 1968,
chaps. 3 and 4.

CLARK, J. DESMOND. "A Comparison of the Late Acheulian Industries of
Africa and the Middle East," in *After the Australopithecines:
Stratigraphy, Ecology and Culture Change in the Middle Pleistocene*.
Chicago: Aldine, 1975.

COLE, SONIA. "A Spanish Camp of Stone Age Elephant Hunters."
New Scientist, 18 October 1962.

DEVORE, IRVEN, AND WASHBURN, S. L. "Baboon Ecology and Human
Behavior," in *African Ecology and Human Evolution*. Chicago:
Aldine, 1963.

EDELMANN, CLAUDE. "Camping on the Riviera in 2,000,000 B.C." *Realités*,
English ed., September 1968.

FREEMAN, LESLIE. "Acheulean Sites and Stratigraphy in Iberia and the
Maghreb," in *After the Australopithecines: Stratigraphy, Ecology
and Culture Change in the Middle Pleistocene*. Chicago: Aldine, 1975.

HOWELL, F. CLARK. "Observations on the Earlier Phases of the European **433** Lower Paleolithic (Torralba-Ambrona)." *Recent Studies in Paleoanthropology, American Anthropologist Special Publication,* April 1966, pp. 111–140.

ISAAC, GLYNN. "The Diet of Early Man: Aspects of Archaeological Evidence from Lower and Middle Pleistocene Sites in Africa." *World Archaeology,* June 1969.

_____ "Middle Pleistocene Stratigraphy and Cultural Patterns in East Africa," in *After the Australopithecines: Stratigraphy, Ecology and Culture Change in the Middle Pleistocene.* Chicago: Aldine, 1975.

LUMLEY, HENRY DE. "A Paleolithic Camp at Nice." *Scientific American,* May 1969.

MOVIUS, H. L. "The Lower Paleolithic Cultures of Southern and Eastern Asia." *Transactions of the American Philosophical Society* (new series) 38, pt. 4 (1948).

OAKLEY, KENNETH P. *Man the Tool-Maker,* 6th ed. University of Chicago, 1976, pp. 39–70.

_____ *Frameworks for Dating Fossil Man.* Chicago: Aldine, 1964, pp. 217–240.

PFEIFFER, JOHN. "Man the Hunter." *Horizon,* Spring 1971.

SCHALLER, GEORGE B., AND LOTHER, GORDON R. "The Relevance of Carnivore Behavior to the Study of Early Hominids." *Southwestern Journal of Anthropology,* Winter 1969.

SOLHEIM, WILHELM G. "Southeast Asia and the West." *Science,* 25 August 1967.

SPETH, JOHN D. *The Role of Hunting and Meat-Eating in Early Hominid Evolution.* In press.

7.   ORGANIZING FOR SURVIVAL: THE RISE OF TRADITION AND TABOOS

CRAIK, K. J. W. *The Nature of Explanation.* New York: Cambridge University Press, 1952.

DENHAM, WOODROW W. "Population Structure, Infant Transport, and Infanticide among Pleistocene and Modern Hunter-Gatherers." *Journal of Anthropological Research,* Autumn 1974.

EISELEY, LOREN C. "Man the Fire-Maker." *Scientific American,* September 1954.

FOX, ROBIN, "The Evolution of Human Sexual Behavior." *New York Times Magazine,* 24 March 1968.

_____ "Sexual Selection and the Evolution of Human Kinship Systems," in *Sexual Selection and the Descent of Man.* Chicago: Aldine, 1972.

_____ "Primate Kin and Human Kinship," in *Biosocial Anthropology.* London: Malaby Press, 1975.

ISAAC, GLYNN LL. "Chronology and the Tempo of Cultural Change During the Pleistocene," in *Calibration of Hominid Evolution.* Edinburgh: Scottish Academic Press, 1972.

LASHLEY, K. S. "Persistent Problems in the Evolution of Mind," *Quarterly Review of Biology,* March 1949.

LAWICK-GOODALL, JANE VAN. *In the Shadow of Man.* Boston: Houghton Mifflin, 1971.

LINTON, SALLY. "Woman the Gatherer: Male Bias in Anthropology." Paper read at 69th Annual Meeting of the American Anthropological Association, San Diego, Calif., 1970.

MACLEAN, PAUL D. "New Findings Relevant to the Evolution of Psychosexual Functions of the Brain." *Journal of Nervous and Mental Disease,* October 1962.

MANN, ALAN. "Australopithecine Demographic Patterns," in *African Hominidae of the Plio-Pleistocene.* London: Duckworth, 1976.

OAKLEY, KENNETH P. "Fire as Palaeolithic Tool and Weapon." *Proceedings of the Prehistoric Society* XXI (1955).

PFEIFFER, JOHN E. The Human Brain. New York: Harper & Row, 1955, chaps. 2 and 3.

———— "When *Homo Erectus* Tamed Fire He Tamed Himself." *New York Times Magazine,* 11 December 1966.

REYNOLDS, V. "Open Groups in Hominid Evolution." *Man,* December 1966.

TANNER, NANCY, AND ZIHLMAN, ADRIENNE. "Women in Evolution. Part I: Innovation and Selection in Human Origins." *Signs,* Spring 1976.

THOMAS, ELIZABETH MARSHALL. *The Harmless People.* New York: Knopf, 1959.

TIGER, LIONEL, AND FOX, ROBIN. *The Imperial Animal.* New York: Holt, Rinehart and Winston, 1971.

TRIVERS, ROBERT L. "The Evolution of Reciprocal Altruism." *Quarterly Review of Biology,* March 1971.

YOUNG, J. Z. "The Organization of a Memory System." *Proceedings of the Royal Society* 163B (23 November 1965).

8. THE SEARCH FOR REMAINS OF THE EARLIEST MODERN-TYPE PEOPLE

CAMPBELL, BERNARD. "The Centenary of Neanderthal Man: Part I." *Man,* November 1956.

———— "The Centenary of Neanderthal Man: Part II." *Man,* December 1956.

———— "Quantitative Taxonomy," in *Classification and Human Evolution.* Chicago: Aldine, 1963.

HOWELL, F. CLARK. "The Evolutionary Significance of Variation and **435**
Varieties of 'Neanderthal' Man." *Quarterly Review of Biology,*
December 1957.

HOWELLS, WILLIAM. "Mankind in the Making." New York: Doubleday,
1959, chaps. 13 and 15.

LEROI-GOURHAN, ARLETTE. "The Flowers Found with Shanidar IV, a
Neanderthal Burial in Iraq." *Science,* 7 November 1975.

OXNARD, CHARLES E. "Some African Fossil Foot Bones: A Note on the
Interpolation of Fossils into a Matrix of Extant Species." *American
Journal of Physical Anthropology,* July 1972.

SMITH, FRED H. *The Neanderthal Remains from Krapina.* University of
Tennessee, Department of Anthropology, Reports of Investigation
15, 1976.

SOLECKI, RALPH S. "Shanidar Cave." *Scientific American,* November 1957.

_____ *Shanidar—The First Flower People.* New York: Knopf, 1971.

_____ "Shanidar IV, a Neanderthal Flower Burial in Northern Iraq."
Science, 28 November 1975.

STRAUS, WILLIAM L., AND CAVE, A. J. E. "Pathology and the Posture of
Neanderthal Man." *Quarterly Review of Biology,* December 1957.

SULLIVAN, WALTER. "200,000-Year-Old Skull of Man Is Found." *New
York Times,* 13 October 1971.

9. DEVELOPMENTS IN THE SCIENTIFIC STUDY OF NEANDERTHAL PEOPLE

BANFIELD, A. W. F., "Migratory Caribou." *Natural History,* May 1961.

BINFORD, LEWIS R. *An Archeological Perspective.* New York: Seminar
Press, 1972.

_____ AND BINFORD, SALLY R. "A Preliminary Analysis of Functional
Variability in the Mousterian of Levallois Facies," in *Recent
Studies in Paleoanthropology.* American Anthropologist, special
publication, April 1966.

_____ "Interassemblage Variability—The Mousterian and the
'Functional' Argument," in *The Explanation of Culture Change:
Models in Prehistory.* University of Pittsburgh Press, 1973.

BINFORD, SALLY R., AND BINFORD, LEWIS R. "Stone Tools and Human
Behavior." *Scientific American,* April 1967.

BORDES, FRANCOIS. "Mousterian Cultures in France." *Science,* 22
September 1961.

_____ *A Tale of Two Caves.* New York: Harper & Row, 1972.

HOWELL, F. CLARK. "Isimila: A Paleolithic Site in Africa." *Scientific
American,* October 1961.

KELSALL, J. P. *The Caribou.* Ottawa: Canadian Wildlife Service, 1968.

KLEIN, RICHARD G. "The Mousterian of European Russia." *Proceedings
of the Prehistoric Society* XXV (1969).

LAVILLE, HENRI. "The Relative Position of Mousterian Industries in the **436**
Climatic Chronology of the Early Wurm in the Perigord." *World
Archaeology*, February 1973.

PFEIFFER, JOHN E. *The Search for Early Man.* New York: American
Heritage, 1963, chaps. I and IV.

10. THE DISAPPEARANCE OF NEANDERTHAL PEOPLE AND
THE APPEARANCE OF MODERN PEOPLE

BAKER, JOHN R. "Cro-Magnon Man, 1868–1968." *Endeavour,* May 1968.

BINFORD, LEWIS R. "Post-Pleistocene Adaptations," in *New Perspectives
in Archeology.* Chicago: Aldine, 1968.

———— "Nunamiut Demographic History: A Provocative Case," in
Demographic Anthropology. University of New Mexico Press, 1976.

BINFORD, SALLY R. "Early Upper Pleistocene Adaptations in the Levant."
American Anthropologist, August 1968.

———— "Late Middle Paleolithic Adaptations and Their Possible
Consequences." *Bioscience,* 1 March 1970.

BRACE, C. LORING. "The Fate of the 'Classic' Neanderthals: A Consideration of Hominid Catastrophism." *Current Anthropology,*
February 1964.

BRICKER, HARVEY M. "Upper Palaeolithic Archaeology." *Annual Review
of Anthropology* 5 (October 1976).

BROTHWELL, DON. "Where and When Did Man Become Wise?"
Discovery, June 1963.

BURCH, ERNEST S., JR. "The Caribou/Wild Reindeer as a Human
Resource." *American Antiquity,* July 1972.

COHEN, MARK NATHAN. *The Food Crisis in Prehistory.* New Haven: Yale
University Press, 1977.

FRAYER, DAVID W. "Metric Dental Change in the European Upper
Paleolithic and Mesolithic." *American Journal of Physical
Anthropology,* January 1977.

FREEMAN, L. G., AND ECHEGARAY, J. GONZALES. "Aurignacian Structural
Features and Burials at Cueva Morin (Santander, Spain)." *Nature,*
23 May 1970.

FRISON, GEORGE C., WILSON, MICHAEL, AND WILSON, DIANE J. "Fossil
Bison and Artifacts from an Early Altithermal Period Arroyo
Trap in Wyoming." *American Antiquity,* January 1976.

GARROD, DOROTHY A. E. "The Relations Between Southwest Asia and
Europe in the Later Paleolithic Age." *Journal of World History,*
July 1953.

HOWELL, F. CLARK. "Upper Pleistocene Stratigraphy and Early Man in
the Levant." *Proceedings of the American Philosophical Society*
103 (1959).

KLEIN, RICHARD G. "Ice-Age Hunters of the Ukraine." *Scientific American,* June 1974.

LAVILLE, H., AND RIGAUD, J.-PH., "The Perigordian V Industries in Perigord: Typological Variations, Stratigraphy and Relative Chronology." *World Archaeology,* February 1973.

MANN, ALAN, AND TRINKAUS, ERIK. "Neandertal and Neandertal-Like Fossils from the Upper Pleistocene." *Yearbook of Physical Anthropology* 17 (1973).

MONGAIT, A. L. "Archaeology in the U.S.S.R." Baltimore: Penguin Books, 1961.

MULVANEY, D. J. "Prehistory from Antipodean Perspectives," *Proceedings of the Prehistoric Society* XXXVII, pt. II (December 1971).

PERICOT-GARCIA, L. "A New Site with the Remarkable Parpallo-Type Solutrean Points." *Current Anthropology,* October 1961.

PFEIFFER, JOHN. "Man the Hunter." *Horizon,* Spring 1971.

———— *The Search for Early Man.* New York: American Heritage, 1963, chap. VI.

SACKETT, JAMES R. "Method and Theory of Upper Paleolithic Archeology in Southwestern France," in *New Perspectives in Archeology.* Chicago: Aldine, 1968.

SHEETS, PAYSON D., AND MUTO, GUY R. "Pressure Blades and Total Cutting Edge: An Experiment in Lithic Technology." *Science,* 11 February 1972.

SMITH, FRED H. "The Skeletal Remains of the Earliest Americans: A Survey." *Tennessee Anthropologist* 1 (Fall 1976).

———— "A Fossil Hominid Frontal from Velike Pecina (Croatia)." *American Journal of Physical Anthropology,* January 1976.

SMITH, PHILIP E. L. "The Solutrean Culture." *Scientific American,* August 1964.

———— "Solutrean Origins and the Question of Eastern Diffusion." *Arctic Anthropology* 1, no. 1 (1962).

SONNEVILLE-BORDES, DENISE DE. "Upper Paleolithic Cultures in Western Europe." *Science,* 18 October 1963.

STRAUS, LAWRENCE GUY. "A New Interpretation of the Cantabrian Solutrean." *Current Anthropology,* June 1976.

WHITMORE, FRANK C., et al. "Elephant Teeth from the Atlantic Continental Shelf." *Science,* 16 June 1967.

11.   THE GOLDEN AGE OF PREHISTORY

BAUMAN, HANS. *The Caves of the Great Hunters.* New York: Pantheon Books, 1954.

BORDES, FRANCOIS. "Physical Evolution and Technological Evolution in Man: A Parallelism." *World Archaeology,* June 1971.

BRODRICK, A. H. *Father of Prehistory*. New York: Morrow, 1963.   **438**

COLLINS, DESMOND. "Prehistoric Art." *Discovery*, May 1965.

DAMS, LYA, AND DAMS, MARCEL. "Cave Art of La Pileta." *Illustrated London News*, April 1976.

———— "Prehistoric Rock Art Discoveries." *Illustrated London News*, November 1973.

———— "Prehistoric Rock Art of the Spanish Levant." *Illustrated London News*, March 1973.

FLANNERY, KENT V. "The Origins of Agriculture." *Annual Review of Anthropology* 2 (1973).

FRITZ, MARGARET CONKEY. *The Evolution of Style: Some Thoughts on the Cantabrian Upper Paleolithic*. Paper read at 73rd annual meeting of the American Anthropological Association, Mexico City, 21 November 1974.

———— *The Structure of Paleolithic Design: A Preliminary Study of the Nature of Variability Among Engraved Bones*. Paper read at 74th annual meeting of the American Anthropological Association, San Francisco, 3–7 December 1975.

———— "An Analysis of Design Structure: Variation in Engraved Magdalenian Bone Assemblages from Cantabrian Spain, and the Sociological Implications Thereof." Doctoral dissertation, University of Chicago, 1976.

GIEDION, S. *The Beginnings of Art*. New York: Pantheon Books, 1962.

HARLAN, JACK R., AND ZOHARY, DANIEL. "Distribution of Wild Wheats and Barley." *Science*, 2 September 1966.

HARRIS, DAVID R. "New Light on Plant Domestication and the Origins of Agriculture." *Geographical Review*, January 1967.

HOLE, FRANK, FLANNERY, KENT V., AND NEELY, JAMES, A. "Prehistory and Human Ecology of the Deh Luran Plain." Memoirs of the Museum of Anthropology, no. 1, University of Michigan, 1969.

HOPE, FRANCIS. "Cave." *New Statesman*, 27 October 1972.

KUHN, HERBERT. *On the Track of Prehistoric Man*. New York: Random House, 1961.

LAMING, ANNETTE. *Lascaux*. Baltimore: Penguin Books, 1959.

LEROI-GOURHAN, ANDRE. "The Evolution of Paleolithic Art." *Scientific American*, February 1968.

MARSHACK, ALEXANDER. "Lunar Notation on Upper Paleolithic Remains." *Science*, 6 November 1964.

———— *The Roots of Civilization*. New York: McGraw-Hill, 1972.

PFEIFFER, JOHN E. "Man's First Revolution." *Horizon*, September 1962.

———— "The First Food Crisis." *Horizon*, Autumn 1975.

SIEVEKING, ANN, AND SIEVEKING, GALE. *The Caves of France and Northern Spain*. London: Longacre, 1962.

UCKO, PETER, AND ROSENFELD, ANDRÉE. *Paleolithic Cave Art*. London: Weidenfeld and Nicolson, 1967.

WOBST, H. MARTIN. "Stylistic Behavior and Information Exchange." **439**
Museum of Anthropology, Anthropological Papers, no. 61,
University of Michigan, 1976.

12.   PRIMATE STUDIES AND REVISED BELIEFS ABOUT ANIMAL BEHAVIOR

BUIRSKI, PETER, et al. "A Field Study of Emotion, Dominance, and Social
Behavior in a Group of Baboons *(Papio anubis)." Primates*, March
1973.
DEVORE, IRVEN. "Mother-Infant Relations in Free-Ranging Baboons," in
Maternal Behavior in Mammals. New York: Wiley, 1963.
————— AND HALL, K. R. L. "Baboon Ecology," in *Primate Behavior.*
New York: Holt, Rinehart and Winston, 1965.
DENHAM, WOODROW W. "Energy Relations and Some Basic Properties of
Primate Social Organization." *American Anthropologist*, February
1971.
EISENBERG, JOHN F. "The Social Organization of Mammals," *Handbuch
der Zoologie* 10, no. 7 (1965).
HALL, K. R. L., AND DEVORE, IRVEN. "Baboon Social Behavior," in *Primate
Behavior.* New York: Holt, Rinehart and Winston, 1965.
LANCASTER, JANE BECKMAN. "In Praise of the Achieving Female
Monkey." *Psychology Today*, September 1973.
RUSSELL, W. M. S. "The Wild Ones." *The Listener*, 5 November 1964.
WASHBURN, S. L. "Behavior and the Origin of Man." *Rockefeller
University Review*, January–February 1968.
WRIGHT, R. V. S. "Imitative Learning of a Flaked Stone Technology—
the Case of an Orangutan." *Mankind*, December 1972.

13.   CHIMPANZEES: OUR CLOSEST RELATIVES

BISCHOF, NORBERT. "Comparative Ethology of Incest Avoidance," in
Biosocial Anthropology. London: Malaby Press, 1975.
CHANCE, M. R. A. "Köhler's Apes—How Did They Perform?" *Man*,
September 1960.
CHISHOLM, JAMES S. "On the Evolution of Rules," in *The Social Structure
of Attention.* New York: Wiley, 1976.
FOX, ROBIN. "Primate Kin and Human Kinship," in *Biosocial
Anthropology.* London: Malaby Press, 1975.
HALLOWELL, A. IRVING. "Behavioral Evolution and the Emergence of the
Self," in *Evolution After Darwin.* University of Chicago Press, 1960.
HARDING, ROBERT, AND STRUM, SHIRLEY, "The Predatory Baboons of
Kekapey," *Natural History*, 85 (1976):46–53.
ITANI, JUNICHIRO, "Twenty Years With Mount Takasaki Monkeys," in
Primate Organization and Conservation. New York: Wiley, 1975.

_____ AND SUZUKI, AKIRA. "The Social Unit of Chimpanzees." *Primates* 8:355–381 (1967).

KORTLANDT, ADRIAAN. "Chimpanzees in the Wild." *Scientific American,* May 1962.

KOYAMA, NAOKI. "Changes in Dominance Rank and Division of a Wild Monkey Troop in Arashiyama." *Primates,* December 1970.

LAWICK-GOODALL, JANE VAN. "My Life Among Wild Chimpanzees." *National Geographic,* August 1963.

_____ *My Friends the Wild Chimpanzees.* Washington, D.C.: National Geographic Society, 1967.

_____ "Mother-Offspring Relationships in Free-Ranging Chimpanzees," in *Primate Ethology.* Chicago: Aldine, 1967.

_____ "The Behavior of Free-Living Chimpanzees in the Gombe Stream Reserve." *Animal Behaviour Monographs* 1 (1968).

MISSAKIAN, ELIZABETH A. "Genealogical Mating Activity in Free-Ranging Groups of Rhesus Monkeys *(Macaca Mulatta)* on Cayo Santiago." Master's thesis, Rockefeller University, New York, 1971.

PETERSON, JAMES D. "Ecologically Differentiated Patterns of Aggressive and Sexual Behavior in Two Troops of Ugandan Baboons, *Papio anubis.*" *American Journal of Physical Anthropology,* March 1973.

PFEIFFER, JOHN E. "The Apish Origins of Human Tension." *Harper's Magazine,* July 1963.

REYNOLDS, VERNON. "The 'Man of the Woods.' " *Natural History,* January 1964.

_____ "Chimpanzees of the Budongo Forest," in *Primate Behavior.* New York: Holt, Rinehart and Winston, 1965.

_____ "Kinship and the Family in Monkeys, Apes and Man." *Man,* June 1968.

ROWELL, T. E. "Forest-Living Baboons in Uganda." *Journal of Zoology* (London) 149:344–364 (1966).

_____ "A Quantitative Comparison of the Behavior of a Wild and a Caged Baboon Group." *Animal Behavior,* October 1967.

_____ "Variability in the Social Organization of Primates," in *Primate Ethology.* Chicago: Aldine, 1967.

SADE, DONALD STONE. "Determinants of Dominance in a Group of Free-Ranging Monkeys," in *Social Communication Among Primates.* University of Chicago Press, 1967.

STRUM, S. C. "Primate Predation: Interim Report on the Development of a Tradition in a Troop of Olive Baboons." *Science,* 28 February 1975.

TELEKI, GEZA. "Chimpanzee Subsistence Technology: Materials and Skills." *Journal of Human Evolution* 3:575–594 (1974).

_____ "The Omnivorous Chimpanzee." *Scientific American,* January 1973.

_____ "Primate Subsistence Patterns: Collector-Predators and Gatherer-Hunters." *Journal of Human Evolution* 4:125–184 (1975).

WRANGHAM, RICHARD WALTER. "The Behavioral Ecology of Chimpanzees **441**
in Gombe National Park, Tanzania." Doctoral dissertation,
University of Cambridge, 1975.

14. OBSERVATION AND EXPERIMENTATION WITH LIVING PRIMATES AND CARNIVORES

ALTMANN, STUART A. "Sociobiology of Rhesus Monkeys. II: Stochastics
of Social Communication." *Journal of Theoretical Biology* 8, no. 3
(1965).
_____ "Baboons, Space, Time, and Energy." *American Zoologist*
14:221–248 (1974).
BECK, BENJAMIN B. "Cooperative Tool Use by Captive Hamadryas
Baboons." *Science*, 9 November 1973.
ESTES, RICHARD D. "Predators and Scavengers." *Natural History*,
February and March, 1967.
_____ AND GODDARD, JOHN. "Prey Selection and Hunting Behavior of
the African Wild Dog." *Journal of Wildlife Management*, January
1967.
FOX, M. W. "A Comparative Study of the Development of Facial
Expressions in Canids: Wolf, Coyote and Foxes." *Behaviour*
36:49–73 (1970).
_____ "Socio-Ecological Implications of Individual Differences in Wolf
Litters: A Developmental and Evolutionary Perspective."
Behaviour 41:298–313 (1972).
GALLUP, GORDON G., JR. "Chimpanzees: Self-Recognition." *Science*,
2 January 1970.
_____ "Chimps and Self-Concept." *Psychology Today*, March 1971.
_____ "Towards an Operational Definition of Self-Awareness," in
Socio-ecology and Psychology of Primates. Chicago: Aldine, 1975.
HARLOW, HARRY F., AND MARGARET K. "Social Deprivation in Monkeys."
Scientific American, November 1962.
_____ AND SUOMI, STEPHEN J. "Social Recovery by Isolation-Reared
Monkeys." *Proceedings of the National Academy of Sciences*, July
1971.
_____ AND ZIMMERMANN, ROBERT R. "Affectional Responses in the
Infant Monkey." *Science* 130:421–432 (August 1959).
HARLOW, M. K., AND H. F. "Affection in Primates." *Discovery*, January
1966.
HINDE, R. A. "Rhesus Monkey Aunts," in *Determinants of Infant Behavior*,
vol. III. New York: Wiley, 1965.
_____ "The Study of Mother-Infant Interaction in Captive Group-Living
Rhesus Monkeys." *Proceedings of the Royal Society*, B, 169 (1968).
_____ "Effects of Brief Separation from Mothers on Rhesus Monkeys."
Science, 9 July 1971.

_____ ROWELL, T. E. AND SPENCER-BOOTH, Y. "Behaviour of Socially Living Rhesus Monkeys in their First Six Months." *Proceedings of the Zoological Society of London* 143, pt. 4 (1964).

KING, GLENN E. *The Evolution of Human Behavior.* Chicago: Aldine, forthcoming.

_____ *The Tribe in Human Evolution.* Paper read at Annual Conference of the Southwestern Anthropological Association, Santa Monica, Calif., 13 April 1974.

KUHME, WOLFDIETRICH. "Communal Food Distribution and Division of Labor in African Hunting Dogs." *Nature,* 30 January 1965.

MASON, WILLIAM A., AND KENNEY, M. D. "Redirection of Filial Attachments in Rhesus Monkeys: Dogs as Surrogate Mothers." *Science,* 22 March 1974.

REDICAN, WILLIAM K., AND MITCHELL, G. "Play Between Adult Male and Infant Rhesus Monkeys." *American Zoologist* 14:295–302 (1974).

SCHALLER, GEORGE B. "The Tiger and Its Prey." *Natural History,* October 1966.

_____ *The Deer and the Tiger.* University of Chicago Press, 1967.

_____ *Serengeti—A Kingdom of Predators.* New York: Knopf, 1972.

_____ *The Serengeti Lion.* University of Chicago Press, 1972.

SHANNON, CLAUDE E., AND WEAVER, WARREN. *The Mathematical Theory of Communication.* University of Illinois Press, 1949.

THOMPSON, PHILIP R. "A Cross-Species Analysis of Carnivore, Primate, and Hominid Behavior." *Journal of Human Evolution* 4:113–124 (1975).

ZIMEN, ERIK. "Social Dynamics of the Wolf Pack," in *Social Ecology of Canids.* New York: Van Nostrand, 1973.

15. CONTEMPORARY HUNTER-GATHERERS: LAST REPRESENTATIVES OF THE STONE AGE

ELKIN, A. D. *The Australian Aborigines.* New York: Doubleday, 1964.

GOULD, R. A. "Notes on Hunting, Butchering, and Sharing of Game Among the Ngatatjara and Their Neighbors in the West Australian Desert." Kroeber Anthropological Society Papers, no. 36, Spring 1967.

_____ "Chipping Stones in the Outback." *Natural History,* February 1968.

_____ "Living Archeology: The Ngatatjara of Western Australia." *Southwestern Journal of Anthropology,* Summer 1968.

_____ *Yiwara: Foragers of the Australian Desert.* New York: Scribner, 1969.

_____ "The Archaeologist as Ethnographer: A Case from the Western Desert of Australia." *World Archaeology,* October 1971.

_____ "The Un-Seasonal Condition of the Western Desert Aborigines of Australia," in *Seasonality in Prehistory.* University of New Mexico Press, forthcoming.

JONES, RHYS. "The Demography of Hunters and Farmers in Tasmania," in *Aboriginal Man and Environment in Australia.* Australian National University Press, 1971. **443**

MULVANEY, D. J. "The Prehistory of the Australian Aborigine." *Scientific American,* March 1966.

PETERSON, NICOLAS. "Totemism Yesterday: Sentiment and Local Organisation Among the Australian Aborigines." *Man,* March 1972.

—————— "Hunter-Gatherer Territoriality: The Perspective from Australia." *American Anthropologist,* March 1975.

STREHLOW, T. G. H. *Aranda Traditions.* Melbourne University, 1947.

—————— "Culture, Social Structure, and Environment in Aboriginal Central Australia," in *Aboriginal Man in Australia.* Sydney: Angus and Robertson, 1965.

TINDALE, NORMAN B. "The Pitjandjara," in *Hunters and Gatherers Today.* New York: Holt, Rinehart and Winston, 1972.

WHITE, CARMEL, AND PETERSON, NICOLAS. "Ethnographic Interpretations of the Prehistory of Western Arnhem Land." *Southwestern Journal of Anthropology,* Spring, 1969.

16.   THE BEHAVIOR OF PRIMITIVE PEOPLES

BINFORD, LEWIS R. *Nunamiut Ethnoarchaeology.* New York: Academic Press, 1977.

BIRDSELL, JOSEPH B. "Some Environmental and Cultural Factors Influencing the Structuring of Australian Aboriginal Populations." *American Naturalist,* supplement, May–June 1953.

—————— "Some Population Problems Involving Pleistocene Man." *Cold Spring Harbor Symposium On Quantitative Biology* XXII (1957).

—————— "On Population Structure in Generalized Hunting and Collecting Populations." *Evolution,* June 1958.

DRAPER, PATRICIA. "Social and Economic Constraints on !Kung Childhood," in *Kalahari Hunter-Gatherers.* Cambridge: Harvard University Press, 1976.

—————— "!Kung Bushman Childhood." Doctoral dissertation, Harvard University, 1972.

HEINE-GELDERN, ROBERT. "Vanishing Cultures." *Scientific American,* May 1957.

HELM, JUNE, AND LEACOCK, ELEANOR BURKE. "The Hunting Tribes of Subarctic Canada," in *North American Indians in Historical Perspective.* New York: Random House, 1971.

LEE, RICHARD B. "Subsistence Ecology of !Kung Bushmen." Doctoral dissertation, University of California, Berkeley, 1965.

—————— "Trance Cure of the !Kung Bushmen." *Natural History,* November 1967.

—————— "Eating Christmas in the Kalahari." *Natural History,* December 1969.

_____ AND DEVORE, IRVEN, eds. *Man the Hunter.* Chicago: Aldine, 1968. **444**

_____ AND DEVORE, IRVEN. *Kalahari Hunter-Gatherers.* Cambridge: Harvard University Press, 1976.

MURDOCK, GEORGE P. Personal communication to the author, 20 December 1967.

PFEIFFER, ANTHONY J. "A Cultural, Ecological View of Some Aspects of Pygmy Life." Unpublished manuscript, 1972.

SERVICE, ELMAN R. Primitive Social Organization. New York: Random House, 1962.

THOMAS, ELIZABETH MARSHALL. *The Harmless People.* New York: Knopf, 1959.

WATANABE, HITOSHI. "The Ainu." *Journal of the Faculty of Science,* University of Tokyo, 30 July 1964.

WOBST, H. MARTIN. "Boundary Conditions for Paleolithic Social Systems: A Simulation Approach." *American Antiquity,* April 1974.

YELLEN, JOHN. *Archeological Approaches to the Present: Models for Interpreting the Past.* New York: Academic Press, 1977.

17. EXPERIMENTAL ARCHEOLOGY

CALLAHAN, ERRETT. *The Pamunkey Project: An Overview.* Paper read at 41st annual meeting, Society for American Archeology, St. Louis, Mo., 7 May 1976.

CHILCOTT, JOHN H., AND DEETZ, JAMES J. "The Construction and Uses of a Laboratory Archeological Site." *American Antiquity,* January 1964.

CRABTREE, DON E. "A Stoneworker's Approach to Analyzing and Replicating the Lindenmeier Folsom." *Tebiwa* (journal of the Idaho State University Museum) 9, no. 1 (1966).

_____ "Notes on Experiments in Flintknapping." *Tebiwa* (journal of the Idaho State University Museum) 10, no. 1 (1967)

_____ AND BUTCHER, B. ROBERT. "Notes on Experiments in Flint-knapping." *Tebiwa* (journal of the Idaho State University Museum) 7, no. 1 (1964).

_____ AND DAVIS, E. L. "Experimental Manufacture of Wooden Implements with Tools of Flaked Stone." *Science,* 26 January 1968.

GOULD, RICHARD A., KOSTER, DOROTHY A., AND SONTZ, ANN H. L. "The Lithic Assemblage of the Western Desert Aborigines of Australia." *American Antiquity,* April 1971.

HARLAN, JACK R. "A Wild Wheat Harvest in Turkey." *Archaeology,* June 1967.

ISAAC, GLYNN. "The Diet of Early Man: Aspects of Archaeological Evidence from Lower and Middle Pleistocene Sites in Africa." *World Archaeology,* February 1971.

JEWELL, P. A. "An Experiment in Field Archaeology." *Advancement of Science,* May 1961.

KEELEY, LAWRENCE H. "Technique and Methodology in Microwear Studies: A Critical Review." *World Archaeology*, February 1974.

PFEIFFER, JOHN E. "Dr. Leakey and His Olduvai Digs." *Think Magazine*, September 1963.

SEMENOV, S. A. *Prehistoric Technology*. London: Cory, Adams and MacKay, 1964.

SWANSON, EARL H. "An Introduction to Crabtree's Experiments in Flintknapping." *Tebiwa* (Journal of the Idaho State University Museum) 9, no. 1 (1966).

TURNBAUGH, WILLIAM A. "An On-Campus Alternative to the Archaeological Field School." *American Antiquity*, April 1976.

WITTHOFT, JOHN. "The Art of Flint Chipping." *Ohio Archeologist*, October 1956–July 1957.

18. THE HUMAN INFANT: A STUDY IN LIVING PREHISTORY

AINSWORTH, MARY D. SALTER. *Infancy in Uganda*. Baltimore: Johns Hopkins Press, 1967.

———— "Attachment and Dependency: A Comparison," in *Attachment and Dependency*. New York: Wiley, 1972.

———— "The Development of Infant-Mother Attachment," in *Review of Child Development Research*, vol. 3. University of Chicago Press, 1973.

———— BELL, SYLVIA M., AND STAYTON, DONELDA J. "Infant-Mother Attachment and Social Development: Socialisation as a Product of Reciprocal Responsiveness to Signals," in *The Integration of the Child into a Social World*. New York: Cambridge University Press, 1974.

ALTMANN, STUART A. "Primate Social Signals," in *Animal Communication: Techniques of Study and Results of Research*. Indiana University Press, 1968.

ANDREW, R. J. "Evolution of Facial Expression." *Science*, 22 November 1963.

———— "The Origin and Evolution of the Calls and Facial Expressions of the Primates." *Behaviour* XX (1963).

————"The Origins of Facial Expressions." *Scientific American*, October 1965.

BEACH, FRANK A., AND JAYNES, JULIAN. "Effects of Early Experience upon the Behavior of Animals." *Psychological Bulletin*, May 1954.

BOWLBY, JOHN. "An Ethological Approach to Research in Child Development." *British Journal of Medical Psychology* XXX, 4 (1957).

————"The Nature of the Child's Tie to His Mother." *International Journal of Psychoanalysis* XXXIX, pt. 5 (1958).

———— "Ethology and the Development of Object Relations." *International Journal of Psychoanalysis* XLI, pts. 4 and 5 (1960).

FREEDMAN, D. G., AND CHINN, NINA. "Behavioral Differences Between Chinese-American and European-American Newborns." *Nature*, 20 December 1969.

JONES, N. G. BLURTON. "Comparative Aspects of Mother-Child Contact," in *Ethological Studies of Child Behaviour*. New York: Cambridge University Press, 1972.

_____ AND LEACH, GILL M. "Behaviour of Children and their Mothers at Separation and Greeting," in *Ethological Studies of Child Behaviour*. New York: Cambridge University Press, 1972.

KAGAN, JEROME. "Do Infants Think?" *Scientific American*, March 1972.

LETTVIN, J. E., et al. "What the Frog's Eye Tells the Frog's Brain." *Proceedings of the Institute of Radio Engineers*, November 1959.

PFEIFFER, JOHN E. "Vision in Frogs." *Natural History*, November 1962.

PFEIFFER, TONY. "Some References to the Study of Human Ethology." *Man-Environment Systems*, May and September 1971 (published by the Association for the Study of Man-Environment Relationships, Box 57, Orangeburg, N.Y. 10962).

19. THE EVOLUTION OF LANGUAGE

ANDREW, R. J. "Evolution of Intelligence and Vocal Mimicking." *Science*, 24 August 1962.

BLOUNT, BEN G. "Studies in Child Language: An Anthropological View." *American Anthropologist*, September 1975.

_____ "The Evolution of Language," in *Anthropology*. New York: Harper & Row, 1977.

BORDES, FRANCOIS. "Physical Evolution and Technological Evolution in Man: A Parallelism." *World Archaeology*, June 1971.

BROWN, ROGER. *A First Language: the Early Stages*. Cambridge, Mass.: Harvard University Press, 1973.

FLEMING, JOYCE DUDNEY. "The State of the Apes." *Psychology Today*, January 1974.

FOSTER, MARY LECRON. "The Symbolic Structure of Primordial Language," in *Perspectives in Human Evolution IV*. Staples Press, 1976.

FOUTS, ROGER S. "Acquisition and Testing of Gestural Signs in Four Young Chimpanzees." *Science*, 1 June 1973.

GARDNER, R. ALLEN, AND BEATRICE T. "Teaching Sign Language to a Chimpanzee." *Science*, 15 August 1969.

_____ "Early Signs of Language in Child and Chimpanzee." *Science*, 28 February 1975.

GESCHWIND, NORMAN. "The Development of the Brain and the Evolution of Language." Monograph series of *Languages and Linguistics*, no. 17 (April 1964).

GLASERSFELD, ERNST VON. "Signs, Communication, and Language." *Journal of Human Evolution* 3:465–474 (1974).

GREENBERG, JOSEPH H. "Language Universals," in *Current Trends in Linguistics.* The Hague: Mouton, 1966.

HALDANE, J. B. S. "Animal Communication and the Origin of Language." *Science Progress* 23 (1955).

HARNAD, STEVAN, STEKLIS, HORST, AND LANCASTER, JANE. "The Origins and Evolution of Language and Speech." *Annals of the New York Academy of Sciences* 280 (1976).

HAYES, C. *The Ape in Our House.* New York: Harper & Row, 1951.

HEWES, GORDON W. *Language Origins: A Bibliography.* Department of Anthropology, University of Colorado, 1971.

_____ "Primate Communication and the Gestural Origin of Language." *Current Anthropology*, February–April 1973.

HOCKETT, CHARL F. "The Origin of Speech." *Scientific American*, September 1960.

_____ "Comments on 'Current Trends in Linguistics.' " *Current Anthropology*, April–June 1968.

_____ AND ASCHER, ROBERT. "The Human Revolution." *Current Anthropology*, June 1964.

KELLOGG, WINTHROP N. "Communication and Language in the Home-Raised Chimpanzee." *Science*, 25 October 1968.

KEYSER, SAMUEL J. "Our Manner of Speaking." *Technology Review* February 1964.

LANCASTER, JANE B. "Primate Communication Systems and the Emergence of Human Language," in *Primates: Studies in Adaptation and Variability.* New York: Holt, Rinehart and Winston, 1968.

LEMAY, M., AND GESCHWIND, N. "Hemispheric Differences in the Brains of Great Apes." *Brain, Behavior and Evolution* 11:48–52 (1975).

LENNEBERG, ERIC. H. *Biological Foundations of Language.* New York: Wiley, 1967.

_____ "The Biological Foundations of Language." *Hospital Practice*, December 1967.

MACDONALD, CRITCHLEY. "The Evolution of Man's Capacity for Language," in *Evolution After Darwin*, vol. 2. University of Chicago Press, 1960.

_____ "The Nature of Animal Communication and its Relation to Language in Man." *Journal of the Mount Sinai Hospital*, May–June 1961.

MENZEL, EMIL. "Chimpanzee Spatial Memory Organization." *Science*, 30 November 1973.

_____ "Natural Language of Young Chimpanzees." *New Scientist*, 16 January 1975.

_____ AND HALPERIN, STEWART. "Purposive Behavior as a Basis for Objective Communication Between Chimpanzees." *Science*, 22 August 1975.

MILLER, GEORGE A. "Some Psychological Studies of Grammar," *American Psychologist*, November 1962.

_____ "The Psycholinguists." *Encounter*, July 1964.

_____ "Communication and the Structure of Behavior," in *Disorders of Communication*, vol. XLII. Research Publications, Association for Research in Nervous and Mental Disease, 1964.

_____ "Linguistic Communication as a Biological Process," in *Biology and the Human Sciences*. Oxford University Press, 1972.

ORR, WILLIAM F., AND CAPPANNARI, STEPHEN C. "The Emergence of Language." *American Anthropologist*, April 1964.

PASSINGHAM, R. E. "Changes in the Size and Organization of the Brain in Man and His Ancestors." *Brain, Behavior and Evolution* 11:73–90 (1975).

PREMACK, DAVID. "The Education of Sarah." *Psychology Today*, September 1970.

_____ "A Functional Analysis of Language." *Journal of the Experimental Analysis of Behavior*, July 1970.

_____ *Intelligence in Ape and Man*. Hillsdale, N.J.: Lawrence Erlbaum Associates, 1976.

_____ "Language and Intelligence in Ape and Man." *American Scientist*, November–December 1976.

_____ AND SCHWARTZ, ARTHUR. "Preparations for Discussing Behaviorism with Chimpanzee," in *The Genesis of Language*. Cambridge, Mass.: M.I.T. Press, 1966.

RUMBAUGH, DUANE M. "Comparative Primate Learning and its Contributions to Understanding Development, Play, Intelligence, and Language," in *Perspectives in Primate Biology*, vol. 9. New York: Plenum, 1974.

_____ AND GILL, TIMOTHY V. "The Mastery of Language-Type Skills by the Chimpanzee *(Pan)*", in *The Origins and Evolution of Language and Speech. Annals of the New York Academy of Sciences* 280 (1975).

_____ GILL, TIMOTHY V., AND GLASERFELD, E. C. VON. "Reading and Sentence Completion by a Chimpanzee *(Pan)*." *Science*, 16 November 1973.

SEBEOK, THOMAS A. "Discussion of Communication Processes," in *Social Communication Among Primates*. University of Chicago Press, 1967.

YENI-KONSHIAN, GRACE H., AND BENSON, DENNIS A. "Anatomical Study of Cerebral Asymmetry in the Temporal Lobe of Humans, Chimpanzees, and Rhesus Monkeys." *Science*, 23 April 1976.

20. STUDY OF HUMANS: THE POWER OF THE PAST AND POTENTIAL FOR CHANGE

BEKOFF, MARC. "The Development of Social Interaction, Play, and Metacommunication in Mammals: An Ethological Perspective." *Quarterly Review of Biology*, December 1972.

BRANNIGAN, CHRISTOPHER R., AND HUMPHRIES, DAVID A. "Human **449** Nonverbal Behavior, a Means of Communication," in *Ethological Studies of Child Behavior*. Cambridge University Press, 1972.

CHANCE, M. R. A. "A Biological Perspective on Convulsions." *Colloques Internationaux du Centre National de la Recherche Scientifique* no. 112 (1963).

DEMENT, WILLIAM C. "Toward an Evolutionary Theory of Dreaming." *American Journal of Psychiatry*, August 1966.

DENHAM, WOODROW W. "The Detection of Patterns in Alyawara Nonverbal Behavior." Doctoral dissertation, University of Washington, 1973.

——— "Infant Transport Among the Alyawara Tribe, Central Australia." *Oceania*, June 1974.

——— "Population Structure, Infant Transport, and Infanticide among Modern and Pleistocene Hunter-Gatherers." *Journal of Anthropological Research* 30 (3):191–198 (1974).

DISSANAYAKE, ELLEN. "An Hypothesis of the Evolution of Art from Play." *Leonardo* 7(3):211–218 (1974).

ESSER, A. H. "Interactional Hierarchy and Power Structure on a Psychiatric Ward," in *Behavior Studies in Psychiatry*. New York: Pergamon Press, 1970.

FAGEN, ROBERT. "Play as Innovation: Models of the Origin, Transmission and Fixation or Loss of Novel Behaviors in Animal 'Cultures.'" Doctoral dissertation, Harvard University, 1974.

——— "Exercise, Play and Physical Training in Animals," in *Perspectives in Ethology* vol. 2. New York: Plenum, 1976.

——— "Modelling How and Why Play Works," in *Play: Its Role in Evolution and Development*. New York: Viking, 1977.

——— "Selection for Optimal Age-Dependent Schedules of Play Behavior." *American Naturalist*, 1977, in press.

FOX, ROBIN. "Human Mating Patterns in Ethological Perspective." *Animals*, July 1967.

——— "In the Beginning: Aspects of Hominid Behavioural Evolution." *Man*, September 1967.

——— AND FLEISING, USHER. "Human Ethology." *Annual Review of Anthropology* 5 (October 1976).

GEIST, VALERIUS. *Mountain Sheep—A Study in Behavior and Evolution*. University of Chicago Press, 1971.

GOOD, ROBERT A. "Disorders of the Immune System." *Hospital Practice*, January 1967.

GRANT, EWAN C. "An Ethological Description of Some Schizophrenic Patterns of Behaviour." *Proceedings of the Leeds Symposium on Behavioural Disorders*, March 1965.

——— Human Facial Expression. *Man*, December 1969.

HAMBURG, DAVID A. "The Relevance of Recent Evolutionary Changes to **450** Human Stress Biology," in *Social Life of Early Man*. Chicago: Aldine, 1961.

HOLLOWAY, R. L. "Human Aggression." *Natural History*, December 1967.

HUMPHRIES, D. C., HUMPHRIES, D. A., AND DRIVER, P. M. "Erratic Display as a Device Against Predators." *Science*, 30 June 1967.

HUTT, CORINNE. "Exploration and Play in Children." *Symposia of the Zoological Society of London* no. 18 (1966).

_____ "Specific and Diversive Exploration," in *Advances in Child Development and Behavior* vol. 5. New York: Academic Press, 1970.

JONES, N. G. BLURTON. "An Ethological Study of Some Aspects of Social Behaviour of Children in Nursery School," in *Primate Ethology*. Chicago: Aldine, 1967.

_____ "Emotional Behaviour in Children and Monkeys." *Animals*, November 1966.

_____ "Nonverbal Communication in Children," in *Nonverbal Communication*. Cambridge University Press, 1972.

_____ "An Ethologist Looks at Socialisation and Nursery School," in *The Integration of the Child into a Social World*. Cambridge University Press, 1972.

MACKENZIE, NORMAN. "Sweating It Out with B-P." *New Statesman*, 15 October 1965.

MCGREW, W. C. "Aspects of Social Development in Nursery School Children, with Emphasis on Introduction to the Group," in *Ethological Studies of Child Behavior*. Cambridge University Press, 1972.

MILLER, STEPHEN. "Ends, Means, and Galumphing: Some Leitmotifs of Play." *American Anthropologist*, February 1973.

OMARK, DONALD R. "Peer Group Formation in Young Children. Action." Doctoral dissertation, University of Chicago, 1972.

_____ AND EDELMAN, MURRAY S. "A Developmental Study of Group Formation in Children," in *The Use of Direct Observation to Study Instructional-Learning Behavior in School Settings*, Learning Research and Development Center, University of Pittsburgh, 1974.

PRICE, JOHN. "The Dominance Hierarchy and the Evolution of Mental Illness." *Lancet*, 29 July 1967.

_____ "Genetics of the Affective Illnesses." *Hospital Medicine*, July 1968.

SCHNEIRLA, T. C. "Instinct and Aggression." *Natural History*, December 1966.

SOUTHWICK, CHARLES L. "Rhesus Monkeys in North India," in *Primate Behavior*. New York: Holt, Rinehart and Winston, 1965.

TIGER, LIONEL. *Men in Groups*. New York: Random House, 1969.

_____ AND FOX, ROBIN. *The Imperial Animal*. New York: Holt, Rinehart and Winston, 1971.

_____ "The Zoological Perspective in Social Science," *Man*, March 1966.

TINBERGEN, N. "Aggression and Fear in the Normal Sexual Behavior of
    Some Animals," in *The Pathology and Treatment of Sexual Deviation*.
    New York: Oxford University Press, 1964.

—— "On War and Peace in Animals and Man." *Science*, 28 June 1968.

WHITE, ROBERT W. "Motivation Reconsidered: The Concept of
    Competence." *Psychological Review*, September 1959.

EPILOGUE: OUR FUTURE AS FORMER HUNTERS, IN A WORLD WITH NO PLACE FOR HUNTERS

ALEXANDER, CHRISTOPHER. *The City as a Mechanism for Sustaining Human
    Contact*. Institute of Urban and Regional Planning, University of
    California, Working Paper no. 50 (October 1966).

DAWKINS, RICHARD. *The Selfish Gene*. New York: Oxford University
    Press, 1976.

DILLON, WILTON S. *Gifts and Nations*. The Hague: Mouton, 1968.

GRAHAM, MICHAEL. "Crowds and the Like in Vertebrates." *Human
    Relations* 17, no. 4 (1964).

JONGE, DERK DE. "Applied Hodology," *Landscape*, Winter 1967–8.

MASCIONI, JOHN. *Report of Probes Conference on Government Office
    Buildings*, 15–17 June 1967. Institute for Applied Technology,
    National Bureau of Standards.

MORISON, ROBERT S. "Where Is Biology Taking Us?" *Science*, 27 January
    1967.

PARR, A. E. "Urbanity and the Urban Scene." *Landscape*, Spring 1967.

PFEIFFER, JOHN E. "Machines That Man Can Talk With." *Fortune*, May
    1964.

—— "New Look at Education: Systems Analysis in Our Schools and
    Colleges." New York: Odyssey, 1968.

—— "The Tribe That Talks Peace and Makes War." *Horizon*,
    January 1977.

SAGAN, CARL. "Direct Contact Among Galactic Civilizations by
    Relativistic Interstellar Spaceflight." *Planetary and Space Science*
    II (1963).

—— SALZMAN, LINDA, AND DRAKE, FRANK. "A Message from Earth."
    Science, 25 February 1972.

TANNER, J. M. "Earlier Maturation in Man." *Scientific American*,
    January 1968.

WILSON, E. O. "Sociobiology: the New Synthesis." Cambridge, Mass.:
    Harvard University Press, 1975.

INDEX